The Russian Question

The Russian Question

Nationalism, Modernization, and Post-Communist Russia

Wayne Allensworth

ROWMAN & LITTLEFIELD PUBLISHERS, INC.
Lanham • Boulder • New York • Oxford

ROWMAN & LITTLEFIELD PUBLISHERS, INC.

Published in the United States of America
by Rowman & Littlefield Publishers, Inc.
4720 Boston Way, Lanham, Maryland 20706

12 Hid's Copse Road
Cumnor Hill, Oxford OX2 9JJ, England

Copyright 1998 by Rowman & Littlefield Publishers, Inc.

British Library Cataloguing in Publication Information Available

Library of Congress Cataloging-in-Publication Data

Allensworth, Wayne, 1959–
    The Russian question : nationalism, modernization, and post-
Communist Russia / Wayne Allensworth.
       p.   cm.
    Includes bibliographical references and index.
    ISBN 0-8476-9002-4 (cloth: alk. paper).—ISBN 0-8476-9003-2
(pbk. : alk. paper)
       1. Russia (Federation)—History—Philosophy. 2. Nationalism—
Russia (Federation) 3. Patriotism—Russia (Federation) 4. Post
communism—Russia (Federation)   I. Title.
DK510.555.A45   1998
320.947'09'049—dc21   98-24157
                                                                        CIP

Printed in the United States of America

⊗ ™ The paper used in this publication meets the minimum requirements of
American National Standard for Information Sciences—Permanence of Paper
for Printed Library Materials, ANSI Z39.48–1984.

To the memory of
Oliver Armstrong Allensworth, 1898–1988

I go the way of all the earth:
be thou strong therefore, and shew thyself a man.
1 Kings 2:2

Contents

Preface

A few years ago, a friend of mine and I were watching a news program about sweeping changes that have occurred in Russia since the collapse of the Soviet Union. The producers of the program had uncritically adopted the still prevalent view that the opening of the Moscow Mc-Donald's and the supposed ascension of westernizing "democrats" (the triumph of mass democracy and consumerist capitalism, as it were) were not only desirable events but were the only possible alternatives to communist totalitarianism. The Russians, the program's viewers were told, had embraced the Western model of development.

But not all Russians were prepared to accept the premise that Reeboks, Big Macs, and the political equivalent of fast food were a blessing devoutly to be wished for without reservation. In fact, some "nationalists" were adamantly opposed to adopting the Western model, calling for Russians to find their own way out from under the rubble of communism's collapsed edifice. A report on a mob scene at a Michael Jackson concert in Moscow and a sequence on the ready availability of pornography, much of it recycled from Europe and the United States, prompted my friend to groan, "No wonder they hate us." All I could do was nod in agreement.

I admit to feeling a pang of sympathy for the nationalists. They seemed to feel no need to seek validation from Westerners. They loved Russia and the Russians, the land, the culture, and the people; they thought Russia unique and feared that "westernization" meant losing something that they couldn't quite put their finger on. They felt no need to rationalize their feelings or to explain them to others. Nationalism was taken as a given; patriotism as the norm for any healthy community.

This book began as an attempt to explain to myself why I had felt sympathy—more for their *emotions* than for their policy prescriptions—for these people in the first place. Since World War II, nationalism, as either an emotion or a policy, had inhabited a political purgatory ruled by the shade of Adolph Hitler, cast there by the guardians of respectable opinion. A certain kind of "patriotism" was socially acceptable, if eccentric, in enlightened circles, but nationalism was *verboten*. It seemed to me, however, that the Russian nationalists were on to something, a something that was as intellectually elusive for me as it had been for them.

What were they afraid of losing? Why did they consider nationalism and patriotism as normal and necessary as food and shelter? And why had Russian nationalism, and many others besides, adopted a stance that was so anti-Western (other than out of sheer cussedness, usually characterized in the West as an inexplicable xenophobia)? It could partly be explained by the imperatives of pursuing the national interests of particular nations, but when the Russians spoke of a "Western invasion," they seemed to have in mind something less concrete (most of the time, at least) than the massed divisions of a revived *Wehrmacht*. In any event, it was plain that not all of the nationalists were anti-Western as such; they were insisting that the Western model could not be adopted wholesale in Russia. But what is nationalism, and who is a "nationalist"? How can one nationalism be distinguished from another?

It was a truism by the early 1990s that the end of the cold war had removed whatever restraints the requirements of ideological conflict had had on potential ethnic or nationalist conflict. The fall of the Berlin Wall and the collapse of communism might help explain the clash of Georgian and Abkhazian, Czech and Slovak, Moldovan and Russian, or Hungarian and Rumanian. But what about confrontations between Irish Catholics and Protestants, or between Francophone and Anglophone Canadians? Were these nationalist conflicts as well? Even the supposedly domesticated Scots had been making nationalist noises in recent years, and Italy appeared to be dividing along regional lines. Hadn't all these questions of identity (what these conflicts were about at heart) been settled by the consolidation of the "nation state"? Did the apparent escalation of nationalist and ethnic conflict around the world have anything to do with the resurgence of nationalism in Russia?

In attempting to explain myself to myself, I had inadvertently opened a Pandora's box of related questions about the nature of nationalism, the condition of the modern world, and human nature, for it seemed to me that nationalism was somehow natural. Was it also necessary? If I were to make sense of the various Russian *nationalisms*, it appeared that I must also tackle some of these very daunting questions that came along with the familiar Russian baggage.

Like Lewis Carroll's walrus, I was to speak of many things as seemingly unrelated as cabbages and kings and, in some cases (Russians who claimed that Josef Stalin was a model *Russian* patriot, for example), as improbable as pigs with wings. If my reach has exceeded my grasp, I can only plead that we who have expertise in a given area must attempt to make use of the research of widely divergent fields of study, if we are not to fall into the trap of talking only to each other, thus becoming the proverbial experts who know more and more about less and less. As this study began to take shape, I felt that neither Russian nationalism nor the various distinct manifestations of that phenomenon could be explained without considering the wealth of information available outside what is nowadays called "Russian studies."

The book undoubtedly has many shortcomings. Tackling something as big as the "Russian question"—the question of Russian identity that so many nationalists in that country have wrestled with for centuries—has left me a little more tolerant and less inclined to attack those who disagree with me. Vladimir Lukin, former Russian ambassador to the United States, has said that Russia is less a choice than a fate, and I have learned that the battle lines drawn between human beings are more often lines drawn by fate or providence than by the individuals themselves.

Chapters 1–2 address the problems of defining nationalism (as well as some other important terms used in the remainder of the book), explaining its primal emotional power, and describing how Russian nationalism came to be a social and political force to be reckoned with in the eighteenth and nineteenth centuries. Making sense of contemporary Russian nationalism requires an understanding of what nationalism is, and the discourse of post-Soviet Russian nationalists simply wouldn't make sense without an explanation of where the concepts common to all Russian nationalists came from. Chapters 3–9 describe the particulars as well as the overlapping folds of contemporary Russian nationalisms, and reach some conclusions about which form of nationalism is likely to dominate the Russian political scene in the near term. It will become apparent to the reader that one of the underlying assumptions of this study is that Russia will go, in fact has already gone, nationalist. Chapter 10 returns to the attempt to put contemporary Russian nationalism, particularly its tendency toward anti-Westernism, in a proper world historical context. It analyzes just what the nationalists (not only in Russia) fear they are in danger of losing when their governments pursue a course of Westernization.

I have not attempted to hide any of my own prejudices or inclinations. We all have them. Like Chesterton's undesirable jurist, someone who brings no preliminary impressions to a serious (and widely discussed) problem is probably too ignorant to render an opinion that anyone else should take seriously. My ideas and opinions evolved considerably as I worked on this project. If my views fly in the face of the conventional wisdom or prove inconvenient for some, I can only confess to the reader that what I came to regard as the truth about the nature of nationalism and its post-cold war efflorescence has proved inconvenient for me as well.

Acknowledgments

I owe a debt of gratitude to the following people for their advice, encouragement, criticism, and other services rendered: Bill Crimmins, Bob Otto, Alynn Nathanson, Peter Reddaway, Jamila Abdelghani, Zbignew Rau, John Haskell, Edward Ericson, Ignat Solzhenitsyn, Alexis Klimoff, Walker Connor, John Dunlop, Richard Rowsen, Susan McEachern, Jim Chapman, and Gretchen Sandels. I would like to thank the Rockford Institute and the editors of *Chronicles* magazine, especially Thomas Fleming and Ted Pappas, for giving me the opportunity to fine-tune some of my ideas in the pages of their magazine and reproduce certain passages from those articles. As always, I owe special thanks to my wife, Stacy. The views expressed in this book are, of course, mine alone and do not reflect those of the Foreign Broadcast Information Service or any other agency of the federal government.

1

The Nationalist Imperative

The processes known as "modernization" are the primary cause of the efflorescence of nationalist phenomena in modern times. These processes tend to threaten social arrangements that underpin a people's sense of identity, a necessary element of human community. In any event, the powerful attachments of kinship, which are the bedrock of human identity, are ingrained in human nature and must be accounted for in any discussion of nationalist phenomena. "Nationalism" is the expression of the community's sense of identity and purpose as articulated by a myth-symbol complex. The power of nationalism is explicable if we recognize its connection with the sense of kinship. As the rationalizing forces of modernization expand globally, we should expect a sharp particularist—especially nationalist—reaction, as national communities' self-awareness is awakened by the encounter with the "other."

Historian John Lukacs once described nationalism as a modern phenomenon essentially different from what he called "patriotism." "Patriotism," he wrote, "grows from a sense of belonging to a particular country; it is confident rather than self-conscious; it is essentially defensive. Nationalism is self-conscious rather than confident; it is aggressive, and suspicious" of all those "who do not seem to agree with some of the popular nationalist ideology." "Patriotism," according to Lukacs, is premodern and traditionalist whereas "nationalism is ideological." "Patriotism is rooted to the land; nationalism to the mythical image of a people, of a community that is so often not a real community." Referring to the ideological content of "nationalism," Lukacs wrote that "patriotism is not a substitute for religion, whereas nationalism often is. It may fill the emotional needs of insufficiently rooted people." He then got to the heart of the matter, to the core of what is most often associated with "nationalism" in the West: "It [nationalism] may be combined with hatred—and, as [G. K.] Ches-

1

terton said, it is not love . . . but hatred that may unite otherwise very disparate men and women."[1]

Lukacs, to be sure, does not deny that "nationalist phenomena appear . . . earlier in history" but steadfastly associates "nationalism" with the modern era and a particular sort of jingoism, the most extreme form of which was German National Socialism.[2] Thus he sees "nationalism" as a chauvinistic ideology that displays aggressive tendencies, whereas "patriotism" is the simple, traditional, (and natural?) love of any man for what he views as his own. Lukacs's statement is an eloquent one, one that cuts close to the bone with a particular insight: both "nationalism" and "patriotism" are manifestations of a duality in the human heart. The same kinds of emotional attachments can generate quite different ideas and actions, which brings to mind the old saw about love and hate being but two sides of the same coin. Still, his definitions seem a bit fuzzy and unclear in their particulars. His references to attachments to the land obscure rather than illuminate what he means by the "nation." Is a nation a polity, a state? It *can* mean that, but Lukacs appears to use the term to mean both a people (a community that has generated a particular tradition) and a state. When Lukacs wrote that "patriotism" is, in part at least, a sense of "belonging to a particular country" and "nationalism" a mythical image of a people, does he mean that patriotic Frenchmen are loyal to their "country" (the state? a locality?) before their people? Could a "patriotic" German support "nationalistic" protectionist programs or immigration restrictions?[3] As far as myths go, it seems unlikely that any community has ever been able to generate a sense of solidarity without them.

To be fair, Lukacs was not attempting to address any of these issues, and a lack of clarity in using words like "nation," "nationalism," and "patriotism" is all too common, as is Lukacs's feeling that nationalism is a modern phenomenon. This common (among intellectuals at any rate) assumption is not, however, undisputed.

The Nationalist Debate

Sociologists and historians who have studied the concepts of nation and nationalism have historically been divided (unevenly) between the currently dominant modernist and the older minority primordialist schools of thought.

The primordialist sees nations as the stuff of history, a universal attribute of humanity since the Bronze Age, at least. The predominance in recorded history (and suggested in archeological evidence of prehistory) of primordial ties "based on language, religion, race, ethnicity

and territory" led primordialists to "claim that nations and ethnic communities are the natural units of history and integral elements of the
human experience" and that "there is nothing particularly modern
about nationalism, nor is it likely to disappear with any marked alter-
ation of 'modern conditions.' "[4]

The history of the ancient Hebrews is surely the history of a nation
in the eyes of the primordialist, complete with genealogical records, a
unique religion, and a sense of ethnic solidarity. Palestine remained
the promised land even after the dispersion of the Jews as a people,
thus adding a territorial dimension. Hebrew remained the scriptural
language of Judaism in exile and diaspora.

Moreover, the Jews were not the only nation to see themselves as
unique (a chosen people) and possessing a destiny set by God (or the
gods), the motif of chosenness being common throughout recorded
history. Modern Englishmen and Americans, for example, have taken
up the white man's burden and subdued barbarians in the name of
Manifest Destiny. Ancient Greeks and Romans regarded all peoples
who did not live in city-states or did not share their cultures as barbarians. In the ancient world "we find movements that appear to resemble
modern nationalism in several respects, notably a desire to liberate territories conquered by aliens, or to resist foreign encroachments, like
the Ioanian resistance to Persian expansion in the late sixth century
BC or in the Gallic resistance to Caesar's campaigns."[5] Primordialists
perceive "an ancient analogue for the modern system of nation-states
in the Tell-el-Amarna period of the 14th century BC, when a number
of powerful states—New Kingdom Egypt, the Hittite Empire, the kingdom of Mitanni and Kassite Babylon—were engaged in a complex network of diplomatic and military alliances and conflicts, such as was
much later to characterize Europe in the modern period."[6]

Modernists, however, tend to see nations and nationalism as wholly
modern phenomena whose naturalness is only assumed by people living in the "age of nationalism."[7] They explain this by pointing to the
changes in social, political, and economic structures that have defined
modernity. Premodern agrarian societies, which required a stable and
sedentary way of life in order to ensure food production, encouraged
social stratification. The great mass of humanity in such societies must
preoccupy itself with food production while a small minority devotes
itself to administrative functions or highly specialized arts and crafts.
Literacy is necessary for the minority of scribes, priests, and court functionaries, but not for the masses. Interaction between polities (city-
states, kingdoms, empires) is the purview of the ruling stratum. All of
the various classes, castes, or estates may be of differing ethnic background and religion or, at the very least, adhere to varying "high" and

"low" traditions that have little in common, including language. Each must know his place and station in a society that lacks mobility and social fluidity. Thus, caste, class, and other divisions are highlighted; the law of taboo, of custom and tradition, governs social behavior. Status and privilege determine outcomes in disputes. Persons who belong to a "high" tradition culture of functionaries, such as priests and rulers, identify primarily with their class or caste; members of a "low," or folk culture, identify with their immediate kinship group and village.

Some modernists stress the importance of structural, or socioeconomic, qualities in determining the nature of a given society, a view maintaining that ideas and ideologies are, for the most part, generated by the necessities of the economic and social superstructure and not vice versa. Agrarian societies generate a more or less standard worldview in which religion explains man's existence and purpose (discouraging those inclined to question the particulars of that existence and purpose and thereby disrupt the social structure). Birth more or less determines one's occupation and status, and caste or class privilege determines legal standing. Custom and tradition provided whatever social lubricant was necessary for the functioning of day-to-day affairs. Ideas per se are only of secondary importance (at best). This is particularly true of nationalist ideologies and ideologues who "did not really make much difference" to the movement toward nationalism because the situation determined that "if one of them had fallen, others would have stepped into his place."[8] Others stress the importance of ideas in generating changes in the socioeconomic superstructure but this appears to be a minority persuasion.[9] Modernists see nationalism and nations as an impossibility under premodern conditions, despite some vague analogies that can be made with nationalist-looking ideas and movements in the distant past.

The age of nationalism was preceded, say the modernists, by changes in social organization, particularly in changes related to political and economic centralization and the development of industrialism.[10] Neither a bureaucratic functionary of a blossoming mercantile state nor the merchants and manufacturers of early modern Europe could stand for the maintenance of a social system that fused "labour, technique, material and mould, prescribed by custom, tied to a social order and rhythm" when "his progress and the advancement of the economy of which he is a part hinges . . . on his untrammeled selection of whatever means, in the light of evidence and nothing else, serves some clear aim such as the maximization of profit" or the material aggrandizement of the state, particularly as improved agricultural techniques gradually lessened the importance of the peasantry and a stable, even stagnant, social order.[11] Indeed, under premodern feudal-ism people would have been "hard put to it to single out a solitary, isolable criterion of success. Profit for them would have been merged in a number of inseparable other considerations, such as the mainte-nance of their positions in the community."[12]

The humanist thinkers of the Renaissance began the process of pro-viding the new order with its ideological justification, ideas that were further developed during the Enlightenment. Rationalism provided the stuff of the new ideologies. Two elements were prominent in the new rationality: consistency, or the "like treatment of like cases," which provided the basis for a systematic and regular standardization, and efficiency, or "the cool rational selection of the best available means to . . . clearly formulated and isolated ends."[13] The two concepts easily fit the requirements of the bureaucratized and centralized mer-cantile state and the expanding manufacturing and capitalist strata who required a single legal, linguistic, and monetary space in order to work effectively. In short, the new order demanded the breakup of the old. The new economic situation demanded a mobile workforce, a standardized idiom and a homogenized culture. The old world of "multiple, not properly united, but hierarchically related sub-worlds, and the existence of special privileged facts [known but to specialized castes, classes, or priests]" retarded the growth of the new system.[14] All systems of thought, social organization, or economic production that could not be rationalized, that is, justified by serving a clearly formulated and isolated purpose, were disposable.

The state, through the agency of positive law, began the gradual breakup of the old system by attacking the patchwork of classes, guilds, and special privileges and by providing a standardized legal and monetary system for the industrialists and capitalists. The move toward centralization and the destruction of the feudal order was facil-itated by the new "modern" ideologies of liberalism and democracy. The new order systematically undermined the old, replacing the priestly class with the intelligentsia as the guardians of the Word, and creating centralized state educational systems to produce reasonably literate workers who could function in the standardized idiom of the new world of interchangeable parts, both human and material. The new idiom demanded a standardized ethic to mobilize the masses (who were replacing classes) as well as national traditions. Myths were concocted by elites to turn provincials whose primary identity had been at the village level into Frenchmen, Germans, and so on.

Modernists maintain, however, that the creation of the new system did not proceed without a measure of pain. The dislocated masses, deprived of the certainty and continuity of the old world and crowded

into rapidly industrializing metropolitan areas, were prone to mob behavior, and the old world did not always "go gentle into that good
night," as demonstrated by the violence of the French revolution. New
identities had to be forged, and the displaced provincial had but two
choices: conform or wither in the stagnant village. Some, because of the
prominence of their differences with others (race, ethnicity, divergent
religious traditions), could not, or would not, be easily homogenized
into the new "nation." Some groups suffered from their former privileged status as outsiders who had performed necessary functions, such
as usury, that had been forbidden to others by religious strictures and
ethical norms. Having had no valuable experience in such fields put
members of the new "nation" at a competitive disadvantage with the
formerly privileged group and caused social friction under the newly
minted egalitarian ethic that disdained class privilege and special
status. The minority's "otherness" was now a liability.

The social lubricant of the new order, as viewed through the modernist prism, was the promise of ever expanding material wealth. Rationalism, egalitarianism, and the promise of scientific discovery and
continuous economic growth became the coin by which the new nations were bought off. Few had any doubt that the rationalization of
social and economic relations combined with new discoveries would
provide for an ever expanding pie for the nation. Progress was the
watchword for the proud nations of new Europe; nationalist and pro-
gressivist ideologies relegated traditional religious faith to a support-
ive role at best.

Europe, having learned the secrets of the universe and the key to
earthly progress, absentmindedly conquered the world, partly by force
and partly by superior social, economic, and political organization that
enabled Europeans to circumnavigate the globe, cure previously incur-
able diseases, build arsenals of advanced weaponry, and produce
wealth such as the world had never seen. To put it bluntly, the non-
European world had to "modernize" or face conquest or stagnation.
Elites in Asia, in Latin America, and later in Africa began to attempt
to apply European developmental models at home. "Nation building"
was their task.

Because nations have largely been built on mythical elements concocted by elites to provide a standardized ethic and baseline homogenized culture as a means of generating solidarity and social cohesion,
there may be reason to think, according to the modernist argument,
that nations themselves will someday be superseded by something
larger. If nations are the products of social organization and ideology,
there is no reason to doubt the possibility of creating a world nation, a
nation that is coextensive with humanity, especially as classical eco-

nomic theories involving a division of labor between nations break down in the face of transnational corporations and world quasi-governmental organs working to lower protectionist barriers and impediments to capital mobility. A world without borders would ensure labor mobility, and moves toward global economic integration would ensure investment worldwide. Moreover, the "rationalization" of economic relations appears to be the goal of the developed nations; the broad outlines of a world culture, based on the manufactured pop culture of the first world, are already visible in the second and third worlds. Nationalism, then, is "not necessarily a form of particularism."[15]

Modernist Dissent and the Nationalist Babel

Modernist notions of nations and nationalism have been significantly modified by the work of British sociologist Anthony D. Smith. Smith, while criticizing both modernist and primordialist approaches to the question of nationalism, proposed a synthesis of the old positions in his 1986 book, *The Ethnic Origins of Nations.*

Smith's theory is that "modern nations are not as 'modern' as modernists would have us believe." Moreover, "if they were they could not survive," for "nations require ethnic cores if they are to survive. If they lack one, they must 'reinvent' one."[16] Smith presents a mountain of evidence to show that nations do require an overarching common culture, a language, and a certain degree of uniformity in customs, religion, and so forth. It is doubtful, however, that such commonalties can be entirely manufactured. The mythologies of successful nations (those that have successfully integrated varying provincial and cultural groups into a new nation) must have psychological resonance for the masses. Thus a totally counterfeit "myth-symbol" complex and constitutive myth, or mythomoteur—one that does not build on certain commonalties already present—is doomed to failure. Structural changes by themselves do not account for the feeling of solidarity among citizens of modern nations, which requires a credible identity if the individual citizen is to to feel at home within the national community, something that the standard modernist argument tends to discount.

Following Smith's argument to its logical conclusions, it is much easier to make Frenchmen (using the Parisian cultural baseline) out of Gascoqne provincials than Algerian Arabs, even when they speak French and Algeria was at one time considered a department of the French Republic. Algerians have a ready made Muslim (or Arab) identity that is very much alive, an identity that has the power to generate a particularist solidarity in a people whose physical appearance also differs from that of the ethnic core of the French nation. The myth-symbol complex of France, with its Christian Frankish emperors and Joan of Arc cultural motifs, as well as its Napoleonic and revolutionary mythomoteur, may not be flexible enough to absorb them, at least in large numbers. Efforts by African states to "build nations" that cut drastically across ethnic and cultural lines have failed largely because not enough commonalties among the groups can be found to generate "national" solidarity.[17] Moreover, it has been difficult enough for France to make Frenchmen out of Bretons, who have maintained a separate Celtic myth-symbol complex to this day, to say nothing of Basques and Corsicans. The modern state of Israel has been largely successful in generating national solidarity among disparate peoples probably because of the successful incorporation of Hebrew constitutive histories (the calling of Abraham, the Exodus, King David, the revolt of the Maccabees) in a new national mythomoteur that gives credibility to an Israeli identity through Jewish nationalism.[18]

Socialization within a potentially "national" group is itself no easy task, particularly if competing mythomoteurs and mythic motifs vie for the loyalty of the nation's potential citizens. Following Smith, we can deduce that the American Civil War was in large part a result of competing mythomoteurs and the competing identities they generated. Thus both sides claimed to be upholding the tradition of the founders but had markedly different notions about what they had founded in the first place. Alexander Hamilton's centralizing and mercantile program was a part of the legitimizing myth-symbol complex of a Northern society that embraced the constitution as a charter for an indivisible and "mystical union." The divisibility of the union was inconceivable to people attached to this image of America. The Southerners saw the Northerners as the betrayers of the founding, the Yankees' centralizing tendencies counteracting the very rights the founders had seen as the heritage of their people. The divisions have long outlived the original quarrel. The same could be said of royalists and republicans in France, prorepublic and pro-Franco Spaniards, and countless others for whom the loss of a particular symbol, the destruction of a particular monument, or the rewriting of the history of a particular event can be tantamount to a denial of their identity.

Class differences may impede the formation of a national identity as the prime mover of a society, particularly an agrarian one whose class differences (and local and clan identities) have so stratified the population that speaking of it as a single nation is sometimes quite problematic. The answer (according to Smith) to the complex problem of national socialization lies in successfully combing elements of "high" and "low" traditions that cut across class lines, as the ancient Hebrews and the modern Israelis did in combining dynastic legitimizing stories and genealogies of kings with communal ones of the tribes and the people.

Smith notes a certain rough uniformity in various constitutive myth motifs or myths of ethnic origins and descent that constitute a pool of potential materials for the myth maker to choose from. These include

1. a myth of origins in time; i.e. when the community was 'born';
2. a myth of origins in space; i.e. where the community was 'born';
3. a myth of ancestry; i.e. who bore us, and how we are descended from him/her;
4. a myth of migration; i.e. whither we wandered;
5. a myth of liberation; i.e. how we were freed;
6. a myth of the golden age; i.e. how we became great and heroic;
7. a myth of decline; i.e. how we decayed and were conquered/exiled; and
8. a myth of rebirth; i.e. how we shall be restored to our former glory.[19]

A dominant ethnic group wishing to absorb lesser ones and create a nation must, in Smith's view, have a myth-symbol complex and constitutive mythology that draws on the various types of mythic motifs listed above and that has enough commonalties with the lesser groups to be the baseline for a common national identity. Thus Castilian mythology was a (mostly) successful baseline for integrating the Iberian peninsula and creating the nation of Spain. The founders of the new nation then incorporate civic elements of common citizenship, a common legal and linguistic space, and a common economic zone to flesh out the nation-state.

By the fusion of ethnic mythology and civic elements, Smith created a sort of neomodernism that does not reject the general structural arguments about types of nationalism. Generally, the two main types are described by modernists as Western nationalism, which emphasizes civic membership, and Eastern nationalism, which leans more heavily on the ethnic element of national community. Western nationalism tends to be more democratic, emphasizing egalitarianism, and is potentially a model for the world nation some modernists foresee. Diaspora nationalism tends to be more Eastern, since the diaspora community's sense of solidarity is usually reinforced by pariah status.[20] Smith, by emphasizing the importance of the "ethnic" element evident even in Western nationalism, partially rehabilitates the primordialists while acknowledging the importance of standardized education systems, centralized administration of state and economy, and the civic elements of modernism.

Terminological Confusion and Ethnonationalism

None of this, however, helps clear up our original confusion about just what scholars mean when they use words like nation and nationalism, and how "nationalism" might differ from "patriotism." The answer lies in the fact that different scholars from varying backgrounds and disciplines are very often talking about *different concepts* even when they use the same word.[21] Structuralists use the words *nation* and *nationalism* in conjunction with the concept of "nation-building." They emphasize economic determinism and give little attention, generally speaking, to things they call "ethnicity" or "race." When structuralists (and other modernists as well) write about nation-building they are speaking of a particular form of socioeconomic and political organization; in other words they are describing the formation of what are erroneously (in most cases) called "nation states." France is a nation-state, an industrial society with a centralized political, legal, and (to a certain degree) economic system that operates within a given territory, and whose citizens constitute a highly mobile, literate, and (for the most part) culturally homogeneous population. All citizens participate in the rituals of the "civic religion" of the state, and the intellectual climate of the nation is secular, rationalist, and liberal democratic. Since we are speaking of artificially contrived, modernized, egalitarian (to varying degrees), highly individualistic societies, whose highest values are material and personal aggrandizement, it is no surprise that modernists downplay ethnicity and race, think Eastern nations and African "nation builders" may need some tutoring on this score, and speak of "tribalism," "racism," or "chauvinism" as impediments to nation building.

Thus, nations are modern *states*, nationalism an ideology associated with justifying structural reorganization of society through *nation building*,[22] and "nationality" is a synonym for *citizenship*. "National" means *state-wide*, and patriotism usually means loyalty to a *state*.

It is no wonder, then, that many modernists see nations and nation-states as a passing phase in the social, political, and economic evolution of humanity; that nation building is a progressive step up the evolutionary ladder for third world Africa, Asia, and Latin America; and that a world federation is the future of mankind. Thus "trans-national" or "multi-national" actually means *trans-state* and *multi-state*, and the United Nations (scholars aren't the only ones who are terminologically confused) is a prototype world federation government.

Primordialists use the word nation in a sense that is closer to the word's origins in the Latin *natio* "birth," and patriotism in the sense of *patria* "fatherland." Indeed, Greeks, Germans, Russians, and many others have referred to their country, their territory as it were, as their fatherland. The nation is the people, the extended kinship group bound by blood, common experience, and history; the *patria, Vaterland, or Otechetsvo* is the "land of my fathers." The tie that binds *is not* the territory or polity itself but the sense of common ancestry that is given concrete reality in national mythology, religion, art, customs, language, and folkways. Landscapes and national memory are intimately connected, of course, but diaspora nations such as Armenians and Jews, as well as diaspora Chinese and Greeks, have managed for centuries to survive "territorially" on the strength of an image of a historical homeland. Primordialists assert that such kinship bonds constitute the strongest human tie. This is what they mean when they say that nations are a "natural" thing, that nations are, in some cases at least, very old, and are extensions of earlier tribal, clan, and family units. A state is most decidedly not a nation, and nation building, the extension of the kinship-based group, is an enormously complicated task that must rest on an ethnic foundation whose primary tie is blood.

Whereas the work of Smith begins to build a bridge between the two schools, it is the work of political scientist Walker Connor that has clarified the issues (and the terminological chaos) and offered yet another alternative to modernism and primordialism that may be called "neoprimordialism."[23]

Connor cuts through the structuralist problem and proceeds to the heart of the matter: Nationalism means ethnonationalism, loyalty to the *ethnos*, the nation; the nation is the largest group of people who imagine themselves to be related; nationality designates the nation that one belongs to; and patriotism as commonly used by scholars means loyalty to state and not to the nation, while loyalty to the fatherland is merely an extension of loyalty to the nation for those fortunate enough to identify the state with the nation, either as a true nation-state or in the guise of a *Staatvolk* state. Moreover, there are quite few true nation-states, states whose inhabitants are members of a single, distinct nation with a sense of national purpose and destiny; the age of the multinational state is over; and the age of nationalism is far from played out. The myth of economic man is comforting to structuralists and those who dream of a world nation, but the truth is that material aggrandizement is very often trumped by the nation's sense of self-preservation. Finally, the chances of assimilation of aliens by "immigrant" states is highly problematic under modern conditions.

Japan, Germany, and Iceland are true nation-states. Some states, such as France, Spain, China, and Russia, are dominated by a particular nation that is the heart and soul of the state. These are *Staatvolk* states. Others, including most of the third world states of Africa and

Asia, Belgium, and Canada, as well as the former Yugoslavia and Soviet Union, are properly called binational or multinational states. Thus
the age of the nation-state has only structural significance, according
to Connor, and in fact most of the so-called nation-states which had
modernized decades or centuries before are showing signs of nationalist conflict that has in no way been abated by modernization, which
more likely exacerbates national tensions and helps to incite calls for
nations to establish independent states.

In order to see where nationalism, especially in the form of a nation
demanding its own state, as well as modernization fit in to Connor's
theories, we must first go back to the question of political, economic,
and administrative centralization and bureaucratization that preceded
the age of nationalism, which roughly coincides with the period of the
Enlightenment and the concept of popular sovereignty.

Connor accepts the picture of revolutionary social change presented
by the structuralists. But the real nature of the states created as a result
of the destruction of feudal arrangements is not (by and large) that of
nation-states, but of what Connor calls the "integrated state," a state
wherein little escapes the new bureaucratic, economic, and political
structures. In fact, the very nature of the integrated state, with its lust
for administration, standardization, and centralization, as well as its
tendency to break up older social structures, vitalizes a dynamic of
expansion of the integrated society that cannot allow for autonomous
and nonstandardized communities.

The integrated state arose in tandem with liberalism and democratism, which asserted that the consent of the governed was required for
a state's legitimacy. Thus popular sovereignty and Rousseau's "general will" became the slogan of mass democracy. But whose general
will would be asserted? "All sovereignty resides essentially in the Nation. No body, no individual can exercise authority which does not
explicitly emanate from it," reads article 3 of the Declaration of the
Rights of Man and Citizen.[24] But which nation? There were, after all,
Bretons, Basques, Corsicans, Normans, and Parisian Frenchmen of the
kingdom's heartland who could claim nationhood. The Parisian heartland offered a ready-made high culture, as well as an administrative
center and numerical dominance to build on. The henceforth classless
people would be a French nation or, to be more precise, they would be
absorbed by the French nation. The nation was deified as the new
source of mystical power, the state was seen as the locus of the general
will, and the cult of civic religion replaced Catholicism as the faith of
the realm. In this way modern nationalism was intimately connected
with democracy and mass society. Modern France was created as a
Staatvolk state, and the Parisian culture was strong enough and shared

enough in the way of mythic motifs to successfully homogenize most (but not all) provincials.

The revolution, however, unleashed more than democratic, egalitarian nationalism and the liberal cult of individualism. Both the dynamic of social and economic revolution through structural change and the logic of individualism demanded the breakup of old social structures, from the class system to the autonomous family unit itself. State centralization was required for both. The powerful bureaucratic state administration could then proceed with the task of breaking up traditional society. This may appear to contradict liberal theory, but if one is to be liberated from the social bonds that have prevented mobility and a fluidity of social relations, and simultaneously build an industrialized society whose reason for being is "progress," centralization and state intrusion are necessary. Discerning the general will can also be a problem, particularly as democracy has a tendency to run aground on the shoals of group special interests. Thus revolutionaries took on the mantle of being the vanguard of the general will, which was always (theoretically) aimed toward furthering ideological aims. The French Revolution carried within it not only the seeds of democracy and liberalism but of totalitarianism as well, in both its "red" and "brown" varieties. It gave birth to the revolutionary slogan Liberty, Equality, and Fraternity, but also to national chauvinism in a new, mobilized form.[25] They were, after all, intimately connected at the beginning, but the logic of the civic nature of Western nationalism, with its emphasis on the social contract instead of nationality per se (as defined by Connor) leads some to universalize the egalitarian contract principle, whereas others emphasized the national element to the detriment of all other values.[26]

Feudalism, the Multinational State, and National Consciousness

Feudalist regimes had operated on a principle of homage, duty, service, and obligation in the context of an agrarian social order. Separate communities existed more or less in isolation from one another. Contacts with outsiders were relatively few and far between. In short, multinational empires based on feudal social arrangements did not require centralization, standardization, or uniformity. No general idiom was necessary for decentralized food production; education was a matter for the local community to deal with; the workforce was ready-made; specialists trained apprentices in their trades and crafts. It simply did not matter, at least as far as day-to-day matters were concerned, who ruled or what language was spoken at court. This arrangement's relative success and longevity accounts for the modernist emphasis on social, political, and economic structures and their assertion that human identity is (probably) an artificial construct that (perhaps) has an infinite range of flexibility.[27] It is most difficult for modernists, particularly structuralists and nation builders, to accept ancient Greeks or Hebrews as a real nation not because they lacked national self-awareness or the capability to mount temporarily concerted efforts in war or diplomacy but a nation-state, a modern, classless, centralized, integrated state that is capable of mobilizing a national community and directing coordinated action toward specific aims defined by the general will through the agency of that state. Some modernists can have it both ways: On the one hand, nations and nation-states are modern, and that's that; on the other, who says multiethnic states are risky enterprises?

As modern arrangements replaced feudal ones and as the integrated state displaced fiefdoms, principalities, kingdoms, microstates, and empires as the fundamental political unit of modernity two developments emerged. First, prenational groups, slumbering nations whose people may not have been aware of the fundamental commonalities they shared with other tribes or clans in adjacent regions, developed a national consciousness. The dominant group in a *Staatvolk* state or a new nation-state develops a sense of nationhood (if it hasn't already, à la the ancient Hebrews or Greeks), aided by the modern revolution in communications (everything from the printing press to radio and TV), the increased frequency and duration of contacts with other members of the emerging nation through improvements in transportation (everything from railroads to jet airliners), the experience of industrial labor in factories and life in larger towns and cities, the indoctrination of the masses in the national mythomoteur, and mass mobilization for war. Thus Frenchmen were molded, in some sense, *after* the French state was created.

But there are those troublesome pariah groups and small nations of the old polity to consider. What happens to their consciousness? The pariah group, almost by definition, already has a sense of otherness. But what of those Bretons, Basques, Catalonians, Irishmen, Kurds, Sikhs, and the like? Diverse nations were able to exist more or less peacefully for some time in Ethiopia, for example. Ethiopia has a three-thousand-year history behind it as a multinational polity. But in modern times the Ethiopian state has experienced conflict within as a result of persistent national separatist movements in Eritrea and Tigre. Thailand, another multinational state with a long history, has experienced similar difficulties with the Lao and Malay peoples in the past quarter century. The same could be said of many other African and Asian states that escaped colonialism in the 1960s, states which were created out of largely decentralized colonial administrative units.[28]

The answer as to why this happens, once we have grasped the processes of modernization in the first world, is not at all difficult to perceive. If centralization, standardization, and more or less forced cultural uniformity successfully homogenized like groups in modernized states by increasing national consciousness or creating a new mythomoteur out of familiar mythic motifs, it has the exactly opposite effect on small national groups. "As a result of this new presence [the integrated state in the forms described above], resentment of foreign rule has become an important political factor for the first time" in such states. "In addition to the question of who rules [raised by the ubiquitous gospel of popular sovereignty and democracy trumpeted throughout the world by the communications revolution], there is the matter of cultural preservation." Feudal systems or undeveloped unintegrated states do not necessarily pose a "serious threat to the lifeways" of the small nations, but the communications and transportation improvements that accompany modernization increase the duration and frequency of intergroup contacts. Industrialization threatens traditional lifeways and puts the "other" in competition with the dominant group for jobs, economic development of the homeland, state subsidies, and so forth. Standardized educational institutions threaten the very cultural survival of a nation through homogenization and assimilation.[29]

The member of the small nation too becomes more aware of his likeness with other clan or tribal kinship groups of his own nascent nationality. He also becomes more conscious of what separates him from the dominant group, and the more disparate the nations by way of race, religion, language, as well as other "badges" of identity, the more likely the small nation is to want to go it alone.[30] Rule by aliens in conditions of modernity is not something that most people can accept without reservation. True, some may assimilate, but the possibility of assimilation, as the modernists perceive, may be partly limited by external factors. There is also the psychological aspect to consider.

Modernists are in some sense correct in saying that national identity is a myth. Nations are built on common experience and history, a shared constitutive myth, a common set of mythic motifs, and other factors that tend to reinforce national identity, such as language, literature, styles of dress, national cuisine, religion, and a hodgepodge of folkways. The shared experiences of the ancient Hebrews helped to form their constitutive myth and forge a nation out of tribal groups. Other commonalties cemented the pact. A similar process now seems to be happening with the Palestinian Arabs. All of these psychological factors are part and parcel of what nationalists call the national character. They are subjective and internalized and thus are mythic in quality.

Nations, like other types of human associations, depend on constant revitalization—on passing on mythic motifs and constitutive myths from generation to generation. A fear of extinction excited by modernization and the loss of national consciousness in the face of the homogenizing influences of the integrated state is not an unreasonable one. One telling sign of the resilience and persistence of particular identities in the modern world is the fact that a national group may lose many of the external attributes of national distinctiveness, or even wholly change its constitutive myth, yet retain a powerful sense of otherness. Modern Egypt's Copts, for example, claim descent from the inhabitants of the land of the pharaohs (the word *Copt* is derived from the Greek word for Egyptian), yet their myth-symbol complex and constitutive mythology revolves around their Christian faith. In their case, a wholly different mythic identity was formed around religion to replace the pharaonic myth that had lost its vitality. Today the Copts are afloat in the Middle Eastern sea of Islam, and it is Christianity that provides one of their badges of Egyptianness and binds them to the land of the Nile. A more vital unifying experience has kept alive a sense of national separateness after the old myths died.[31] The Egyptians of King Tut are long gone, but Egyptianness lives on in a new form.

External physical factors account for part of the strength of particular identities. But physical factors are not a necessary element of particularism, and national consciousness can survive the loss of many of the nonphysical attributes of separateness. Connor has noted the powerful sense of otherness that is evident among the Irish, a sense of uniqueness and consciousness that outlived the loss of their native language. The Irish nationalists of the nineteenth and early twentieth centuries, for instance, stressed the importance of Gaelic in uniting the Irish people against the hated English, "but postindependence attempts to resurrect Gaelic have been spurned." In Northern Ireland the vitality of Irish identity is often masked by confusion as to the nature of the Ulster conflict, which is partly due to a tendency among persons of English and Scottish extraction to use a sort of nationalist shorthand for describing the other, in this case the Irish minority. The Irish are often described as Catholics, and the Irish refer to the alien as "Prod." The casual observer may therefore be forgiven for mistaking the Ulster conflict for a religious clash. Like the Copts in Egypt, the Irish have lost their language and many other external signs of "otherness." They now partly depend on identification with a religion, in this case Catholicism, as a badge of uniqueness. The commonly heard term "Irish Catholics" suggests that being Catholic in Ireland is somehow doctrinally different from being Catholic in Spain.[32]

Research into the national identifications of Ulster residents supports such a conclusion. A survey conducted in the 1960s found that residents of Northern Ireland chose to identify themselves as "Irish" (43 percent), "British" (29 percent), "Ulster" (21 percent), or "mixed, other, or uncertain nationality" (7 percent). We may assume "on the basis of the ethnic and religious histories of the island, that there exists a close correlation between self-identification as Irish" and at least nominal Catholicism. The "British" or "Ulstermen" have, it appears, developed a separate identity *in opposition to* the Irish. Any talk of the Ulster conflict as a religious quarrel between "Irishmen" is therefore misleading. The religious dimension of the conflict is largely a cover for conflicting national identities, something that is illustrated vividly by the tendency on the part of the region's population to ignore any call for peace by religious leaders of either group.[33] Moreover, materialistic Marxism has served as a vehicle for some militants to pursue "Irish Catholic" nationalist aims. Religion and religious ceremony remains a powerful unifying force for nations, even if belief itself is only skin deep.

If some observers have mistaken the Irish-Ulstermen conflict for a religious one on the basis of the nonphysical elements of "otherness," the same can be said of conflicts between Walloons and Flemings (supposedly over language), or Ukrainians and Russians (language, religion). The truth is that no one nonphysical factor determines national consciousness and that the specific conditions of the particular conflict determine which attributes, or badges, become the focus of what are essentially disputes between nations over territory and national identity. But if nations identify themselves to the outsiders on the basis of largely dispensable nonphysical badges, what is the essence of national identity? What explains the tenacity of national passions that animate the struggle of "us" against "them"? Connor takes the sense of family found in national communities to its logical ends. The nation is a self-defining unit (the Palestinians are a nation because they say they are, which means also that they may decide who is Palestinian and who is not) whose sense of national consciousness is ultimately based on the foundation of common ancestry. We are speaking of a *mythic* blood tie. All that is necessary to give any national consciousness vitality is a sense of common ancestry that is given concrete reality in external badges and myths, above all in a communal experience that forever binds the community together as an extended family. This is the essence of the nation, of an identity that, in a test of loyalties, trumps all others. In this way, American black nationalism, and recurring Scotch, Welsh, Irish, Breton, Basque, Kurd, Afrikaner, and French Canadian nationalism are explicable. The Scots and Welsh, long since thought to have been made "British" through assimilation, have lost their languages and many other nonphysical signs of separateness, but as long as any shred of separateness remains, the sometimes mythic blood tie can be reasserted in the face of the external threat.

As Connor points out, this feeling of common ancestry explains the "psychological depth" of nationalism's power. It is a *feeling*—adoptive parents fight for their children—that will survive any scientific evidence about the roots of the German nation's lying in a mixture of Celtic and Teutonic tribes or historical facts about Napoleon's or Stalin's origins. But this feeling *must* have as its binding tie the internalized sense of blood relation. Connor notes how even "immigrant states" refer to the land of "our Fathers" and speak of "founding Fathers," implying both legitimacy through lineage and a limitation to the ability of such states to assimilate foreigners, especially those for whom the *image* of the founders is not plausible due to either physical factors or nonphysical consciousness. In the modern world, loyalty to a state is primary only when the state is coterminous with the nation and the conditions of modernity, both objective (social, political, and economic systems) and subjective (popular sovereignty, national self-determination), have made all such multinational integrated states vulnerable to nationalist conflict.

The sense of family that animates nations explains why economic considerations are not sufficient to either dampen or explain nationalist agitation. To be sure, uneven development in multinational states may help spur conflict between a national minority and the dominant group, and the slogans of class interest and Marxism may be used by the minority (as they were against colonial regimes in Asia and Africa), but economic improvement is highly unlikely to stop such frictions, whose sources lie elsewhere. The notion of economic viability has not stopped the formerly Soviet Baltic states from going their own way, and the same could be said of Chechnya and Abkhazia, to say nothing of Slovakia in eastern Europe or of Ireland in western Europe.

Our argument up to this point asserts that whereas integrated states are modern and many prenations developed a national consciousness as a result of that modernization, the psychological force of nationalism is primordial and based on the sense of common ancestry. We have, therefore, fused modernism with Smith's myth-symbol complex explanation of national identity and Connor's "ethnonationalism." Modern nations are the extensions, real or imagined, of kinship ties that once animated family, clan, or tribe, giving the members of such kinship groups a sense of belonging and purpose. National myths, as well as physical and nonphysical badges, demarcate the boundaries of the national group, enabling its members to tell "us" from "them." The dynamics of modernization and the imperatives of the integrated state make multinational states extremely vulnerable to nationalist conflicts and further complicate the already complex problem of assimilating foreigners in immigrant states. Nationalism is a primary identity, an identity that asserts itself against all others in a test of loyalties.

What our argument has implied but has not explicitly stated so far is that nationalism, tribalism, clannishness, or whatever it may be called, is natural and thus an unavoidable, even necessary, element of human community. Modernists' assumptions about human nature lead them to envision a world nation, a vision that rejects both the physical and nonphysical attributes of nations as secondary (at best) to other factors relevant to nation building. Despite our argument's recognition of the mythic and subjective quality of a nation's badges, and even, in many cases, the imagined sense of common relation that animates nationalism and underpins national consciousness, we assert that these elements have an objective base in human nature, something that neither Smith nor Connor explicitly maintain. This nature is objective, though it manifests itself at different times in different ways and provides the boundaries for human action against which all theories of nationalism must be tested.

Nationalism and Human Nature

C. S. Lewis once wrote that when we speak of love, we also refer to the object of affection. We say "he loves so and so," attaching the love of an individual to a particular object. The phrase "he loves" simply doesn't make sense. Man must have an object *to love*; "love" (or hate, for that matter) in the abstract is virtually meaningless. True, one often hears that "God is love," but surely what we mean is that "God loves *us*." God loves His creation, a domain so vast, and filled with such an enormous quantity of beings and objects as to be practically incomprehensible to the human mind. Only God can comprehend all that He has created. Only a Being who is without beginning and end Himself could grasp this vast universe we inhabit.

Man himself is a finite, limited creature. Our horizons cannot match those of the Creator. "The universe," like "a billion dollars," is a catchphrase thrown about without much consideration of the fact that for most of us it is an abstraction, a phrase perhaps meant to convey a field so vast, a sum so large, as to be overwhelming to the listener. There is really no thought that the listener will picture "the universe" in his mind. The best he may manage is to conjure up an image of the Crab Nebula or the Milky Way, dots of brilliant light shining in a mysterious black firmament, a vault so huge that we can only grasp its vastness by picturing a tiny section of the sky, the light from the distant stars already older than the world by the time our pitifully limited minds can receive and form an image of it.

Our own world is, indeed *must* be, limited to a scale we can grasp. Our minds are capable of processing only so much information at a single time, our imaginations bound to the store of knowledge we already have at hand. The frame of reference for most of us is our own home, our workplace, and the places we have visited or have seen on television. Yet even those we have visited vicariously through television or films, or heard tell of, remain something of an abstraction; there remains an air of unreality about them. We can attribute smells, tastes, and other sensory perceptions to them as we wish, having had no experience of them ourselves.

The words "humanity" and "mankind" have the same quality about them that words like universe and infinity have, a quality that is related to the number of people involved, the scale of distances theoretically measured, the meaninglessness of incomprehensible numbers. Humanity must remain, for the most part at least, the purview of philosophical speculators, scholars, or theologians, who are trained to think in such terms. Most of us find it difficult enough to keep track of our own extended families. Besides the limitations of our minds in processing the enormous quantities of information and sensory perceptions that we are bombarded with each day, we are also limited by a finite quantity of emotional capital available to us to deal with the ins and outs of our everyday existence.

During the horrific Ethiopian famine of the early 1980s, I had a conversation with a friend about the ability of ordinary people to gasp with shock at the hellish images of the starving unfortunates and then go about their business. His reply has stuck with me to this day: He said that spending time contemplating the deaths of strangers, however distressing the circumstances, drains people of the emotional energy necessary to deal with the uncertainties of their own lives and responsibilities. They would probably be driven mad as well. Our minds would simply overload, overheat, and shut down as a nuclear reactor does during a meltdown.

The ability to feel empathy is limited and must be so. It is part of our built-in survival mechanism. Writing on humanity's aggressive impulses, ethologist Konrad Lorenz put it this way: The "Cro-Magnon warrior had plenty of hostile neighbors against whom to discharge his aggressive drive, and he had just the right number of reliable friends to love. His moral responsibility was not overtaxed by an exercise of function which prevented him from striking, in sudden anger, at his companions with his sharpened axe." If the scope of required loyalties is too broad, "a man's capacity for personal love" is overtaxed, and the intensity of his emotional attachment to those claiming his loyalty diluted. Man *must* have a limited cultural and social environment in which to live, or be left utterly bewildered and drained of emotional and moral energy.[34]

It is entirely natural that many black Americans react sharply to the suffering of black Haitians, that diaspora Chinese keep one eye cocked toward the Middle Kingdom, and that Orthodox Russians are emotionally involved in the fate of Serbia. Still, few are volunteering to cast aside their direct responsibilities and head off for Port-au-Prince, Beijing, or Belgrade. It may be another matter entirely, however, if we are speaking about, for instance, Russians residing in the former Soviet republics. It is no accident, to borrow Stalin's phraseology, that this issue is one that has become a matter of grave importance to Moscow, for the "badges" of identity we all have and wear appear to trigger emotional responses in those who share them. Again, we are speaking of that mysterious quality called human nature, which is itself a boundary, a limit on the flexibility of human action.

Sociobiology and the Roots of Human Nature

Sociobiologists, scientists who attempt to explain human behavior patterns through biological mechanisms, have in recent years succeeded in corroborating through their research what village elders have always known: Human nature is real. Moreover, it is explicable through the scientific method. The work of various scientists working in a broad range of disciplines tends to support this view.

Linguists Noam Chomsky and Jerry Fodor, for instance, have mounted a serious challenge to behaviorism, claiming to have research that indicates an innate ability of very young children to understand the sentences of their elders and construct new ones, which cannot be reduced to B. F. Skinner's "stimulus-response" pattern. Our minds at early stages of development appear to process thoughts in an innate universal language.[35] This "innateness" lends credence to the notion of human nature, of a preexisting mold that represents the flexible but not infinitely elastic character of humanity.

Other scientists have probed the nature of sexual dimorphism, including the role of hormones in determining secondary sexual characteristics, differing responses to various physical stimuli among males and females, and differing modes of cognition in the sexes.[36] The work of the sociobiologists suggests the scientific equivalent of something very much like a law of nature, and that law of nature appears to be the objective quality that provides the biological foundation for natural law.[37]

Philosophers have frequently acknowledged the existence of natural law. C. S. Lewis restated an old Christian position on the subject in his book *The Abolition of Man* by taking note of the nearly universal quality of what he called, after the Chinese, the "Tao," the laws seemingly etched in the hearts of all men everywhere. Lewis divided the Tao into eight sections in the book's appendix and pulled quotations from sources as diverse as Aristotle and Australian aboriginal tradition to give an overview of the universal law, the system of "thou shalts" and "thou shalt nots" that have existed for uncountable centuries, supported by a near universal system of custom, taboo, and social convention. Three of the sections deal with special responsibilities to kinfolk. "Has he insulted his elder sister?" inquires the Babylonian List of Sins.[38] The Old English epic *Beowulf* states plainly enough that "nothing can change the claims of kinship for a right thinking man."[39] Christian Scripture (1 Timothy 5:8) maintains that "if any provide not for his own, and specially for those of his own house, he hath denied the faith."[40]

Christians have long recognized the division of sacred and temporal duties ("Render unto Caesar . . ."), and have prioritized accordingly, but the notion was not new in the world. Cicero wrote, "Part of us is claimed by our country, part by our parents, part by our friends," and that "the union and fellowship of men will be best preserved if each received from us the more kindness in proportion as he is more closely connected with us."[41] The question remains as to how the sociobiologist's law of nature is connected to the philosopher's natural law, particularly, for our purposes, in the area of the strength of kinship bonds.

The collapse of the two-parent nuclear family in America's inner cities, as well as growing pressures on the family generally, have revealed something else about human beings: The family is an essential intermediary between its members and the larger society. As the primary vehicle for the socialization of children, the family is an indispensable element of civilization. The roving predatory street gangs and increasingly deviant behavior of children raised in a society that facilitates divorce, illegitimate births, and fatherless families gives credence to those sociologists who have identified the family, not the individual, as the fundamental unit of society.[42] It is a universal attribute of human community that does not exhibit extreme variation in form in cross-cultural studies.[43]

The strength and universality of the kinship bond reflects the importance of family for human society and is grounded in the built-in survival mechanisms of humans and other creatures. In the early 1970s, evolutionary biologists began to study the development of altruistic behavior among animals, believing that according to the logic of evolutionary theory this behavior should be linked to the reproductive success of individual organisms. For the animal in question reproductive success means that "one set of genes was winning out in a competition with other sets."[44] According to evolutionary biologists, the willingness of living creatures to put themselves at risk for the sake of others may well have its origins in biology—they are inclined to take risks for the sake of others according to "the probable amount of genetic material" they have in common, in short, according to the degree of kinship.[45] Thomas Fleming, synthesizing the work of evolutionary biologists and sociobiologists, with reference to their notions of cultural evolution, put it this way: "Altruistic behavior would be most likely to evolve in a 'family-structured population' in which individuals could recognize each other or, at least, be in a position to reciprocate acts of kindness. Mankind has the best opportunity to develop group-related characteristics of more generalized altruism, since human beings have the intelligence and foresight needed to 'transcend the limits of family relationships.' "[46]

As man has evolved culturally, he has been able to partly transfer the altruism concept to larger groups—clan, tribe, village, city-state, and, eventually, nation—by envisioning the larger group as an extended family. None of this rules out his most basic responsibilities to his immediate family members or dissolves the tangible qualities of mutual respect we associate with the family itself. On the other hand, Lewis's Tao applies universally: "Thou shalt not kill"—shall not murder a fellow human being—is a recognition of our ultimate relatedness as God's children and acts as a sort of universal social control, a brake on man's aggressive instincts that can be self-destructive if uncontrolled.

We agree with Fleming that what we identify as good is also good for us, though at times very unpleasant. Therefore, we say that the altruism concept has evolved along with human society, but we are nevertheless bound to our immediate responsibilities, viewing our responsibilities to the larger groups as extending outward in a series of concentric circles, the more distant, the less immediate and important. This is "good for us" in two ways. First, the emotional capital and physical ability of humans to interact is limited and must be reserved for immediate concerns; moreover, this is part and parcel of man's limited cognitive horizons. Second, as Fleming notes, altruistic behavior develops best in a situation wherein mutual reciprocity is possible—in short, we become virtuous by performing virtuous acts personally in a "face-to-face" situation: "The experience of modern urban civilization

does not suggest that universalized benevolence flourishes in a society
of mobile and deracinated individualists."[47]

Finite Groups Versus a Worldwide Regime

Because of these very real limits on finite human beings and their
ability to deal emotionally and physically with the often complex situations of day-to-day living, humans appear to have developed a system
of badges enabling individuals to identify "us" and "them" and to
prioritize their actions as related to others. These badges are both physical and nonphysical in character. They seem to trigger emotional responses in humans in reaction to signals from others that differ in psychological resonance according to the ability of each badge to convey
a sense of relatedness to the observer. Humans therefore tend to associate with each other in finite groups that may be expandable but are not
elastic enough to include all of humanity. Clannishness, tribalism, and
nationalism are as unavoidable as the urge to eat or sleep but unlike
hunger or drowsiness can manifest themselves in varying forms. Some
nationalisms, or nationalist ideologies, are quite healthy and reaffirm
the vitality of a people, whereas others fail to properly harness man's
capacity for uncontrolled aggression[48] and are potentially self-destructive. But the notion that the mass of humans are capable of transcend-
ing the kinship group on a day-to-day basis is sheer folly.

Following Connor, most people's reaction to efforts around the
world to build a sort of world regime based on interstate quasi-governmental bodies and transstate corporations, organizations that by definition cannot tend to the national or parochial interests of the web of
clans, tribes, and nations that the mass of humanity sees as the source
of their primary identity will be hostile, or at least suspicious. Moreover, as the ubiquitous pop culture of the first world intrudes on the
second and third worlds, we can expect a violent reaction (as in Iran)
from those who see the expansion of the transstate regime and the
influence of consumer driven pop culture as a threat to the cultural
survival of their people, a point we will take up again at the end of this
study. Add to this the shaky foundations of multinational states in the
modern era, and Connor's contention that the world has not yet seen
the end of the "age of nationalism" but perhaps only its beginning
takes on meaning. Nationalism can be a road to, a result of, and a
reaction to, modernization, i.e., the building of an integrated state and
the spreading of the integrated state's rationalization process over regions and continents with the concomitant diffusion of global pop culture.

A Word on Terminology

One of the frustrations of studying nationalism is that one can never be quite sure what various scholars mean when they use terms like nationalism, nationalist, nation, patriotism, or, especially in the case of Russia, words like conservative, right, and right-wing. This study, taking its cue from both Anthony Smith and Walker Connor, will utilize their nomenclature throughout as a sort of baseline. At this juncture, however, it may be useful to define some terms as they are used in this book.

Nationalism

We have already seen the use of the term *nationalism* in several different contexts: (1) *structural nationalism* refers to the process of *nation building*, meaning the construction of a modern integrated state; (2) *political science nationalism* is the desire of a particular group for an independent state; (3) *ideological nationalism* means the ideological or philosophical expression of nationalist (however defined) ideas; and (4) *ethnonationalism* designates loyalty to the nation, in the sense of the (often mythically) ancestrally related group. The last definition (unless otherwise stated) is the one we shall use in this study. We will also refer to *nationalisms*, the various ideological and philosophical forms the nationalist impulse takes. The term *nation-state* will generally be replaced by *integrated state*, unless nation and state are coterminous. Thus a *nationalist* is someone who is particularly conscious of his loyalty to the *nation*—the mythically related group—and acts on that consciousness in public life. *Patriotism* will be used in the sense of its original meaning, the feeling of connection between the nation and the homeland (whether an actual nation-state, an ancestral homeland in a multinational state, or a *Staatvolk* polity), with all the emotional power of real and mythic landscapes the term conveys to those who use it in that sense.

Right, Right-wing, Left-wing, Conservative

The imprecise use of these terms has been a particular source of confusion when observers attempt to describe the political landscape in Russia. The Communist Party of the Russian Federation, the largest of the "red" political parties, persists in calling itself a leftist or left-wing party. Some observers, however, call them a party of the Right. The confusion arises because of a tendency to use the terms *left* and *right* in an economic sense, identifying left with socialist, social-democratic, and communist programs, which are generally hostile to capitalism, private property, and the like. On the other hand, the communists wish to return to the recent past in some sense, to restore socialist property and the rule of the vanguard party, so, as some observers reason, they must be conservative and right-wing, or even reactionary. The terms *left* and *right* also may be used to juxtapose the clash of traditionalist and progressive.

The economic and social content of the terms has been dominant in the West for some time, but there is also present in these words, as a result of communism's call for proletarian brotherhood, a sense that the Left inclines toward internationalism, the Right toward national-ism. Internationalism itself may be a loaded term, meant either in its Marxist guise as the replacing of national and state loyalties with global ones, or as a policy of cooperation, even fusion (through the administrative control of interstate organizations) between states. In either case, what is apparent on closer examination is that the terms are used as weapons in the clash between particular interests and uni-versalism. Clannishness, tribalism, nationalism, and patriotism are all efforts to assert a particular interest or identity over the universalist tack the modern world has taken. Some nationalist ideologies are mod-ernist but nevertheless attempt to protect the particular over the uni-versal. In this book the terms *right* and *right-wing* designate those who incline to nationalism and particularism; *left* and *left-wing* refer to those who favor internationalism and universalism. This is the essence of what Samuel Huntington calls the "clash of civilizations" that is desta-bilizing much of the world at present.[49]

Conservative and *conservatism* are also quite confusing terms, particu-larly in the context of contemporary Russia. Many observers use these terms in quite different ways. *Instrumental conservatism* denotes a phi-losophy of action that favors caution and gradual change over rapid reform or revolution; *content conservatism* takes a particular view of mankind and society that assumes the imperfect (or "fallen") state of man to preclude utopian plans for his perfection by political, eco-nomic, social, or scientific manipulation. It is true enough that the two often accompany each other, but this is not necessarily so. The conser-vative tends to favor tradition and experience over experimentation and innovation, but he is not always a traditionalist. He may be a cau-tious individual who will always be inclined to favor the status quo, whatever it may be. On the other hand, the content conservative may desire sweeping social change in certain circumstances, particularly if the status quo is the result of radical experimentation that either rubs against the grain of human nature or brings out the worst features of man's character. A *reactionary* is usually meant to be someone who either is dead set against all change in principle or who wishes to reanimate an old regime that has long since passed away. Again, Russia is a particular problem in this regard since Communists may wish to bring back a Stalinist regime, while other "reactionaries" pine for a simon-pure Czarism. This is something the reader will have to keep in mind.

Empire, Imperialism

Russia is often accused of harboring "imperialist" sentiments and of desiring to reconstitute her "empire." But empires, vast territories housing disparate nations ruled by a metropolitan center whose head is a feudal hereditary monarch, no longer exist anywhere. The Soviet Union was not by definition an empire but a multinational integrated state headed by a party dictatorship. For this reason, the state was not nearly as stable as many true empires were for centuries in the past, and could be held together only by a Stalinist regime of mass terror. To avoid getting sidetracked by terminological arguments, we will allow the somewhat romantic characterization of the Soviet Union as an "empire," with the caveat that an "imperialist" is not always a Stalinist monster; he may be one of those who believe that multinational harmony is still somehow a real possibility or that *Pax Sovieticus,* however flawed, served the interests of the peoples of the old union better than the current arrangement. Our notions concerning the "age of nationalism" make that dream a shaky proposition, but the hope of many Russians that the union will be reconstituted does not necessarily mean they intend to use force or terror to do so. On the other hand, some imperialists are attached to the notion of a vast empire precisely because it meant that Russia was a respected and feared great power. Brute force is implicit (and sometimes explicit) in their ideologies.

Notes

1. John Lukacs, "The Patriotic Impulse," *Chronicles*, July 1992, 19.
2. Ibid., 19–20.
3. Lukacs seems to think so, since he himself decries "Americans whose vision of American history begins with Ellis Island." Moreover, Lukacs recognizes America as the product of a particular people connected by a feeling of more than mere "civic" solidarity. Commenting on a biography of fellow immigrant Vladimir Nabokov, which claimed that though Nabokov and his wife eventually left America, they "would always remain proudly American," Lukacs wrote, "Well, good luck to them, and they indeed deserved some; but

an American passport does not a proud American make." Lukacs, "Patriotic Impulse," 20.

4. Anthony D. Smith, *The Ethnic Origins of Nations* (New York: Basil Blackwell, 1986), 12.

5. Ibid., 11.

6. Ibid., 11.

7. A concise argument of the modernist view is made in Ernest Gellner, *Nations and Nationalism* (Ithaca, N.Y.: Cornell University Press, 1983).

8. Ibid., 124.

9. In this way, modern ideas help to produce modern (that is, nationalist oriented) superstructures. This is one of many chicken-and-egg questions that arise in discussions among scholars concerning the origins of the modern world. See Liah Greenfeld, *Nationalism: Five Roads to Modernity* (Cambridge: Harvard University Press, 1992), 19–21, for an argument that takes issue with some of the structuralist positions.

10. As opposed to capitalism, since the same fundamental principles apply in noncapitalist industrialized societies. In this view, modernism is identical with the changes in social organization and economy that accompany industrialism. Modernist ideologies merely justify and explain the changes after the fact.

11. Gellner, *Nations and Nationalism*, 23.

12. Ibid., 23.

13. Gellner is here using Max Weber's notions of rationality. Ibid., 20.

14. Ibid., 21.

15. Greenfeld, *Nationalism*, 7.

16. Smith, *Ethnic Origins of Nations*, 212.

17. Not that they haven't tried. See ibid., 188, for Zimbabwe's efforts to claim the ruins of the elliptical temple of an ancient African civilization as a part of a "Zimbabwean" myth-symbol complex.

18. Though even here, the credibility of the myth-symbol complex and mythomoteur as legitimizing motifs have been strained by the question of the black African Jewish Falashas, who claim to be descended from Solomon and the Queen of Sheba.

19. Smith, *Ethnic Origins of Nations*, 192. One might also include stories of renowned wise men who attempted to lead the people back to the right path or warned them of impending destruction. A cult of heroes is always part of "golden age" stories.

20. Gellner, *Nations and Nationalism*, 88–101.

21. See Walker Connor, *Ethnonationalism: The Quest for Understanding* (Princeton: Princeton University Press, 1994), 89–117 for a stinging critique of "terminological confusion" in discussions of nations and nationalism.

22. Though the process may take on ethnic connotations, as in establishing an independent nation of Scots, Basques, or French Canadians who may feel that the prevalent state structures retard their social mobility and "life chances."

23. Walker Connor has synthesized nearly thirty years of work on national-

ism in *Ethnonationalism*. The characterization of his work as neoprimordialist is mine.

24. Cited in Greenfeld, *Nationalism*, 172.

25. Mussolini called fascism an "organized, centralized, authoritarian democracy," and Hitler called the Third Reich a "Teutonic democracy" based on the "free choice of the leader." Cited in Robert Nisbet, *The Quest for Community* (San Francisco: Institute for Contemporary Studies, 1990), 174.

26. Robert Nisbet builds a compelling case for such an interpretation of the modern state's development in *Quest for Community*.

27. I do not mean to dismiss the fact that such polities often had a dominant *Staatvolk* and that the threat of force played a role in keeping the peace. The point is, rather, that the coercive tools available were relatively crude by today's standards, yet the impulse of the small nation to assert itself, paradoxically, appears, as we shall see, to have grown in the modern era.

28. Connor, *Ethnonationalism*, 36–37.

29. Ibid., 36–37.

30. The opposite holds true as well. The less evident the badges of national identity, the more likely that the national group will be absorbed by a dominant *Staatvolk*. The Belorussians, for example, have yet to display any signs of having a national consciousness. They are suspended in a prenational state, probably because there is simply not enough to distinguish them from the Russians to prompt feelings of otherness. One must remember that the mere presence of some differing cultural factors is not sufficient to develop national consciousness and that like groups tend to homogenize in modern conditions.

31. Smith, *Ethnic Origins of Nations*, 87.

32. Connor, *Ethnonationalism*, 105.

33. Ibid., 45.

34. Konrad Lorenz, *On Aggression* (New York: Bantam Books, 1967), 244.

35. Thomas Fleming, *The Politics of Human Nature* (New Brunswick: Transaction, 1988), 33.

36. See ibid., 73–101, for a discussion of sexual dimorphism.

37. Fleming's argument for a "natural politics" is based on the relation between natural law and the laws of nature. He devotes a chapter to discussing this aspect of his argument. See *Politics of Human Nature*, 45–72.

38. C. S.Lewis, *The Abolition of Man* (New York: Collier Books, 1955), 101.

39. Ibid., 102.

40. Ibid., 103. One might add that the rest of the verse reads "and is worse than an infidel." My Bible also notes an alternate translation of "house" as "kindred."

41. Cited in ibid., 102.

42. Fleming follows Comte and Durkheim in this regard, calling the family "a sort of system—like an organism." Fleming, *Politics of Human Nature*, 108. George Gilder makes an argument of a similar sort in his *Men and Marriage* (Gretna: Pelican, 1986), an expanded version of his 1973 book, *Sexual Suicide*. For more on the pressures straining the American family, see Allan Carlson, *From Cottage to Work Station* (San Francisco: Ignatius Press, 1993).

43. See Fleming, *Politics of Human Nature*, 101–34.

44. Ibid., 58.

45. Ibid., 59.

46. Ibid., 61.

47. Ibid., 62. Entomologist Edward O. Wilson, originator of the term sociobiology, makes a similar argument, calling reciprocal altruism "soft altruism," and claiming that man is inclined toward "soft" altruism rather than self-annihilation ("hard altruism"), which is evident in insect societies. See Edward O. Wilson, *On Human Nature* (Cambridge: Harvard University Press, 1978), 149–167.

48. Konrad Lorenz maintained that man was not particularly aggressive as animals go and therefore lacked the proper internal mechanisms for controlling his aggressive impulses when he began to use weapons and became a hunter and warrior. Cultural institutions, taboos, and rituals provide the necessary brake on these impulses. See Konrad Lorenz, *On Aggression*. See also Fleming, *Politics of Human Nature*, 58 for discussion of Lorenz's theories on human aggression.

49. A restatement of Huntington's thesis concerning the "clash of civilizations" can be found in the anthology *History and the Idea of Progress*, ed. Arthur M. Melzer, Jerry Weinberger, and M. Richard Zinman (Ithaca: Cornell University Press, 1995), 137–154. Huntington sees the conflicts between East and West, North and South that are heightening after the cold war as the West and its notion of universal progress clashes with various particularisms.

2

——————

The Historical Background

The myth-symbol complex of postcommunist nationalist discourse was formed in the nineteenth century clash of Slavophiles with Westernizers, both of whom borrowed heavily from European Romanticism. The clash itself was the result of Russia's encounter with the West, with Peter the Great acting as the agent of modernization ("westernization" or "Europeanization"), a process that disoriented Russian society and raised Russian national self-awareness. The quest for a Russian identity ("the Russian Idea"), heretofore never fully articulated, dates from this period and is connected to the Russian intellectual effort both to defend the community from the corrosive forces of modernization and to find a place (a "mission") for Russia in the new post-Petrine world.

Philosophers, both wittingly and unwittingly, have helped to destroy great empires and build new ones with the power of their ideas—ideas that have informed, perhaps motivated, and surely justified (in the eyes of partisans) political and social action by both moderate reformers and brutal tyrants of every political persuasion. By the time the idea has been retooled to fit a particular demagogue's agenda, it may bear only a slight resemblance to the philosopher's own, but few would deny that it matters greatly what ideas prevail in any society. A dominant weltanschauung, or worldview, helps to form society's political, social, and economic institutions and informs the very notion of the citizenry's identity. Liberalism, conservatism, fascism, and socialism are thus, to a great degree, a state of mind.

The programmatic formulations commonly identified as nationalist in Russia in the last decade of the twentieth century do not form a single ideology, much less a common weltanschauung. Various nationalist politicians and public figures have different notions of what the total content of a patriotic or nationalist program should be, and many of them subscribe to worldviews that vary greatly from those of other patriots. What the entire Russian Right has in common, besides its particularist tendencies, is a cultural system,[1] or myth-symbol complex—a reservoir of expressions, symbols, and historical interpretations that are in large part the legacy of the nineteenth century's controversies over Russian identity, purpose, and socioeconomic structure that erupted in the wake of the forced westernization and modernization begun by Peter the Great more than a hundred years earlier. The essentials of the controversy were defined by the midcentury ideological struggle between two intellectual schools, the Slavophiles and the Westernizers.

Russian Westernizer Alexander Herzen once described the controversy between the liberal Westernizers and the conservative Slavophiles as that of a Janus whose two heads—one looking to the past and the other looking to the future—were warmed by the same heart. It is true that many Westernizers were motivated, at least in part, by a love of Russia that was no less intense than their opponents'. Still, the forward-looking, modernizing head of the Westernizers was pointed toward a secularized universal ideal that would eventually deny the particular identity and interest of the Russian heart. Some of the modern epigones of the Westernizers, especially today's neocommunists, would turn inward, rejecting the universal for the particular, mixing ideas of Slavophile origin with those of a much different pedigree in ways that both the Slavophiles and the Westernizers would have found alarming.

This phenomenon is not difficult to grasp in light of Herzen's notion of the Janus. Modernity itself is a Janus, divided in one of its many dual manifestations between socialism and capitalism, and in another between modern nationalism and internationalism, with either head nourished by the same ideological heart, a heart whose life's blood is the idea of progress in varying forms. These ideologies offer different paths to utopia but share a common faith in Man's ability to mold the world to his liking. Nationalisms in Russia today represent the continuing struggle between the universal and the particular and, at least in some tactical sense, carry on the struggle of the Slavophiles. Though many of today's nationalists are not truly antimodern, as the Slavophiles essentially were, they stand for a particular identity and oppose the general drift of social and political transformation, even if they do not recognize the modernist assumptions that lie at the heart of their own ideologies, assumptions that work to erode the very peculiarities they profess to cherish. Others carry on the Slavophiles' antimodernist struggle against today's manifestations of the secular uinversalist ideals that their deceased mentors so detested. All nationalist trends tend to be grouped together, though fundamental ideological assumptions irrevocably divide them.

Slavophiles and Westernizers[2]

The great nineteenth century controversy which peaked during the 1840s between the Slavophiles, the defenders of traditional Russian "organic" society, and the Westernizers, who looked to the West for models of Russian development, had as its initial impetus the social, political, and economic transformations brought about by Peter the Great (1672–1725), the "revolutionary czar" who would eventually transcend the ideological ferment and revolutionary turmoil he helped to unleash, finding defenders on both the Right and the Left. Nevertheless, the origins of the Slavophile-Westernizer controversy lie in an earlier controversy between Peter's supporters and his detractors. Conservative historian and precursor of the Slavophiles, Nikolai Karamzin, wrote disapprovingly that during the reign of the great innovator, "we began to be citizens of the world, but we ceased in some measure to be citizens of Russia."[3] The Westernizer Belinsky, in contrast, described Peter as "the most extraordinary phenomenon" in the history of mankind, "a deity who has called us into being and who has breathed the breath of life into the body of ancient Russia."[4]

Belinsky's observation that Peter had "called us into being," "us" being the Western-educated intellectuals who would be the progenitors of the ideological and political struggles of the nineteenth century, was not lost on his Slavophile opponents, who realized that their own philosophizing was done within the intellectual parameters of the European thinkers who so influenced both themselves and the Westernizers. Moreover, Christianity, the cornerstone of the Slavophile school, connected Russia with the West in a broader sense. The originators of classical Slavophile thinking tended not to be anti-Western in an ideological sense, but criticized the "wrong turns" taken by the West, especially during the Enlightenment, which, in their view, had bred freethinkers, revolutionaries, and atheists by way of its rationalism, skepticism, and positivism.[5] For their part, some of the Westernizers, Herzen in particular, would eventually seek the fulfillment of the West's promise in traditional Russian institutions, particularly as the social dislocations produced by the bourgeois liberal-capitalist regimes in the West became clearer.

Peter was the father of the Slavophile-Westernizer Janus. He had established Russia as a European power, having brought foreign teachers and technicians to Russia to effect the modernization of education,

trade, and industry, as well as to aid in establishing a navy and reforming the army. He had followed the model of "enlightened despotism"
set by Europe's great monarchs, centralizing the Russian state on the
basis of an expansive bureaucracy. Peter, the Enlightenment free-
thinker, subjugated the Russian Orthodox Church to the interests of
the state by abolishing the patriarchate and establishing the church as
a state institution in the guise of the Holy Synod, a subjugation from
which Russian Orthodoxy has yet to recover. He forced Western modes
of dress and manner on the people of Russia and built Saint Petersburg, at great cost in human life, on the swampy shores of the Baltic
as his "window on the West." Peter undermined the traditional position and prerogatives of the hereditary nobility by establishing his
Table of Ranks, which opened up the possibility of nonnobles' gaining
noble rank by way of work in the bureaucracy, and by abolishing the
Council of Boyars (*Boyarskaya Duma*), which had represented the interests of the old noblity. His policy of expansion had brought Russia
victory in war over Sweden, then one of Europe's great powers, and he
annexed parts of Finland and the Baltic states. Russia also expanded in
the south, making war on Turkey and Persia. Peter, who had traveled
and worked in Europe, recognized the sources of the West's power,
of the wealth and technological innovation that enabled the European
powers to gain mastery over nature itself and dominate the world. He
acted accordingly.[6]

Peter's revolution had both objective and subjective aspects. When
he demanded the institution of Western dress and the building of Saint
Petersburg along Western architectural lines, he was attacking the objective reality of Russia's outward appearance. His opening to Western
ideas, particularly those of Enlightenment scientism and rationalism,
attacked the subjective foundations of the old Russian order, which
rested on the bedrock of Orthodox Christianity, and helped to spur on
the objective technological innovations he sought. The Table of Ranks
established the basis for a bureaucracy fit to manage a modern state,
and the creation of the Holy Synod objectively undermined another
restraint on the absolutism he so desired. He also took the title Emperor and weakened the subjective, ideological tie to the past that the
notion of the czar as the defender of Holy Orthodox Russia had engendered.

The revolutionary czar did not forgo any methods, however brutal,
to achieve his aims. When the *Streltsy* (the old military corps established by Ivan the Terrible) revolted, the nightmare of torture and murder that ensued in retaliation shocked an empire that had seen much
of both. When churchmen, armed with the icon of the Blessed Virgin,
approached Peter to ask for mercy for the condemned, he asked them

what business they had to interfere in an affair of state. Henceforth the priesthood itself fell under suspicion, and priests suspected of sympathy for the rebels were executed along with the other wretched captives of Peter's wrath.[7]

Peter was not an ideological Westernizer but a practical ruler and empire builder who made use of advanced Western technology and organizational know-how to begin the process of modernizing Russia, which he aimed to make a feared and powerful state. The Tartar invasion and domination of Russia, which lasted from the thirteenth to the end of the fifteenth century, was never far from Russian rulers' minds. Subsequent invasions by Poles, Frenchmen, and Germans only stoked the fires of Russian suspicion of outsiders. The Russia of Peter's time appeared vulnerable in the presence of the technologically advanced West, but henceforth she would be a player in the European great game of power. Western ideas facilitated, and in some cases justified, the revolution, but Peter was not interested in abstractions or ideals (as subsequent Westernizers were). His importance for our purposes lies in the intellectual ferment that resulted as a reaction to, and evaluation of, the sweeping and disorienting changes that had taken place in Russia during and after his reign. Peter, like many of his successors, had thought that he could have his technological cake and eat it too. He had no intention of allowing the opening to the West to infect the Russian organism with the ideas of liberalism and egalitarianism, which boiled over in France at the end of the eighteenth century. What he did not realize is that modernity comes in a single package. Many of his countrymen would spend the next century, and the century after that, puzzling over how to enjoy the material progress of the West without the side effects of, on the one hand, the dissolution of traditional social bonds or, on the other, the advancement of the "capitalist stage" of socioeconomic and political development. These questions have yet to find their answers.

Ancient and Modern Russia

Andrezej Walicki wrote in his *The Slavophile Controversy* that the ideas which became Slavophilism were born of "retrospective criticism" of the Petrine reforms by means of a dual contrast between "ancient" and "modern" Russia and between Russia and Europe. The critics of Peter's reforms owed much to the conservative thinkers of Europe, for many of the criticisms of Russia's Europeanization, as well as the notion of contrasting ancient and modern society, were based on yet a third antithesis that had been an ideological weapon of Western conservatives, that of ancient and modern Europe.[8] Although the con-

servative criticism of Peter emerged when the "foundations of the feudal system [in Russia] were not yet threatened,"[9] and the European
conservatives were attacking the already emerging capitalist and liberal type of socioeconomic formation, the Russian trend would nevertheless be bolstered by the traditionalist arguments of Burke and Coleridge in England and the "conservative romantics" of Germany.[10]
"One might say," wrote Walicki, "that an essential (though not in itself
sufficient) prerequisite of Slavophilism was the appearance of an ideological situation in which Russian conservative criticism of the Petrine
reforms could merge organically with Western philosophical romanticism and the conservative-romantic criticism of capitalism."[11]

The criticism of Peter's reforms that emerged during the reign of
Catherine II ("the Great," she reigned from 1762 to 1796) was largely
the product of what became known as the aristocratic opposition,
which was tied to the interests of the old nobility. The leading critic
was Prince Mikhail Shcherbatov.[12] Shcherbatov, to be sure, appeared
to be no Slavophile prototype. He was a Mason and deist who borrowed many of the forms of his criticisms from European Enlightenment thinkers. His criticisms of Peter recognized that the very education he had received was the product of the opening to the West, and
he acknowledged Peter's role as builder of a Russia that was objectively
stronger in an economic and military sense. Still, Shcherbatov represented a trend that would influence the Slavophiles, particularly in his
attacks on the brutality, radicalism, and antireligious nature of Peter's
revolution, and in his contrast of ancient and modern Russia.

A historian and a polemicist, Shcherbatov defended the prerogatives
of the old aristocracy against the despotism of the absolutist autocracy
established by Peter and attacked the corrupting influence of his expansive bureaucracy. His historical works (the seven-volume *History of
Russia*) attacked the notion that autocracy was the time-honored form
of Russian government (he saw Ivan the Terrible's reign of terror as a
deviation from the norm that more or less proved his point), claiming
that in old Russia the czars' powers were limited by the prerogatives
of the aristocracy and the moral influence of the church, which had
not yet been wholly subjugated to the will of the despot. Shcherbatov
defended a notion of class and hierarchy that was based on mutual
obligation and responsibility, tempered by Christian mercy and restraint. Only such a system could maintain the ideas of Honor and
Liberty against the onslaught of rationalist contractarianism and bureaucratic intrusion. Like the European conservatives, he thought of
the development of traditional social arrangements as natural and organic and viewed with suspicion artificial rationalist attacks on the living organism of society. The Mason and enlightened aristocrat in this

way found himself defending tradition and custom against rationalist radicalism, which disrupted society and weakened social bonds. He particularly attacked bureaucracy and the subsequent growth of careerist individualism that it engendered, the autocracy and the servility it demanded, and the selfish materialism of the luxury laden court.

Shcherbatov was a conservative in both the instrumental and "content" senses. If reform was judged beneficial, let it come gradually so as not to disturb the historical continuity of the community; but the essential nature of that community must be defended. He was subtle enough a thinker to recognize the nature of trade-offs in social reform. Peter's European Enlightenment educational reforms and general deportment had attacked the traditional religion of the community, and the prince noticed "less superstition" in the religious views of the people of Russia after Peter, but also "less faith." "The former servile fear of Hell disappeared," he noted, "but so did love of God and his holy laws."[13] The reforms had been needed but had been applied too quickly and too brutally. Peter had simply gone too far. Shcherbatov did not envisage a return to pre-Petrine Russia but rather the limitation of the monarchy and the bureaucracy by increasing the influence of the nobility. Increasing the influence of the church would bolster public morality.

If Shcherbatov pioneered the comparison of ancient and modern Russia in the historiography of the day, then Nicholai Karamzin appears to have cemented it in the bedrock of conservative nationalist thought by way of his twelve-volume *History of the Russian State* (still referred to by the nationalist intelligentsia today) and his *Memoir on Ancient and Modern Russia*, which first appeared in 1811. Karamzin wrote during the time of Alexander I (he reigned from 1801 to 1825), who led the forces of monarchy and tradition (he had earlier been something of a liberal) against the whirlwind that was Napoleon, and he had witnessed the early days of the French revolution while traveling in Europe. "France has been struck by lightning," he wrote, later noting that the "revolution clarified our ideas."[14] Karamzin came to view autocracy, albeit in a circumscribed form, as the only true guardian of society.[15]

Karamzin's early writings praised the "virtuous and simple life of our ancestors," a time when "Russians were Russians,"[16] wore traditional dress, spoke Russian (the upper classes of his day often spoke French), and "adhered faithfully to the strict customs of old."[17] He wrote glowingly of the liberty of ancient Russia, particularly of the citizens' assembly, the *Veche*, which shared power with the princes of the cities of Novgorod, Pskov, and Vyatka. But autocracy triumphed in the end. The independent cities and principalities of ancient Russia were unable to act in concert at moments of common danger, particularly against the Tartar threat, and the domination of Muscovy was the instrument of Russia's salvation. Sadly, in his view, the protorepublicanism of ancient Russia had to go by the wayside, but that did not imply that Karamzin was a backer of unlimited absolutism.

Karamzin viewed the czar's power as undivided: the czar alone, after consulting with learned citizens, should make the most important state decisions. His power should not extend to the social sphere, however, to the sacred area of family and private discourse. Karamzin's ideal monarchy would be limited in scope. Like Shcherbatov, Karamzin preached a strict observance of custom in relations between state and society as a kind of Russian common law. He advised a more independent role for the church as a moral force in society, thereby providing the cultural and social equilibrium necessary for civil society to function without state interference. Though a member of the landholding class himself, he did not favor increasing the influence of what he considered a corrupt aristocracy.

Karamzin influenced the Slavophiles through (1) his criticism of unlimited autocracy, (2) his favorable view of ancient Russia (he too thought many of Peter's reforms beneficial, but he judged the method of their implementation harsh and damaging to society), (3) his principled stand for a moral regeneration of a society too much influenced by Enlightenment individualism, (4) his disapproval of the widening cultural gap between rulers and ruled, and (5) his contrasting of ancient Russia with Europe. He saw modern Europe as corrupted by a "wrong turn" in the form of French Jacobinism, and he urged resistance to the further influence of European political and social ideas. Karamzin thought of medieval Russia as a freer place than the Europe of his own time and, at the end of his life, professed sympathy for ancient Russian republicanism.

Another historian who influenced the development of the Slavophile worldview, and at the same time stoked the fires of future chauvinist circles, was Mikhail Pogodin (1800–1875).[18] Pogodin was a *raznochinets*, a man of nonnoble birth who had been educated and had won his academic positions as a result of bureaucratic reforms begun under Peter the Great. His father had been a serf. His historical writing diverges from that of the earlier aristocratic scholars, though he appears to have borrowed much from Karamzin.

Pogodin became a great defender of the bureaucratized autocratic state, whose ideology, called "official nationality," was summed up in the phrase *Pravoslaviye, Samoderzhaviye, Narodnost* (Orthodoxy, Autocracy, Nationality),[19] which was a conscious counterpart to the Liberty, Equality, Fraternity formulation of the French revolution.[20] This tripartite formulation was an attempt at forging an ideology that claimed a bond between the people and the autocrat as an organic, patriarchal extension of the hierarchy of ancient Russia. As such, the formula conspicuously left out the old nobility, while implying that the bureaucratic state had replaced older social bonds. The formula borrowed organic aspects from the regime's critics (particularly in the notion of the czar as *batyushka*, "father," of his people) who had stressed the natural, patriarchal harmony of old Russia, while preserving a modernized form that mirrored to some extent the formation of the integrated state in the West, with its democratic pretensions of classlessness, as well as its centralization and standardization. The "official nationality" ideology constituted a step toward the gradual dissolution of the feudal and agrarian social bonds of the old order, while simultaneously hoping to give an ideological basis to the maintenance of the monarchy and, at first, serfdom. Essentially, the idea of "official nationality" justified right-wing modernization. It suffered from the inadequacies of all such efforts, particularly the internal contradiction of progressive modernism (in the form of technological and administrative reformation) tying itself to the person of the imperial monarch. The monarchy naturally displayed a reluctance to follow the modernizing line to its logical conclusions, which would have meant transforming Russia from an empire into an integrated nation-state. The unrest and turmoil of Russia in the last half of the nineteenth century and the subsequent revolutions of 1905 and 1917 bear this out.

In any event, it was not Pogodin's defense of what would become a bureaucratic police state[21] that influenced the Slavophiles themselves but rather his notions of Russian distinctiveness and destiny. Pogodin is the first historian in Russia[22] to claim a distinct origin and development for Russian society and culture that would later be used to justify notions of a separate path of development for Russia or a Russian way of political, social, and economic evolution by politicians and thinkers of every conceivable persuasion. The Slavophile Yuri Samarin directly acknowledged his debt to Pogodin: "Among the professors [at Moscow University], the one who influenced me . . . most strongly was Pogodin. . . . He showed us that it was possible to look at Russian history and Russian life in general from a completely new angle. Western formulas are not applicable to us; the Russian way of life is an expression of specific principles unknown to other nations; our evolution is subject to its own laws that have not yet been defined by scholarship."[23]

Pogodin's essential teaching involved his interpretation of the development of the Russian state. He borrowed from French thinkers the notion of Europe's having developed in the direction of class struggle, culminating in the turmoil of the French revolution, because of its initial division between conquerors and conquered, between medieval knight and vanquished peasant. The West was built by the cult of violence, a distorted beginning that guaranteed social enmity and strife. The Russian state began, however, with what Pogodin called a "voluntary invitation to rule."[24]

Ancient Russia, according to Pogodin, had no native ruling class and had "invited" the Normans to rule. The church, like the other elements of society, had submitted to state authority, only wishing to operate in its own sphere and allowing the rulers to rule and society to develop harmoniously and peacefully. Russia was heir to the Eastern tradition of Byzantium, not of Western Rome, and represented a distinct form of civilization.

In Pogodin's theorizing this did not rule out crossgermination with the West, to which Russia was connected both physically and historically through certain elements common to both, such as the Christian faith (albeit in a distinct Eastern form). In fact, Pogodin, as the logic of his thinking dictated in view of his support of the absolutist regime whose modernizing tendencies had made his public career possible, admired Peter the Great and praised him at length in his works. "Russia is part of Europe," he wrote, "together they form a geographical whole, and she must therefore, from sheer physical necessity, share her fate and take part in her development, like a planet obedient to the laws of the solar system."[25] It was simply useless and futile to attack Peter and his reforms in his view, for the Russia of Pogodin's time was *Peter's* Russia, from the newspapers the intelligentsia read to the very foods they ate; all were Peter's innovations. The navy was his creation, the victories of Russian armies his own, the might of Russia his legacy. Moreover, Pogodin revamped the old notion of Russia's mission as guardian of Orthodox Christian doctrine and culture and gave it a secular face. In its fully developed form, the idea juxtaposed "young" and dynamic Russia with "old" and strifetorn Europe, envisioning a time when Russia would act as the agent of civilization's salvation by synthesizing East and West, Rome and Byzantium, thesis and antithesis.

Pogodin, a prototype *gosudarstvennik*, or proponent of state power, believed that the state was the only truly creative force in Russian history. The Russian people, as borne out by the "invitation to rule," were merely passive and indifferent subjects of the central power, which made them fit material for shaping by the state apparatus in the interests of the empire. Thus, the brutality and cold calculation of Peter's revolution was completely justified. In Pogodin's eyes, Russia was entering a new age of greater glories, an age when she could realize the full development of native potential without depending on the West.

The Slavophile Weltanschauung

Andrezej Walicki, author of a classic study of the Slavophiles, *The Slavophile Controversy*, identifies three men as the most important formulators of "classical" Slavophilism: Ivan Kireevsky (1806–56), Aleksey Khomyakov (1804–60), and Konstantin Aksakov (1817–60). Important contributions to Slavophile thought and public activities were also made by men such as Petr Kireevsky (Ivan's brother, 1808–56), Ivan Aksakov (Konstantin's brother, 1823–86), and Yuri Samarin (1819–76), among others. All came from noble families (some of ancient pedigree) and all participated in the salon debates and polemical fireworks of the era, when Russia had begun developing what may be called public opinion, the public being, of course, the educated classes who could serve the state well enough but lacked an avenue for political activity.

The Slavophiles developed a conservative weltanschauung that was influenced not only by their Russian precursors but the Romantic movement[26] in Europe as well, especially the German romantic conservatives from whom the Slavophiles borrowed many of their initial ideas, particularly as related to their theory of human personality, which complemented their Orthodox theology and socioeconomic theorizing. The Slavophile weltanschauung is discussed here (in a simplified form) in terms of its views on *personality*, as well as its *religious* and *socioeconomic* aspects. The discussion concludes with an examination of the Slavophiles' overall conception of Russia's place in the world and her historical fate.[27]

Personality

The Slavophile idea of the "integral personality" was developed by Ivan Kireevsky[28] and informs the whole of Slavophile doctrine. The integral personality is founded on the bedrock of Kireevsky's concept of "integral reason," which assumes a unity and "wholeness" (*tselostnost*) of man's psychic powers, including nonrational and rational elements. "Natural reason" is the mental faculty that transforms sensory perception and individual experience into empirical knowledge. The ability to reason in such a manner is innate in man, though each person's empirical knowledge is a product of learning and experience. "Integral reason" enables individuals to perceive with the whole of their purely mental and purely spiritual powers by concentrating and merging the faculties of natural reason, will, feeling, and conscience. Individuals can thereby ascertain higher truths than mere empirical verities. These faculties were intended by the Creator to work together to integrate man's capacities for thought and feeling and to provide the voice of a priori knowledge that must inform all empirical knowledge if man is to live a proper life. The result of integration is faith—the bedrock of human existence.

Rationalism is the result of disconnecting natural reason from integral reason, which amputates the faculty of the psyche that integrates all forms of knowledge and connects the material with the spiritual. Rationalist truths are fragmentary and partial, and cannot serve as the basis of either a harmonious society or a content individual.[29] Rationalism "acts as a disintegrating force," encouraging the separation of natural reason from integral reason and transforming "reality into a collection of isolated fragments bound together only by a cobweb of abstract notions and relationships."[30] The thrust of Kireevsky's notion of the integral personality is an individual who experiences internal harmony and external contentment, in the juxtaposition of natural and integral reason.

Religion

The Slavophiles identified three historical components that constituted the West, which in their philosophical writings was less a concrete, geographical entity than an ideological structure. The constituent components of the West were the cultural heritage of classical Greece and Rome, the barbarian tribes of Dark Age Europe who would succeed Rome as the bearer of Western civilization, and Christianity in its Roman Catholic form.

The Slavophiles thought of Roman Catholicism as having been poisoned at the source. Like other Orthodox Christians, they considered Orthodoxy the oldest surviving form of Christian worship, the form most consistent with the early Christianity practiced by the first believers of the ancient world. Orthodoxy's church fathers were Byzantine Greeks, and their theology did not follow the scholastic tradition of the West as particularly manifested by Thomas Aquinas. Scholasticism, in this view, was merely the rationalism of classical Greece and Rome applied to theology. Thus scholasticism's inherent rationalism paved the way for a second Fall. As man, following Lucifer's example, had cut himself off from God by rebelling against Him, so rationalism's identity with natural reason cut man away from faith. When reason triumphed over faith, it was only a matter of time before individualism, the product of efforts to justify faith by the individual's reason, would triumph over the unity of the church, which, by all accounts, had fallen into worldliness by becoming preoccupied with temporal affairs under the power-seeking popes of the Middle Ages. "Christianity in the West," wrote Ivan Kireevsky in 1839, "yielded to the lawless influence of the classical world," thus ensuring the "triumph of rationalism" over "internal spiritual" wisdom.[31]

The Reformation completed the demolition of the church in the West. Though Luther was sincere in his efforts to reconstitute the faith, Protestantism followed the logic of classical rationalism and individualism by rejecting authority.[32] The "priesthood of all believers," as asserted by Luther, compounded the confusion in Western Christianity by atomizing the community of believers, which left all vulnerable to the forces of individualism. The believer could not justify faith by his own intellectual constructions, the product of the second Fall, and Europe was steadily succumbing to the forces of Enlightenment scientism, deism, and, finally, agnosticism and atheism. The chaos of the French revolution and the phenomenon of Napoleon, the new revolutionary whose real enemy was God, were thus entirely explicable.[33]

Society and Economy

Russia, though connected to the West by virtue of the Christian faith, had followed a different path, according to the Slavophiles. Whereas Europe had inherited the rationalist bias of classicism via ancient Greece and Rome, Russia had accepted Eastern Christianity via Byzantium. Orthodoxy was pure in its faith, true in its adherence to Christian tradition. The communalism of the early believers was preserved among the Orthodox. Rationalism and individualism were alien to Orthodox believers. Simple faith and humble acceptance of authority were part and parcel of the harmonious "inner life" of ancient Russia, which had had no need of the "external" restraint of a bureaucratized state to enforce public order.

Ancient Russia had been formed not by conquest but by the "invitation to rule" extended to the Normans. Thus the cult of force was alien to Russian society, and the shared faith and common culture of all Russians ensured harmony between social classes. Peasant and noble were distinctly Russian and Orthodox, and social pretension was little known. Society had been harmonious and patriarchal, each knowing his station and keeping his obligations. The fundamental unit of society was the peasant commune, the *obshchina*, which was founded on common holding of property, shared responsibility, and adherence to tradition, both religious and social. The *obshchina* was governed by the *mir*, a council of elders who settled disputes, distributed land, and kept the peace in the community not by enforcing statutory law imposed from above (as the Western heirs of Roman law did) but by observing custom and tradition. In fact, all Russian law was a variety of common law. Justice was thus served by observing communal custom informed by the wisdom of countless generations of the community's forebears, tempered by Christian mercy. Thus the Slavophiles maintained that "through the Church individual communities merged into larger units functioning according to the same principles and in the same way. The whole of Russia was one large *mir*, a community of land, faith, and custom embracing the entire nation."[34] The Slavophiles' notion of the ideal of Russian harmony—the integral personality living within an integral society—was called *sobornost*, or communal togetherness. In such a society, consensus rather than majority rule (which was derived from rationalism, legalism, and individualism) determined decision making.

The ideal Slavophile deliberative body was the ancient Land Assembly, or *Zemskiy Sobor*, which was called together by Muscovite czars and included representatives of all "the estates of the realm, including boyars, clergy, gentry, and sometimes burghers and peasants."[35] The *sobor* considered matters of great importance and elected Michael Romanov czar in 1613. Moreover, the assembly sought the endorsement of the whole of Russia before making the decision final, thus extending the corporate principle throughout the realm.[36] The first assembly was called by Ivan IV in 1549 and met continually as an advisory body until 1622. Peter the Great, however, abandoned the tradition of calling the *sobor*.[37]

The Slavophiles identified the concept of the primacy of private property with Western individualism and saw it as a corrosive agent that would dissolve the *obshchina*, atomize society, and undermine the possibility of achieving *sobornost* as an ideal. Class conflict and social corruption would surely follow the capitalizing of Russia. They continued the tradition of the aristocratic opposition in attacking bureaucratic absolutism (arbitrary external control), Peter's reforms, and finally by opposing capitalist economics.[38]

The Russian Idea

The Slavophile weltanschauung developed as the result of a deliberate attempt to define Russianness and Russia in opposition to the West, and the Petrine revolution served as the impetus for its evolution. The formulators of classical Slavophilism were influenced by both their Russian predecessors and by European conservatives, especially the German romantic conservatives, who provided the Slavophiles with the rudiments of a conservative worldview, particularly in the concepts of gemeinschaft and gesellschaft, which were the prototypes of Ivan Kireevsky's people and society (*narod* and *obshchestvo*).[39]

The Slavophiles saw the Russian common people as the true carrier of the traditions of organic society, Russia's gemeinschaft. Their precursors in the aristocratic opposition had still viewed the nobility as the prime bulwark against autocracy and Westernization. But by the middle decades of the nineteenth century, the Slavophiles, themselves of noble extraction, were certain that the upper and educated classes had become so alienated (the Russian equivalent of gesellschaft, an artificial social grouping alien to organic society) from the traditions of their own country and the monarchy, so committed to bureaucratic modernization that only the peasant commune, which still carried on the communal and Orthodox traditions of ancient Russia, could be the basis of Russian renewal. The rulers had become too distant from the ruled and a dangerous gap was evident in Russian society. This situation was only exacerbated by continued modernization and capitalization and class war and chaos were waiting ahead.

At the heart of the communal relations that so defined Russia in the Slavophiles' eyes was the peasant family, often an extended one. The organic nature of Russian society had its deepest roots in the kinship bonds of the *obshchina*. Historian Nicholas Riasanovsky has noted that the Slavophile notion of integralness begins with the integral personality and proceeds upward through "the family [which] represented the principle of integration in love," the same integralness that could "pervade other associations of men" once again, as they had in ancient Russia, if Russia returned to native principles and cultivated *sobornost*. External coercion could be held to a minimum, the bureaucratic state would be done away with, and Russia could be cured of the effects of the West's modernizing virus she had been forcibly infected with by Peter.[40] They were unalterably opposed to legalism and constitutionalism as manifestations of rationalism and individualism, though their support of autocracy remained historical and functional and, therefore, relative.[41] The historian Riasanovsky has characterized the Slavophiles as "religious anarchists," though this may more accurately describe Tolstoy.[42]

The Slavophile worldview was a profoundly conservative one in the content sense, but its views of the autocratic bureaucracy and the Russian *narod* led it away from reaction toward an instrumentally conservative reformism. The Slavophiles' stance puzzled and sometimes angered the authorities, and their publications were often censored. They supported emancipation of the serfs and a concept of monarchy close to that of Karamzin, that is, one limited by the weight of Russian custom and the functional division of state and land, the state being limited to its sphere and the land, organic Russian society, being left to function in a natural manner. Konstantin Aksakov made his own vision clear enough: "Man was created by God as an intelligent and a talking being" and thus should be granted freedom of conscience and speech.[43] Their concept of the relationship between state and land was one of mutual noninterference.[44]

The Slavophiles acknowledged their debt to the West and did not consider a wholesale return to ancient Russia possible or desirable under the prevailing social conditions. They also did not underestimate the accomplishments of Western rationalism in certain areas. "I have no intention of writing a satire about the West," wrote Ivan Kireevsky, "no one values the conveniences of social and private life that have come out of . . . [Western] rationalism more than I. . . . I belong to it [the West] by way of my education, my personal habits, [and] my tastes."[45]

The Slavophiles' nationalism was ignited by Peter's revolution,[46] by the confrontation with the Other in the guise of the Napoleonic wars, and by the cultural ferment unleashed by Russian exposure to Western ideologies and philosophies. Their debate with the Westernizers manifested a desire to construct a worldview consistent with Russian history and national character. Intellectuals that they were, they wanted to make a specifically Russian contribution to the world. While seeking answers to questions about Russia's heritage and future, they began an intellectual quest for a unifying principle (subsequently called the "Russian Idea"), which they found in *sobornost*, and a clue as to Russia's purpose in history. They finally judged her mission to be that of unifier and synthesizer. Having absorbed elements of the Western experience in the period after Peter, Russia would turn back to her own traditions and develop in her own way. Her spiritual strength restored, she could then serve as an example to the West. Europe, long dependent on external coercion as a result of losing her integral wholeness, first among individuals and then among the nations, could learn from Russia and effect a new synthesis of East and West. Russia, therefore, could be the agent of civilization's regeneration through the principle of *sobornost*.

The Slavophiles, it should be noted, tended not to be national chauvinists. Walicki, in *The Slavophile Controversy*, noted that the philosophy of Ivan Kireevsky was "not narrowly nationalistic" because "he did not ascribe the superiority of ancient Russian civilization to specifically Russian features but only to the fact that Christian principles in Russia had been saved by certain historical circumstances from the distortions suffered by Western civilization."[47] Moreover, their "missionism" does not necessarily amount to messianism since "messianism requires faith not in a 'mission' but in a 'Messiah'—that is in a chosen people."[48] Missionism tends to play out by example, whereas messianism requires the deified national messiah to *act* on the external subjects of its intended salvation, sometimes through aggression. Messianism also tends toward universalist assumptions, whereas missionism tends to have more limited goals. Admittedly, there are gray areas, and many of the epigones of classical Slavophilism would, through Pan-Slavism, begin the transformation of Russian missionism (Russia as the "Third Rome" and bearer of Orthodox civilization; Russia as the regenerative agent of civilization in both East and West) into messianism.

The Slavophiles are often said to have been utopians.[49] Their philosophy, in this view, had no practical suggestions for Russia. Although they were subjected to censorship, many of them did nevertheless advise the government of Alexander II on land reform and emancipation. Moreover, their views on politics are often misunderstood by liberals. When the Slavophiles called for the noninterference of the state in the affairs of the land they had in a mind a conservative concept of freedom *within* a community and not any assumptions related to liberal notions of the autonomous individual. The individual could only develop fully within a given set of norms and within an organic community. Their ideal was the freedom to live and develop *outside* of politics, which would also be circumscribed, limited to the immediate affairs of state. For the Slavophiles, the essential element binding society together and defining its character was religion. Limitations on arbitrary powers were fundamentally limitations imposed by the Christian faith. Law was a lasting and valid reflection of society only when it was based on the organic nature of Russian communities, which were built on the bedrock of Orthodoxy. Khomyakov, for example, defined *sobornost* as "freedom in unity."[50]

The Westernizers, Romanticism, and Hegel

The Westernizers' clash with the Slavophiles is not only important because of the Slavophile intellectual framework generated by the debate but also because of what the Westernizers' development can tell us about later manifestations of Russian nationalism and its relation to romanticism and idealism.

The Slavophiles owed much to the romantic movement in Europe, from which they freely borrowed ideas and arguments.[51] But the endpoint of classical Slavophilism was *not* romantic nationalism—if one means by that the idea of a nation as a spiritually and organically united force of its own acting as the agent of history. This differs qualitatively from the concept of a national mission that may or may not be carried through by sinful men. Romantic nationalism internalized pantheism in the idealistic form that inspired so much of early romantic art and was associated with radicalism in Europe. The "Idea," "History," "Consciousness," or "Will" as the expression of the Ultimate Reason of the universe had taken the place of a personal God—the Slavophiles viewed Hegelian philosophy not as the negation of Enlightenment rationalism but as its fullest expression.

Romantic nationalism so defined prepares the ideological ground for deification of the nation and thereby moves us into new territory. History as such must remain a mystery for Christians, since the particulars of God's plan are inscrutable to humans and saying that everything and everyone is part of the eternal One (especially if that eternal supraindividual force is the nation) is heresy. Though the lay theologians of Classical Slavophile persuasion were not always orthodox in their handling of spiritual questions in the narrow sense of the term, their spiritual and ideological journey after their initial immersion in European Romanticism led them back to the familiar hearth of traditionalism. They were conservative nationalists who borrowed romantic ideas and expressions to form their own arguments for a traditional social order.

Romanticism in art was associated with pantheism; in philosophy with idealism. The romantic notions of the power of intuition and consciousness as opposed to the hard empiricism of much of Enlightenment thought[52] thus had appeal for those unsatisfied with the implications of that worldview, and had some utility for the conservatives of the era. Indeed, many of the Slavophiles passed through a Hegelian idealist phase before turning to conservatism, as Coleridge, for example, turned from his initial embrace of idealism and pantheism to Christian orthodoxy and conservatism.[53]

The Westernizers were also heavily influenced by idealism and romanticism, though they did not promulgate a coherent or consistent weltanschauung. They were a diverse group whose ideas differed even in their particulars. All that can be said with a fair degree of certainty about them is that they believed in progress, and that their European intellectual mentor was Hegel. Indeed, Hegel's dialectic, the clash of opposites, of thesis, antithesis, and synthesis; his ideas of historical development and progress and an end point (the "end of history") as the "realization of the ethical Idea"[54] make him "the preeminent philosopher of the nineteenth century."[55]

What both the Slavophiles (even after their turn to conservatism) and Westernizers had in common was the Hegelian conceptual framework. Each nation expresses some particular idea (the Russian Idea) or purpose as set out by the Ultimate Reason that "governs the world."[56] In Hegelian philosophy, nations are the key actors in world history and history travels "from East to West, for Europe is absolutely the end of

History."[57] Thus Westernizers turned to Europe for models of development.

Both Slavophiles and Westernizers internalized the thesis-antithesis-synthesis formula of the Hegelian dialectic, though only the Westernizers continued to see it as "the mechanism, the dynamic essence or cause of the pattern that progress has taken in the world."[58] Europe and Russia, East and West, were thesis and antithesis; the synthesis would be either the westernization of Russia (Russia had been left out of "history," an idea especially strong in Petr Chadaaev's historical interpretations[59]) or the Russification of the West.

Hegelian philosophy could support either Right or Left. Its stress on national destiny and the national will would be picked up by the Right, whereas his statism could support centralizers of both persuasions.[60] Finally, his nationalism appealed to some elements among both Westernizer liberals and radicals. Herzen, for example, embraced the Slavophiles' notion of the peasant commune as the ideal socioeconomic unit after his exposure to industrialized, urbanized Europe. A socialist, Herzen was repelled by the very things the Slavophiles themselves rejected in modernism, especially capitalism. In 1847 in his *Letters from France and Italy* he wrote "long live the Russian village—it has a great future."[61] Herzen took up "a new faith—faith in Russia and Slavdom, in 'Russian socialism' based on the village commune idealized by the Slavophiles."[62] His cause was subsequently taken up by the right wing element in Russian populism in the 1870s and 1880s.[63] Herzen's socialism idealized precapitalist social and economic relations and thus combined "a romantic and essentially conservative critique of capitalism with a belief in democracy and revolution."[64]

Herzen's "Russian socialism" would live on in the influence it exerted among Russia's anarchists and terrorists. Anarchist Mikhail Bakunin, for example, looked to the Russian peasantry as the revolutionary force in Russian society and at one time "raised the banner of a 'revolutionary Pan-Slavism.'"[65] They would, through the prism of class struggle (*narod* and *obshchestvo*), present an ideology that paralleled that of the Slavophiles. Russian radicals would "go to the people" in search of a revolutionary class, while idealizing the romantic revolutionary as a type.

Westernizers dissatisfied with "right" Hegelianism, the notion that the end of history would be constitutional monarchy and a liberal order combined with a doctrine of necessity, or necessary stages of development, turned, as the Bolsheviks later would do, to a philosophy of action and materialism as the justification for immediate revolutionary activity. Whether they realized or not, the Russian radicals confirmed what the Slavophiles had always suspected: Hegelianism was but the idealist phase of Enlightenment individualism and skepticism. The thrust of the philosophy of action was the assertion of the individual will; the radicals had revolted against the Idea as they had earlier revolted against God. "Buddhist" Hegelianism threatened the individual's autonomy, which was the whole point (in the eyes of many radicals) of the rationalization of social and economic relations and the breakup of traditional social bonds. Ironically, but with a certain logic, their dream reached its end of history in communist totalitarianism, which itself combined materialist (Marxist-Leninist) trends with romantic ones (the idealization of "history").[66]

Early on, the universalist-particularist Janus was evident in the westernizer trend. If Herzen would go back to the people and place his hopes for a new order in Russian socialism, Chadaaev could bitterly write that Russia, cut off from history, had "given nothing to the world": "We have disfigured everything we have touched of that [human] progress. From the very first moment of our social existence, nothing has emanated from us for the common good of men; not a single useful thought has sprouted in the sterile soil of our country; not a single great truth has sprung from our midst."[67] The westernizers' universalist strain sometimes turned to self-hatred and manifested itself in the supreme power of the radical revolutionary notion of "negation," even the negation of one's own country, expressed vividly in the poetry of one embittered radical: "How sweet it is to hate one's country" he wrote. "And eagerly await her destruction / And to see in the destruction of one's country / The dawn of a world reborn."[68]

Synthesis

Classical Slavophilism degenerated when its leading lights died. By the end of the 1860s, the Great Reforms had taken place and the serfs were emancipated. The modernizing trends of the bureaucratic autocracy continued. The peasant's land hunger was not satiated by the reforms, nor was the appetite for revolution among Russian radicals, who were becoming bolder. Alexander II, after six unsuccessful attempts, was assassinated in 1881. His successor would tighten the reins of the developing police state and attempt to reverse the reformist trend begun by the "Czar Liberator." The political momentum on the Right had passed to the adherents of the "official nationality" and those who saw Russia's historical mission in Pan-Slavist chauvinism. The 1905 revolution would give birth to the quasi-fascist Black Hundreds.

By the time 1905 had come and gone, the language of Russian nationalism was fully formed. The cultural system of Russian nationalism, the litany of expressions, concepts, and assumptions was by then quite familiar. Russia was distinct from the West; or perhaps between East and West. She had a separate destiny and mission and her own way of developing. Orthodoxy was the bedrock of Russianness and the communalism of the peasant was the ideal social arrangement. Autocracy was the most suitable form of government for the Russians, who wished to remain aloof from (or were simply incapable of taking part in) affairs of state. The cultivation of *narodnost* would be Russia's salvation. The contamination of Russia by Western ideas must be avoided. Endurance, patience, kindness, and piety were the distinguishing characteristics of the Russian people. Russia needed a unifying principle, a Russian Idea, to unite the people and the state and rekindle *sobornost*. Above all, Russia must remain indivisible and whole, either to preserve the integral society or to defend herself against potential enemies, both external and internal. It is in this language—the nationalist myth-symbol complex—that the polemics of contemporary Russian nationalists are conducted.

The nationalist myth-symbol complex arose from an intellectual struggle that reached its peak in the controversy between the Slavophiles and Westernizers, and between romanticism and idealism (not necessarily the mystic elements in Russian Orthodoxy or Russia's Byzantine past)[69] and played the crucial role in its development. That is not to say that the ideological struggle and subsequent Russian nationalisms (in the sense of distinct ideologies or persuasions) were self-generating. They arose in reaction to Russia's contacts with the West and as a response to the disorienting forces of modernization that were unleashed by Peter the Great. After that, it is a problematic "chicken or egg" question to ask "what came first?" Social and economic dislocations, war, political instability, official policies, and ideology are all part and parcel of the fate that befell Russia in the twentieth century.

Notes

1. I have borrowed the term from a scholar of German nationalism, Jeffrey Herf of the College of the Holy Cross in Worcester, Massachusetts.
2. The analysis of the Slavophile-Westernizer controversy offered here is derived in large part from the work of Polish scholar Andrezej Walicki. His two classic works covering this subject are *The Slavophile Controversy* (1975) and *A History of Russian Thought: From the Enlightenment to Marxism* (1979).
3. Cited in Robert K. Massie, *Peter the Great: His Life and World* (New York: Ballantine, 1980), 878.
4. Ibid., 879.
5. By rationalism I mean a worldview that rejects the accepted norms of

a traditional, premodern society, norms that are the product of the organic development of that society and its customs. Traditionalism accepts the wisdom of corporate experience, whereas rationalism tends to rely on the reason of the autonomous individual as a guide to conduct and philosophy. The Slavophile traditionalists did not reject rational modes of thinking (how could they have debated the Westernizers if they had?) but rather rejected the notion that autonomous individuals could construct, by way of their own reason, an independent set of values and social ideals disconnected from the wisdom of the community.

6. For an account of Peter's reign that places him in the perspective of his times, see Massie's *Peter the Great.*

7. Ibid, 265–266.

8. Andrezej Walicki, *The Slavophile Controversy* (Notre Dame, Ind: University of Notre Dame Press, 1989), 19.

9. Here Walicki uses the term feudal in the way that it will be used throughout this study, that is, as indicative of a socioeconomic system based on mutual obligation and hierarchy and not dependent on the cash nexus for sustenance. Thus lands held by nobles in ancient Russia were held as a reward for service to the crown. Nobles were responsible for the well-being of the serfs, and serfs were responsible for working the land and turning over a portion of the crop to the feudal lord. Homage, obligation, and service are the hallmarks of feudal agrarian systems. Peter's reforms did not completely supplant the feudal system, since the bureaucratic nobility was rewarded with land and the right to hold serfs. The ongoing modernization of Russia in the nineteenth century thus involved the continued struggle of feudal economic and social institutions against the forces of industry, bureaucracy, and capitalism on the one hand and modernist ideologies with traditionalist conservatism and religion on the other. As noted earlier, the Romanov dynasty never resolved the conundrum facing them in simultaneously modernizing and preserving the monarchy.

10. See particularly Edmund Burke, *Reflections on the Revolution in France* (New York: Bobbs Merrill, 1955).

11. Walicki, *Slavophile Controversy*, 9.

12. Shcherbatov's views are discussed at length in ibid., 20–32. His aristocratic views of liberty and anti-autocracy would influence some of the Decembrists, a group of army officers who took part in an anticzarist revolt in December 1825. Many others were inspired by the republicanism they had encountered in Europe during the Russian army's campaign against Napoleon. Thus the Decembrists can be claimed, in some sense, by both Left and Right as either revolutionary precursors of 1905 and 1917 or as Russian patriots acting in the name of traditional Russian liberties.

13. Cited in Walicki, *Slavophile Controversy*, 29.

14. Cited in ibid., 33.

15. Karamzin's views are discussed at length in ibid., 32–44.

16. Cited in ibid., 33.

17. Ibid., 33.

18. Pogodin's views are discussed in ibid., 47–63.

19. The word *narodnost* means "nationality" and "national roots" or "national character."

20. Walicki, *Slavophile Controversy*, 46.

21. See Richard Pipes, *Russia Under the Old Regime* (New York: Scribner's, 1974), for an elaboration of this view of nineteenth century Russian development.

22. Walicki, *Slavophile Controversy*, 48.

23. Cited in bid., 49.

24. Cited in ibid., 48.

25. Cited in ibid., 53.

26. In view of the oftmade connection between the romantic movement and fascism and nazism (as if a direct line from romantic modes of thought and expression necessarily progresses to Hitler via Wagner), it is necessary here to clarify what I mean by the "romantic movement." Romanticism rejected Enlightenment era neoclassicism, empiricism, and materialist worldviews in art and philosophy and emphasized emotions, imagination, and intuition. That by no means automatically assumes a nationalist, right-wing, or conservative agenda, and Rousseau's views bear this out. The Westernizers, for example, attached themselves, via Hegel, to a view of historical progress that was romantic as well.

27. Slavophile here denotes both the originators of Slavophile thought (and not necessarily their precursors) and direct participants in the public and private debate between Slavophiles and Westernizers that peaked in the 1840s. These are Walicki's "classical Slavophiles." Many philosophers, polemicists, and writers would subsequently identify themselves as "Slavophiles," in spite of their many deviations from "classical Slavophile" thought.

28. Kireevsky's "integral personality" concept is discussed in Walicki, *Slavophile Controversy*, 150–160.

29. Ibid., 152.

30. Ibid., 155.

31. Ivan Kireevsky, "A Reply to A. S. Khomyakov" ["V Otvet A. S. Khomyakovu"], *The Russian Idea* (Russkaya idyeya), ed. Mikhail Maslin (Moscow: Respublika, 1992), 67.

32. The authority of Christian tradition and not necessarily that of the visible church.

33. See Kireevky's comments on Napoleon in this context in his "Reply," 67.

34. Walicki, *Slavophile Controversy*, 143.

35. John Paxton, *Companion to Russian History* (New York: Facts on File, 1983), 447.

36. Nicholas Riasanovsky, *A History of Russia*, 5th edition (Oxford: Oxford University Press, 1993), 173.

37. Paxton, *Companion to Russian History*, 447.

38. Many of the Slavophiles made their peace with commercialized agriculture after the reforms of the 1860s, though not with private landholding as

such. In fact, some Slavophiles who participated in advising the czar on land reform and the abolition of serfdom insisted on maintaining the *obshchina* as the fundamental unit of Russian society. Their real enemy was implicitly modernization as such, of which industry and urbanization represented the most dangerous components to the agrarian society they idealized. Kireevsky explicitly links industrialism with Western rationalism in his "Reply to A. S. Khomyakov," written as a response to Khomyakov's article "On the Old and the New," both of which were written in 1839. Their epigones would continue the struggle on that basis.

39. See Walicki, *Slavophile Controversy*, 168–78.

40. Riasanovsky, *History of Russia*, 363.

41. Riasonovsky, ibid., 363.

42. Riasanovsky, ibid., 363.

43. Within limits, presumably, since the Slavophiles were not liberals by any means, advocating adherence to tradition and the absolute truth of the Orthodox faith. Liberal notions of "pluralism" would not have met with their approval. Riasonovsky, *History of Russia*, 363.

44. So that society could develop organically. Ibid., 364.

45. Kireevsky, "Reply to A. S. Khomyakov," 67.

46. One should not underestimate the powerful reaction Russian society had to the prevalence of foreigners at Peter's court. That reaction, combined with the forced acceptance of foreign ways, was enough to incite a people who resented the perceived arrogance of the outsiders, who were afforded privileges and separate settlements in a land whose people had become, in the eyes of many of them, cannon fodder for Peter's wars and human material for his many collectivist projects. This resentment helped to spark the Astrakhan revolt of 1705. See Riasanovsky, *History of Russia*, 223.

47. Walicki, *Slavophile Controversy*, 144.

48. Ibid., 149.

49. The subtitle of Walicki's study of the Slavophiles is *History of a Conservative Utopia in Nineteenth-Century Russian Thought.*

50. Andrezej Walicki, *A History of Russian Thought: From the Enlightenment to Marxism* (Stanford: Stanford University Press, 1979), 105.

51. For a discussion of the romantic movement that notes the borrowing of ideas (organic society for one) by the Slavophiles and their relation to Romanticism, see Nicholas Riasanovsky, *The Emergence of Romanticism* (Oxford: Oxford University Press, 1992).

52. Riasanovsky dates the "emergence" of Romanticism as the 1790s, making it both a reaction to and a wing of Enlightenment thought.

53. Riasanovsky, *Emergence of Romanticism*, 77–79. For a discussion of Coleridge's conservatism, see Russell Kirk, *The Conservative Mind: From Burke to Elliot*, 7th ed., rev., (Washington, D.C.: Regnery Gateway, 1993), 133–46.

54. Robert Nisbet, *History of the Idea of Progress* (New York: Basic Books, 1980), 278.

55. Ibid., 276.

56. Cited in ibid., 278.

57. Cited in ibid., 278.

58. Ibid., 277.

59. See Walicki, *Slavophile Controversy*, 83–117.

60. See Nisbet, *History of the Idea of Progress*, 276–286, for a discussion of the statism and romantic nationalism evident in Hegelian philosophy.

61. Cited in Walicki, *Slavophile Controversy*, 582.

62. Ibid., 585.

63. For a discussion of populism, see ibid., 580–601.

64. Ibid., 596.

65. Walicki, *History of Russian Thought*, 269.

66. For a description of Vissarion Belinsky's turn to the "philosophy of action," see Walicki, *History of Russian Thought*, 370–78. Nisbet in his *History of the Idea of Progress* comments on the eventual "Hegelianizing of Marx," 276.

67. Cited in Walicki, *History of Russian Thought*, 100.

68. Cited in ibid., 101.

69. Riasanovsky holds this view, assigning a certain priority to romanticism in the development of Slavophile thought. See *Emergence of Romanticism*, 94, n. 73.

3

—————

Solzhenitsyn and the Russian Questions

Contemporary Russian nationalisms all borrow from the myth-symbol complex established by the nineteenth century Slavophile-Westernizer clash. Aleksandr Solzhenitsyn is often identified as a "Slavophile" by critics who consider the appellation a stain on his reputation. However, unlike the Slavophiles, he has developed a brand of nationalism that attempts to deal with social-structural questions in a way that his precursors seldom did, while reasserting their view of Russian uniqueness. Solzhenitsyn's program appears to take account of human nature and the nationalist imperative in a way that no other contemporary Russian public figure does. His keen perception of the sources of modern man's alienation could point the way to a viable postmodernization for Russia.

Aleksandr Solzhenitsyn's identification of the most important Russian questions, his attempts to address them, as well as the dramatic sense of expectation that surrounded his return to Russia, underscore his importance as a cultural figure and an exponent of a nationalism that is not inherently hostile to the West, however cognizant its originator may be of the cultural encroachment of the "other." His Russophile, or neo-Slavophile, ideas take up where the classical Slavophiles and their epigones left off. His expression of such views in the 1970s made the West aware that Russian nationalism had remained a potent cultural force within the nominally internationalist USSR. An examination of Solzhenitsyn's life and views is, therefore, the best place to start our review of contemporary Russian nationalism (chapters 3–9).

An End and a Beginning

Aleksandr Solzhenitsyn's odyssey began on a "pallid" February morning in 1945 somewhere in a "narrow salient on the Baltic Sea"[1] when he was arrested by Soviet counterintelligence for making disparaging remarks about the Great Leader and Teacher himself—he had referred to Stalin as *pakhan*, a leader of thieves,[2] in a letter to a friend. "The brigade commander," he wrote in *The Gulag Archipelago*, "called me to his headquarters and asked me for my pistol; I turned it over without suspecting any evil intent, when suddenly . . . two counterintelligence officers stepped forward hurriedly . . . and . . . shouted theatrically: 'You are under arrest!' "[3]

Forty-nine years later, in May 1994, he returned to Russia after twenty years' exile in the West, no longer puzzled, as he had been as an artillery captain in the Soviet army as to the reason for his arrest (" 'You are under arrest!' Burning and prickling from head to toe, all I could exclaim was: 'Me? What for?' "[4]), certain now that it had all been to a larger purpose and thankful for it: "Looking back, I saw that for my whole conscious life I had not understood either myself or my strivings. . . . And that is why I turn back sometimes to the years of my imprisonment and say, sometimes to the astonishment of those about me: *'Bless you, prison!'* "[5] Aleksandr Solzhenitsyn, one time Soviet captain of artillery, Gulag prisoner for eight years, exiled teacher, and Nobel Prize-winning author, had fulfilled the prophecy he himself had made: He would return one day to his homeland, his literary mission accomplished, the course of his life and, perhaps, the last stage of its purpose not yet finished. The role he could play in Russia's life has been the source of much discussion in a country where writers have for some two centuries served as the conscience of the Russian nation.

Russia Ponders Solzhenitsyn's Role

Russian media coverage of Solzhenitsyn's return to his homeland focused on the question of his role in postcommunist Russia. Would Solzhenitsyn take sides in the ongoing political struggle? Was he a "democrat"? Would he, as some of his most vociferous critics maintained, find his real home in the amorphous "red-brown" coalition of "White" and "Red" "patriots," at the center of which beat the living heart of what Yeltsin had dubbed "communo-fascism"? Was Solzhenitsyn a Khomeini-like figure, as some observers alleged, prepared to act as the center of gravity for the formation of a new Orthodox fundamentalist order, the kind that Russian chauvinists of the last century swore would be the salvation of Holy Russia? Worse, was he merely irrelevant, a grandstanding has-been whose sense of his own self-importance had alienated him from ordinary Russians?

Solzhenitsyn himself kept the media chatterboxes busy enough. After his plane arrived in the Russian Far East in May 1994, he began a fifty-five-day journey by train from Vladivostok to Moscow, stopping along the way to meet ordinary citizens, some of whom greeted him as a hero and prophet of the coming Russian rebirth while others saw him as a conduit for their complaints and personal travails, a messenger to Czar Boris in Moscow carrying petitions from the denizens of the beleaguered hinterlands. To diehards, Solzhenitsyn was the destroyer of the Soviet homeland, the man who had done so much to bring about the collapse of the communist regime and with it the security and stability of Soviet socialism, not to mention the glories of superpower status. His arrival in Moscow brought out a mixed crowd of dignitaries, well-wishers, and not-so-well-wishers, partisans of the old order who heckled him during a short speech in the rainy weather, making clear their hostility to a man whose book *The Gulag Archipelago*, had undermined the Soviet Union perhaps as much as any other external phenomenon, attacking the foundations of the Soviet regime's ideological fortress with a hundred armored divisions of Truth. The communists' Lie was bound to lose such a struggle.

Pravda, although critical of Solzhenitsyn, barely took note of his return, save to print the words of Eduard Limonov, one-time member of Vladimir Zhirinovskiy's shadow cabinet, describing Solzhenitsyn as a self-styled savior who had actually done much, through his attacks on the old regime, to spread what Limonov considered a "false image of Russia and the Russians" in the West, an image of a "dangerous nation" and a "dangerous people."[6] The image of Solzhenitsyn as destroyer was seconded by fellow writer Valentin Rasputin, who claimed that Solzhenitsyn was partly responsible for the degraded and chaotic condition of Russia, since he had continued his attacks on the old regime beyond the point where "war against communism became war against . . . Russia."[7] Another critic told readers of the nationalist newspaper *Zavtra* that the mere fact that Solzhenitsyn's return had prompted enthusiasm from many "democrats" (partisans of a Westernizing reform line) signified what now appeared obvious: Only the "utopian radicals" among the "democrats" could expect anything favorable from Solzhenitsyn, a man who had "shocked" many in the anti-Yeltsin camp by his contacts with the current regime.[8] Amid *Zavtra's* relentless attacks playwright Viktor Rozov asked what he, and apparently many others, considered the "central question": "Who will Aleksandr Isayevich line up with?"[9]

That Rozov could even ask such a question in view of Solzhenitsyn's reputation as an anticommunist, as well as his writings and public statements from the past about the desirability of giving up the empire, something that had particularly mussed the ideological feathers of many nationalists, speaks volumes about the lack of any real understanding of Solzhenitsyn's literary and polemical works among so many Russians who should know better. The reason why any members of the "patriotic" coalition could entertain the possibility of an alliance with the Nobel Laureate (considered by many to be the moral conscience of the nation) for the political battle against what they viewed as a pro-Western and anti-Russian regime is that Solzhenitsyn himself had confused (and disappointed) westernizers by his sharp criticisms of the government's reforms. The thrust of Solzhenitsyn's comments was that the reforms had been pursued too hastily, that the same old tired bureaucratic faces were still running things, that "false democrats" were taking advantage of the chaotic privatization program to enrich themselves, and that Russians in the "near abroad"— the former Soviet republics—had been left to fend for themselves on what was often hostile territory. Having told a welcoming crowd in Vladivostok that "I know that your lives are . . . hard, that there is no clear future for you or your children," he flatly stated that "I refuse to recognize that [any kind of] reform is taking place." Moreover, and more encouraging from the nationalist viewpoint, Solzhenitsyn constantly stressed the importance of Russian patriotism and Orthodox religion for any program of Russian rebirth.[10]

The Critics' Opening Salvo

The patriots were not alone in either their attacks on Solzhenitsyn or their confusion about what he stood for. In fact, the attacks began even before his return to Russia. *Nezavisimaya Gazeta*, probably reacting to Solzhenitsyn's criticisms of the current Russian situation, characterized him as a man still a prisoner, this time of his own "lack of understanding" of the country's condition, a man so insulated by his own "eternal" Gulag that he "does not understand anything in Russia or the West." Solzhenitsyn was a man "with a Hollywood beard," a has-been who was staging a dramatic entrance to attract attention to himself.[11] The newspaper's chief editor, Vitaliy Tretyakov, continued the attacks, likening him to a man "on a white horse" who had carefully orchestrated a grand entry "from the east" like the sun itself (the editorial was titled "Solzhenitsyn, Like the Sun, Rises in the East"). Tretyakov asserted that despite Solzhenitsyn's "subjective intentions," in particular his stated intention to remain above politics, his return could not help being political in view of the attention his every step would attract.[12] Tretyakov was moved to sarcastically assert, after quoting another commentator's characterization of Solzhenitsyn as "[our] doctor" and the country as the patient, that he, for one, was "healthy in spirit and body" and not in need of doctoring of any sort. He also voiced the hope that Solzhenitsyn, as promised, would not take part in the partisan political struggle.[13]

Defenders of Solzhenitsyn

Some stood up to defend Solzhenitsyn. One defender called his return "a victory for Russia" as well as a vindication of the man who had predicted that communism would fall in his own lifetime. Thus, Solzhenitsyn's life was the unfolding of a personal mission to enlighten the Russian people about their own history, so obscured by the communists. His life, in this defender's estimation, demonstrates for all the necessity of purpose, of a higher aim not just for individuals but for "nations and humanity in general," a purpose that, as a Christian, Solzhenitsyn felt (so the defender wrote) was a reflection of "Divine Providence."[14] Another defender, dismissing as naive the assertions of unnamed democrats that Solzhenitsyn, absent for twenty years, was out of touch and would not recognize the "red-brown" danger for what it was, noted that "communism is still communism" and that Solzhenitsyn would recognize the enemy when the time came. Solzhenitsyn is "bigger than any politician," a man who will act as a moral guide and defender of civilization, a man who, like Tolstoy, is always above ordinary experience.[15]

The notion that Solzhenitsyn would eventually recognize the enemy is interesting in coming from an observer who wrote as if he understood Solzhenitsyn's beliefs and intentions. This note of tentativeness and uncertainty ran through many of the essentially defensive articles and broadcasts about his return, and a careful reader might be forgiven for wondering whether the defenders themselves were all that sure about the subject of their ruminations. The popular weekly TV newsmagazine program *Itogi*, for instance, carried a report on Solzhenitsyn's arrival in Russia that was defensive in tone but followed up with a subsequent interview with the man himself in which *Itogi* anchorman, well-known democratic journalist Yevgeniy Kiselev, returned several times to the questions that both patriotic and democratic partisans had wondered aloud about, namely, would Solzhenitsyn get involved in partisan politics? If so, whose side would he be on?[16]

The initial report called Solzhenitsyn's arrival in Russia "the principal event of the week" and noted the high degree of interest[17] that his return seemed to have sparked in Russian society. Kiselev considered it "obvious" that Solzhenitsyn's return "will change Russian politics." Despite the interest already noted, the report adopted a more condescending tone when it implied that Solzhenitsyn's actual ideas and writings enjoyed a fairly limited audience. Kiselev attempted to interpret Solzhenitsyn for the audience, noting that nationalism was on the rise in Russia (he described Solzhenitsyn's views themselves as nationalist) but asserting that many Russians nonetheless failed to understand that the "nationalism of Solzhenitsyn and the nationalism of the Russian ultras"[18] diverged considerably. Kiselev felt compelled to tell his viewers that Solzhenitsyn's nationalism was without "xenophobia or geopolitical ambition," something that needed to be explained, apparently, to many Russians who had not "read Solzhenitsyn carefully."[19] What this says about Kiselev's trust or distrust of the Russian public, as well as his true feelings about Solzhenitsyn (was Kiselev hoping that he would come out on the right side of the political struggle?) is not entirely clear, but the anxiety among democrats about Solzhenitsyn's possible political impact was apparent in the subsequent interview.

The interview is noteworthy for two reasons. First, Kiselev harped on now familiar themes, repeating the all important political questions asked elsewhere, thereby demonstrating the uncertainty about Solzhenitsyn in Russia. Did Solzhenitsyn realize that his criticisms of the government might play into the hands of the communists and "ultras"? Would Solzhenitsyn play an active role in politics? Did he realize that his every move was under media scrutiny and, therefore, was bound to have a "political" effect? What did he think of Yeltsin? Kiselev was respectful and apologized occasionally for bringing up questions Solzhenitsyn had undoubtedly heard before. The question that wasn't asked was nevertheless screaming between the lines: Just whose side was Solzhenitsyn on? Second, the interview provided the former political exile with his first opportunity to directly address the broader Russian public at any length.

Solzhenitsyn calmly reiterated his intention to remain outside of the partisan political struggle (he preached against party politics). But he asserted that "Russia is in trouble"[20] and no responsible citizen could abandon the field at this critical time. As to the question of his subjective impact on the political scene, he flatly rejected any such concerns, emphasizing his devotion to truth and the objective reality of Russian life, certain aspects of which appeared not to have penetrated the hardened sociopolitical "ellipsoid" that encased the capital.[21] He had pledged to convey the realities of the peoples' troubles to those in power and intended to do so, no matter what politicians of whatever stripe tried to make of it.

Solzhenitsyn: Prophet of Postmodernism

So what does Aleksandr Solzhenitsyn believe and why does it matter? The criticisms leveled at him since his return to Russia have been heard before, an echo of attacks launched against him in both the Soviet Union in the late 1960s and early 1970s, and in the West after his exile in 1974. Mainstream critics have charged him with being messianic, dictatorial, a Russian chauvinist, an anti-Western fanatic, a Russian Khomeini, a self-promoting has-been, or an arrogant blowhard whose ideas are irrelevant to either Russia or mankind at the end of the twentieth century. All of these charges are false, either wrongheaded or simply mean-spirited. Solzhenitsyn's ideas matter very much, both for Russia and for the West. His ideas are a critique of modernity itself, voiced in a language and style that is jarring to the modern ear and modern sensibilities, East and West.[22]

Solzhenitsyn, by answering a particular question in a particular way ("What should men live by?"), offers alternative answers to the Russian questions that have so vexed his countrymen since Peter the Great's time: What is Russia?, Who is Russian?, What is to be done?, and, perhaps most important, Who is to blame?, for many Russians have long dissipated the nation's energies on uncovering enemies (often imagined) and assigning blame for the many disasters that have befallen her in this century. His answers present Russia with a nationalist program (for he is a nationalist, a conservative, and a man of the Right as we have defined those terms) that speaks to the best in his nation, thus undermining the "red-brown" temptation. Solzhenitsyn's ideas may well represent the wave of the future, for, in spite of what the critics say, his eye is always on the future, particularly future generations of Russians, and is not fixated on a fantasy of a utopian past. That future may well bring a reassessment of mankind's destiny that takes us beyond the modern era that so many observers claim is already at an end.

Since Solzhenitsyn's message is delivered in a language and style that is, unfortunately, no longer familiar to us (which, in part at least, explains the various misinterpretations of his work and philosophy), in order to understand the man and his message we must begin at the beginning and briefly review his pilgrim's progress from Leninist to Christian, from Soviet officer to exile, in order to correctly interpret what he has to say to us. Only then can he be judged fairly.

The Pilgrim's Progress[23]

Aleksandr Isayevich Solzhenitsyn was born on December 11, 1918, at Kislovodsk in the North Caucasus to a family of Russian and Ukrainian peasant stock. He was raised by his mother, the elder Solzhenitsyn having volunteered for army service while a student at Moscow University, serving (as his son would in the next European conflagration) as an artillery officer. He was killed some six months before Aleksandr's birth. Solzhenitsyn's widowed mother moved the family to Rostov-on-Don, where the child grew up, absorbing along the way the Orthodox Christian beliefs of his forebears. In a 1989 interview, he said that he had been "raised by my elders in the spirit of Christianity, and almost through my school years, up to 17 or 18, I was in opposition to Soviet education."[24] He once recalled how the old people explained the disasters that had befallen Russia: "Men have forgotten God; that's why all of this has happened."[25] Later the atheistic program of his Soviet tutors did its work, and as a young man in his twenties, Aleksandr Solzhenitsyn became a Marxist-Leninist.

By the time Solzhenitsyn left school in 1936, he already harbored literary ambitions, planning to someday write a story about the Russian military defeat at Tannenberg in 1914, a story that became *August 1914* some decades later.[26] He entered Rostov University to study mathematics and physics but never gave up his ambition to become a writer. "I never intended to devote the rest of my life to mathematics," he would say later. "Literature was the greatest attraction, but I realized that mathematics would at least provide me with bread and butter."[27] Solzhenitsyn excelled at his studies and graduated with honors in 1941. In the meantime, he won a Stalin scholarship and enrolled in a correspondence course in literature at the Moscow Institute of Philosophy, Literature, and History. During this period he also authored his first stories, which were rejected by the journal *Znamya*.

Solzhenitsyn was twice rejected for military service on medical grounds (he attempted to enlist shortly after the outbreak of the war). In 1941 he took a post as a physics teacher at a secondary school in the Rostov region, moving there with his wife, chemistry student Natalya Alekseevna Reshetovskaya, whom he had married the previous year. By the fall of 1941 the Soviet army's situation was such that problems previously judged as grounds for rejection were now being overlooked. Solzhenitsyn was called up for military service on October 18, 1941. He began his time in the army "like Nerzhin in *The First Circle*" as a "driver of horse drawn vehicles, although he knew nothing about horses."[28] His career as a Russian-style muleskinner was to be short lived, he qualified for artillery school and received a commission in 1942. He saw action in the battle of Kursk and took part in the march into East Prussia. Eventually, Solzhenitsyn was promoted to captain, having been awarded the Order of the Patriotic War Class II and the Order of the Red Star.

After his arrest during the battle of Konigsberg in February 1945, he was taken to Lubyanka prison in Moscow and interrogated.[29] He was convicted by an NKGB[30] tribunal under Article 58, the famous catch-all "political crimes" provision of the Russian Republic's criminal code and sentenced to eight years hard labor, "the normal sentence for most 'crimes' under Article 58 at the time."[31] Solzhenitsyn was initially interned in one of the labor camps near Moscow, going into the city each day to work on various building projects. But, beginning in 1946, he was sent to work in a special research institute (*sharashka*) staffed by Gulag prisoners, an experience that he later translated into art in the *First Circle*.[32] Like the novel's protagonist, Gleb Nerzhin, he was later transferred from the relative comfort of the *sharashka* to serve the last three years of his term in the camps, in this case in central Kazakhstan near Karanga. In the camp, the future novelist first conceived the story that would become *One Day in the Life of Ivan Denisovich*, and like the story's namesake he worked as a bricklayer.

In the camp at Karanga Solzhenitsyn suffered the third great ordeal of his life: he was stricken with cancer. An operation failed to cure the malady that afflicted him. Solzhenitsyn was released from the camp in March 1953 and lived in exile in the village of Kok Terek (Green Poplar) in Kazakhstan, working as a school teacher. A former school administrator remembered him as "a tall man with a pale face and deep set eyes, straight hair combed back and nervous hands fumbling with a worn old fur hat. He was wearing discolored riding breeches and patched boots. None of this was in accord with the man's disarming simplicity and charm."[33] He was popular with students and administrators, an able teacher and agreeable colleague.

While living in Kok Terek his condition worsened. Near death, he made his way to a clinic for cancer patients in Tashkent, Uzbekistan, where he made a startling recovery. The clinic, as well as the village of Kok Terek, provided the background for *Cancer Ward*, and the polyphonic novel's center of gravity, Kostoglotov, took over from *The First Circle*'s Nerzhin (and, to some extent from Ivan Denisovich) the role of "the chief embodiment of Solzhenitsyn's own experience."[34]

Solzhenitsyn benefited from Khrushchev's de-Stalinization program in 1956, when the military tribunal of the Soviet Supreme Court reviewed his case and threw out the charges against him. He returned to European Russia, eventually settling with his wife in Ryazan. Here Solzhenitsyn began his writing career, completing *Ivan Denisovich* in 1958. He waited until 1961, when the atmosphere seemed right, to contact Aleksandr Tvardovskiy, editor of the leading "liberal" literary journal of the day, *Novy Mir*. *Novy Mir*'s publication of the short novel (with Khrushchev's approval and sponsorship) caused a sensation in

Russia and around the world and marked Solzhenitsyn as an enemy of the revanchist forces that would launch a neo-Stalinist crackdown a few years later. Solzhenitsyn's recalcitrance and civic courage, his call for an end to Soviet censorship, and his involvement with dissident circles (and especially the seizure of his *The Gulag Archipelago* manuscript) prompted the Soviet authorities to expel him in 1974. Until the Gorbachev period, *Ivan Denisovich* would remain the only one of his major works to appear in the Soviet Union, though clandestine typescripts (*samizdat* "self-publishing" versions) of his works had been circulating for some time.

The traumatic experiences of his life had not been without effect. Aleksandr Solzhenitsyn's odyssey had brought him full circle: He became a Christian. In *The Gulag Archipelago* he described his conversion experience as a slow ascent out of the spiritual pit he had fallen into. "In the seventh year of my imprisonment I had gone over and re-examined my life quite enough and had come to understand why everything had happened to me: both prison and, as an additional piece of ballast, my malignant tumor. And I would not have murmured even if all that punishment had been considered inadequate. Punishment? But . . . whose? Well, just think about that—*whose?*"[35]

Solzhenitsyn's self-examination had been prompted not simply by the fact of his own suffering but by the jarring and inspiring behavior of a few of his fellow prisoners, men who proved to him that imprisonment need not be the end of life, that freedom and spiritual meaning were not automatically destroyed by the barbed wire and guard dogs. A good life, a meaningful life, even a free life, in many ways freer than the life of those Soviets still living "out there," was possible, even in the Gulag. In the camps, the 58s (political prisoners) spoke more or less freely since they had precious little left to lose. This was their liberation: to know themselves as "free" men seldom do and in that self discovery experience an awakening of the spirit. Among the fellow *zeks* who would influence him the most were Dr. Boris Kornfeld and the devout Baptists he met during his incarceration, men who found their highest freedom with Daniel, in the lions' den.

In *One Day in the Life of Ivan Denisovich*, the saintly Alyoshka the Baptist draws for the reader a composite portrait of the simplicity and piety of the many Baptists the author encountered and learned from in the Gulag: "[Alyoshka] [t]he Baptist was reading his Bible, not altogether silently, but sort of sighing out the words. . . . 'But let none of you suffer as a murderer, or a thief, or a wrongdoer, or a mischiefmaker: yet if one suffers as a Christian, let him not be ashamed, but under that name let him glorify God.' "[36] Alyoshka remains something of an enigma to his fellow *zeks*, even to the good-hearted Ivan Denisovich Shukhov: "Looking through the wire gate, across the building site and out through the wire fence on the far side you could see the sun rising, big and red, as though in a fog. Alyoshka, standing next to Shukhov, gazed at the sun and a happy smile spread from his eyes to his lips. Aloyshka's cheeks were hollow, he lived on his bare ration and never made anything on the side—what had he got to be happy about? He and the other Baptists spent their Sundays whispering to each other. Life in the camp was like water off a duck's back to them."[37] Shukhov is fond of Alyoshka and gives the Baptists their due: "Never says no, that Alyoshka, whatever you ask him to do. If everybody in the world was like him I'd be the same. Help anybody who asked me. Why not? They've got the right idea, that lot."[38]

Shukhov, if he has not (yet?) crossed the spiritual river that Alyoshka has, is not an atheist. Something, perhaps the whisper of his own conscience (or like the young Solzhenitsyn, his elders' folkish wisdom) tells him that God exists: " 'Where I come from they used to say God breaks up the old moon to make stars.' The captain laughed. 'What savages! I never heard anything like it! So you believe in God, do you, Shukhov?' Now Shukhov was surprised. 'Of course I do. How can anybody not believe in God when it thunders?' "[39]

Solzhenitsyn met Kornfeld during his stay in a camp hospital for his initial cancer surgery. It was here that his ascent may well have been completed. Kornfeld visits the ailing Solzhenitsyn and speaks to him of matters of the soul:

Following an operation, I am lying in the surgical ward of a camp hospital. I cannot move. I am hot and feverish, but nonetheless my thoughts do not dissolve into delirium—and I am grateful to Dr. Boris Nikolayevich Kornfeld, who is sitting beside my cot and talking all evening. The light has been turned out—so it will not hurt my eyes. He and I—and there is no one else in the ward. Fervently he tells me the long story of his conversion from Judaism to Christianity . . . I am astonished at the conviction of the new convert, at the ardor of his words. . . . It is already late. All the hospital is asleep. Kornfeld is ending up his story thus: "And on the whole, do you know, I have become convinced that there is no punishment that comes to us in this life on earth which is undeserved."[40]

Solzhenitsyn tells his readers that "by that time I myself had matured to similar thoughts." Nerzhin and Kostoglotov also begin to "mature" during the course of *The First Circle* and *Cancer Ward*, both renouncing the temptation of "surviving at any price."[41] Like *The First Circle*'s Innokenty Volodin, who warns an acquaintance of his impending arrest by the NKVD, and thereby seals his own fate, both men sacrifice themselves to a Truth that is not altogether clear to them yet moves them by a mysterious compulsion to do what each knows is right and just. The Gulag is a metaphor in Solzhenitsyn's literature for the Soviet Union itself, a gigantic Gulag where the temptation to "survive at any price" may forever torment those unfortunates who haven't found the answer to the ultimate question that haunts the characters in the author's novels: What should men live by?

Solzhenitsyn's answer is to live by the Truth, which is transcendent and eternal, a Truth that burns in each man's soul, which is created in the image of God. Only this can save one from the horror of becoming an animal, driven by animal desires alone;[42] only this gives meaning and purpose to human life. Rejecting the Truth does not open up vistas of independent life but rather the lid of the hellish cauldron that is Stalin's Soviet Union. Justice and Good are objective qualities in a universe that has meaning and purpose. Rejecting them is the path to self-destruction, spiritually as well as physically. True freedom begins with accepting the Truth. As moral agents possessing free will, we choose the path that we (and through the individuals who compose them, our nations and countries) will take. The choices are the same at all times and in all places, though the Soviet Union provided the artist with an exaggerated variant of the troubles that have confronted all of mankind in one way or another.

The process of spiritual ascent, as described by Solzhenitsyn, begins "as soon as you have renounced that aim of 'surviving at any price,' "[43] enabling the human soul to "ripen with suffering"[44] and to understand the problem of evil: "It was granted to me to carry away from my prison years . . . this essential experience: *how* a human being becomes evil and *how* good. In the intoxication of youthful successes I had felt myself to be infallible, and I was therefore cruel. In the surfeit of power I was a murderer, and an oppressor. In my most evil moments I was convinced that I was doing good. . . . Gradually it was disclosed to me that the line separating good and evil passes not through states, nor between classes, nor between political parties either—but right through every human heart. . . . This line shifts. Inside us, it oscillates with the years. Since then I have come to understand the truth of all the religions of the world: They struggle with *the evil inside a human being* (inside every human being)."[45]

Having accepted the Christian view of the fallen nature of Man, created in the image of God, but willful and rebellious, Solzhenitsyn came to believe that "it is impossible to expel evil from the world in its entirety, but it is possible to constrict it within each person." Thus the strength of a given society depends on its degree of acceptance of this truth and an understanding of the fallen state of the world, created (and proclaimed "good" by the Creator) in harmony with the natural order and its natural laws but fallen away from that harmony through the conscious choice of Man to do evil and disrupt the natural order. Since Man is imperfect, the line between good and evil within him must be regulated by observance of the natural laws that are stamped on his very soul. The moral health of society depends on the moral health of its individual members.

Since he was created in God's image, Man's conscience is the voice of Truth in all of us, a Truth that cannot be replaced by pseudoreligions, ideologies, and false truth—the Lie that Solzhenitsyn so often has called on his countrymen to reject.[46] The basis of the Lie is a belief in Man's ability to transform his own nature, to manipulate the universe and create an earthly heaven, a terrestrial utopia, but Man's nature is more or less constant: "Human nature, if it changes at all, changes not much faster than the geological face of the earth."[47] In the modern era, Solzhenitsyn believes the Lie is embodied in the ideologies that Man has constructed to substitute for God's truth: "I have come to understand the falsehood of all the revolutions in history: They destroy *those carriers* of evil contemporary with them (and also fail, out of haste, to discriminate the carriers of good as well). And they then take to themselves as their heritage the actual evil itself, magnified still more."[48]

In the 1970s, some critics wondered when exactly Solzhenitsyn's conversion had taken place.[49] After all, none of his major protagonists were Christians, not Nerzhin, not Volodin, not Kostoglotov, not even Ivan Denisovich. Matryona of the short story *Matryona's House* keeps icons in her simple home but is not particularly pious, at least not when compared to secondary characters in Solzhenitsyn's literature like *Ivan Denisovich*'s Alyosha. The problem lies within the critics, their minds having been formed by a secular age, who, first, misinterpreted Solzhenitsyn's work as a sort of secular humanist liberal manifesto[50] and, second, failed to see (or ignored) the clues in Solzhenitsyn's works that might have forced a somewhat different interpretation of the unfolding drama being played out in his successive novels and stories. Characters such as Nerzhin and Kostoglotov portray the author's slow ascent and conversion, representing the dawning of a new consciousness for themselves that comes, as it does for most people, slowly, like the sunrise; few appear to experience the thunderclap of the apostle Paul's vision, as unbelievers might expect. In Solzhenitsyn's literature, unbelievers who manage to respond to the Truth etched in their hearts, like Volodin, convey the possibility of redemption to the reader, which Christians believe was bought for them by the suffering of Christ. Solzhenitsyn had been slowly revealing himself through his literature.

Christianity and Criticism

> In our time Christian writers cannot expect a reception based on
> an understanding of their position.
>
> —Donald Treadgold[51]

Solzhenitsyn believes that "by intuition and by his singular vision of
the world, a writer is able to discover far earlier than other people
aspects of social life and can often see them from an unexpected angle.
This is the essence of talent. . . . It is incumbent upon the writer to
inform society of all that he is able to perceive and especially all that is
unhealthy and cause for anxiety."[52] In Russia, where political and social activity has often been restricted by the state, the writer has traditionally played the role of society's watchdog and conscience. Solzhenitsyn continues that tradition today. Both in terms of his art and his
social role he ranks with the great writers of the past, most often being
compared with Tolstoy and Dostoevsky. It is through the prism of this
view of the writer's social role that Solzhenitsyn's insistence on being
heard must be judged.[53] It is not a role he chose for himself, but one
that he inherited as part and parcel of the writer's life. The writer has
a social mission and function to perform through his art and, if need
be, in the public forum. Literature provides the artist's message with a
forum that is both universal and timeless.

Nevertheless, what really appears to disturb moderns about Solzhenitsyn is the message itself, probably not the style of the messenger
or his assumptions about the importance of art, since our own Congress sees fit to hear the opinions of movie stars, among others, on
everything from animal rights to abortion. This became clear when
Western critics began savaging the exiled writer[54] in the 1970s. Curi-
ously, it was only after the publication of more overtly religious (and
implicitly conservative) works, such as *August 1914* and *The Gulag Archipelago*, that such critics, many of whom had been previously sup-
portive, began to attack Solzhenitsyn, even going so far as to attack his
literary reputation retroactively.

The attacks, which began before Solzhenitsyn's public (and friendly)
criticisms of the West,[55] particularly his Harvard address of 1978 that
so roused the indignation of some American elites, many of whom had
perhaps themselves occasionally used harsher terms to attack their
own society.[56] Edward Ericson, in his *Solzhenitsyn and the Modern World*,
took note of the "chilling effect" that Solzhenitsyn's public revelation
of his Orthodox Christianity had on Western opinion makers, accompanied with "a kind of foreboding of more bad news to come."[57]

The "bad news" was confirmed with the publication of the English translation of *August 1914*[58] in 1972. In keeping with Solzhenitsyn's worldview, it attacked the pre-Revolutionary Russian intelligentsia for their utopian, atheistic radicalism, revealed Solzhenitsyn's heartfelt Russian patriotism (as opposed to the liberal internationalism of his critics), and, worst of all, rejected the core of modernity by attacking the Enlightenment heritage of the West, a heritage that had inspired men to believe in the possibility of utopia, an earthly version of paradise to be constructed by the secular high priests of political religion. It became clear that Solzhenitsyn, like Dostoevsky before him, imagined a Godless world as one in which everything is permissible and the end justifies the means. This heritage, in the form of Marxism, had resulted in the disaster of Soviet communism. Solzhenitsyn was not merely antimaterialist and anti-Stalinist but anti-Leninist and even antimodern!

If modernism (not merely its Marxist derivative) is not above criticism, it follows that neither would Western-style democracy be considered the true and only heaven.[59] Modernity's secularism, in Solzhenitsyn's eyes, had fostered a rebellion against God whose form was new, but whose essence was as old as Adam: Man "dismisses God as an agent in the drama of human life" and usurps "the role of supreme moral arbiter" for himself.[60] For Solzhenitsyn's Western critics (like their Soviet counterparts), politics was the standard by which a man should be judged, and Solzhenitsyn's religion precluded the adoption of their secular faith. This was his real transgression.

A particular passage in *August 1914* helped to prompt one Western critic to accuse Solzhenitsyn of spreading "medieval rubbish."[61] Professor Andozerskaya, a teacher of medieval history tells her startled students something of her view of the Middle Ages, and its meaning for the West, which they all profess to admire:

"If you reject the Middle Ages, the history of the West collapses, and the rest of modern history becomes incomprehensible." . . . Varya from Velikie Luki: "But, practically speaking, the history of the West, and everything we need to know about it, begins with the French Revolution. . . ." Varya from Pyatigorsk: "With the Age of Enlightenment" . . . Her lips slightly pursed, Olda Orestovna listened to all those objections as though they were familiar. "That's an error of overhasty thinking—to point to the branch and claim that it's the whole tree. The Enlightenment is only one branch of Western culture, and perhaps by no means the most fruitful. It grows out of the trunk, not from the root." "Which branch is more important, then?" "Well, if you like, the spiritual life of the Middle Ages is more important. Mankind has never known a time, before or since, when there was such an intense spiritual life predominant over material existence." (Could she mean it? What about obscurantism, Roman Catholicism, the Inquisition?) Both Varyas: "But really! How can we in the present day spend our time on the Western Middle Ages? How is it going to help to emancipate our people? How will it help progress in general?"[62]

The students soon get to the heart of the matter: transcendent religion is irrelevant; materialism is their faith, doctrine, and guide: "Surely for practical purposes all we need today is an analysis of the contemporary social environment and material conditions? What can the Middle Ages add to that?" Andozerskaya has an answer for that too:

> "That would be so if the life of the individual really were determined by his material environment. It would be much easier then: the environment is always at fault, so all you have to do is change it. But apart from the environment there is also a spiritual tradition. . . . There is, too, the spiritual life of the *individual,* and therefore each individual has, perhaps in spite of his environment, a *personal* responsibility—for what he does and for what other people around him do."[63]

Well, what about obscurantism (Solzhenitsyn knows about that firsthand) or the Inquisition? Solzhenitsyn is no reactionary dreamer, lost in a fantasy of an idealized lost world; his Christian faith tells him there is no possibility of perfection on earth. No. He understands the rejection of the medieval period's excesses, of its "intolerable despotic repression of man's physical nature in favor of the spiritual one."[64] What he cannot endorse is the wholesale negation of man's spiritual side that is at the heart of modernity. Its rosy view of the perfectibility of Man in another manifestation takes the form of a rejection of the very notion of evil by way of relativism: "The humanistic way of thinking . . . did not admit the existence of intrinsic evil in man, nor did it seek any task higher than the attainment of happiness on earth. It started modern Western civilization on the dangerous trend of worshipping man and his material needs."[65]

Solzhenitsyn's religion, as well as his criticisms of the Enlightenment and the modern condition, began the cycle of vicious, often personal attacks that have continued to this day in the West. His entertaining of the notion in the *Letter to the Soviet Leaders* (published in 1974) that Russia may need a period of authoritarian but law-based rule to smooth the path away from communist totalitarianism evoked a spasm of hysteria from critics who were no less hidebound and doctrinaire than the Soviet communists.[66] Man is perfectible, Western liberalism (replacing Soviet socialism in many minds) is to be the vehicle of utopia's creation, and nothing less than a complete, immediate revolution was acceptable. One *New York Times* critic let lose a barrage of nasty invective, describing Solzhenitsyn as "messianic, patriotic, utopian and religious in tone; anti-democratic, anti-Western."[67] Such critics doubtless thought of the Gorbachev period in Russia, authoritarian but not murderous, as transitional in nature, not a time of reactionary obscurantism.[68]

By the mid-1970s it became apparent that many critics were simply ignorant of the things Solzhenitsyn was speaking of. Many of them really seemed to equate Solzhenitsyn's conservative and religious worldview with czarist reaction, inquisitions and tyranny, obscurantism and chauvinism, if not outright "fascism," whatever that may mean. Some of these critics, who never missed a chance to proclaim their own commitment to open-mindedness and free inquiry, reacted to Solzhenitsyn much as the Soviet regime's lackeys had earlier. Solzhenitsyn himself suspected that many of the West's erstwhile intellectual leaders simply never bothered to read his books, preferring to take their cues, and opinions, from the op-ed page of the *New York Times*.[69] Their Russian counterparts were merely following suit when they began similar attacks after his return to Russia in 1994. A close examination of Solzhenitsyn's essays on Russia's fate, however, which began with his *Letter to the Soviet Leaders*, presents a different, and fuller, picture of his political, social, and economic views. The stature he enjoys in his homeland demands such an examination if we are to determine what significance he may have for contemporary Russia and what direction the nationalist mood of the country could take.

Solzhenitsyn and Russia's Fate

Solzhenitsyn has used the media since his return to Russia to attempt to convey his vision for the salvation of the country and its peoples. His program, briefly outlined in the *Letter to the Soviet Leaders*, was fleshed out in his 1990 essay "Rebuilding Russia" and was reiterated in "The Russian Question at the End of the Twentieth Century," an essay published in *Novy Mir* in 1994. Its key elements include a rejection of imperialism, the peaceful reunification of the Eastern Slavs, and a unique Russian path of development.

Solzhenitsyn attempts to answer the perennial Russian question, What is to be done? In doing so, he also answers the other Russian questions that Slavophiles and Westernizers, nationalists and communists, democrats and patriots, have grappled with since the beginning of the Russian empire's modernization efforts under Peter the Great. What is Russia? Who is Russian? Who is to blame for the disasters that have plagued the homeland? He answers these questions in a way that diverges considerably from any other prominent nationalist figure, probing the condition of modern Man in a manner that is more thoughtful, and more perceptive, than others.

Russia's Moral Crisis

> For the third year [of the Yeltsin regime] we have heard about nothing besides the economy. But the present crisis in our country is a much deeper one, it is a crisis of morality, a crisis so deep that we must not consider [that the solutions will come in a] decade—or [even] a century.[70]
>
> —Aleksandr Solzhenitsyn

In Solzhenitsyn's view, the moral health of society is contingent on the spiritual condition of its individual members, that is, no amount of legislation, legal framework, or constitutional order alone can make a decent society. He sees society shaped from the bottom up, not from the top down, stressing the social underpinnings of any just and decent state system and viewing the moral stability of society as a product of religious faith, which precedes legal and social stability.

For this Christian writer, the strength of a society "depends more on the level of its spiritual life than on its level of industrialization." Neither capitalism nor democracy is a magic bullet, a panacea that will solve society's ills: "Neither a market economy nor even general abundance constitutes the crowning achievement of human life. . . . If a nation's spiritual energies have been exhausted, it will not be saved from collapse by the most perfect government structure or by any industrial development: a tree with a rotten core cannot stand." For Solzhenitsyn, the most "terrifying thing of all" for Russians to contemplate is "the destruction of our souls" that took place under the communists, which any effort to revive Russia must address.[71]

Solzhenitsyn maintains that the disasters of Russia's past, including the victory of the Bolsheviks in 1917, are not mere "accidents" but indicate a deeper crisis that already afflicted Russian society: "Fundamental flaws in the state and in [our] spirituality lead to these [disasters.]"[72] The loss of faith by the Russian intelligentsia[73] preceding the revolution and the un-Christian acts of theft and vengeance by individual Russians themselves in 1917 (here Solzhenitsyn has in mind the mass desertions the Russian army suffered in that year and the soldier-peasants' looting of their neighbors in the mass scramble for land afterward) were part and parcel of a moral crisis that helped to pave the way for the Bolsheviks.

Personal and National Repentance

> West Germany was suffused with the feeling of repentance before
> the coming of their economic boom. But in our country no one has
> even begun to repent. And our *glasnost* is bedecked . . . with the
> same old . . . lies. . . . This is a recipe for warped development.[74]
>
> —Aleksandr Solzhenitsyn

Because Solzhenitsyn sees society's moral health as the aggregation
of the relative moral healthiness of individuals, he has stressed the
importance of the confession of sins (*pokayaniye*) and repentance
(*raskayaniye*) as the path to both individual and national reconciliation.[75] Henceforth, the Golden Rule should be the standard for the personal behavior of individuals and should serve as a guide to state policy. Russia desperately needs both individuals and the nation as a
whole to accept the truth about the past and Russian guilt in what
transpired. Reconciliation with those who suffered under the communists, which all of those guilty of the crimes and abuses perpetrated
under the communist regime should seek (and, Solzhenitsyn maintains, all Russians need to seek with each other, given the depraved
conditions everyone resigned themselves to during the Soviet period)
is the key to putting to rest the misdeeds of the past.

Progress, Empire, and Self-Limitation

> The concept of unlimited freedom is closely connected in its origin
> with the concept of *infinite progress*, which we now recognize as
> false. Progress in this sense is impossible on our earth with its
> limited surface area and resources. . . . It would be . . . so much
> easier to adopt the principle of self-limitation—and to achieve it
> through *prudent self-restriction*.[76]
>
> A society with unlimited rights is incapable of standing up to ad-
> versity. If we do not wish to be ruled by a coercive authority, then
> each of us must rein himself in.[77]
>
> —Aleksandr Solzhenitsyn

Solzhenitsyn laments the foothold that the Western notion of progress
gained in Russia under Peter I, an idea that justified Peter's reforms
(often carried through with brute force) and which in some ways foreshadowed the forced collectivization and industrialization of the country spurred by the communists' materialist Prometheanism. As interpreted by Solzhenitsyn, under Peter Russia became a player in the
European great game of empire (indeed, that had been the primary

goal of Peter's misguided modernization program), and the empire began to calculate its interests in terms of imperialist aggrandizement, while subordinating the interests of the Russian people to great power expediency.

Solzhenitsyn sees nations, like individuals, as the expression of the many-faceted beauty of God's creation, each having its own intrinsic value. He therefore maintains that the minority nationalities of the Russian federation should enjoy cultural autonomy within their own national communities. He has advocated allowing the peripheral Caucasian republics (Chechnya, for example) the option of independence from the Russian federation but rejects as impractical the independence of the national republics (such as Tatarstan) that do not have an external border and, in any event, generally lack majorities of the nominal nationalities.

In Solzhenitsyn's view, Russia should give up pretensions of great power status. He considers imperialism and tyranny to be mutually supporting phenomena partly responsible for the disasters that have befallen Russia in the past and for the retardation of the natural development of the country. In his view, both czars and communist dictators wasted Russia's natural and human resources on grandiose projects, all carried out with the aim of securing Russia (or the Soviet Union) the attendant prestige and status of a great power. In *Rebuilding Russia*, he bluntly told the Russian people that "we don't have the strength," economically or morally, to hold on to the trappings of empire. "Let this burden fall from our shoulders," he wrote, noting with alarm that "the awakening Russian national self-awareness" had so far been unable to "free itself of great-power thinking and imperial delusions. . . . The time has come for an uncompromising choice between an empire . . . and the spiritual and physical salvation of our own people. . . . Holding on to an empire means to contribute to the extinction of our own people. . . . We must strive, not for the expansion of the state, but for a clarity of what remains of our spirit."[78]

He rejects Pan-Slavism out of hand as still another justification for empire and another impediment to national development. Referring to the faulty reasoning that pushed Russia into the First World War, he links Pan-Slavism, imperialism, and Russian weakness: "The defense of the Balkan Slavs from pan-Germanism was not our task; and any violent inclusion of all [those] Slavs into Austria [would] only have weakened that . . . empire and its position against Russia."[79]

It follows from Solzhenitsyn's view of Russian history and his Christian view of human nature, as well as his criticism of the Western scientism that lies behind the doctrine of progress, that he ties national reconciliation and future Russian stability to what he calls "self-limitation." Self-limitation is nothing more or less than an acceptance of Man's finite, fallen nature—a recognition of the limitations of human possibility and an acceptance of the imperfectibility of terrestrial existence. The author's criticisms of Western consumerism are one expression of his notion of self-limitation: The drive for economic growth has forced us to pay a grievous price for our insatiable appetites, both in terms of the human spirit and the destruction of the earth itself. Man's vision of material aggrandizement as the be all and end all of life has bred a malaise that is one of the indicative characteristics of modernity. Solzhenitsyn, therefore, views a life that is abundant in material goods but barren in terms of the spirit, as empty existence, no life at all.

On the level of individuals, the failure to limit personal appetites lies behind the decadence that so afflicts modern society, a decadence that is both manifest in and fed by the cultural "liquid manure" of a "self-indulgent and squalid" mass culture.[80] In any event, the repentant individual can find meaning and purpose only within the confines of family and community.[81]

Solzhenitsyn's Way: A Russian Path to the Future

> Spengler correctly pointed out that the very concept of the state is differently understood in different cultures and that there is no definitive "best" form of government which needs to be borrowed from one culture for use in another. . . . For a given people, with its specific geography, history, traditions, and psychological makeup, the task is to set in place a structure that will lead to a flourishing of this people rather than its decline and degeneration.[82]
>
> —Aleksandr Solzhenitsyn

Society precedes the state in Solzhenitsyn's philosophy. Hence, attempts by ideologues to construct earthly utopias based on abstractions, independent of the culture and society in which they are to operate, are doomed to produce chaotic or tyrannical dystopias. Solzhenitsyn has offered a third, uniquely Russian, way of development that is based on the particular features of Russian culture within the broader traditions of Western Christian civilization.

Solzhenitsyn supports a unique path of development for Russia, one that will "save our character, our national traditions, our national culture, our historical path [of development]," natural developments that were sidetracked by imperialism, Pan-Slavism and, most of all, communism, a path of development now threatened by "a new explosion of materialism, this time a 'capitalist' one." This new materialism undermines the moral base of civilization—religion. Capitalist materialism "threatens all religions," according to Solzhenitsyn.[83]

This third way would draw on Western civilization, including current technology and economic know-how, but with an eye to strengthening those features of the Russian experience that would provide a specifically Russian framework for liberty, particularly through the revival of the pre-Revolutionary *zemstvo* system of local self-rule.[84] Russia's people, ideally morally healthy individuals finding meaning and purpose within the fundamental social units of family and community,[85] would be able to exercise responsibility for managing their own affairs at the most personal, decentralized level.

Solzhenitsyn is skeptical of mass democracy, seeing it as particularly vulnerable to manipulation by organized minorities or as threatening a tyranny of the majority.[86] His plan for reviving the *zemstvo* system therefore focuses on direct elections only at the lowest levels of representation, with indirect elections gradually replacing the current system over a period of years. For Solzhenitsyn, what is important in what he loosely calls "democracy" is its "essence," which he determines consists of "individual freedom" and "a government of laws." Even here, however, he is careful to separate a healthy respect for individuals as children of God from the Western democracies' relentless focus on rights, ever expanding, over duties and obligations, ever diminishing.[87] A law-based state, one limited in scope and power, would, he believes, curtail the traditional Russian bane of arbitrary rule.[88]

Solzhenitsyn's third way would break up collective agriculture, supporting the creation of the free peasantry that Stoylipin envisioned for Russia. But it would limit the use, sale, and accumulation of land in an effort to revive village life. Land ownership via land transfers from the collectives to family farms would be granted with the proviso that the land be used for agricultural production. His great fear is that an unregulated breakup of the collectives would lead to another situation in which poor peasants were pushed aside by speculators. Therefore he supports limits on the accumulation and sale of land. The revival of the village is a key point in Solzhenitsyn's program, for only in face-to-face situations can Russia hope to revive the traditional communitarian virtues. He appears to hope that Russians alienated by the atomization of life in the decrepit metropolitan areas will be attracted to a new life in the countryside, where he hopes they will come to love the land, a fundamental element of patriotism.[89]

In a similar vein, Solzhenitsyn supports decentralization in industry, expressing hope that new technologies will promote extensive, decentralized, small-scale production over intensive heavy industry. He supports the breakup of gigantic monopolistic Soviet-era concerns and the conversion of defense and heavy industry, in order to redirect Russian industrial production toward internal markets and the production of civilian goods, which would raise the Russian people's standard of living and diminish the massive concentration of power in the old military-industrial complex.[90]

As in all things, humility and self-limitation must be a key ingredient of the new Russia's economy in Solzhenitsyn's vision. It was noted earlier that Solzhenitsyn is no partisan of the notion of progress. Improvement, yes, but dreams of perfection or endless economic development, no. In his *Letter to the Soviet Leaders*, he noted that Prometheanism was not limited to the Soviet regime but is part and parcel of all modern ideologies, capitalist or socialist. As a Russian, he is keenly aware of the potential for destruction that inheres in modern technologies combined with utopian economic plans. The Soviet planners diverted rivers, dried up lakes, polluted the air, and devastated the countryside, demolishing villages and throwing up dehumanizing (and ugly) concrete apartment blocks. At that time he proposed a zero-growth economy as the long term goal for Russia.[91]

What Westerners, confident of capitalism's superiority, should keep in mind is that Solzhenitsyn sees the root of Russia's economic and environmental woes not so much in socialism per se but in modern man's lack of humility. In the wake of Chernobyl and the Challenger disaster, his call for self-limitation in all spheres of human activity no longer appears so eccentric. In fact, environmentalism of a sort has been a staple of Russian nationalist thought at least since the 1960s. Solzhenitsyn's environmentalism must be viewed both within the context of the Russian experience and his own religion, which sees man as a steward of God's creation. At any rate, his views on environmental concerns appear to be far less extreme than some of those tossed about by Western environmentalists.[92]

A New Role for the Church

> We must build a *moral* Russia, or none at all—it would not then matter anyhow. . . . Will the Orthodox Church help us? It was ravaged more than anything else in the Communist years. In addition, it was undermined internally by its three-century long subordination to the State and lost the impulse for strong social actions.[93]
>
> —Aleksandr Solzhenitsyn

Solzhenitsyn calls for the spiritual renewal of the Russian people, based on the Christian concepts of confession, repentance, and reconciliation, as the first step to a national renaissance. He wants to end the historical fusion of the state and the Orthodox Church, arguing that Peter the Great's virtual incorporation of the church into the state system undermined the authority and honesty of the nation's primary spiritual institution. By making the church an arm of the state, the Petrine reforms, according to Solzhenitsyn, removed the church from its role as the spiritual and moral lodestar of Russia. Under the communists, the church was further corrupted, making its peace with the regime after a long period of persecution. The church can and should be socially active, Solzhenitsyn believes, but it must first repent of its own sins. Prerevolutionary Russia was, however marred in many respects, still a Christian society. It is this break with the past that Solzhenitsyn laments the most. Only with the spiritual renewal of the nation can the reforms he advocates make any sense. "Political activity," wrote Solzhenitsyn in "Rebuilding Russia," "is by no means the principal mode of human life. . . . The more energetic the political activity in a country, the greater is the loss to spiritual life."[94]

Who Is Russian?

When we say "nationality," we do not mean blood, but always—a spirit, a consciousness. For centuries the Russian soul and the Russian culture have existed [and] whoever . . . by consciousness [belongs to that spirit and culture] they are Russians.

—Aleksandr Solzhenitsyn[95]

Only suffering love gives one the right to chastise one's own nation.

—Sergey Bulgakov[96]

Although Solzhenitsyn is proposing that Russia turn inward, focusing on her own internal development by revitalizing certain aspects of traditional Russian culture, his conception of what constitutes the Russian people is broad and cultural rather than narrow and nationally exclusive. He rejects the arguments of some nationalists who maintain that blood alone can determine Russian identity. He does not deny (as no nationalist[97] would) the ancestrally related core of the Russian nation. But he recognizes the power of national consciousness, which may transcend all else. The sprawling Russian empire and the Russified Soviet state spread Russian culture, traditional practices, religion, and language among neighboring peoples, making many of them in effect Russians as well. Solzhenitsyn adopts a version of self-determination as the standard for identity: Those who consider themselves Russians are Russian.

Solzhenitsyn's concern for national identity is tied to the question of the fate of Russians living in the former Soviet republics, now a common theme in nationalist circles in Russia. He would clearly prefer that those who wish to return to Russia be given the opportunity to do so. This would remove a major point of friction with many of the now independent republics, though Solzhenitsyn realizes that such a repatriation may not be immediately feasible. In the meantime, Russia must take responsibility upon herself for the protection of the Russian diaspora, which has found itself in a precarious position in many instances, often (unjustly, he would say) blamed for the crimes of the Soviet regime.[98]

None of this is even remotely chauvinistic or "racist," much less "fascist," charges critics still fling at Solzhenitsyn.[99] In "Rebuilding Russia," Solzhenitsyn wrote, "When our fathers and grandfathers threw down their weapons during a deadly war [World War I], deserting the front in order to plunder their neighbors at home, they in effect *made a choice for us,* with consequences for one century so far, but who knows, maybe for two."[100] Thus the chaos that made the Bolshevik coup possible was set in motion by the decision of Russian peasant-soldiers to abandon the front and seize the land of their more prosperous countrymen. Solzhenitsyn calls for Russia to seek national revival first through personal repentance, for, in his view, Russia's travails are not the result of blind historical forces, nor are they wholly caused by the machinations of internal and external enemies. They are chiefly the fruit of the decisions and actions of individual Russians.

Solzhenitsyn is a Russian nationalist. He sees his country reborn within the framework of her own history and traditions, but he is also a practicing Christian who recognizes that the sin of Adam is also the sin of Russians. To nationalists of Solzhenitsyn's persuasion, the Russian nation is an extended family, not an ideology separate from the people themselves; such nationalists do not indulge in the "deification" of the nation. Russia is not a savior or messiah for the world (though she may play a special role in it), because for these nationalists, Christ will suffice.

Solzhenitsyn attacked the arrogance of imperial Russia in *August 1914* and was more explicit in his condemnation in *The Russian Question.* Years before, in an article appearing in the symposium *From under the Rubble,* he dealt with the phenomenon of National Bolshevism, briefly outlining and ridiculing the chief postulates of that ideology as he saw them:

The Russian people are the noblest in the world; its ancient and modern history are alike unblemished; czarism and Bolshevism are equally irreproachable; the nation neither erred nor sinned either before 1917 or after . . . there are no nationality problems in relations with the border republics, Lenin and Stalin's solution [of the question] was ideal . . . communism is in fact unthinkable without patriotism; the prospects of Russia-USSR are brilliant; blood alone determines whether one is Russian or non-Russian. . . . Orthodoxy is not the least more Russian than Marxism, atheism, [or the] scientific outlook . . . God need not be written with a capital letter, but "the Government" must be. . . . Their general name for all this is "The Russian Idea."[101]

Solzhenitsyn recognizes that Stalin to some extent fused the traditional great power mentality of imperial Russia's official nationality ideology, together with its sense of world historical mission, with that of world revolution. Atheist materialism, however, was the core of communist ideology and is one of the major breaking points with old Russia that Solzhenitsyn believes betrays the falsity of National Bolshevism, which sees the Soviet Union as the successor to (not a replacement for) the Russian empire. Solzhenitsyn attacks this as a perversion of Russian national identity.[102]

What Is Russia?

The trouble is not that the USSR broke up—that was inevitable. The real trouble, and a tangle for a long time to come, is that the breakup occurred mechanically along false Leninist borders. . . . In several days we lost 25 million ethnic Russians—18 percent of our entire nation—and the government could not scrape up the courage even to take note of this dreadful event, a colossal historical defeat for Russia, and to declare its political disagreement with it—at least in order to preserve the right to some kind of negotiations in the future.[103]

—Aleksandr Solzhenitsyn

Solzhenitsyn believes that the Russian state should unite the Eastern Slavs—Russians, Ukrainians, Belarussians—with Kazakhstan or, perhaps, the northern, Russian populated sections of Kazakhstan, thus joining the peoples of old Rus, rooted in the same historical and cultural soil, in a more compact political structure, which he calls the Russian Union (*Rossiyskiy Soyuz*).[104] He expresses the hope that Ukraine would join such a union but does not support forced integration of the Slav republics or Kazakhstan with the Russian Federation. On occasion he has written that Russia may wish to work toward an agreement with Kazakhstan or Ukraine, failing integration, allowing the self-determination of the predominantly Russian portions of eastern Ukraine and northern Kazakhstan. Obviously Solzhenitsyn rejects any dreams of reconstituting the Soviet state, an entity that was, in his opinion, doomed in any event, though in "Rebuilding Russia," true to his conservative instincts, he wrote of a more gradual approach to dissolving the Soviet Union.

Solzhenitsyn's desire for a Russian union is based on both cultural and practical grounds. First, "Russia" is a vast cultural unity; the three great branches of the Russian national tree share the same roots and, in his eyes, are destined to grow together, nourished by the same historical and cultural soil. Second, there is such an overlap in economic, trade, military, and social concerns among the Eastern Slavs as to preclude any true separation. There is also the problem of identity, with Russian predominating as the primary language among all three branches of the Russian (*Rossiyskiy*) family, not to mention the shared religious and cultural inheritance that all three enjoy via Kievan Russia, making the formation of three full blown nations problematic. A whole tangle of questions (the question of the rightful ownership of the Crimea, historically tied to Great Russia but claimed by an independent Ukraine, for instance), more complex even than those between Russia and non-Slavic republics, justify Solzhenitsyn's concerns. None of this will convince Ukrainian nationalists, of course, and he recognizes that some accommodation is better than the possibility of another debilitating internal conflict.

The Russian Questions

The late Mikhail Agursky, contributor to the *From under the Rubble* symposium, once wrote of Solzhenitsyn's "Letter to the Soviet Leaders" that

> It appears quite obvious that the sole realistic alternative for those who would truly desire to revive Russian life in its fundamental form would be the acceptance . . . of the humanistic program proposed by Solzhenitsyn in his *Letter to the Soviet Leaders*. Unfortunately, Western public opinion views this program as something of an extreme form of Russian nationalism. It does not understand that this is the only humanistic alternative in Russia to racism and neo-Nazism.[105]

What may have appeared cryptic some time ago (Agursky was writing in 1977) seems evident now. Russia's westernizing democrats, who carry with them a considerable amount of internationalist baggage,

have been steadily waning in popularity since their victory over revanchist forces in 1991; any Russian regime of the future will be nationalist. Indeed, it is one of the basic assumptions of this book that a nationalist revival is virtually inevitable when internationalism begins to
assert itself anywhere. The Zhirinovskiy phenomenon and the relative
electoral success of the "patriotic" neocommunists makes Agursky's
comments seem all the more prophetic: Russia is at a crossroads. A
choice must be made, not between nationalism and internationalism
but between Russian *nationalisms.*

It is altogether too simplistic to regard the controversy that has ensued between the democrats and the patriots in present-day Russia
as a mere replay of the Slavophile-Westernizer controversy of the last
century. To be sure, broadly speaking, one side inclines toward Western models and the other towards a Russian path, but such a simple
dichotomy loses the nuances and shades of differences separating the
many subgroups participating in the present struggle, as the various
shades of opinion (as well as the many similarities) between the early
Slavophiles and the Westernizers of the 1840s and 1850s were lost in a
historical blur, Slavophile coming to designate virtually anyone seeking a Russian path, including those close to the spirit of classical Slavophilism and those not.

The parallels between Solzhenitsyn and the early Slavophiles are obvious: the emphasis on the internal and spiritual over the external and
material; the stress on the social and spiritual underpinnings of any
just regime; criticism of untrammeled autocracy; the detection of a psychological gap between rulers and ruled; the importance of freedom,
both freedom from state censorship and spiritual freedom; criticism of
modern industrial and bureaucratic states; the fervent Russian patriotism and deeply felt Christianity (and criticism of the institutional
church); the importance of the village and traditional family life; a
wariness about Western legalism displayed by a preference for traditional Russian consensus politics, *sobornost;* attacks on the revolutionary intelligentsia; and a sympathetic view of the common man.

Solzhenitsyn diverges from classical Slavophilism on some important matters. Solzhenitsyn is no starry-eyed idealist, much less a reactionary, who imagines an idyllic Russia of the past as his utopia. If
given a stark choice, he would prefer the spiritual emphasis of the past,
with all its injustices, to the even worse alternative of modern secular
society. In another way, however, he is truer to Christian ideals than
the early Slavophiles: However sympathetic he may be, he harbors no
illusions about the nature of Man, common or no. Russians, even the
idealized peasants of the Slavophiles, are humans, created in the image
of God, but fallen away from Him. The Russian village commune

(which he does not seek to revive, seeing it as a product of serfdom) and Christian perfection are not coterminous. He loves Russia not because she is perfect but because he belongs to her, and she to him.[106] However wayward a parent she may be, she is still Mother Russia. Despite the significance of Solzhenitsyn's comments for the West, it is Russia that demands her son's attention first of all. He has returned to share her fate.

Solzhenitsyn once again differs sharply with theorists of liberal democracy on the national question. The national framework is (as noted in chapter 1) attractive to some liberal democrats for purposes of nation-building. For Solzhenitsyn, as noted earlier, the nation has intrinsic value of its own as a link in God's hierarchical great chain of being. He is spiritually bound to the Russian nation and has responsibilities to his nation not unlike those of a member of a family. Indeed, this is one of the great intellectual divides that makes communication between nationalists and liberal internationalists, or nation-builders, so difficult. Each fails to understand the assumptions of the other.

Solzhenitsyn has identified himself directly with the authors of *Vekhi* (*Landmarks* or *Signposts*), a symposium written in the wake of the aborted Revolution of 1905.[107] The book's contributors include a host of Russian thinkers who, having jettisoned the Marxism of their youth, returned to an earnest spirituality and belief in Christianity as an antidote to the materialist poison the Russian intelligentsia had succumbed to. They saw in revolutionary ideology a nihilism whose only solution to Russia's plight was destruction, a suicidal impulse to destroy (rather than reform) the old social order. *Vekhi* contributors Sergey Bulgakov and Nikolay Berdyayev, as well as the spiritual mentor of the *Vekhi* writers, Vladimir Solovyov, are frequently referred to in Solzhenitsyn's polemical writings, and the title of the symposium *From under the Rubble* is a wordplay on the title of the second symposium pieced together by many of the *Vekhi* authors, *Iz Glubiniy* (*From the Depths*),[108] written after the Bolshevik revolution, when the nature of the Bolshevik regime (and a harbinger of what was to come) had become clear to the authors.

It would be mistaken to think that Solzhenitsyn's ideas wholly derive from this intellectual source: He can think for himself, and his ideas were formed by a later period. The context is different. Solzhenitsyn concerns himself with structural and external matters in a way that neither the classical Slavophiles nor the *Vekhi* authors did.[109] The author of "Rebuilding Russia," while stressing the internal antecedents of any stable social order, appears to hold a view of modern society that closely parallels that of many Western social critics and sociologists. Robert Nisbet in his seminal *Quest for Community* sees the roots of modern alienation in the social atomization concomitant with the development of industry, the dissolution of agricultural society, and the formation of the modern centralized state. Solzhenitsyn's comments on the shared assumptions of modern socialist and communist societies with those of capitalism are similar in some respects to James Burnham's critique of what he called the "managerial" state, and his positive view of village life connects readily with that of the American southern agrarians. Western thinkers from Edmund Burke to Russell Kirk and Christopher Lasch are among those whose ideas resemble Solzhenitsyn's in many important respects. Solzhenitsyn's ruminations on the pros and cons of various forms of government are derived from Plato and Aristotle, once again confirming that he sees Russia as tied to the Western tradition in many respects.[110]

Nisbet in particular appears to hope that a new, postmodern order will draw on the experience of face-to-face communities, small in scale, personal, and more agreeable to the spirit of community than the decrepit megalopolis of the late twentieth century. Solzhenitsyn, like so many Western thinkers, appears to believe that Mankind is on the verge of a new era.[111] A choice has to be made, a road taken. Solzhenitsyn, by speaking so eloquently to his countrymen, may have some insights we in the West may have need of as well.

Few would now deny that modern ideologies have unleashed horrors in this century, or that efforts to construct a moral framework in societies schooled in materialism and relativism have failed. The vital importance of family and community has been stressed by thinkers from both the conventional Left and the mainstream Right, and the widespread belief that Man has abused the earth informs a body of opinion that transcends the environmentalist movement itself. What is missing is a weltanschauung that gives shape and purpose to a postmodern order. Solzhenitsyn's Christian worldview speaks to that as well, a view of life that is so old that it seems strangely new. If modern societies can shake off their own prejudices, they may find something of value in what he has to say.

Like all nationalists in Russia from Peter's time on, Solzhenitsyn is grappling with modernity. He believes that the ideologies and social structures of the modern era have shown themselves to be inadequate to the task of containing the evil in Man that is the legacy of original sin. Solzhenitsyn is not attempting to carry out a successful modernization of Russia, as other nationalists and liberal internationalists may hope to do, but a *postmodernization* that involves construction of new sociopolitical and economic structures that, together with their internal antecedents, take into account a Christian view of human nature.[112]

Solzhenitsyn recognizes that a materialist and environmentally driven structuralism ignores the spiritual side of Man and gives the animal nature of humans a predominant and destructive role. Thus the cognitive and spiritual precedes the material. Unlike many other Christian moralists, Solzhenitsyn appears to recognize that some structural conditions are more conducive than others to encouraging observance of natural law and supporting religious belief. We construct the societies that our worldviews demand. Solzhenitsyn is doing much more than merely preaching about "family" or "traditional" values. He is attempting to wrestle with both the internal (spiritual) and external (social-communal, economic) supports of such values.

Solzhenitsyn believes that "the presence of good" as the divine spark of conscience in humans "legitimates and even requires action on behalf of the moral uplifting of human beings."[113] He does not subscribe to Tolstoy's view of Man as a helpless creature at the mercy of historical forces beyond his control. Human beings possess free will and can change the tide of events for good or ill. His views are similar not only to those of Dostoevsky but also to those of French philosopher Jacques Maritain, who developed the notion of "personalism," the idea that "individuals develop themselves only by realizing their responsibilities before others and in particular before their family and society." Personalism became a key element of European Christian Democratic movements at their inception, and "Christian personalism" captures the essence of Solzhenitsyn's philosophy.[114]

Solzhenitsyn's impact on the times he has lived in has been much greater than that of any other Russian writer. "Gulag" has joined "holocaust" as a word that has seeped into the vocabulary and imagination of the whole literate world. Solzhenitsyn deserves a large measure of credit for undermining the entire communist edifice, not only in the Soviet Union but everywhere in the world. His moral and civic courage were like a firebell in the night signaling the beginning of the end for the legitimacy of communist ideology. Those who are inclined to listen may be able to hear the rest of his message, and only if he is heard and justly evaluated can his true significance as an artist and as a public figure be determined. Let history judge.

In the Arena

On October 28, 1994, Aleksandr Solzhenitsyn addressed the Duma, the lower chamber of Russia's parliament. He attacked the incompetence and hastiness of the government's reform program and described the troubles of the Russian people he had met on his long journey across Russia. He did not spare the patriots, and his very independence appears to have flustered some observers who didn't quite know what to make of him.[115]

Two weeks after his address to the Duma, Solzhenitsyn had a four-hour meeting with President Boris Yeltsin. Yeltsin's press secretary told reporters that the two men had discussed "the most crucial and urgent problems facing Russia."[116] Between his arrival in Moscow on July 21 and his speech to the Duma on October 28, Solzhenitsyn had continued to travel into the hinterlands, packing auditoriums and drawing crowds in Voronezh and Rostov-on-Don, among others. During one meeting in Voronezh, a heated debate broke out between members of "mutually hostile political currents." Solzhenitsyn reproached both sides, saying that the outburst was an "example of the way we have let ourselves go these past seven to ten years" and calling on all present to "listen and try to understand one another, to feel like citizens of the same country."[117] In August Solzhenitsyn was named by *Nezavisimaya Gazeta* as number twelve on their periodic list of the "one hundred leading politicians in Russia" for the month of July, having risen from eighty-eighth place in May at the time of his return to Russia. An accompanying commentary proclaimed that Solzhenitsyn had "come close to the pinnacles of political influence,"[118] an astonishing feat for an artist who eschews party politics.

Solzhenitsyn kept up the busy pace of his public activities in 1995. In February he spoke at a conference on local self-government in Moscow, pushing his notions of reviving the *zemstva* and endorsing the decentralizing approach of a presidential draft law. Solzhenitsyn told the conference participants, who included administrators and officials from all across Russia as well as the central government, that the "future of our country" depended in part on the development of local self-government. He attacked the centralized state that had denied the "forgotten" Russian people any chance to "direct their own fate." He further noted that a "chasm" now divided the people from the state authorities. In closing, Solzhenitsyn rocked the government's boat once more, saying that the draft law was not explicit enough. He called on Russian legislators to revive a full-blown system of local *zemstva*.[119]

In September 1994, Russian state television began broadcasting a series of programs entitled *A Meeting with A. I. Solzhenitsyn*, following the main nine o'clock newscast. For a year, Solzhenitsyn was given a twice monthly platform to speak directly to the Russian viewing public; then the program was suddenly dropped without warning from the schedule. "Solzhenitsyn's program does not satisfy the viewers any longer," one official claimed. Natalya Solzhenitsyn, however, suggested that "his criticism of the government was being stifled before the parliamentary elections" planned for December. She told reporters that "the first reason is the electoral campaign. They want to take off the air all broadcasts that are critical of the current state of things. The general reason, unfortunately, is like it was thirty years ago. They don't want to hear the truth. They don't want to hear disagreeable things." The director of the series claimed that ratings were rising, despite government officials' claims that the show was unpopular. The *Washington Times* summarized the government's claims this way: "To many, his words are not welcome." More telling, perhaps, was the report's characterization of Solzhenitsyn's "somber themes" as "unappealing to modern audiences."[120]

Notes

1. Aleksandr Solzhenitsyn, *The Gulag Archipelago I*, trans. Thomas P. Whitney (New York: Harper & Row, 1973), 18.
2. Christopher Moody, *Solzhenitsyn* (New York: Harper & Row, 1975), 6.
3. Solzhenitsyn, *Gulag I*, 18.
4. Ibid., 18.
5. Aleksandr Solzhenitsyn, *The Gulag Archipelago II*, trans. Thomas P. Whitney (New York: Harper & Row, 1975), 615–16.
6. *Pravda*, 24 May 1994.
7. *Zavtra* 21 (June 1994).
8. *Zavtra* 21 (June 1994). Solzhenitsyn had spoken with Boris Yeltsin by telephone prior to his return and had maintained a personal correspondence with Vladimir Lukin, former ambassador to the United States.
9. *Zavtra* 21 (June 1994).
10. *Sovetskaya Rossiya* (2, 9 June 1994), which supports the Communist Party of the Russian Federation, selectively quoted Solzhenitsyn's comments to crowds in the Russian Far East.
11. *Nezavisimaya Gazeta*, 27 April 1994.
12. *Nezavisimaya Gazeta*, 24 May 1994.
13. *Nezavisimaya Gazeta*, 28 May 1994.
14. *Obshchaya Gazeta*, 27 May 1994.
15. *Izvestiya*, 24 May 1994.
16. The initial report was aired on the May 29, 1994, broadcast; the interview followed on 24 July.
17. According to a June 15, 1994, report broadcast on Russian television's *Vesti* (news program), 58 percent of those responding to a poll conducted in Moscow acknowledged that they were "following all the details" of reporting on Solzhenitsyn's return to Russia. However, only 15 percent of the respondents felt that his return would improve the situation in the country. According to the report, 44 percent of the respondents had never read a single one of Solzhenitsyn's books. The interesting fact here, particularly from an American perspective, is that the report failed to mention the 56 percent of respondents who had read at least one of Solzhenitsyn's works. This observer doubts that

the works of Mark Twain, for example, would fare so well in such a poll in New York or Los Angeles.

18. Kiselev's reference to "ultras" is to chauvinist elements among nationalists, commonly dubbed "ultranationalists" by the Russian press.

19. Moscow NTV, *Itogi*, 29 May 1994.

20. Moscow NTV, *Itogi*, 24 July 1994.

21. Moscow NTV, *Itogi*, 24 July 1994.

22. Solzhenitsyn's ideas, as well as the criticisms of them, are masterfully dealt with in Edward E. Ericson, *Solzhenitsyn and the Modern World* (Washington, D.C.: Regnery Gateway, 1993). I owe much to Ericson's treatment of the subject.

23. This biographical section is derived from Moody, *Solzhenitsyn*, 1–28, and from Ericson, various pages.

24. Cited in Ericson, *Solzhenitsyn and the Modern World*, 31.

25. Cited in Ibid., 25.

26. Solzhenitsyn did draft some sections of the story at the time that were eventually integrated into the *Red Wheel*. See Aleksandr Solzhenitsyn, *August 1914: The Red Wheel I*, trans. H. T. Willets (London: Penguin, 1990), p. v.

27. Cited in Moody, *Solzhenitsyn*, 5.

28. Ibid., 6.

29. Solzhenitsyn drew on this experience to describe the interrogation of Innokenty Volodin in the novel *The First Circle*, and to describe the psychological effect of arrest, as well as the various methods of arrest and interrogation favored by the secret police, in *Gulag I*.

30. The Soviet secret police as it was designated from 1943 to 1946, when it was renamed MGB and then, in 1953, KGB.

31. Moody, *Solzhenitsyn*, 7.

32. Ibid.

33. Cited in ibid., 8.

34. Ibid.

35. Solzhenitsyn, *Gulag II*, 614.

36. Aleksandr Solzhenitsyn, *One Day in the Life of Ivan Denisovich*, trans. H. T. Willetts (New York: Alfred A. Knopf, 1991), 23.

37. Ibid., 39.

38. Ibid., 96.

39. Ibid., 102.

40. *Gulag II*, 612.

41. *Gulag II*, 610.

42. Solzhenitsyn has written that some he met in prison spoke more freely than those on the "outside," but there is more than that to the freedom his fictional characters frequently make reference to. Their lack of material possessions in effect has freed them from the temptation to toady to the jailers, and allowed them to find fulfillment, satisfaction, and even joy, in every breath, every friendship, every morsel of simple food, and, if they are able to see it, in the knowledge of a higher plane of existence.

43. *Gulag II*, 610–11.

44. *Gulag II*, 611.
45. *Gulag II*, 615.
46. Solzhenitsyn has *The First Circle*'s Lev Rubin, who has remained a convinced communist even in prison, attempt to devise a civic religion to inculcate virtues in the demoralized and degraded citizenry. The author implies that Rubin's efforts are as fruitless as the efforts of the Soviet authorities to construct religion without God, Christianity without Christ, redemption without repentance.
47. *Gulag I*, 562.
48. *Gulag I*, 616.
49. Christopher Moody in his critical biography *Solzhenitsyn* seemed particularly confused and uncertain about this.
50. The book jacket of the 1968 edition of *The First Circle* calls the novel "a sublime hymn of praise to man, an outpouring of love and pride." Pride, of course, is one of the seven deadly sins. The author of those lines passed over the many religious references in the story, beginning with the title of the novel. Life in the *sharashka*, the research institute staffed by Gulag prisoners wherein the main action of the novel takes place, is, like Dante's first circle of Hell, only one step from the abyss of the camps. But it is also an appropriate place for the novel's intellectuals to conduct their soul-searching discussions, like Dante's vision of the pagan philosophers in their own first circle, still in a pre-Christian state.
51. Cited in Ericson, *Solzhenitsyn and the Modern World*, 82.
52. Cited in Moody, *Solzhenitsyn*, 2.
53. He insisted during the Gorbachev period, for instance, that only after his works were published in the Soviet Union would he return to his homeland.
54. Initially living in Switzerland, he eventually moved to Cavendish, Vermont, where he lived until his return to Russia in 1994 with his second wife and their three sons.
55. Solzhenitsyn once said "I am not a critic of the West . . . For nearly all our lives we worshiped the West—note the word 'worshiped.' We did not admire it, we worshiped it. I am not a critic of the West. I am a critic of the weakness of the West. I am a critic of a fact which we can't comprehend: how one can lose one's spiritual strength, one's will power, and possessing freedom, not value it, not be willing to make sacrifices for it." Cited in Ericson, *Solzhenitsyn and the Modern World*, 126.
56. Solzhenitsyn's address, which attacked the loss of religious belief and the concomitant growth of superficial materialism in contemporary America, appeared to him to be merely a piece of friendly criticism honestly rendered. He once told an earlier American audience, "I have come . . . as a friend of the United States. . . . There is a Russian proverb: 'The yes-man is your enemy, but your friend will argue with you.' It is precisely because my speech is prompted by friendship, that I have come to tell you: 'My friends, I'm not going to give you sugary words.'" Cited in ibid., 127.
57. Ibid., 62.
58. It is interesting that few critics of the novel commented on the devastat-

ing depiction of the late czarist regime's incompetence and corruption. After *August 1914*, Solzhenitsyn was frequently accused of harboring fantasies of a czarist restoration, despite the unflattering picture of the regime painted by the novel. Critics, zeroing in on Solzhenitsyn's Orthodox religion and nationalistic bent, mistake the author's sympathetic portrayal of loyal czarist officers for something it is not. Since freedom and stability are his primary concerns for the future Russia, he is willing to discuss at length the merits and drawbacks of various systems of government, drawing on the classical example of Plato and Aristotle. If he does not condemn monarchy outright, it is because his view of the nature of Man precludes the notion that any particular political system can perfect that nature; evil is possible under any system.

59. "Let us note that in the long history of mankind there have not been so very many democratic republics, yet people have lived for centuries without them and were not always worse off. They even experienced that 'happiness' we are forever hearing about. . . . They preserved the physical health of the nation. . . . They preserved its moral health, too, which has left its imprint at least on folklore and proverbs—a level of moral health incomparably higher than that expressed today in simian radio music, pop songs and insulting advertisements: could a listener from outer space imagine that our planet had already known and left behind it Bach, Rembrandt, and Dante?" Aleksandr Solzhenitsyn, "As Breathing and Consciousness Return," in *From under the Rubble* (New York: Bantam Books, 1975), 21.

60. Ibid., 145.

61. Raymond Rosenthal, reviewing both *August 1914* and Solzhenitsyn's Nobel Lecture in *The Nation*. Cited in Ericson, *Solzhenitsyn and the Modern World*, 70.

62. Aleksandr Solzhenitsyn, *August 1914*, trans. by Michael Glenny (New York: Farrar, Straus and Giroux, 1972), 547–548.

63. Ibid., 548–549.

64. Cited in ibid., 146.

65. The last two quotes are from Solzhenitsyn's Harvard address. Cited in ibid., 146.

66. Only one of the many reviews of the letter took notice of the legitimacy of Solzhenitsyn's asking the question, What is the best form of government? "His answer is that no one form is best in practice because governments must grow out of the character of the people being governed." Richard and Judith Mills, cited in ibid., 80.

67. Nan Robertson, cited in ibid., 84.

68. Ericson makes a similar observation on Solzhenitsyn's gradualism. His views on a transitional period for Russia's political system are discussed in ibid., 302–30.

69. Ericson deals extensively with Solzhenitsyn's Western critics, ibid., 46–125.

70. Aleksandr Solzhenitsyn, "Russkiy Vopros v Kontse Dvadstatovo Veka" (The Russian question at the end of the twentieth century), *Novy Mir* 7 (July 1994). An English translation by the author's son Yermolai was published by

Farrar, Straus, and Giroux in 1995. All quotations are my translations from the Russian text, unless otherwise noted.

71. Aleksandr Solzhenitsyn, *Rebuilding Russia* (New York: Farrar, Straus, and Giroux, 1991), 49–50.

72. Solzhenitsyn, "Russkiy Vopros," 174.

73. See especially his essay "The Smatterers" from the symposium *From under the Rubble*, for a critique of the old intelligentsia, comparing them with the intellectuals of the Soviet period. He mounted a counterattack against the Russian intellectuals of the mid-1980s (who had joined in the attacks on him) in his essay "Nashi Pluralisty" ("Our pluralists").

74. Solzhenitsyn, *Rebuilding Russia*, 52.

75. Solzhenitsyn first proposed national repentance as the path to reconciliation, both between men and God and among Russians themselves, in "Repentance and Self-Limitation in the Life of Nations," in *From under the Rubble*.

76. Ibid., 137.

77. Solzhenitsyn, *Rebuilding Russia*, 54.

78. Ibid., 10.

79. Solzhenitsyn, "Russkiy Vopros," 157. In *August 1914*, the author has many of his characters question the wisdom of Russia's entry into World War I, an event that Solzhenitsyn links with the victory of the Bolsheviks in *The Red Wheel*, of which *August 1914* forms the first part. Solzhenitsyn believes that the country had had a chance for peaceful reform under Prime Minister Pyotr Stolypin, who attempted to solve the problem of peasant land hunger (which the Bolsheviks exploited masterfully in 1917) by encouraging the growth of a class of freeholders, independent of the peasant commune. Stolypin's plans were cut short by the war. The inept conduct of the war discredited the czarist regime and opened the door for the Bolsheviks to call on the peasant soldiers to seize the land once and for all, land reform having been the policy of the provisional government that was proclaimed after the czar's abdication. Land seizures had already begun in any case. The revolutionary intelligentsia's nihilism is attacked repeatedly in *August 1914*, and Solzhenitsyn's rejection of it lies behind his criticism of the postcommunist regime's hasty reforms, Solzhenitsyn himself preferring a more gradualist and less disruptive approach.

80. Solzhenitsyn, *Rebuilding Russia*, 44.

81. Solzhenitsyn sees the family playing a fundemental role in Russia's salvation. He further calls for what was once known as the "family wage," a wage rate that allows the father, as head of the household, to support a family, leaving the mother to raise the children, long the wards of the state. Ibid., 42–44.

82. Ibid., 60–61.

83. Aleksandr Solzhenitsyn, *The Russian Question at the End of the Twentieth Century*, trans. Yermolai Solzhenitsyn (New York: Farrar, Straus, and Giroux, 1995), 108.

84. *Zemstva*, which date back to the sixteenth century in Russia, were introduced as a state institution in 1864 with the election of assemblies at the local and provincial level, as part of the great reforms of the "Czar Liberator," Aleksandr II. *Zemstvo* representatives were elected indirectly by all classes of Rus-

sians (though representation was tied to property ownership) and were involved in financing and operating schools, roads, and public health facilities, among other things. They were abolished by the Bolsheviks in 1918. For Solzhenitsyn, the only true democracy is the democracy "of small areas." *Rebuilding Russia*, 82–86.

85. It would greatly distort Solzhenitsyn's ideas to describe him as some sort of individualist, something that it is all too easy for moderns to do because he writes so powerfully about the importance of individual free will and responsibility. His Christian faith and traditionalist worldview make the philosophy of individualism, based as it is on Enlightenment notions of personal autonomy, anathema to this most Christian of writers. Solzhenitsyn's frequent allusions to individual moral health are, rather, an expression of his Christian belief in free will and personal salvation. The Deity is a personal God who acted through Christ to secure the redemption and salvation of humanity. He is definitely not some impersonal deist or pantheist "life force," or merely another name for history, much less a New Age universal spirit who sanctions all avenues to self-realization.

86. Solzhenitsyn discusses the pluses and minuses of democracy in part two of *Rebuilding Russia*.

87. *Rebuilding Russia*, 64.

88. During the gradual transition period he does, however, support a strong presidency as a stabilizing factor. *Rebuilding Russia*, 95–99.

89. Agriculture and the village are discussed in *Rebuilding Russia*, 30–34. Solzhenitsyn frequently makes reference to the need to develop the Russian north country, something he first mentioned in "Letter to the Soviet Leaders." Among other things, developing the north would encourage Russians living in metropolitan areas to move to less populated regions.

90. *Rebuilding Russia*, 34–39.

91. He repeated the argument in "Repentance and Self-Limitation in the Life of Nations," in *From under the Rubble*, 137.

92. Beginning with the Christian view of Man as the flawed pinnacle and steward of God's "good" creation rather than simply another species having no more intrinsic value than others.

93. *Russian Question*, 108.

94. *Rebuilding Russia*, 49.

95. "Russkiy Vopros," 174.

96. Cited in "Repentance," *From under the Rubble*, 120.

97. In fairness to Solzhenitsyn's own self definition, he prefers the term patriot to nationalist, probably because so many of his detractors have used the term as a synonym for "racist" or the still fuzzier "fascist," or because he may define the term differently than we have for our purposes, meaning someone for whom the nation is exalted above any other value or aim. By this definition, a nationalist cannot in any meaningful sense be a Christian. "I am a patriot. I love my motherland. I want my country, which is sick . . . and is on the very edge of death, I want it to come back to life. But this doesn't make me a nationalist. I don't want to limit anyone else. Every country has its patriots who are

concerned with its fate." (Cited in Ericson, *Solzhenitsyn and the Modern World*, 176) For our purposes, however, the term as defined in chapter 1 fits.

98. He discusses the fate of the diaspora in part one of *Rebuilding Russia*, and returns to it in "Russkiy Vopros." Solzhenitsyn, like other Russian nationalists, maintains that Russians themselves suffered most of all under the communists, providing the bulk of the human material for the communist experiment. The plight of the Russian diaspora is a popular theme on the Russian Right, and some revanchists repeat the claim of Russian suffering, tied to claims that the Russian "center" paid dearly for the maintenance of both the empire and the Soviet state (Solzhenitsyn concurs), with a seemingly paradoxical nostalgia for the Soviet Union. Needless to say, Solzhenitsyn does not share such views.

99. Alexander Yanov, an émigré journalist, has popularized such a view of Solzhenitsyn in his books *The Russian New Right* and *The Russian Challenge and the Year 2000*. Such charges are usually accompanied by a further libel: Solzhenitsyn is accused of anti-Semitism. We will take up the convoluted history of anti-Semitism as an element of some Russian nationalisms in the next chapter, but the charges in Solzhenitsyn's case are usually cooked up around a "content analysis" review of his novels. Critics claim they depict Jews, more often than not, as villains. Though little attention is given to the positive portrayals of Jews, every negative or ambiguous Jewish character is grasped as an indicator of "anti-Semitism." From the mountain of literature Solzhenitsyn has produced, his portrayals of the assassin Bogrov in *The Red Wheel* and of Parvus in *Lenin in Zurich* are pointed to as the defining element of his worldview. That's all his critics have to go on, other than his nationalism, which a particular brand of bigotry sees as an indicator of anti-Semitism, evidence or no. Solzhenitsyn, for his part, has dismissed the charges as "an unscrupulous technique" of attack (Ericson, *Solzhenitsyn and the Modern World*, 205) used by his ideological opponents to discredit him. A prominent list of cultural and scholarly defenders have refuted such charges, including Elie Wiesel, Mstislav Rostropovich, Adam Ulam, Robert Conquest, Vladislav Krasnov, Lev Lossev, Mikhail Agursky, and Solzhenitsyn's second wife, Natalya, herself half Jewish (Ibid., 203). Ironically, Soviet critics at one time attacked Solzhenitsyn as a philo-Semite, as someone who had depicted Jews in his literature too favorably. Zhores Medvedev tells a tale of KGB efforts to attack Solzhenitsyn by claiming that he was a Jew: "The person known to you as Solzhenitsyn is really Solzhenitser and he's a Jew" (Ibid., 202).

100. *Rebuilding Russia*, 13.

101. "Repentance and Self-Limitation in the Life of Nations," 118–19. It may have been better if Solzhenitsyn had used the word *gosudarstvo*, "the state," instead of *pravitelstvo*, "the government," (I checked the original, republished in the literary journal, *Zvezda* 6, 1994) in describing what National Bolsheviks, and many others besides, consider the locus of the national will. The difference, as we shall see in subsequent chapters, is significant in Russian nationalist circles, the state being an abstraction embodying the will, destiny, territory, values, population, and military might, as well as the mundane government bodies, of Russia as *derzhava*, or great power. Many nationalists are today criti-

cal of, if not hostile to, the government, meaning the prime minister and his cabinet, or Yeltsin, the cabinet, and the legislature. The distinction is important. 102. In the Stalin chapters of *The First Circle*, Solzhenitsyn imagines the aging despot picturing himself as the leader of the Russian people. His interpretation of Russian history and its relation to the Soviet regime is the source of Solzhenitsyn's dispute with some historians (he has attacked Richard Pipes in particular) over the question of continuity or discontinuity in Russian-Soviet history. Solzhenitsyn always distinguished between the two. When he spoke of "my country" while in exile, he meant Russia and not the Soviet Union. In his literary memoir *The Oak and the Calf*, Solzhenitsyn noted that the real difference between himself and his friend Aleksandr Tvardovskiy, editor of the literary journal *Novy Mir*, was Tvardovskiy's commitment to Soviet literature, whereas Solzhenitsyn identified himself with the Russian tradition.

103. Solzhenitsyn, *The Russian Question*, 90.

104. *Rossiyskiy* is a broad term with cultural and geographic overtones, whereas *Russkiy* has a narrower, "ethnic" meaning.

105. Cited in Ericson, *Solzhenitsyn and the Modern World*, 219.

106. "As we understand it patriotism means unqualified and unwavering love for the nation, which implies not uncritical eagerness to serve, not support for unjust claims, but frank assessment of its vices and sins, and penitence for them. We ought to get used to the idea that no people is eternally great or eternally noble . . . that the greatness of a people is to be sought not in the blare of trumpets—physical might is purchased at a spiritual price beyond our means—but in the level of its inner development, in its breadth of soul . . ." "Repentance," 119.

107. See especially "The Smatterers" in *From under the Rubble*. Solzhenitsyn dissects the Soviet intelligentsia of the 1970s, using the earlier collection as an intellectual guide. Solzhenitsyn also has one of the characters in *August 1914* read (and praise) *Vekhi*.

108. A new translation of *Vekhi* by Marshall Shatz and Judith Zimmerman was published by M. E. Sharpe in 1994. A single volume edition of *Vekhi* and *Iz Glubiniy* in Russian was published by the Pravda publishing concern in 1991.

109. Some of the *Vekhi* contributors, most notably Bogdan Kistiakovskiy, did concern themselves with "external" legal matters involved in building the foundation for a law-abiding regime, but they did not delve deeper in socio-economical "structural" matters as Solzhenitsyn does. Indeed, "social structure precedes any political program and is a more fundamental entity." *Rebuilding Russia*, 34.

110. Besides his frequent references to the *Vekhi* authors and other neo-Slavophiles such as Ivan Ilyin and George Fedotov, in *Rebuilding Russia* Solzhenitsyn borrows ideas from a wide range of Western thinkers including Plato, Aristotle, Montesquieu, John Stuart Mill, Karl Popper, and Joseph Schumpeter. He sees Russia as a nation different in many ways from, but tied to, the West via Christianity. This, as well as his admiration for the early American republic (and the founders), the Swiss confederation, and the New England town meetings he observed while in exile, confirm him as a widely read thinker with

none of the reflexive antiwesternism so characteristic of many other Russian nationalists. He believes that a decentralized government (and economy) working in a Christian society is the best form of socioeconomic and political structure for Russia. When Solzhenitsyn is criticized for being "anti-Western," one may ask which "West" is being referred to, that of the American founders and the tradition of Western Christendom, or the West as a modern political and geographic entity that has rejected its Christian legacy? One could easily claim that it is Solzhenitsyn's most tenacious modernist critics who are themselves "anti-Western."

111. For a discussion of the view that the modern era is passing away and that Solzhenitsyn, among others, may be having an influence on a postmodern order, see Ericson, *Solzhenitsyn and the Modern World*, 331–70.

112. Solzhenitsyn believes that the monarchist's restorationist dream is just that—that something new that draws on past experience must be constructed, but that resurrecting the past, even if desirable, would be impossible. A monarchy without feudal socioeconomic structures can operate in contemporary conditions only as a figurehead institution and not as the embodiment of the principle of Russian *sobornost* that some monarchists appear to believe will automatically arise with a restoration. The best available form of governance for Russia under postcommunist conditions is some form of representative constitutionalism. Solzhenitsyn, as noted earlier, prefers republican decentralization to Jacobin centralized democracy.

113. Ericson, *Solzhenitsyn and the Modern World*, 35.

114. Richard Sakwa, "Christian Democracy in Russia," *Keston Journal: Religion, State and Society* 20, 2 (1992): 136.

115. See, for instance, commentaries in *Izvestiya*, 1 November 1994, *Kommersant*, 29 October 1994, *Rossiyskiye Vesti*, 1 November 1994, and *Nezavisimaya Gazeta*, 1 November 1994.

116. RIA news service, 17 November 1994.

117. During his initial trip across Russia, he visited many towns and cities along the way; see, for instance, reports in *Vecherniy Novosibirsk*, 15 July 1994, and an Interfax news service report, 20 July 1994. For more on later trips, see *Komsomolskaya Pravda*, 20 September 1994, and, for the quotation, *Rossiyskaya Gazeta*, 8 October 1994.

118. *Nezavisimaya Gazeta*, 2 August 1994.

119. *Rossiyskaya Gazeta*, 11 March 1995.

120. *Washington Times*, 26 September 1995.

4

Christian Nationalism and the Black Hundreds

For many Russians, adherence to Orthodox Christianity is an indispensable part of Russian identity. Nevertheless, important distinctions between varying types of Christian nationalism remain, not the least of which is the identification by some Orthodox nationalists of Stalin's collectivist Soviet Union with Russia, the legacy of turn of the century Black Hundredism. Many Christian nationalists dissent from this view, especially those who profess Christian democracy, which has attempted to grapple with the difficult questions of identity, statehood, and religious faith in the modern world, as well as the implications of globalization. The Christian democratic version of nationalism has yet to realize its full potential, though it could yet prove a promising—and sane—option for postcommunist Russia.

Aleksandr Solzhenitsyn's nationalism is peculiar in that his embrace of Orthodoxy has not led him down the path to imperialism. In Russia, the national, imperial, and religious missions are often fused in the nationalist mind, and the circumstances of the Soviet Union's collapse have prompted many a Christian nationalist to part company with Solzhenitsyn over the issue of empire. The question of Orthodoxy's relationship with a particular Russian identity has spawned mutations of Christian nationalism within Russia that are different, but are difficult for the outsider to separate. Russian nationalists who embrace Orthodoxy must wrestle with a difficult spiritual problem: Are we Orthodox because we are Russian? Or are we Russian because we are Orthodox?

Religion and Nationalism

Nationalist movements have often used religion to mobilize the rebirth of the nation. The IRA rallies its followers, Marxist or no, as members of a national-religious community, the "Irish Catholics," and British Unionists in Northern Ireland, churchgoers or not, are invariably identified by their nominally papist enemies as "Prods." Nationalists thus make use of the collective memory of national communities, drawing on images of churches and familiar religious symbolism to designate badges of identity that separate them from outsiders. Nations possessing historic nation-based religions, the Jews or the Armenians, for example, have an even deeper well of national memory from which to draw images, symbols, and rituals that are connected to the origins of the nation itself and thus are indivisible from the collective identity of a people. The Hebrew people, believers or not, are forever tied to the Jewish faith. Like Irish Catholics, they are identified with it as a part of their cultural heritage, part of what makes them Jews. In the same way, Russia's cultural heritage and national identity is tied by history to Orthodox Christianity.

Russian Christian Nationalism

Kievan Origins

The Orthodox Church has traditionally based itself in national formations, with a patriarch presiding over the national community of believers. In Russia, the birth of the national church and national culture as such is tied to the mission of the monks Cyril and Methodius. Sent from Byzantium before the Great Schism, they worked out an alphabet for the Slavic tribes, which they used to compose a vernacular text of the Gospels. They labored for some thirty years (855–885) chiefly among the Western Slavs, though Cyril (d. 869) traveled as far east as the Crimea. Still, the spread of Christianity to the Eastern Slavs would have to wait. The Magyar invasions squelched Christianity as far west as Moravia, for instance, and Methodius, who had been concentrating on the Bavarians, died in 885. Their lasting contribution to Russia was the invention of an alphabet based on Greek characters that evolved into present day Cyrillic script. The language of the Eastern Slavic Church is known as Old Church Slavonic, the vernacular that the monks used to compose their version of the Gospels.[1] The seeds of a national culture had been planted.

Oleg, successor to Rurik, ruler of the northern city of Novgorod, united the southern Eastern Slav city-states with his northern holdings in the ninth century. Oleg recognized the importance of Kiev as a guardian to the trade routes south to the Black Sea and Byzantium and made it the capital of old Russia. Kievan Russia's connection to Byzantium would be a momentous one, for Vladimir, ruler of Kiev from 980, adopted the Christian faith in 988. The key point is that he chose (the *Nestor Chronicle* tells us that he made a conscious choice after studying Judaism, Islam, and the Roman Church's ritual[2]) the Eastern Church, whose center was Byzantium, thus tying Russia, after the Great Schism, to "the East," separating her from Western Christendom. Vladimir probably viewed the connection with Byzantium as a strategically important step for Kiev; indeed he married the sister of the Byzantine emperor. From Byzantium, Russia would inherit the claim of legitimacy as the center of the true church, and Moscow would eventually claim for itself the mantle of the "third Rome," the true successor to the imperial heritage of Rome and Byzantium, rivaling Western claims of "Holy Roman" emperors.

Christianity from the tenth century began to exert its cultural influence in Russia. Literature based on the Old Church Slavonic language flourished following the conversion of Vladimir and the baptism of Kiev's population in 990. Christianity appeared to have filled a spiritual void among the pagan Eastern Slavs. Despite lingering heathen superstitions among the people, it exerted itself socially as well as culturally: "Christian principles did affect life in Kievan Russia. Their influence can be richly illustrated from Kievan literature and especially its ethical norms, such as the striking concept of the good prince which emerges from Vladimir Monomakh's *Testament*, the constant almsgiving of the period, and the sweeping endorsement of Christian standards of behavior."[3] Metropolitan Hilarion, who served in the eleventh century and was one of the leading intellectuals of Kievan Russia, glorified Vladimir and the baptism of the Kievan Russians in these words:

> All countries and cities and people
> honor and glorify their teacher,
> who taught them the Orthodox faith . . .
> our teacher and guide
> the great sovereign of our land Vladimir.[4]

Hilarion noted that Vladimir had brought Christianity to "Russian land," a territorially based concept of national religious community that was "dear to Kievan writers and preachers," one that would remain "in the Russian consciousness" after the shift of power to Moscow. A case can be made that a Russian identity was already present and strong. This identity was born of the fusion of Rurik's dynasty with Eastern Christianity and Kievan culture, was cemented in Russian soil, and endured the collapse of Kiev and the "the dark first hundred years following the Mongol conquest" into the middle decades of the fourteenth century.[5]

The literature of the period reflected on the Mongol yoke: "The churches of God they devastated, and in the holy altars they shed much blood. And no one in the town remained alive: all died equally and drank the single cup of death. . . . And all this occurred to us for our sins."[6] Holy Russia, keeper of the True Faith, had suffered the first of many calamities, the pall of foreign (and pagan) invasion and conquest stamping indelibly on the Russian historical memory the vital importance of what had united them—their suffering and their church; "In that period the persistence of these bonds ensured the survival of the Russians as a major people."[7]

The folklore of old Russia not only saw her defeat and domination by the heathen Mongols as God's judgment on a sinful people but portrayed the victory of Dmitriy, grand prince of Moscow, over the Mongols at Kulikovo in 1380 as a sign of God's favor, further binding Russia to Orthodoxy in the popular consciousness. St. Sergey of Radonezh, founder of Russia's largest monastery (1337), the Troitsa-Sergeyeva Lavra, had blessed Dmitriy before the battle, and Aleksandr Nevskiy's victory over the Teutonic Knights in 1242 was forever merged with Orthodox Christianity by his canonization. The image of Holy Russia would live on in the most unholy of times: the freethinking Peter The Great founded a knightly order in Nevskiy's honor, and Josef Stalin himself authorized its (limited) revival during the Great Patriotic War. Stalin had followed Peter's lead in other matters as well, reviving the prostrate Russian church to rally the people against Hitler's latter-day Teutonic invaders in return for its loyalty to the Soviet state. The price for institutional survival was subjugation.

By blood and soil are nations made and by the blood of St. Aleksandr Nevskiy and the soil of Holy Russia the Russian consciousness has reaffirmed itself time and again against the Teutonic knights, the Poles, Napoleon, and Hitler. For many Russians, to be Russian is to be Orthodox, and in the postcommunist quest for identity and purpose, the church once again beckons, calling Russia home.

During the Gorbachev era, the church was again revived by a turn of political events. Thousands of Orthodox parishes were reactivated or established in Russia alone, and in the March 1990 Soviet parliamentary elections some three hundred clergymen were elected at various levels.[8] The restoration and rebuilding of churches desecrated or demolished by the communists began with *perestroika* and continues today. Charitable organizations and restoration societies work steadily in very difficult economic and social conditions, gathering money and materials and restoring, often with volunteer labor or the help of Russia's new business class, the architectural landscape of what was once

Holy Russia, a land marked by shimmering crosses atop golden cupolas.

It remains to be seen whether the fascination with religion in post-communist Russia[9] is anything more than an assertion of national identity or a mere tasting of what was once forbidden fruit. No politician in postcommunist Russia can afford not to be seen lighting a candle in an Orthodox church at Easter or heard praising the role of Orthodoxy in Russian history. But some observers could confuse nationalist rhetoric disguised as religious faith for the genuine article. The pertinent question relating to Christian nationalism in Russia, the notion that Russian national rebirth is first and foremost organically tied to the reanimation of Russian Orthodoxy, or at least the institutional church, is whether it is predominantly Christian or predominantly nationalist in content. The two are not mutually exclusive, but the accent placed on one or the other can have important consequences for the ideas and direction of Christian nationalism as espoused by various nationalist leaders.

Christian Democracy in Postcommunist Russia

The first Russian socio-political organizations of any significant size espousing a variant of Christian nationalism emerged during the late Gorbachev period and called themselves "Christian democratic."[10] They self-consciously drew on the ideas of West European Christian democracy and in some instances have joined international Christian democratic organizations.

Western Europe's Christian democratic movement was born in the late nineteenth century as a response to the growth of socialist parties. It spread quickly and emerged as a potent force in Europe's parliaments in the first quarter of the twentieth century. Since World War II, Christian democratic parties have more or less dominated the politics of some European countries, particularly West Germany and Italy, and have played a significant role in the politics of Belgium, Holland, Luxembourg, Austria, and Switzerland.[11] Christian democratic parties have proved particularly strong in some of the formerly communist Central European countries as well, especially Hungary and Slovakia.[12]

European Christian democracy has tended to be associated with Roman Catholic traditions, particularly as the church developed its social philosophy in the late nineteenth century following Pope Leo XIII's encyclical *Rerum novarum* of 1891, in which "the Church discussed the main social problems of a nascent industrial society: labor problems and conditions, fair wages, rights to property and human dignity." The encyclical "thus sought to establish a new role for the church by developing a distinctive social philosophy that criticized the excessively materialist tradition of socialism while being careful not to capitulate into uncritical adulation of liberalism."[13] The church was thus attempting to grapple with the socioeconomic dislocations of modernity and adapt its teachings to the new conditions.

The two ideological pillars of European Christian democracy—the social market economy and the notion of personalism—evolved from the socioeconomic ideas first set forth in *Rerum novarum* and further developed by a series of later papal encyclicals. The former was developed by the German Christian Democrat Ludwig Erhard, the latter by French philosopher Jacques Maritain.[14] Erhard recognized the importance of property rights and the superiority of market relations in producing wealth and sustaining a decent standard of living but refused to turn over society's fate wholly to the "invisible hand," thus laying the philosophical groundwork for a regime of welfare capitalism. Maritain, as noted in chapter 3, stressed the importance of the individual while not lapsing into individualism. Christian Democrats, proceeding from the ideas of Maritain and Erhard, tend to stress their commitment to "pluralism" within a framework of parliamentary style democracy as the political vehicle for any just social order in the modern era.[15]

The Christian democratic paradigm has proved to be particularly alluring in postcommunist Russia. Its rejection of Marxist socialism, its criticism of modern secularism, its "patriotic" content via personalism, and its embrace of the capitalist welfare state are particularly attractive to many Russian Christian nationalists who reject communism, but are wary of Western materialism in the form of consumerism and individualism. They fear the threat of social upheaval if reforms should proceed without a social "safety net" for the Russian people, many of whom have suffered severe economic and social dislocations as a result of the collapse of the old order. Christian democracy's commitment to "pluralism" dovetailed nicely with the Christian nationalists' early demands for freedom of conscience for believers, and parliamentarism was long seen by many as the political system of the "civilized world," which stood out in sharp contrast to the Soviet regime's repression.

Russia had no pre-Revolutionary Christian democratic party, though a group of state Duma[16] deputies formed a Christian Democratic caucus and the Constitutional Democratic (Kadet) Party boasted a Christian Democratic group internally from 1905 on.[17] A Christian democratic party was formed following the February (old style) revolution of 1917 but "made almost no impact on political life."[18] Since the late Gorbachev period, five parties and movements calling themselves "Christian Democratic" have been founded and, in some cases, all but disappeared. Aleksandr Ogordnikov, a former prisoner of conscience (he was in Soviet labor camps from 1978 to 1987) and political activist, founded the Christian Democratic Union (CDU) of Russia at a Moscow conference in August 1989.[19]

The CDU held a second conference in December of that year which attracted some three hundred delegates from around Russia. The aim of the party was to nominate candidates for the parliamentary and local elections held in spring 1990. CDU candidates (five in all) won seats in local assemblies, including three in Leningrad (now St. Petersburg).[20]

Ogorodnikov's relative success, however, was not to last. Russian political parties of the pre-Revolutionary period enjoy a well-deserved reputation for schism, and factional infighting may have been their one shared characteristic. Latter-day political parties and movements have proved no less prone to splitting, even atomizing, into often minuscule groups. One often reads of the "posttotalitarian" nature of present day Russian politics, a view that points out overpersonalized leadership styles and a tendency to schism (based on ideological hairsplitting) as the generic characteristics of political parties that have inherited such tendencies from the communist regime. Others see this as an example of a specifically Russian maximalism, wherein each adherent of a particular ideological line imagines himself to be in possession of the Truth, which cannot be compromised.[21] Whatever the reason, Ogorodnikov's organization splintered after a series of leadership quarrels.[22]

The CDU survived but tended to concentrate on charitable activities rather than politics. The party's schismatics formed the Russian Christian Democratic Party, whose leader, Aleksandr Chuyev, became a member of the council of Democratic Russia, an umbrella organization that united westernizing democrats and other reformers. Chuyev's party claimed 1,500 members in ten cities and towns, not an inconsiderable number as Russian parties went in the late 1980s.[23] The CDU's organizations in Moscow and Saint Petersburg broke away as well, creating a United Christian Democratic Union of Russia in December 1990. The organizations involved could claim only a few hundred members, but the Saint Petersburg group, organized by human rights activist Vitaliy Savitskiy, remained quite active in local politics.

Aksyuchits, Yakunin, and The Great Divide

By far the largest and most influential of the Christian democratic parties to form in the late Gorbachev period was the Russian Christian Democratic Movement (RCDM). Following the repeal of article six of the Soviet constitution, which granted the Communists a monopoly on political power, the RCDM became the fifth new party to register in mid-1990. The RCDM claimed some 15,000 members, making it one of the largest sociopolitical organizations in Russia and the Soviet Union, for branches had quickly been established in many of the fifteen Soviet republics. By 1992, the RCDM was claiming 28,000 members in 150 local and regional organizations both in Russia and the former Soviet republics.[24] For a time, the RCDM demonstrated the appeal that Christian democracy could have in Russia, its members serving in local, regional, and all-Russian legislative bodies. Its parliamentary deputies and their allies were able to have a significant effect on public policy, their most notable accomplishment being the passage of a law on freedom of conscience in October 1990.[25] The RCDM combined the activities of party and movement, members of the movement (who did not necessarily belong to the political arm) organized charitable and Christian educational organizations in the regions, while its party members were actively engaged in the political struggle.[26]

This too, did not last. By mid-1992 many local organizations were disassociating themselves from the national leadership and hereafter it became very difficult to gauge the RCDM's approximate size or influence. At the top, a leadership battle had earlier flared up around two men, Viktor Aksyuchits and Gleb Yakunin, both of whom had fought the good fight against Soviet repression during the dark years of stagnation[27] but increasingly found themselves on opposite sides of the political struggle. Despite its potentially broad appeal, Christian democracy in a Russian form has yet to coalesce, remaining something that is in the air of postcommunist Russia, but not (yet?) in its political bloodstream, visible via the many Orthodox Christian educational and charitable organizations as well as in various public figures' references to individual responsibility and the desire for a "social market economy." But it is no more than a minor current in political life. Christian nationalism in a broad sense, however, is an important part of the ideological landscape of postcommunist politics in Russia. It remains to be seen if the Christian element will trump the nationalist in the popular imagination, or if politics itself will consume whatever there is that is Christian in public life. The great divide represented by the Aksyuchits-Yakunin split is twofold. First, it is a divide within nascent Russian Christian democracy. Second, and more important, is another divide between Aksyuchits's truly *Christian* nationalism and the temptation of the Black Hundreds.

Father Gleb and Christian Nationalism

The Bolsheviks, true to the atheist word they put their faith in, began an all-out assault on the Russian church after their seizure of power in

October (old style) 1917. By 1922, the dreaded Cheka, the first incarnation of the Soviet secret police, had arrested Patriarch Tikhon. It executed, imprisoned, or exiled thousands of priests, closed churches, and confiscated church property. The Bolsheviks were more than mere anticlerics; their program called for the eradication of religion, root and branch. Churches and monasteries were converted into institutions devoted to the promulgation of atheism. The apocalypse had come in Russia.[28]

Tikhon died in 1925, and his eventual successor, Metropolitan Sergey, attempted to make peace with the Bolsheviks. Sergey issued the Declaration of Loyalty, which called the Soviet Union his "civic motherland." The future patriarch proclaimed his civic loyalty to the regime, stating plainly that "her [the Soviet Union's] happiness and success" is "our happiness."[29] "Sergeyism" was to be the policy of the Russian Church throughout the remaining decades of the Soviet period. Church representatives would later argue that Sergey had no choice—that the survival of the Church itself was at stake, and that only accommodation would ensure that survival. Such apologetics beg the question: *Survival as what?* No Christian believer who has not faced the hangman can unequivocally condemn those who have. Forgiveness is available to all who will avail themselves of it, and believers are duty bound to grant forgiveness to the penitent. In the case of the Russian church, however, there have been few who have asked for it, which implies that many of those who toadied to the Soviet regime felt justified in doing so. The Russian church served the Soviet regime loyally, an obedient lapdog that did not dare to yelp even when the repression Sergey may have hoped to curtail continued. The church survived as a skeleton organization whose priests were eventually not even allowed to visit sick and dying parishioners, such few as there were. Institutionally the church lived on, but the attack on the body of Christ, the community of believers, continued.

When Stalin allowed its limited revival during World War II, the church proved a potent national symbol to rally the Soviet Union's core Russian population for a defense of the homeland. In doing so, he may have recalled an alarming fact revealed by the suppressed Soviet census of 1936, namely, that 55 percent of the Soviet Union's population still claimed to be believers. His intuition, often accurate in such matters, told him that religious nationalism would prop up his regime where Soviet atheist ideology would not.[30] His political nose served him well on this occasion: Metropolitan Sergey supported the Soviet war effort fervently. This support "must have impressed Stalin," particularly since "the religio-patriotic appeals of Sergei" were "obtaining results." "The Russian faithful responded to Sergei's (and Stalin's) overtures by collecting huge sums of money for the war effort. Sergei provided equipment for a tank battalion named in honor of St. Dmitry Donskoy; on Red Army Day in 1942, the Moscow churches and clergy contributed a sum of 1,500,000 rubles. The total Church contributions during the war amounted to a staggering 150 million rubles."[31]

In 1943, Stalin permitted Sergey's election as patriarch, a post that had remained vacant since Tikhon's death nearly twenty years earlier. Some parish churches had been reopened since the beginning of the war, and grand religious services were held from time to time to honor the Great Leader of the Peoples, particularly on his birthday, praised by his priestly quislings as "chosen by God," "savior of the Fatherland and the Church," and "wise builder of the happiness of the people."[32] This is not to say that anything like religious tolerance was being practiced. The church was firmly under control, heavily infiltrated by secret police agents and informers. The authorities chose the church hierarchs, the regime eventually putting the church (and all other confessions) under the thumb of the Council on Religious Affairs and Cults. Such measures kept the "revival" under control.

The church had paid a heavy price for limited results, and Khrushchev later renewed antireligious repression. Once again uncooperative priests (and many believers of all persuasions as well) were imprisoned. Churches were closed as antireligious propaganda enjoyed a revival of its own. Of the 22,000 churches reopened under Stalin, more than half were closed from 1960 to 1964. The majority of seminaries and monasteries were closed as well. The number of Orthodox parishes was reduced from 30,00 to 14,500 by 1962. By 1975, the Orthodox Church operated a mere 7,500 churches across the Soviet Union.[33] The church heirarchs remained silent. The institutional church had made its choice, preferring institutional survival and physical security to fidelity to the word of God. The regime that the heirarchs aligned themselves with had murdered countless millions, had created the most fully developed instruments of repression that the world had (or has) seen, and had actively sought to eradicate religion from the land. Under these conditions, arguments about rendering unto Caesar what is his lose their meaning. What if Caesar wants it all?

This is the situation that a young priest, Gleb Yakunin, faced in the mid-1960s, when he too made a choice. In December 1965, Yakunin coauthored open letters to the patriarch, all bishops, and the chairman of the presidium of the Supreme Soviet of the USSR, Nikolay Podgornoy, together with another priest, Nikolay Eshilman, protesting the state's treatment of the church, particularly new restrictions on parish activity made in 1961.[34] Yakunin and Eshilman demanded that the authorities stop interfering in the affairs of the church. Both men were suspended from the active priesthood, but Yakunin continued his dissident activities, founding the Christian Committee for the Defense of the Rights of Religious believers in 1976 and frequently writing *samizdat* articles[35] on religious and church affairs. Yakunin was arrested in 1979, charged with anti-Soviet propaganda and sentenced to five years in a strict regime labor camp to be followed by five years' internal exile.

Yakunin's dissent occurred within the context of a flurry of dissident activity that followed in the wake of Khrushchev's de-Stalinization program. Religious and religio-nationalist dissent became a strong current within the dissident ranks, with *samizdat* journals such as *Veche* and *Zemlya* focusing on nationalist and religio-nationalist issues, including the rights of religious believers.[36] In 1976, Aleksandr Ogorodnikov founded an unofficial study group, the Christian Seminar, whose members were active in Moscow, Leningrad, Ufa, Smolensk, Minsk, Grodno, and Lvov. Similar study groups sprang up in other cities, and Christian *samizdat* publications circulated among Christian dissidents, many of whom began to cooperate with human rights activists.[37] The Committee for Human Rights in the USSR, for instance, united Christian nationalists such as Aleksandr Solzhenitsyn with human rights activists Andrey Sakharov and Valeriy Chalidze, who would become associated in dissident circles with Western style liberal tendencies.[38] For the time being, the "Slavophiles" were cooperating with the "westernizers."

Khrushchev's anti-Stalin campaign had unintentionally sparked a cycle of ideological and philosophical ferment in the Soviet Union. The period became a time of soul-searching on the part of thoughtful Soviet citizens. Khrushchev himself apparently did not understand that discrediting Stalin might call into question the fundamental principles of socialism and materialism. The path of ascension traversed by Aleksandr Solzhenitsyn in the 1940s and 1950s was being taken by others in the 1960s. Like the *Vekhi* authors before them, many twentieth-century Russians would turn from Marxism to Christianity and patriotism: "Not without reason is a concentration camp officially called a corrective labor colony. They come in atheists and go out Christians. They have been *corrected*," wrote Vladimir Osipov, who spent seven years (1961–68) in the camps for his dissident activities. Like Solzhenitsyn before him, he was changed by the experience. In 1961 he was a proponent of Yugoslav socialism, but the camps "made me a man believing in God, in Russia, and in the legacy of my forefathers." Osipov would go on to found the nationalist *samizdat* journal *Veche*. [39]

During the mid-1960s an underground organization advocating the armed overthrow of the Soviet regime and the rebirth of Russia along Christian nationalist lines, the All-Russian Social-Christian Union for

the Liberation of the People (VSKhSON), was founded. Its program
(minus the armed rebellion), authored principally by Igor Ogurtsov,
anticipated Solzhenitsyn's advocacy of a postmodernization program
that rejected both capitalism and communism, advocating a "third
way" that stressed social responsibility and traditionalism, decentralization and representative political institutions. The program also
called for the renewal of the church by freeing it from the grip of the
state. VSKhSON was broken up by the KGB in 1967–68.[40]

Veche would also eventually be suppressed in 1974, after publishing
ten issues and "attracting a considerable audience."[41] Two years earlier, Osipov had enumerated the aims of *Veche*, and the list generally
reflects the primary concerns of Christian nationalists of the period
and, with a few possible additions,[42] today, in effect generally defining
Christian nationalism:

1. to protect monuments of material and spiritual culture from destruction;
2. to foster a respect for national shrines and for one's own national
   dignity;
3. to recover Russia's cultural greatness;
4. to support a love for one's own homeland and the Orthodox
   Church;
5. to elucidate and discuss pressing problems related to contemporary national life;
6. to elucidate and discuss problems of contemporary Russian culture.[43]

What Osipov left out, however, began the process of overtly deline-
ating the boundaries of the great divide within Christian nationalism
itself. He failed to call on the church to repent of its association with
the murderous Soviet regime, much less to attack the heirarchs themselves for moral cowardice, as Aleksandr Solzhenitsyn, Viktor Aksyuchits, and Gleb Yakunin would do. Nor did he call for a fundamental
change in church-state relations. Yakunin made criticism of the institutional church the hallmark of his dissent, actively campaigning for ending the church's subjugation by the state. Moreover, he began to be
associated with the neowesternizers of the liberal human rights movement.

The broadening divisions within the dissident movement itself became apparent following the publication abroad of Aleksandr Solzhenitsyn's *Letter to the Soviet Leaders* in 1974. Solzhenitsyn's Christian nationalist program, his emphasis on gradualism, which included the
possibility of an authoritarian transition to a new Russia, and his criti-

cism of Western materialism set the imaginative juices of the westernizers to flowing, with some viewing such ideas as downright dangerous. "These assertions of Solzhenitsyn's are alien to my way of thinking," wrote Andrey Sakharov in his sharp *samizdat* reply to the "Letter." Sakharov went on to emphasize what was already discernible as the real ideological barrier between the Christian nationalist and liberal dissidents—the fact that the liberal group was dominated by an internationalist and secular philosophy: "I am quite convinced . . . that there is no really important problem in the world today which can be solved at the national level. . . . [A] strategy for the development of human society on earth, if it is to be compatible with the continuation of the human species, can only be worked out and put into practice on a global scale." Solzhenitsyn, he asserted, was an "isolationist" who wanted to cut Russia off from the world, a "patriarchal religious" romantic whose ideas might bring out the worst Russian tendencies.[44]

After Solzhenitsyn's exile in 1974, a shift in the center of Christian nationalism's gravity took place. Ludmilla Alexeyeva, author of *Soviet Dissent*, noted that Yakunin's Christian Committee for the Defense of the Rights of Religious Believers "became the center of the Russian nationalist movement" in the late 1970s, since many nationalists viewed Orthodoxy as "inseparable from their national identity."[45] Still, Yakunin focused on the reform of the institutional church and the state's treatment of believers within a "human rights" framework. Alexeyeva assured readers that Yakunin was "not under the influence of nationalist emotions."[46]

Yakunin returned to the center stage of Russian politics during the Gorbachev period, when he became a leading figure in the Democratic Russia (DR) movement, an organization whose stated aims were to implement "the ideas of Andrey Sakharov," which DR's program described as a defense of "freedom" and "democracy," and a commitment to "the rights of man, a multi-party system, free elections, and a market economy."[47] By 1990, when DR was founded, revanchist forces in the Communist Party, the military, and the KGB were already gathering strength, over a year before the August 1991 coup attempt. The revanchists had made use of nationalist slogans and were thought to be behind the organization of National Bolshevik and chauvinist groups such as Pamyat, which the apparatchiks may have viewed as something of a counterweight to the democrats, particularly since pure Marxism-Leninism lacked any broad appeal in the Soviet Union. This is the atmosphere in which DR held its founding conference in January 1990. Many of the conference's speakers attacked what they "perceived as a growing attempt by the Party to turn to chauvinist and racist elements among Russians in an effort to shore up their crumbling power."[48] One speaker warned the conference that the "last support of the partocracy is racism."[49] Yakunin himself told the audience that "Christianity is above nations. . . . [I]t is supra-national."[50]

The domination of Democratic Russia by the liberal, often internationalist intelligentsia did not, however, precipitate a complete break with many nationalist and Christian nationalist activists at that time. The common enemy, the communist regime, remained, and the Left's human rights agenda fit neatly with Christian nationalism's emphasis on the rights of believers. Thus, DR's political goals overlapped considerably with those of many Christian nationalists. DR called for a new constitution for the Russian Federation, the repeal of the communists' constitutional political monopoly, the return of churches to believers, the placing of the KGB under parliamentary control, a declaration of sovereignty for the Russian Federation, and the creation of a "regulated" market economy.[51] All of these were compatible with the goals of the largest of the Christian nationalist organizations, the Russian Christian Democratic Movement, whose governing body, the Duma, included its two most dynamic members, Gleb Yakunin and Viktor Aksyuchits.

Aksyuchits and the Democratic Russia Schism

Viktor Vladimirovich Aksyuchits was born into a peasant family in western Belorussia in 1949. He was reared, however, in Riga, the family having moved there in 1953.[52] Aksyuchits, a Belorussian, probably spoke Russian as his first language. By an early age he had already lived in two of the Soviet Union's republics, Belorussia and Estonia. The Riga of the 1950s was dominated by the Russian-speaking Soviet elites and remains the place of residence of a large number of Russians and Russian speakers. Aksyuchits's Russian identity was apparently a settled fact from the beginning. For Aksyuchits, Russia and the Soviet Union were physically coterminous. The Communists, however, were ideologically occupying the body of the *Otechestvo*, the Russian Fatherland.

Aksyuchits studied at the Riga Marine College from 1965 to 1969 and then spent three years in the Soviet Navy, were he worked as a political instructor. He entered Moscow State University in 1972, where he studied philosophy, concentrating on the early twentieth century Russian religious thinkers. In 1979, after converting to Orthodox Christianity, he left the Communist Party, which he had joined in 1971, convinced that the party "was leading the country to catastrophe."[53] Aksyuchits was excluded by the authorities from further pursuing his academic interests and had difficulty finding work. He eventually became a *shabashnik*, an itinerant construction worker, and became involved in the activities of informal Christian groups. The RCDM would eventually emerge as a fusion of such pre-Gorbachev groups, and in the late 1980s Aksyuchits founded a literary and philosophical journal, *Vybor* [Choice] with fellow Christian nationalist activist Gleb Anishchenko, "soon recognized as the most serious and thoughtful of the post-*samizdat* 'informal' publications."[54] Aksyuchits's cooperation with Gleb Yakunin dates from this period, and in 1990 Father Gleb became a member of the RCDM's ruling body, the Duma.

From its inception, the RCDM's activities were marred by internal division. Despite the organization's nominal association with European Christian democracy, the RCDM membership represented a wide spectrum of political opinion, from the liberal activism of Yakunin to the monarchism of RCDM Duma member Vladimir Karpets.[55] The movement's initial programmatic documents reflected that "enlightened patriotism" was the byword of the RCDM, whose political program called for the convening of a *Zemskiy Sobor*, an old Russian Assembly of the Land, whose task it would be to choose a "legitimate ruling power in Russia,"[56] since historical continuity had been broken off by the Bolshevik revolution.[57] The RCDM's program also called for respect for "human rights," "pluralism," and the institution of a parliamentary democracy, and a social market economy in Russia.[58] The program called for "tolerance, responsibility and respect for one's own and other people's freedom" and denounced "national hatred," "discrimination," and "national egotism." In anticipation of the possibility of some republics' seceding, particularly the Baltic states, the program insisted that "Russia" (in view of the fact that the republics in question would be seceding from the USSR, did that mean that the USSR was "Russia"?) must have a liberal immigration policy for those wishing to remain Russian citizens and that she "must defend the interests of the Russian population" remaining behind.[59]

The RCDM program thus attempted to be all things to all Christian and Christian nationalist activists, including liberal notions of pluralism along with republican ideas on the separation of powers, stressing the importance of a monarchist-inspired Land Assembly while calling for a parliamentary democracy in Russia, urging the separation of church and state and the revitalization of moral life through repentance and individual moral improvement, while asking for state support for some church-related activities.[60] The rock on which the RCDM ship would break up, however, was the perplexing dilemma of defining "Russia." The ambiguity of the RCDM's programmatic statements served only to paper over the fatal differences that would soon surface.

The RCDM and its allies were present at the creation of Democratic

Russia; indeed, onetime Aksyuchits ally, Mikhail Astafyev, leader of
the Constitutional Democratic Party (Kadets), later claimed that he had
named the organization.[61] The "democratic patriots" support of Democratic Russia's call for legal enactment of the Russian Federation's sovereignty did not later appear to many of them to contradict their nostalgia for the union. For many nationalists, religious or not, the
declaration of sovereignty passed by the Russian Republic's Supreme
Soviet with their (mostly) enthusiastic support, simply represented an
assertion of Russian identity and rights against what they by and large
saw as a denationalized, and completely depraved, Soviet regime. For
this reason, Aksyuchits, and others like him, supported Boris Yeltsin
in his power struggle with the "center" in the person of Mikhail Gorbachev. "In my opinion," Aksyuchits said at the time, "our main aim is
to become independent of the present political structure, which is a
force holding back all reforms. That is what the Declaration on the
sovereignty of Russia basically means."[62] Christian nationalists helped
to man the barricades at the Russian White House in August 1991,
defending "Russia" against what they saw at the time as the revanchist
forces of communist atheism.[63] Many nationalists did not appear to be
overly concerned at the time about the Left's agenda, namely, that the
Soviet Union could and should be dissolved as quickly as possible in
order to pave the way for universal democracy among the republics,
though some probably then saw no danger in recasting the Soviet
Union into a "confederation of democratic states" or an Eastern version of the European Union.[64]

A current of resentment, a feeling that the Russian heartland had
been neglected for the sake of the periphery, not entirely unfounded,
was and is a common theme in nationalist circles. It helps explain
many nationalists' early support of Yeltsin and the declaration of Russian sovereignty. Aksyuchits was among those who simply did not
realize that what they were doing helped to speed up the collapse of
the Soviet Union rather than foster an atmosphere wherein all anticommunist forces could work out their differences gradually once the
"center" had been defeated. To Christian nationalists such as Aksyuchits, the notion that the "periphery" would bolt in toto simply did not
seem likely. At the time, he claimed that "I am absolutely convinced
that the nations on the borders of our country are trying to escape from
the communist regime, not from Russia."[65]

The reason for such optimism was a peculiar view of the pre-Revolutionary Russian empire that many Christian nationalists subscribe to,
a vision of the empire as a great and good one for the most part, tolerant of other nations and faiths, united spiritually by the church and
sobornost, resistant to the siren call of Western materialism. For Chris-

tian nationalists of this persuasion, Orthodoxy "provided the ideological sense" that permitted this good empire, this Holy Russia, to exist. Orthodox Christianity was at the heart of old Russia, the essence of the Russian Idea, a "supranational [idea]" but not an antinational one. Within the boundaries of this idea "the nations in the Empire . . . [were able to] raise their own 'normative,'. . . patrimonial 'ceiling,' realizing in themselves possibilities that were not demanded in the pre-imperial state, proving their own ability to realize their national tasks." The negation of the national idea is the "negation of the nation."[66] The mission of the Russian nation, therefore, is to unite the various peoples of the vast landscape from Belorussia to the Kamchatka in a peaceful commonwealth as well as to preserve the faith.

In an article published in the RCDM newspaper *Put* in 1991, Aksyuchits expounded on the "Holy Russia" variant of Christian nationalism.[67] Calling notions about "the imperialist, expansionist character of the Russian people" an "historical myth," Aksyuchits denounced the National Bolshevik version of the Russian Idea, namely, that the Soviet Union was heir to the traditions of the Russian empire. This view meant that "the Russian people are today's occupiers and imperialists," and such notions fueled both anti-Russian sentiment in the various republics and the confusion of National Bolshevism with Russian patriotism properly understood, which was closely connected to Orthodox Christianity.

Aksyuchits did not deny that the Russian empire, like all others, had been created by force, but went on to point out (again, not entirely without foundation) some special characteristics of imperial Russia: Western European empires were built on slavery and the destruction of indigenous peoples by "fire and sword," but in the Russian "struggle for one sixth of the earth" not one culture had been destroyed. He maintained that Russia had been different in other respects as well: "In all [of the other] national empires" the imperial center had enriched itself at the expense of the colonies, whereas in Russia, "the central Russian provinces were, on the whole, poorer" than the periphery. Moreover, serfdom was not extended into newly acquired territories, and Poland and Finland had enjoyed constitutional government under Russian rule. Russia had won the war with Napoleon but had not seized any territories in Europe as one might expect if the Russian people were "eternally" expansionist and aggressive or desirous of enslaving their neighbors. Tolerance was the characteristic that most of all described the Russian national character.

The Soviet Union, Aksyuchits wrote, could not be considered an especially Russian empire, since it was not a "traditional national empire" but an "ideological, internationalist" one, and an atheist one at that. The Russian people were not the "bearers of the imperial idea" in the Soviet Union. If the Russian people had been the beneficiaries and creators of the USSR, then why had they been massacred "by the tens of millions"? Urging patience and tolerance, Aksyuchits went on to write that "for better or worse," the Russia of 1917 had been an "intact state organism," and all of her peoples who shared a single historical destiny should work together to free themselves of communist tyranny rather than spill blood in "separatist" adventures. He reminded his readers, à la Solzhenitsyn, that "the line dividing good from evil runs not between people, but within the human heart." The guilt for "seven decades of captivity" weighs not only on Russians but on the "Jew Trotsky, . . . the Pole Dzerzhinsky, and the Georgians Dzhugashvili [Stalin] and Beria, the Ukrainian Khrushchev." He denounced scapegoating: "The effort to run from one's own conscience and cast the burden of sin on others—either the 'Russian occupiers' or the Jews are guilty—cannot bring [either] liberation or rebirth to anyone."[68]

The RCDM left Democratic Russia in November 1991, as leading members of DR more or less welcomed the impending dissolution of the union, declaring that the Russia Federation itself was not indivisible. For its part, the RCDM attacked the DR activists as radicals, inheritors of the nihilistic traditions of the pre-Revolutionary intelligentsia. By further humiliating Russia, the intelligentsia that had once brought communism to Russia was now seen by RCDM loyalists as laying the groundwork for fascism.[69] Gleb Yakunin had left the RCDM even before the August 1991 coup attempt, accusing it of aggressive imperialism.[70] Aksyuchits himself has often publicly referred to his own conviction that the "rebirth" of Russian (*Rossiyskiy*, it should be noted, not *Russkiy*, is the precise word he used, in keeping with Aksyuchits's vision of the Russians as a *Staatvolk*) traditions should be accomplished without "revolutionary, violent methods of political struggle," emphasizing his functional conservatism.[71]

Aksyuchits attempted to regroup the democratic patriots, forming temporary extraparliamentary alliances with Nikolay Travkin's Democratic Party of Russia, Sergey Baburin's Russian National Union, and Mikhail Astafyev's Kadets within his Russian National Assembly. The alliances, however, proved to be fleeting ones. The main factor uniting them was a rejection of the dissolution of the union and a hope for its peaceful reconstruction,[72] confident that the union's breakup was by and large the work of the left radicals and the republic-level nomenklatura (still struggling to preserve itself) and did not necessarily reflect the wishes of the people themselves. But most other potential allies did not fully share Aksyuchits's view of Russia as an Orthodox "empire."

He did, however, form a political alliance with Aleksandr Rutskoy, Yeltsin's estranged vice president, who himself had revolted at Yeltsin's signing of a pact with Kazakhstan and Ukraine forming the Commonwealth of Independent States, a pact that effectively dissolved the Union. Aksyuchits later briefly became a member of Rutskoy's *Derzhava* movement, then attempted to form an alliance with the anti-Yeltsin film director, Stanislav Govorukhin, before backing Aleksandr Lebed in the 1996 presidential elections.[73]

From Christian Nationalist to Gosudarstvennik

By 1992, the Soviet Union had collapsed, and civil wars were raging in many of the former Soviet republics as the nations settled old scores and secessionist movements gained strength. Russians became the object of scorn in some corners of the old union and, in a few cases, targets for violent attacks by those who identified Soviet communism with Russian imperialism. Within the Russian Federation, the Caucasian republic of Chechen-Ingushetia had broken up as nationalists under former Soviet air force general Dzhokhar Dudayev staked out territorial claims for a Chechen state. Refugees from the various "hot spots," as the Russian press referred to them, particularly Russians and Russian-speaking people, were pouring into the Russian Federation by the thousands and then the millions, and the Russian government simply could not provide shelter or work for all of them.

Internally, the decision by the government of Prime Minister Yegor Gaydar to lift price controls prior to demonopolization was cited by internal dissenters (particularly Vice President Rutskoy) and "demopatriots" as the root cause of rising prices, inflation, and the devaluation of the ruble. Industrial production was steadily dropping, and Aksyuchits and other "enlightened patriots," who had favored a more gradual approach, took to comparing the radical "shock therapy"[74] program of the government with Bolshevik experimentation on the Russian corpus, particularly as news of falling birth rates and increasing mortality became commonplace in Russia media reports. Crime rates soared as public order broke down. The privatization program of the government came under attack by demo-patriots who feared that the speedy process would hand over state property to the "mafia" and the *nomenklatura* managers, while high taxes stifled the growth of an indigenous business class. Factory managers smuggled raw materials abroad to make up cash shortfalls and sock away personal nest eggs.

Socially, the invasion of the Tartars themselves could not have brought about as much culture shock as the Western purveyors of Nike and Pepsi did in catering to the whims of the "new Russians," the new rich spawn of economic reform, many of them speculators connected with the underworld. While war veterans and pensioners peddled Western made candy bars[75] and soft drinks on street corners and workers continued the moonlighting practices they had begun under the Soviets to make ends meet, Western visitors and "new Russians" could while away the hours in one of the many new casinos, topless bars, and night clubs that accepted dollars only. Pornography was now openly available. Religious "cults" were growing along with conventional religion.

While advisers from foreign banks and governments worked out the details of shock therapy with government economists, Russia aligned herself with the West internationally, shunning former allies. The isolation of Orthodox Serb dominated Yugoslavia was particularly galling to nationalist sensibilities. Within the next year, Western governments would support, and even applaud, President Yeltsin's decision to dissolve a recalcitrant (and lawfully elected) Supreme Soviet by less than democratic means, namely, by application of T-72 tank rounds. The Russian news media, which heavily favored the "democrats," tended to portray all critics of the government, particularly nationalists, as "fascists" or "red-browns," lumping together Aksyuchits with the likes of demagogue Vladimir Zhirinovskiy.

This, then, presented from the nationalist perspective, is the context for Aksyuchits's sharp move toward *gosudarstvennik* positions following his break with Democratic Russia. Since the Time of Troubles[76] in the seventeenth century, the threat of chaos had weighed heavily on the Russian mind. National and political unity came to be viewed by many Russian thinkers, particularly the purveyors of the official nationality doctrine of absolutism, as positive values embodied in the centralized state. The situation had changed since the defeat of the Soviet "center." Now the real threat was the "demo-Bolshevik"[77] radical program, particularly the rush (or so the nationalists saw it) to break up the Soviet Union, physical heir to Holy Russia. Aksyuchits was now presenting himself as a *gosudarstvennik* of sorts, a supporter of the "strong state" advocates, whose slogan under the Whites during the Civil War period had been "Russia—United and Indivisible!"

The Holy Russia variant of Christian nationalism provided a bridge to *gosudarstvennik* positions that often embraced a nostalgia for Russia's status as *derzhava*, a respected military power and force in world diplomacy, a great power that had fired sputniks into the cosmos and defeated Hitler. Even anticommunist nationalists were not immune to such sympathies: Aksyuchits once commented that he did not wish to "groundlessly denigrate" the history of the USSR; there had been, after all, some positive aspects to the period.[78]

Aksyuchits and his allies in the Russian Supreme Soviet now found themselves making tactical alliances with the Communists against the Yeltsin regime. The RCDM leader remarked that "at the moment the task of dismantling communism is not [a] pressing [matter]." "Different tasks" were now more urgent, particularly "the salvation of Russian statehood."[79] He had not, however, changed his mind about communism: Aksyuchits conspicuously failed to participate in the activities of the communist-dominated National Salvation Front (NSF), an umbrella organization that for a time became the locus of antiregime activities. At times, he appeared to be in something of a scramble to find acceptable allies for joint activities, as old RCDM comrades like Ilya Konstantinov drifted away from Christian nationalism and into more radical nationalist currents. Indeed, Konstantinov was joined by Astafyev as an NSF activist, and their skepticism about the West, inherent in Russian nationalism, took on a more strident and anti-U.S. tone.[80]

The October 1993 shoot-out that erupted during Yeltsin's standoff with the Supreme Soviet and the continuing U.S. support for the president seemed to confirm their worst fears: Yeltsin and company amounted to a U.S.-sponsored "occupation" regime, one intent on assuring that Russia would never again reassert herself as a great power. Furthermore, Russia would be integrated into the emerging "new world order," the transnational regime that demanded the subordination of national interests to universal rationalist imperatives. In short, the nation would lose control over its own destiny. After "bloody October" no one in opposition to the Yeltsin regime, including Aksyuchits, could doubt that this was the case. A year earlier, Aksyuchits was already asking the rhetorical question, "In whose interests is Russia's transformation, not even into an 'Upper Volta with rockets,' but into a raw material appendage of developed countries, a third rate state with a degraded society and a destitute population?"[81] By that time many nationalists thought that they knew the answer to that question. In any case, many local RCDM chapters had left the fold, the organization thereafter existing only in skeletal form, and Aksyuchits's hunt for allies continued.[82]

The Way of the Gosudarstvennik

In 1991, the monarchist Vladimir Karpets, writing in the RCDM newspaper *Put*, described the Russian Idea as embracing the concepts of the Third Rome, Eurasia, and Holy Russia. As the Roman emperors after Christianity became the state religion, Karpets reasoned, the Muscovite czars were the rulers of a vast Christian empire, the heirs of the converted Constantine, anointed by God. The empire itself eventually stretched from the Baltic to the Pacific, the vital center of the Eurasian landmass, one-sixth of the earth's surface. Holy Russia was the realization of the City of God on earth, Orthodoxy permeating every aspect of the empire's life. Thus the emperor, the g*osudar*, or sovereign, reigns to keep the true faith and keep the Holy Russian *gosudarstvo*, the state, intact as the bearer of the Christian ideal in a fallen world. The only way for the Russian patriot is the way of the *gosudarstvennik*.[83]

The Black Hundreds[84]

Now the serpent was more subtil than any beast of the field which the Lord God had made. And he said unto the woman, Yea, hath God said, Ye shall not eat of every tree of the garden?

And the woman said unto the serpent, We may eat of the fruit of the trees of the garden:

But of the fruit of the tree which is in the midst of the garden, God hath said, Ye shall not eat of it, neither shall ye touch it, lest ye die.

And the serpent said unto the woman, Ye shall not surely die:

For God doth know that in the day ye eat thereof, then your eyes shall be opened, and ye shall be as gods, knowing good and evil.

—Genesis 3:1–5

For I will cast out the nations before thee, and enlarge thy borders.

—Exodus 34:24

We are Russians, God is with us!

—Slogan seen on a banner during a nationalist rally in Moscow

Conspiracy theories have found a ready audience in many countries in many different times. When cataclysmic events shock a country to its foundations, when people feel impotent before history's tidal wave, when war, economic collapse, or political disintegration mark the end of a historical era and, having rendered old points of reference obsolete, signal the beginning of an uncertain future, a certain segment of any society will turn to the comfort of easy, all-encompassing fantasies in order to explain the heretofore inexplicable and to find something, *someone* to blame. Disaster is far easier to digest if an enemy—an evil foe whose destruction will bring the solution of our ills, the end of our pain—is apparent. The steadfast, the loyal, and the strong can then exorcise the demons of uncertainty, and, having identified the enemy, unite the forces of light to strike back at the darkness. The will to action will be satisfied.

In his book *Black Hundred: The Rise of the Extreme Right in Russia* Walter Laqueur attempted to describe the origins of the convoluted set of conspiracy theories that separate Russian nationalists so inclined from those of a more rational complexion. Laqueur chose to concentrate on the "extreme Right" precisely because the ideology he describes, which we may loosely term "Black Hundredism," is not the purview of fringe groups alone. When Vladimir Zhirinovskiy, who subscribes to a modernized version of the Black Hundred mantra, is able to garner nearly a quarter of the vote in a parliamentary election (1993), when the Communist Party of the Russian Federation, whose leader, Gennadiy Zyuganov, preaches a National Bolshevik variant of Black Hundredism, plays a key role in the Russian parliament (the Duma) and wins some 40 percent of the vote in a presidential election (1996), and a country's topmost leadership (from czarist ministers to Stalinist commissars to various public figures in both Gorbachev's and Yeltsin's Russia)[85] frequently allude to dark forces orchestrating world events, then one can safely conclude that we are not dealing with a "fringe" phenomenon.

Man's propensity for seeking absolution via accusation is as old as the race. As Adam blamed Eve (and God Himself) and Eve the serpent for their own trespass, so have men repeatedly killed the messenger, the one who speaks truth to power, the bearer of bad tidings, however much the fix we find ourselves in is tied to our own behavior. In the modern era, particularly since the growth of the power of the integrated state and the dislocations of the industrial age dissolved feudal religious and social bonds, alienation and impotence have become dominant themes in the literature and scholarship of Western civilization.[86] Under these secularized conditions, when the centers of power seem so distant and the inability of ordinary people to cope with the rate and scope of change brought about by transstate political and economic forces is so apparent, appeals based on the acceptance of God's will lose their potency, and old Adam, always ready to relieve himself of the burden of responsibility, falls prey to the ideologies of demagogues who promise to set things right.

The plot mongering of communists, fascists, Nazis, or other tub thumpers has had broad appeal partly because of the element of truth in most modern conspiritalogy: They have merely made the incomprehensible, and self-interested, maneuverings of UN secretaries, international bankers and industrialists, and self-styled Metternichs explicable by reductionism. Instead of the complicated interaction of varied political and economic players, we have the shadowy enemy who orchestrates every occurrence in accordance with a master plan designed years, decades, or even centuries before. In truth, the reaction called for may have little directly to do with the source of our troubles, but it makes us *feel* better, since the unmasking of the enemy simultaneously absolves us of a share of the responsibility for political or economic chaos *and* gives us answers. True, the witch hunters may be simply ignorant, ready to accept any explanation for catastrophes great and small, like medieval villagers who blamed the plague on well-poisoners. Nevertheless it is difficult to imagine that the identification of the Jews as the collective culprit was not related to their status as outsiders, middle-man merchants, and moneylenders. Thus does the thirst for revenge assume the guise of civic action.

The difference between medieval witch hunts and modern campaigns to destroy "enemies of the people" and other subhumans resides in both the scale of destruction that new technologies have made possible and in the vistas of horror opened by modern ideology, absent even a pretense of accountability to a higher Authority.[87] When the Jew is no longer redeemable through conversion, then "scientific" racism takes a hand. In Russia, the Black Hundreds provided the bridge from one era to the next.

Perhaps it was inevitable that the ideology which spawned the Black Hundreds at the turn of the century arose in a country threatened as Russia was at that time by the specter of revolution. Holy Russia had been defeated in war by the Japanese, her armed forces humiliated, her czarist system exposed as inept and corrupt; wild-eyed, atheistic revolutionaries had assassinated the "Czar Liberator" some years before and were now targeting government officials. For some Russian patriots, the time had come for conservative and constructive change. Prime Minister Pyotr Stolypin (served from 1906 to1911)[88] ruthlessly suppressed the disturbances of the 1905 Revolution and then turned to domestic reform, encouraging the growth of a stratum of peasant freeholders, hoping to quench their perennial land hunger while nudging the czarist system toward constitutional monarchy. The *Vekhi* authors and like-minded Christian philosophers preached the Christianity of the Golden Rule as society's moral foundation and attacked the institutional church for its slavishness before the regime and the mechanical Christianity of the official nationality ideology.[89] The program of these early precursors of the "enlightened patriots," who would eventually claim their mantle, amounted to a conservative modernization, one that simultaneously sought to avoid stagnation on the one hand and revolution on the other. Both right and left radicals despised them.

For the Black Hundreds, the years after 1905 were a time of violent backlash in which the obscurantist wing of Russian Orthodoxy, morally and spiritually hobbled by ideological and institutional subjugation, would aim to hunt down the satanic enemies of Holy Russia. It was a time of pogroms. Supported by prominent government ministers and the czar himself, touting the *Protocols of the Elders of Zion* as well as anti-Masonic propaganda, the Black Hundreds would use these conspiratorial tales of machinations by Jewish bankers, the Sanhedrin, and Masonic lodges—all directed toward world domination and the destruction of Holy Russia (as the most spiritually pure and able enemy facing them)—to explain the troubles that had befallen the Fatherland. Like so many others who looked for answers in global conspiracy, the Black Hundreds indulged in simultaneous self-pity and self-glorification. Russia was both innocent, even helpless, victim, and Holy Russia, a chosen people with a destiny marked by the very hand of God. Lurking in the background were the elements of mass movement organization and populist appeals combined with a psuedoscientific racism that was to mark the dawn of a new era in the developed world. Thus the Black Hundreds took the ideas of Slavophiles (the special spirituality of the Russian village and people), the messianism of Pan-Slavism, the mysticism of Holy Russia, as well as the monarchism inherent in "third Rome" Caesaro-papism and the official nationality ideology, and combined them with new elements to move Russian nationalism in a fundamentally new direction.

The Grand Conspiracy

During the Enlightenment, the curious faith called rationalism invited Man to explain the world. Deists claimed to have the key to the history of the universe in the notion of the Great Watchmaker, an impersonal deity who set the iron laws of the universe as a watchmaker wound up one of his creations. The universe-clock was set in motion by the Watchmaker. Although he himself was unknowable, the perpetual motion machine he made, the universe, was knowable through its iron laws. In the nineteenth century, Charles Darwin offered his theories on origins of species as another view of the key to history—evolution had accounted for the development of all life, and natural selection made nature and Man as subject to study and deciphering as Newton's apple. Great forces, unseen but discernible through scientific inquiry, were at work shaping our world. The prospect of unlocking the keys to the history of the universe and the knowledge of the origins of life itself were irresistible to modern Man— "ye shall be as gods"—who looked forward to knowing, maybe even controlling, the heretofore secret trajectory of the universe.

Karl Marx further sweetened the post-Enlightenment intellectual pot with his theory of history as the story of class struggle, explicable through scientific laws and materialist analysis. Like Hegel before him, he thought of history moving forward by way of the clash of opposites, each clash resulting in progress toward a more or less predictable future. Though Marx sometimes denied that the predicted course was inevitable, men latched onto the notion of history as a replacement for the God they could no longer believe in. Theory became dogma, scientific materialism a faith. Immanentism filled history with a life of its own. Perhaps the greatest insight Marxism had to offer was its notion of the economic superstructure's effect on social consciousness. Feudalism had passed away, a new socioeconomic order had been born, and with it a new consciousness. History had destroyed the old order and was moving toward a new one, not yet visible but predictable.

While Marx and Engels were pondering the correlation of forces in newly capitalist Europe, others began to view the Big Picture in a different light. Some saw race, not class, as the fundamental category of existence. "Aryans," speaking prototype Indo-European languages, had struggled with lesser races, and history had progressed as the "Aryans" spread their domain over Europe. Great societies had clashed and were clashing even now, either the races or the larger civilizations themselves being the operative forces. Since Gibbon, the question of whether civilizations' rise and fall were subject to certain laws of historical development had opened another question: Was the process predictable, even controllable? Such historical speculations prompted twentieth century thinkers like Spengler, Toynbee, and H. G. Wells to "outline" history. Was the West declining according to the laws of historical process, or sputtering forward toward a grand future? In nineteenth century Russia, Nikolay Danilevskiy had already anticipated them, suggesting that humanity "expresses itself solely in specific 'historico-cultural' types," each with its own mission. Russia was to unite the Slavonic peoples in a Pan-Slav empire, thus civilizing one sixth and more of the earth and fulfilling the role her "state organism" had been assigned by "scientific evolutionary laws."[90]

If great, unseen forces at work in the universe are knowable through historical and scientific inquiry, then it seemed logical that the great cataclysms of the dawn of the new era, the French Revolution, for instance, were capable of being analyzed in a similar manner.

Secret societies had long been the object of suspicion in the popular imagination. Those inclined to suspect that a hidden hand was at work, shaping history to its own ends, found ready-made culprits in the guise of the Masons. Established authority, after all, had also been suspicious of the Masons. In Europe, the Catholic Church had issued an anti-Masonic bull in 1738, with others to come.[91] Besides, many (if not most) prominent public figures, politicians, and businessmen, including various radicals and freethinkers, had been Masons. Who else could pull the lengthy strings required to orchestrate world historical events? History did not move forward by accident. From that point on, the Masons became a favorite of conspiracy mongers everywhere, but the Masons soon were linked in the conspiratorial mind with another, more ancient foe of civilization: the Jew.

Anti-Semitism

In *The Origins of Totalitarianism*, Hannah Arendt proposed that the origins of modern anti-Semitism[92] are tied to the political, economic, and social development of the modern world.[93] Under feudal regimes Jews had often been granted a special relationship with the feudal lords and kings. As each estate of the realm had its specific relationship to the sovereign based on the concepts of fealty and service, so did the Jews. Thus many Jews performed special economic services for the rulers of the feudal states, securing loans and bankrolling the lord or sovereign but remaining outside the pale of Christian society itself. It was an uneasy relationship, especially since some particularly skillful Jewish financiers enjoyed privileges the rest of their poorer brethren did not, while still becoming the focus of popular imagery of the Jews as a people.

Arendt argued that the situation changed dramatically in the nineteenth century. The rise of the "nation state," our integrated state, brought with it the leveling tendencies of Jacobin democracy: Special privileges or group status were no longer acceptable to the citizens of the new states. Jews too were emancipated (that is, allowed into the fold of popular society), but many prominent Jewish bankers and financial logrollers retained their special international connections with the Jewish financial diaspora in Europe. As capitalism and industrialism developed, and the dislocations of modern urban society deepened, workers' movements and socialist parties stigmatized the banker as robber baron. The Jewish bankers' cosmopolitan network, though still useful, endeared them not at all to their customers, the rulers and industrialists of the bourgeois nationalist state. With the further development of financial institutions in the new states themselves, the Jewish financial class became less useful and, therefore, less likely to be protected, according to Arendt.

The combination of industrialism, the grit and rawness of the burgeoning cities, capitalism's boom and bust cycle, and the growth of a nationalist-based integrated state system undermined the basis for any privileges some Jews may still have enjoyed and fostered resentment among the populace at large. As outsiders, Jews played a prominent

role in radical politics, particularly as the traditional Jewish community was weakened by assimilation or emigration. By the late nineteenth century Jews had moved into other enterprises, including publishing and the arts. The Jews' communal ties had served them well for
centuries; now the image of the tightly knit, wealthy, cosmopolitan
Jewish network was a liability as never before, especially as Christianity itself declined, often to be replaced by a faith in a deified nation or
race. The search for the key to history, as well as crackpot racial "science" set the stage for modern anti-Semitism.

The Protocols

The Protocols of the Elders of Zion remains the bread and butter source of
anti-Semitic conspiratolgy in the modern world, particularly in Russia,
where the *Protocols* have enjoyed a new popularity following the collapse of communism.[94] The *Protocols* ostensibly are the records of meetings of the Elders of Zion, a secret Jewish society allied with the Masonic order and dedicated to establishing Jewish world rule. The
agents of the conspiracy work behind the scenes to foster the breakup
of traditional society through the modern ideologies of socialism and
liberalism. At the same time, capitalism itself is depicted as the creation
of acquisitive Jews, a vehicle for undermining the old order. The con-
spiracies' agents are at work in Jewish-controlled newspapers, political
parties, and social movements to foster revolution and decay, paving
the way for the plotters to seize power through their agents of influence, who may or may not be aware of the grand plot that is in the
offing, making the plotters that much more difficult to unmask.

The *Protocols* had several precursors in the late nineteenth century.
Wilhelm Marr, for example, wrote an 1879 pamphlet in Switzerland
on the Jewish conspiracy, predicting, among other things, the destruction of the czarist state by Jewish revolutionaries.[95] Other versions cited
Jew-Masons as the source of all the major upheavals in history: "All
political assassinations and all major strikes were organized by them.
They induced workers to become alcoholics and created chaotic conditions by increasing food prices and spreading infectious diseases. They
already constituted a secret world government, but since their power
was as yet incomplete, they incited peoples against each other to provoke a world war."[96] The Elders, however, had no intention of sharing
power: "The new government would put down without mercy all
those who opposed it; its former co-conspirators, such as the Masons,
would be liquidated, some killed, others exiled to primitive settlements
overseas."[97]

The standard Russian version of the great plot was published in 1905

by the court printers at Czarskoye Selo, and later at the print shop of
the Troitsa-Sergeyeva Lavra monastery under the auspices of one
Sergey Nilius, "a Russian playboy who after spending several years in
France underwent a religious conversion and retired" to the monastery.[98] The *Protocols* were probably concocted around 1900 by czarist
secret police officials to encourage resistance to efforts to reform the
autocratic system.[99] In any event, it wasn't until after the calamity of
World War I and the Russian Revolution that this early example of
political disinformation began its "veritably triumphal procession
through all European countries and languages; its circulation some
thirty years later was second only to Hitler's *Mein Kampf.*" [100] Be that
as it may, the *Protocols* had already made their mark in Russia: Nicholas initially believed in the authenticity of the pamphlet, changing his
mind only after Stolypin convinced him otherwise. The czarina, Alexandra Fedorovna, remained a true believer. The plot of the Jew-Masons, gradually evolving as the plot of the "Zionists" after the World
Zionist Congress of 1897,[101] was at the heart of the ideology of the Black
Hundreds.

The Black Hundreds[102]

The radical nationalist organizations collectively known as the Black
Hundreds shared a number of generic characteristics that prompted
Walter Laqueur to see them as a "halfway house" from traditional nationalism to racism, from reaction to right wing revolution. The Black
Hundreds were fervent supporters of absolutism but simultaneously
attacked the state bureaucracy as an impediment to unity of czar and
nation. They were upholders of the official nationality ideal but took
the ideology at its word, calling for land reform[103] and improved working conditions for the laboring classes, and supporting the formation
of a consultative *Zemsky Sobor* to institutionalize the bond between czar
and nation. They found supporters among the lower middle classes,
the workers and peasants, as well the dregs of the empire, including
criminals,[104] but they were led by refined and educated aristocrats, law-
yers, and doctors. Former prime minister Count Witte and his successor Stolypin saw them as a threat to public order, but sympathizers
among the czar's ministers, who saw the Black Hundreds as counter-
revolutionaries, made sure they were sporadically subsidized by the
state. Local officials and police often ignored the violence the Black
Hundreds fomented.[105]

The Black Hundreds' militants were organized into paramilitary
groups, one of which took the name of "Yellow Shirts," anticipating
the Brown and Black Shirts of Germany and Italy. Ostensibly isolation-

ist and anticapitalist, portraying the Russian peasant *obschina* as the ideal social organization and denouncing both "Jewish capital" and "Jewish radicalism" as two sides of the same coin, the Black Hundreds were nevertheless ideologically committed to Russia as *derzhava*, and to be a great power meant to be modernized economically and militarily. Black Hundreds shock troops frequently carried icons and professed Orthodox Christianity, while from all accounts remaining largely ignorant of the particulars of the Christian faith. In any event, the anti-Semitism they preached was moving beyond religious boundaries: many Black Hundreds organizations denied membership even to converted Jews.[106]

The Black Hundreds broke new ground, foreshadowing the mass movement right-wing parties of the twenties and thirties, combining populism with political absolutism and statism, and using storm troopers to terrorize their enemies—the Jews, capitalists, liberals, and reformers. Their notions of right-wing state socialism were precursors of Mussolini's corporatism and Hitler's National Socialism. What the Black Hundred ideology amounted to was a radicalized version of the right-wing modernization the monarchy itself had promoted, but the movement was hemmed in by its own attachments to the old regime, to czar and church, ideologically unable to emerge as a full-blown fascist or Nazi-like party. The populist element in the new ideology rarely called for a classless society per se or a sharp break with the past.

At the core of their ideology beat the black heart of dualism, which found its expression in anti-Semitism and the grand conspiracy. If the Russian nation was the purest and most worthy, the Russian state the City of God, then her enemies, who included anyone who favored even modest political reforms, were the spawn of Satan, subhuman and demonic, the agents of the anti-Christ. The Black Hundreds had, in their own minds, deified the nation. The Russian nation itself was God, the empire the body of Christ, the church and the state fused as one, the official ideology their creed. In Black Hundreds ideology the nationalist element had all but extinguished the Christian. Thus blasphemy was committed in the name of the nation and the state: The cross itself was reduced to a political symbol on a par with the swastika or the hammer and sickle, a totem to unite the nation as the image of the all-powerful Jew did. Most disgraceful of all was the support of many of the church hierarchs, including Hermogen of Saratov, Falvian of Kiev, and Antony of Volhynia, for the hateful actions of the Black Hundreds. Some church publications "preached in every issue that reform was sinful and that the Jews were plotters trying to weaken the Russian state, so that the great Jewish financiers could enslave the Russian people." Metropolitan Antony of St. Petersburg and Archbishop Yakov of

Yaroslav were conspicuous among those clergymen who denounced the Black Hundreds, but it seems likely that the majority of the church's leadership at least tacitly approved of them.[107]

The Black Hundreds had their precursor in an organization known as the *Russkoye Sobraniye* (Russian Assembly) founded in 1900 by Prince D. P. Golytsin. The first shock troop formations were not formed until the spring and summer of 1905, when the disturbances of the first Russian revolution rocked the foundations of the empire. The counter-revolutionaries took names like The White Flag, The People's Union, For Czar and Order, The Fatherland Union, and the Union of the Arch-angel Michael.[108] The largest and best organized of these was the Union of Russian People (*Soyuz Russkogo Naroda*) founded by A. I. Dubrovin and V. M. Pruskevich, a former assistant to the interior minister von Plehve, in November 1905. The union "called for the formation of fighting detachments to quell the revolution" but was making a late start: The first round of pogroms had already come off in October of that year.

At the height of their influence in 1905–6 the Black Hundreds formed thousands of loosely knit branch organizations across Russia.[109] They tended to be stronger in the South, the Ukraine, and White Russia, probably because their anti-Semitic message had broader appeal in those regions in and around the traditional Jewish pale of settlement. In fact, all but a few of the pogroms of the period took place in these regions. As revolutionary activity tapered off in 1906, so did the activi-ties of the Black Hundreds, though some members remained politically active in the state Duma, serving as deputies.

The Black Hundreds continued to influence Russian politics during the Civil War period and after, among the White Russian emigration. The catastrophe of World War I and the Bolshevik coup seemed to confirm the worst fears of the conspiratologists. Had not many promi-nent Bolsheviks been Jews? The *Zhidomasonstvo* (Jew-Masons) had not yet outlived their usefulness as an explanatory device, nor had a com-mitment to Holy Russia died, even in the belly of the Soviet beast.

The Revival of the Black Hundreds

On August 1, 1990, the "Union of Russian People" was revived at Mos-cow's House of the Soviet Army.[110] *Glasnost*, as well as the often unseen support of party functionaries and government officials, had made such an organizational revival possible. The neo-Black Hundreds had been preceded by the black shirted hooligans of Pamyat, carrying out demonstrations and creating public disturbances in the name of "God, Czar, and Nation!" Pamyat eventually splintered, but the most active fragment, under photographer and actor Dmitriy Vasilyev, eventually, after several ideological metamorphoses, espoused a pure Black Hundredism: "Zionism," responsible for the Bolshevik seizure of power in 1917, was still attempting to destroy Holy Russia, since Russia and the Russians, "spiritually purer" than other nations, and the "heir of the Aryan race," remained the primary impediment to the *Zhidomasonstvo,* operating under the guise of Western governments already under their sway, the International Monetary Fund, and "transnational corporations," and their plans for world domination.[111]

In the 1990s, simon-pure Black Hundredism could be found in various guises—as a current in the monarchist and Cossack movements, as the ideology of hundreds of continually splintering Pamyat look-alikes such as the new union and Aleksandr Shtilmark's appropriately named *Chernaya Sotnya* (Black Hundred) microparty. Newspaper and literary journals espousing Black Hundred views sprouted like the proverbial Russian mushrooms after the rain. Shtilmark's newspaper is typical, carrying lurid tales of alleged ritual murders of Russian children by Jews, theories on plots and counterplots too numerous to mention, and making the familiar case for a *Zemsky Sobor* to chart Russia's future course.[112] Like all fanatics, the neo-Black Hundreds see everything as allegedly related to the grand conspiracy: nothing is incidental or accidental. If Yeltsin pledges to cooperate with the West on some matter, this is proof of the plot: "We told you so!" If Yeltsin refuses to cooperate with the West on some matter, this too is evidence of the grand conspiracy: He is only trying to induce "patriots" to let their guard down.

None of these organizations is particularly influential. They operate within the general framework of Russian nationalism as an ever present but politically marginal force. The real danger that the Black Hundreds present for Russia today is twofold: First, their ideology, in mutated forms, has penetrated and flourished within other more modernist-oriented parties and social movements, most of whom still pay some homage to the old Orthodox empire as the precursor of a postmodern Russian *derzhava.* Many members of the Russian intelligentsia, particularly writers and journalists, subscribe to Black Hundred views, keeping the ideology alive as an intellectual hothouse wherein more forward looking nationalists incubate their own visions of Great Russia. More important, however, is the struggle for the church, pitting moderates against the heirs of Sergeyism. It is within the church that a form of Black Hundredism is perhaps strongest. In view of the widespread renewal of interest in religion in Russia and the Church's organic connection to Russian nationalism this is where the Black Hundreds have the potential to most influence postcommunist Russia.

Metropolitan Ioann

Reporter: During the past fifty years it has been declared repeatedly that the "Protocols of the Elders of Zion" is a literary falsification.

Ioann: I think this way: There is a saying that the cap burns on the thief. If these Protocols are forged, then what are the Zionists worried about? Of course it is difficult to determine who wrote them, but the program is already in operation.

Reporter: Do you believe in the possibility of a world conspiracy against Russia?

Ioann: It is not just possible, there is one. . . . Zionism is founded not on religious domination but on the Golden Calf, on domination on a global scale.

—From an interview with Metropolitan Ioann of St. Petersburg and Lagoda[113]

In the late 1980s Gorbachev's reform communist regime allowed the reopening of thousands of Orthodox churches, and in 1988 the church celebrated 1,000 years since the conversion of Prince Vladimir with a fanfare unseen since the Great Patriotic War. Today, Patriarch Alexey espouses the church's official position on everything from the Chechen war to economic reforms, and Russian television and print journalists take those views seriously. The church is an important national institution, and Alexey was present at the creation, so to speak, of the new Russia: As a USSR Supreme Soviet deputy he voted in favor of the deletion of article six of the Soviet constitution, thus ending the Communist monopoly on political power; in August 1991 he appealed to the Soviet Army not to shed the blood of their fellow citizens during the aborted coup attempt, probably helping Yeltsin and the democrats to thwart the designs of the revanchists; following the coup, he personally conducted a funeral service for the three defenders of the Russian White House killed during the *putsch,* one of whom was a Jew.[114] More telling of the factional infighting within the church are Alexey's public statements attacking anti-Semitism and particularly his unsuccessful attempt to silence one man—Metropolitan Ioann of St. Petersburg. Before his death in November 1995, he was the most active of the church's Black Hundred hierarchs.[115] A review of Ioann's ideology can tell us much about Black Hundredism in postcommunist Russia, as well as about the evolution of that ideology in the Soviet period, a process that eventually gave life to a new species of nationalism, National Bolshevism.[116]

Ioann's ideology was a variant of "Holy Russia" nationalism that was centered on the nefarious activities of the Jews, modified by a favorable view of Stalin that makes the identification of the Soviet Union with Holy Russia possible. Imperial Russia, according to Ioann, was the Third Rome, having inherited the mantle of imperial rule from the Eternal City and the mandate to preserve the true faith from Byzantium. Eurasia, from the Baltics to the Pacific, is the geographic center of an empire that once was, and can once again be holy if the Russians, blessed by God with special spiritual awareness, choose the path of Orthodox autocracy and *sobornost*. For Ioann *sobornost* meant, above and beyond all else, unity, the "unification of all Russian land around a single spiritual (religious) and political (great power) center, that, after the victory at Kulikovo, by all rights became Moscow." Church and state work together in a "symphony" of power, each undivided in authority, the state acting in a "supraclass" manner to unite the citizenry, the church working to unite all Russia spiritually, though Ioann often blurred the lines between the symphony's sections.

The geopolitical embodiment of Orthodox *sobornost* is empire, which Ioann defined as "great power statehood in the Christian sense," a great power covering vast territories and disparate peoples (under the auspices, to be sure, of a *Staatvolk* and their "higher culture"), ensuring peace and stability for this microcosm of humanity, instituting the City of God on earth. The empire has both spiritual and geopolitical tasks, acting as a beacon for the world while uniting one-sixth of its surface.

Even before the baptism of the Eastern Slavs, Ioann believed that satanic forces worked to thwart God's plan. The Jews, this time in the guise of the Turkic Khazars, who had accepted the faith of the people of the old covenant, attacked the Slavs in the eighth century but were repulsed. God's new chosen people, the bearers of the new covenant, would survive to build his holy empire. After Russia's baptism, the West, infected with pagan rationalism and the power of the Jews, rejected the true faith. The Vatican, along with the *Zhidomasonstvo*, began to work in tandem to destroy Holy Russia, the only barrier to their plans for world domination under the rule of the Antichrist.

All the disasters of Russian history, according to Ioann, were probably rooted in the machinations of the *Zhidomasonstvo*; World War I and the Bolshevik coup were predicted in the *Protocols*. Stalin, to his credit, recognized the power of Russian patriotism and old Russian *sobornost* during the Great Patriotic War. He called off the war on the church and rallied the Russian people to the patriotic cause, consequently restoring the Russian *derzhava* and fulfilling Russia's geopolitical tasks. After his death, however, forces aligned with the Russophobes gained the upper hand and renewed the assault on Holy Russia. They were neutralized to some extent during the Brezhnev era, when the persecution of the church slackened and "patriotic" positions began to float to the surface in Russian literature and the arts. The Russophobes, however, were not yet defeated: Gorbachev led them to ascendancy and completed the ancient task of dismembering Russia, aided by the West, long under the sway of the *Zhidomasonstvo*. Ioann viewed the United States as the locus of the grand conspiracy in recent decades and warned of an American plot to "destroy approximately one hundred million" Russians, as a part of the diabolic plan to depopulate Russia.[117]

The strength of Black Hundredism within the church is evident in the failure of the patriarch to silence Ioann. Even after the patriarch quietly moved to halt publication of Ioann's writings in church publications in January 1993, and his subsequent comment to reporters that the metropolitan did not speak for the church, Ioann continued his public activities, writing articles for nationalist and National Bolshevik newspapers such as *Zavtra* and *Sovetskaya Rossiya*.[118] Moreover, he was supported in print in a declaration signed by five unnamed church bishops.[119] Church-sponsored printing houses continued to spew forth anti-Semitic literature, and antireformers within the church were successful in having Gleb Yakunin defrocked.

If an empire building regime does come to power in postcommunist Russia, it will likely find allies within the institutional church. Despite Ioann's monarchism, with all the supposed ties to feudalism that implies, he was quite prepared to accept something that was both less and more than any traditional reactionary could. He appeared ready to accept something less than an Orthodox autocrat as ruler of Russia—an atheist tyrant who had murdered millions of Russians would do—as long as the institutional church flourished. He was actually nostalgic for something more than Holy Russia, namely, her successor, that great power that dominated Eurasia from Germany to China, that launched men into space and boasted of a military might second to none. He would buy the great power vision of the *gosudarstvenniki* if it meant the restoration of the "empire." Ioann was a man whose religion was absorbed within an ideology, for his ideology merged the spiritual and the temporal. The totalitarian state *was* Russia in his eyes, and Russia, reduced to an abstraction, his god. He seemed to care nothing for the people themselves or for the restoration of agricultural society or a decentralized regime that was the dream of the truly conservative early Slavophiles. His anti-Semitism went beyond any distorted religious basis as well. For him the Jew was a political plotter, a geopolitical strategist, not the heir of the Pharisees. True, he did not indulge in "scientific" racism, but he probably would have accepted much of what "scientific" racists had to say.

The Fate of Christian Democracy

Christian democracy, which appeared to have (and may yet have) a bright future in Russia, was strangled by circumstances. Nevertheless, in the form of the RCDM, what remains of it appears to be moving toward an alliance with reform nationalist trends. Aksyuchits's support for Aleksandr Lebed in the 1996 presidential election and his association with Russian First Deputy Premier Boris Nemtsov may be indicative of this (see chapter 9)—something that may give it a new lease on life, presenting the possibility of a sane alternative to Russia's present course.

Viktor Aksyuchits may have taken the *gosudarstvennik* path, but it was a choice he made with his eyes open: He appears to view the *gosudartsvo* as a vessel for Russian society, not as the abstract expression of the national will or the mere aggregation of dictator, institutional church, army, and bureaucracy.[120] His view of Russia's mission differs from that of the Black Hundreds both in its means (Russia should heal herself first of all) and its aims (Russia as exemplar of the faith, not ruler of the world). His nationalism is communalist, not collectivist, and he, like Solzhenitsyn, the intellectual mentor of all those who call themselves Christian democrats in postcommunist Russia, appears to understand the implications of the modern technological revolution, something that makes the reconstitution by the Russian *Staatvolk* of a multinational commonwealth problematic, at best. In this day and age, salvaging Orthodox *sobornost* from the web of the integrated state, whether dictatorship or parliamentary democracy, will be no small task. For Aksyuchits, it appears that Christian democracy is a means, not an end. After stabilizing the Russian polity via the Erhard model, the daunting task of reconstituting *sobornost* will have only begun. The implications of globalization for Russia—especially, for Aksyuchits, in the form of the cultural invasion (the community might lose its identity, especially as consumerism erodes residual Orthodoxy)—also explains the middling *gosudarstvennik* path he has taken.

The Christian's Dilemma

Both Viktor Aksyuchits and Gleb Yakunin appear to be devout Christians who, by a strange turn in God's plan, have found themselves on opposites sides of the barricades. Neither appears to have been too generous in his assessment of the other, but such are the failings of fragile humans. From Father Gleb's point of view, he is no doubt fighting the forces of "communo-fascism" that wish to once more subvert the holy church and use it for their own aims, killing a few million unfortunates along the way to the millennium. He can be criticized for appearing to put politics first, working foremost to further the aims of the Left, which may include the abandonment of Russians in the "near abroad," free reign for a licentious society wherein pornography flourishes under the banner of freedom of speech, and consumerism, like a dry rot, hollows out the souls of the people. He may be excused for this if he views the communo-fascists as the more immediate threat. The temptation for such men of the cloth is that of confusing the democrats' internationalist agenda with Christianity, for the Christian has duties to his country and people as much as other men.

The views of Christian nationalists who share Aksyuchits's political posture can best be summarized as those of the authors of two articles appearing a few years ago in *Literaturnaya Rossiya*. One stressed tolerance: Orthodoxy would provide Russia "with a moral climate" that will facilitate "humanitarianism, mercy, and human understanding." Orthodoxy, therefore, does not "represent a threat" to the religious freedom of "believers of any religion."[121] The other's theme was nationalism and patriotism, asserting that Russians had a duty to protect their countrymen in the "near abroad" and that the Russian Federation was not necessarily synonymous with Russia: "We are prepared to respect the wishes of those wanting to break up the historical Union," the anonymous patriot wrote, "[but] we cannot, we don't have the right to, allow our own destruction."[122] At a time when their country is collapsing around them and their countrymen in the near abroad under the gun, it is not surprising that such nationalists have rallied around the institutional church as symbol of unity but have failed to purge it of the poison of Sergeyism. The temptation for these Christians is that of Sergeyism via the paths of the *gosudarstvenniki* or the Black Hundreds.

Christians should always be cognizant of such temptations. We are believers because we believe Christianity to be true, not because it has a utilitarian purpose for either the Left or the Right. For the Christian nationalist, the lure is "cultural Christianity," a Christianity that

> has got so mixed up with a whole range of cultural factors that it is no longer possible to extract it in a pure form. Christianity is German [or Russian] culture. Christianity is middle class culture. Christianity is respect for authority. Christianity is for law and order. Christianity is on the side of "positive" social groups in their struggle against anarchy. It is precisely this kind of view which led to very many Christians accepting the National Socialist movement as a religious renewal.[123]

Christian activist Sergei Lezov, pondering the fate of the Christian faith in a century that saw institutional churches capitulate to Nazism in Germany and communism in the Soviet Union, has proposed a new theology, a theology of "pluralism," to ameliorate the corrosive effects of the ideologization of faith.[124] Most Christians would adamantly disagree with some of Lezov's proposals, for example, that Christians should not accept without doubt even Church dogmas about Jesus Christ, which I take to mean even the question of our Lord's divinity. If Lezov's pluralism is merely another kind of relativism, then he has failed to recognize the core of the modern spiritual problem, "philosophical" Christianity being no less dangerous than the "cultural" variety. Still, he has left for believers a nugget of wisdom, something that may be enough to turn them away from the temptations that we have seen all too many Christians succumb to.

"If faith is agreement with the truth of a series of propositions then it is incompatible with doubt, which implies a serious attitude to others' views," wrote Lezov in his article, "The National Idea and Christianity."

> But if, adopting the formula of Paul Tillich, we define faith as the state of being grasped by my ultimate concern, that is to say we understand faith as a way of existence, then doubt becomes an indispensable element of this faith. If faith as absolute surrender ("state of being grasped") is associated with risk . . . then, as Tillich says, "the doubt of a believer is the doubt of a man gripped by an ultimate aspiration with a concrete content." . . . Faith as absolute surrender includes courage—and therefore doubt—in itself. Doubt is a structural element of faith, not a mental state.[125]

For Lezov, such a faith breaks the Christian out of the ideological "world of unbroken assertions," opening to him vistas of a life in Christ.

One can easily criticize Lezov's formula. A life in imitation of Christ must be predicated on the acceptance of at least one assertion: Either Jesus was the Son of God or he wasn't. If, however, we mean doubt about *oneself*, then the notion of doubt as an element of faith has great value—not doubt of Christ, but of our own ability as finite and flawed creatures to apply Christianity, to act correctly as Christians, in every circumstance we face on this earth—can pull us back away from the temptation of a world of "unbroken assertions." The acceptance of such a world risks the transformation of faith into ideology. In such circumstances, "occurs here a diminishing of God that is far from devout, bringing Him down to the level of an idol." If we imagine God's will and the geopolitical concerns of Holy Russia/Soviet Union as consistently coterminous, then we have fallen into the trap. Such a view ignores the truth of tragedy in our lives in this fallen world: Good men, and good Christians, can sometimes fight on opposing sides.

Notes

1. See Walter Kirchner, *History of Russia* (New York: Barnes & Noble, 1976); John Paxton, *Companion to Russian History* (New York: Facts on File, 1983); and Nicholas Riasanovsky, *A History of Russia*, 5th ed. (Oxford: Oxford University Press, 1993) for historical references.

2. The Roman church's ritual was already diverging from that of the Eastern church before the Great Schism in 1054.

3. Riasanovsky, *History of Russia*, 54.

4. Hilarion of Kiev, "A Word on Law and Grace" (Slovo o zakonye i blagodaty), in *Russkaya Idyeya* (The Russian idea), ed. Mikhail Maslin (Moscow: Respublika, 1992), 29.

5. Riasanovsky, *History of Russia*, 63.

6. "The Tale of the Ravage of Ryzan by Batu"; cited in ibid., 67.

7. Ibid., 63.

8. Edward E. Ericson, *Solzhenitsyn and the Modern World* (Washington, D.C.: Regnery Gateway, 1993), 345–46.

9. All religions, not simply Orthodoxy, seem to be attracting new adherents, and anyone who has traveled in Russia in the past few years will probably have noticed the presence of missionaries, particularly Protestants from the United States, in towns and cities large and small. This often well-financed foreign proselytizing distresses many Orthodox Christians, who tend to see it as part and parcel of foreign interference in their country. One often hears Russians comment on the "colonizing" of Russia by foreigners through both economic and religious intrusion. In an open letter to the Patriarch, one Christian nationalist activist warned him of "forces hostile to Russia" who had been "conducting a mass campaign to sway the population in the spirit of Catholicism, Protestantism, and occultism." Open Letter from V. V. Selivanov to the Patriarch. *Nezavisimaya Gazeta*, 5 August 1992.

10. For more on Russian Christianity Democracy, see Richard Sakwa, "Christian Democracy in Russia," *Keston Journal: Religion, State and Society* 20, no. 2 (1992): 135–200; and, in the same issue, Roanne Thomas Edwards, "Russian Christian Democracy from a Regional Perspective: The Case of St. Petersburg," 201–11.

11. Sakwa, "Christian Democracy in Russia," 135.

12. Ibid., 136.

13. Ibid.

14. Ibid.

15. Ibid.

16. The Duma, an elected parliament, was one of the results of the 1905 revolution.

17. Sakwa, "Christian Democracy in Russia," 137.

18. Ibid.

19. Ibid.

20. Ibid., 138.

21. Nikolay Berdyayev in particular took the "Russian" view of the prob-

lem, claiming at one point that "Schism" had become "a characteristic phenomenon of Russian life" after the schism in the Russian Church in the seventeenth century. Berdyayev believed this tendency to schism derived from the "dogmatic" nature of Russian religious belief, and was easily transferred to secular politics. See Berdyayev's *The Origin of Russian Communism* (Ann Arbor: The University of Michigan Press, 1993), 12.

22. Sakwa, "Christian Democracy in Russia," 138.

23. Ibid.

24. Most observers, however, including Sakwa, are skeptical of party membership claims. The new political parties tend to be loosely knit bodies in any event, and few appear to keep, or to be interested in keeping, accurate membership records. This is one of the factors that makes gauging the strength or weakness of any political movement so difficult; since postcommunist Russia has been operating in an ideological vacuum, opinions and alliances are changing constantly.

25. Many of the same people would later work to restrict the activities of Western Protestant evangelists in Russia, seeking to protect the Orthodox Church, still organizationally weak and underfinanced. Some would go further and claim that the evangelicals (and Catholic missionaries as well) were part of an anti-Russian conspiracy. The moves to, in effect, give the Orthodox Church a privileged status disturbed some Orthodox activists (such as Gleb Yakunin) who dreaded the prospect of the church once again becoming an arm of the state. Others, such as Aksyuchits, would support the move, first made in 1992, to force all foreign evangelists to register with the authorities (registration could be refused, of course), citing the danger of the spread of "cults" as well as the desirability of giving the national church an opportunity to revive itself. This is not to say that Aksyuchits has not been concerned with the past subjugation of the church by the state, merely that he views protective measures as necessary. For more on Aksyuchits' sharp criticism of the church's past worldliness, see especially his book *The Rulers of the Darkness of This World* (Miropraviteli tmy veka sego) (Moscow: Vybor, 1994). Such changes to the Russian Federation laws were first proposed by the Russian Supreme Soviet's Committee on Freedom of Conscience, headed by Christian nationalist activist Vyacheslav Polosin. For a criticism of Polosin and the proposed restrictions (later passed by the Supreme Soviet), see "Who Is Afraid of a Man with the Gospels?" (Kto boitsya cheloveka s Evangeliyem?), *Izvestiya*, 15 July 1993. Nevertheless, the debate over the status of the church has continued.

26. Sakwa, "Christian Democracy in Russia," 139.

27. The characterization of the Brezhnev years as the "period of stagnation" during the Gorbachev era became a sort of shorthand describing all that was wrong with the Soviet regime.

28. For more on the church under the communists as it relates to our discussion, see Riasanovsky, *History of Russia*, 587–588; Walter Laqueur, *Black Hundred: the Rise of the Extreme Right in Russia* (New York: HarperCollins, 1993), 222–44; and John Dunlop, *The Faces of Contemporary Russian Nationalism* (Princeton: Princeton University Press, 1983), 3–28.

29. Walter Laqueur, *Black Hundred*, 224.

30. Riasanovsky, *History of Russia*, 588.

31. John Dunlop, *Faces of Contemporary Russian Nationalism*, 19.

32. Cited in Laqueur, *Black Hundred*, 232.

33. Ludmilla Alexeyeva, *Soviet Dissent: Contemporary Movements for National, Religious, and Human Rights*, trans. Carol Pearce and John Glad (Middletown, Conn.: Wesleyan University Press, 1987), 248.

34. See Alexeyeva, *Soviet Dissent*, 249; and Dunlop, *Faces of Contemporary Russian Nationalism*, 180–181. Dunlop describes the restrictions as having "deprived" the parish priest of "any real control over the life of the local parish" through the institution of new twenty member controlling councils that had to be approved by the authorities. It was common for unbelievers to serve on such councils.

35. *Samizdat* "self-publishing" refers to informal and unapproved manuscripts circulated by hand in order to avoid censorship.

36. Dunlop discusses the content and importance of these journals at length in *Faces of Contemporary Russian Nationalism*.

37. Alexeyeva, *Soviet Dissent*, 259.

38. Ibid., 291.

39. Cited in Dunlop, *Faces of Contemporary Russian Nationalism*, 45. Ogordnikov too had converted after his own spiritual-philosophical journey from Marxism through "left radicalism, hippyism, [and] youth counterculture" in the early 1970s. See Ibid., 55.

40. See ibid., 246–54. See also his *The New Russian Revolutionaries* (Norland, 1976) for more on VSKhSON.

41. Dunlop, *Faces of Contemporary Rusian Nationalism*, 45.

42. One might include concern for the welfare of Russians in the former Soviet republics and, for some at least, the revival of the union and Russia as *derzhava*, or great power, as elements in a Christian nationalist platform. Many Christian nationalists of the time tended to go beyond Osipov's conservationist and preservationist program to a broader environmentalism.

43. Cited in Dunlop, *Faces of Contemporary Russian Nationalism*, 45.

44. Cited in Alexeyeva, *Soviet Dissent*, 444–445.

45. Ibid., 445–446.

46. Ibid., 445.

47. Cited in John Dunlop, *The Rise of Russia and the Fall of the Soviet Empire* (Princeton: Princeton University Press, 1993), 93.

48. Ibid., 94.

49. Ibid.

50. Ibid.

51. Ibid., 93.

52. Biographical material on Aksyuchits is drawn from Sakwa, "Christian Democracy in Russia," 163, n14, and *Russian Politicians from A to Z* (Rossiyskiye politiki ot A do Ya) (Moscow: Panorama, 1996), 1: 6–7.

53. Sakwa, "Christian Democracy in Russia," 163.

54. Ibid., 138.

55. Aksyuchits has described himself as a constitutional monarchist, occupying a sort of middle ground between the two. See, for instance, the biographical sketch in his book, *The Rulers of the Darkness of This World*.

56. The Land Assemblies were called occasionally by the Muscovite czars to deal with matters of particular importance. The assemblies included clergy, gentry, aristocracy, and even peasants and burghers on occasion. The first assembly was called by Ivan IV in 1549. In 1613, a Land Assembly convened to pick a new czar, Michael Romanov. Peter the Great discontinued the custom of calling Land Assemblies. See John Paxton, *Companion to Russian History*, 447 for more on the Land Assemblies. Since Aksyuchits believes that the Bolshevik Revolution represented a break in Russia's historical development, he certainly stood behind the inclusion of a call for a *Zemsky Sobor* in the RCDM program.

57. "Fundamental Principles of the Political Program of the RCDM," *Keston Journal* 20, no. 2 (1992): 180.

58. Translations of the RCDM's initial programmatic documents are included in the *Keston Journal* issue cited in the preceding note.

59. "Fundamental Principles," 184–85.

60. See particularly calls for the state to take over the restoration of monasteries and churches, "Fundamental Principles," 181.

61. Cited in Dunlop, *Rise of Russia*, 93.

62. From an interview with Aksyuchits, "Fundamental Principles," 194.

63. Aksyuchits himself "established a radio station in the White House, and helped to convince a key unit of the Tamansky division to turn its tanks round to defend the building." Sakwa, "Christian Democracy in Russia," 151.

64. Dunlop, *Rise of Russia*, 93.

65. Aksyuchits interview, "Fundamental Principles," 194.

66. Tatyana Glushkova, "Na Ruinax Imperskogo Soznaniya" [On the Ruins of the Imperial Consciousness], *Zavtra* 32 (August 1995): 1, 7. Glushkova goes on to chastise those on the Russian Right who supported the declaration of sovereignty and attack the secular nationalists for forgetting Orthodoxy, the heart of the Russian Idea.

67. Viktor Aksyuchits, "Natsionalnoye I Ideologicheskoye" [The National and the Ideological], *Put* 1 (January, 1991): 2.

68. One should bear in mind that Aksyuchits did not—and does not—rule out the possibility of some republics' seeking independence from any renewed Union. In fact, at the time he wrote "The National and the Ideological," he also formed a faction within the Russian Supreme Soviet called Russian Union, after Aleksandr Solzhenitsyn's proposals to unite the three Slavic republics with Kazakhstan. See the announcement of the faction's formation in the same issue of *Put* cited above.

69. See Sakwa, "Christian Democracy in Russia," 152. Aksyuchits himself attacked the left intelligentsia in a polemic published in the nationalist journal *Moskva* (4 April 1994): 77–92, "Orden Russkoy Intelligentsii" [The order of the Russian intelligentsia].

70. Sakwa, "Christian Democracy in Russia," 151.

71. See the Aksyuchits interview in *Moskovskiye Novosti*, 16 August 1992, 11.

72. In the *Moskovskiye Novosti* interview, Aksyuchits expressed his hope that economic imperatives and social realities, particularly the presence of large Russian populations, would compel many of the former republics to "propose a conception of gradual state reunification, in order to lead to integration first in economics and culture, and then in the political sphere."

73. Aksyuchits was named a political adviser to Russian First Deputy Premier Boris Nemtsov in spring 1997 (*Segodnya*, 16 May 1997), underscoring the potential for "reform nationalism" to absorb some forms of Christian nationalism and broaden its appeal. See chapter 9 for more on Lebed, Nemtsov, and reform nationalism.

74. Critics bitterly called the program "shock without therapy."

75. The reverse face of "shock therapy" was the commercialization of the country, often termed by critics the "Snickersization" of Russia.

76. The Time of Troubles (1598–1613) began with the death of Boris Godunov and lasted until the ascension of the Romanov dynasty, when a *Zemsky Sobor* elected Michael Romanov Czar. During the interim period, five pretenders claimed the Russian throne, Russia was invaded by the Swedes and the Poles, and there was widespread unrest in the hinterlands. See Paxton, *Companion to Russian History*, 395.

77. Critics of the shock therapy program liked to point out that many of today's free market economists and democratic politicians had only a few short years earlier been high-ranking communists, while many of their opponents were either not party members or had only been rank-and-file members or low-level functionaries, which one may extrapolate further into a variation of a particular revisionist view of party history, the "two parties thesis" that is taken up in the next chapter. Aksyuchits developed the idea of the old radicals being transformed—figuratively—into the new democrats via a mutation in the ideology of "nonbeing" from Marxism to "demo-bolshevism" in his book *Ideokratiya V Rossii* (Ideocracy in Russia) (Moscow: Vybor, 1995). The driving goal of all ideology, as Aksyuchits sees it, is to struggle against God. Like Dostoevsky, he does not really take atheists at their word.

78. *Sovetskaya Rossiya*, 9 April 1994.

79. Ibid.

80. See *Pravda*, 16 October 1992.

81. *Nezavisimaya Gazeta*, 23 October 1992. Aksyuchits's opinion of the West's role in Russia's degradation has not changed, as evidenced by a lecture given by him (attended by the author) at the Russian-American University in Moscow in September 1996.

82. As early as November 1991, after Aksyuchits's departure from DR, the RCDM had begun to fall apart. Only the Tsaritsyn local followed him out of DR, the other locals going their own way. It is unclear if the locals have remained aligned with DR or its epigones or have remained independent. In any case, Sakwa points out that their failure to follow Aksyuchits out of DR may have had little to do with policy matters: DR was simply the best organized umbrella organization at the time, and the locals may not have wished to give up their connections with such a center of influence. Whether the RCDM's old

activists remain potential followers for Aksyuchits or not, their numbers do represent a pool of potential Christian Democratic activists. Yakunin established the Russian Christian Democratic Union together with Vitaliy Savitskiy in early 1992, but the organization's influence appears not to extend beyond Saint Petersburg, and Yakunin immersed himself in his role as Russian Duma deputy. See Sakwa, "Christian Democracy in Russia," 153–54.

83. Vladimir Karpets, "Idyeya Rossii ili 'Russkaya Idyeya'?" ("An idea of Russia or the Russian idea?"), *Put* 1 (January 1991): 7.

84. The Black Hundreds were legendary Russian warrior monks, who, garbed in their black cassocks, fought against the infidel.

85. Long-time Yeltsin crony Mikhail Poltoranin, who served in the first postcommunist state Duma as a committee chairman from the "Russia's Choice" faction, led by liberal former prime minister Yegor Gaydar, has referred to "Zion" "gnawing Russia to the bone." Poltoranin further claimed that the "growing audacity of pro-Zionist and pro-Israel circles in Russia is such that they are pursuing a systematic campaign against the Russians that could result in horrible massacres." Poltoranin has clearly imbibed, perhaps become intoxicated with, a Black Hundredish ideology. Interview with Poltoranin, *Al-Ra'y*, 29 March 1994.

86. See particularly Robert Nisbet's *The Quest for Community*, for more on the recurrence of such themes. James Burnham's *The Managerial Revolution* described the development of the centralized state and economy, Walker Conner's "integrated state," in the twentieth century.

87. In his *A History of Christianity* (New York: Atheneum, 1976), Paul Johnson observed that "certainly, mankind without Christianity conjures up a dismal prospect. The record of mankind *with* Christianity is daunting enough. . . . The dynamism it has unleashed has brought massacre and torture, intolerance and destructive pride on a huge scale, for there is a cruel and pitiless nature in man which is sometimes impervious to Christian restraints and encouragements. But without these restraints, bereft of these encouragements, how much more horrific the history of these last 2,000 years must have been!" Christianity, notes Mr. Johnson, "supplies hope," and has "cag[ed] the beast" on occasion, acting as a "civilizing agent." "In the last generation, with public Christianity in headlong retreat, we have caught our first, distant view of a de-Christianized world, and it is not encouraging" (517).

88. Stolypin was assassinated by a Socialist Revolutionary terrorist in 1911. Robert K. Massie in his *Nicholas and Alexandra* described Stolypin as "direct, outspoken, brimming with impassioned patriotism and overwhelming in his physical energy." He was "a passionate monarchist" who nonetheless "sensed" that the monarchy would survive only "if the government and the structure of society itself could adapt to the times." Robert K. Massie, *Nicholas and Alexandra* (New York: Antheneum, 1967), 215.

89. I have borrowed the term "mechanical Christianity" from Paul Johnson. He uses it frequently to describe a Christianity that is spiritually emasculated by a rigid emphasis on ceremony in his book *A History of Christianity*. The Orthodox Church in Russia has often been criticized for such an emphasis on

liturgical exactness over spiritual content, particularly with reference to the institutional church's subjugation to the state.

90. Andrzej Walicki, *The Slavophile Controversy* (Notre Dame, Ind.: Notre Dame Press, 1989), 505. A new edition of Danilevskiy's book, *Russia and Europe*, appeared in 1995, published by St. Petersburg University.

91. Walter Laqueur, *Black Hundred*, 38.

92. "Anti-Semitism" represents yet another difficult concept to pin down. The term has become so loosely tossed about that one may be excused for thinking that practically everyone, from a neo-Nazi to a mere critic of Israel, is an "anti-Semite." Here we use the term in the context of our discussion of conspiritalogy—an "anti-Semite" is someone ideologically committed to seeing the Jews as the focus of evil in human history. His worldview revolves around this single concept, seeing all other trends as secondary to the main current of historical development. Ordinary Jew haters are, of course, attracted to the rhetoric of the anti-Semite, but it is the rhetorician himself who concerns us here.

93. See particularly Hannah Arendt, *The Origins of Totalitarianism* (New York: Harcourt Brace & Company, 1975), Part 1, 11–120.

94. The version of the *Protocols* referred to throughout this study was in fact published in the nationalist journal *Molodaya Gvardiya* (10 October 1993). The *Protocols* have been reprinted and commented on countless times in the nationalist press.

95. Laqueur, *Black Hundred*, 32.

96. Ibid., 33.

97. Ibid.

98. Ibid., 35.

99. Hannah Arendt, *Origins of Totalitarianism*, 241. Arendt names the Pan-Slavist Konstantin Pobedonostsev, reactionary procurator of the Holy Synod of the Russian Orthodox Church and political adviser to Czars Aleksandr III and Nicholas II, as the initiator and sponsor of the forgery. He served until 1907.

100. Ibid.

101. Laqueur, *Black Hundred*, 36.

102. For more on the Black Hundreds, see Stephen Carter, *Russian Nationalism: Yesterday, Today, Tomorrow* (New York: St. Martin's Press, 1990), 29–42; F. L. Carston, *The Rise of Fascism* (Los Angeles: The University of California Press, 1982), 41–44; and Laqueur, *Black Hundred*, 16–28, 45–57.

103. But they tended not to favor Stolypin's reforms since they were aimed at breaking up the peasant communes; see Laqueur, *Black Hundred*, 25.

104. "Count Witte, the former Prime Minister, wrote in his memoirs that the Union [the Black Hundreds] was a body made up of plain thieves and hooligans: 'The aims of the Black Hundred are usually selfish and of the lowest character. Their stomachs and pockets dictate their aspirations. They are typical murderers from the dark alleys.' " Cited in ibid., 20.

105. The Black Hundreds took part in some seven hundred pogroms in the turbulent 1905–6 period. See ibid., 21.

106. The Black Hundreds may have been influenced by the writings of one Mikhail Menshikov, who posed "the race problem" as the most pressing issue for Russia. Menshikov appears to have derived his theories from the proto-scientific racists of the turn of the century, particularly Houston Stewart Chamberlain. See ibid., 17.
107. Ibid., 51.
108. Carter, *Russian Nationalism*, 30–31.
109. Ibid., 31.
110. Laqueur, *Black Hundred*, 17.
111. *Pamyat* 1 (January 1995): 6. This newspaper is published by Vasilyev's organization.
112. See *Chernaya Sotnya* 11 (1994), for an article on ritual murder in Russia.
113. *Nezavisimaya Gazeta*, 16 April 1993.
114. See John Arnold, "Patriarch Alexei: a Personal Impression," *Keston Journal*, 20, 2 (1992): 238–39.
115. The Patriarch told *Moskovskiye Novosti*, "The Russian Orthodox Church is free of racial prejudice. To whom is it not clear that to incite inter-ethnic discord in our time is madness?" Cited in John Dunlop, "The Growth of Fascist Tendencies in the Russian Orthodox Church," a paper delivered at a Moscow international forum on the Church in Russia held on 20–22 January 1995. Citations from this paper, and the notes taken in a question and answer session at the conference, will be henceforth attributed to Dunlop, "Church."
116. The synopsis of Ioann's views offered here is based on an article by the Metropolitan, "Soyuz Nerushimiy" (The indestructible union) which appeared in *Zavtra* 30 (August 1994), and a book, *Rus Sobornaya* (roughly, Sobornost Russia) which was serialized in the nationalist literary journal *Nash Sovremennik* in 1994 and 1995. See particularly 8–12 (1994). All quotations are from those sources.
117. Cited in Dunlop, "Church," 2.
118. Dunlop, "Church," 3–4.
119. Dunlop, "Church." Conference participant Zoya Krakhmalnikova mentioned the support for Ioann by bishops Melchisedic, Tikhon, Pitrim, and Gedeon—the identity of the other bishop is not known.
120. See especially his *The Rulers of the Darkness of This World* for more on Aksyuchits's view of the state.
121. Vladimir Belyayev, *Literaturnaya Rossiya*, 6 December 1992.
122. "Raspad SSSR I Russkiy Vopros" ("The collapse of the USSR and the Russian question"), *Literaturnaya Rossiya*, 21 February 1992.
123. Robert Ericksen cited in Sergei Lezov, "The National Idea and Christianity," *Keston Journal* 20, 1, (1992): 39.
124. Sergei Lezov, "The National Idea and Christianity."
125. Ibid.

5

National Bolshevism and the Two Parties

Internationalism, as Lenin understood it, is based on a careful and sensitive relationship to one's culture, mores, and traditions. Trotskyite internationalism, on the other hand, is based on the elimination of national distinctions and the total liquidation of nations in general.

—*Veche*[1]

Via Bolshevism, Djugashvili [Stalin] joined the Russian nation.

—Robert C. Tucker[2]

It is impossible to be both a Communist and a Russian.

—Aleksandr Solzhenitsyn[3]

Internationalist revolutionaries have invariably been forced to fall back on the powerful national bond to prop up their regimes. In Russia, postrevolutionary "Red patriotism" was expropriated by Stalin to fight his political battle with Trotsky and to inspire the Russian masses during the Great Patriotic War. National Bolshevism thus attempts to reconcile the two "streams" of Russian national greatness, "white" and "red," merging them into a "single stream" mythomoteur that proclaims Soviet collectivism the fulfillment of Orthodox sobornost. National Bolshevism, evolving from Black Hundredism and Stalinism, has often manifested itself as a uniquely Russian fascism, a modernist ideology that has channeled the human urge for community into the collectivist, statist project.

Stranger words may never have been heard during this or any other campaign for public office.[4] Gennadiy Zyuganov, Russian Communist Party (CPRF, Communist Party of the Russian Feder-

145

ation) leader and candidate for the state Duma, had a message for voters who were still clinging to the poetic image of the Fatherland as
Holy Russia: "The first communist was Jesus Christ," intoned the
CPRF chairman, "because he wanted justice in this earthly life and
sacrificed his life on the altar of lawlessness, malice and treachery in
order to atone for other people's sins. I support this idea and think it
should be fully developed." To drive his point home, Zyuganov made
election-year pilgrimages to Kulikovo, where Dmitriy Donskoy,
blessed by St. Sergey of Radonezh, defeated the heathen Tartars in the
fourteenth century, and to Borodino, where, during the first Great Patriotic War, the forces of Holy Russia fought the army of the Antichrist,
Napoleon, to a standstill on an autumn day in 1812.[5]

However dubious Zyuganov's theology may have been, he was not
very subtle about tying communism to Russian history in a way that
has had some currency among Russians for a long time, in fact since
shortly after the October 1917 Bolshevik coup. Zyuganov, like many
other Russians, subscribes to what is known as the "single stream"
interpretation of Russian history, a version of the Russian past that
merges the victory at Kulikovo and the messianism of the first Great
Patriotic War with the long march to Berlin during the Second, the
Russian empire with the Soviet Union, and Peter the Great's legacy
with that of Stalin. The October Revolution did not represent a sharp
break with the past, according to Zyuganov's version of the single
stream interpretation but rather a metamorphosis of the Russian *derzhava*. The empire as such no longer served the interests of the *narod*—
the Russian nation—and, like a snake shedding an old skin, the nation
shook off the old czarist institutions, not that Russia should die or her
mission go unfulfilled, but that she might have new life in order to
fulfill a destiny whose engine is the historical dialectic. The legacy of
the nineteenth century westernizers and Slavophiles, the radical populists and the *pochvenniki*, the nationalist "men of the soil," is thus reconciled as the two currents merge in a single stream of national consciousness. Communism is not the negation of Christianity but its
modern twin, shorn of the supernatural element that was no longer
tenable in a scientifically managed society—the communism that
Lenin envisioned would be the fulfillment of Orthodoxy. Lenin and
Khomyakov were both great Russian prophets, Pushkin and Gorky the
bards of the nation, Peter and Stalin her great reformers and *gosudarstvenniki*. Zyuganov, by splicing communist limbs onto the Russian
body, is merely preparing the Fatherland for the next round of a game
that had its origins both without and within the Soviet Union, a game
whose rules were codified by Stalin.

Origins of National Bolshevism

The powerful urge to particularism has pulled more than one universalist revolution off its predicted track. Utopian revolutionaries of the Left, once ensconced in the belly of the state, inevitably make the same discovery that every one of their kind has made before: "Government or the principle of ordered rule is the antithesis of revolution."[6] Moreover, historical continuity always tends to reassert itself "because a revolution is made within certain material and environmental constraints by men who have been politically socialized within specific national conditions."[7] The new state must function in a more or less orderly manner and the anarchists must be restrained. The new regime usually finds its bureaucracy manned by many of the same people the radicals had hoped to eradicate. Geopolitical and economic factors, not often subject to the whims of ideology, assert themselves, and the new regime, like the old, must formulate a foreign policy, that is, recognize itself as a separate entity with definable, particular state interests that are often in opposition to other states. Over time, the regime must justify itself and all of its topsy-turvy shifts in policy, reconciling the old with the new in an often uneasy accord. Thus the French celebrate both the revolution that murdered a Bourbon monarch and the achievements of the French empire under the Bourbons, both a revolution made in the name of egalitarian democracy and the emperor whose armies conquered Europe in the name of France while fighting under the revolutionary banner of Liberty, Equality, and Fraternity. Time and again, leftist revolutionaries have turned to the nation to purchase their own legitimacy, for few men outside radical cafe society will long tolerate the negation of the tribe they belong to. Revolutions must mobilize the masses and internationalism has failed to be attractive to the people in whose name revolution has been made. More telling, perhaps, is the tendency for old revolutionaries to become sincere nationalists themselves as the imperatives of foreign statecraft, with all of its inherent friction with the "other," make them more aware of themselves as representatives of a *Staatvolk* who dominate a particular polity. When this transformation of consciousness takes place, the once leftist regime takes a rightward turn, often finding that it has new allies in the guise of old enemies.

A Change of Landmarks

Again, as in the days of the October Revolution, one suffers from being a Russian; one suffers because Bolshevism, like leprosy, is

eating up the body of Russia. What can we call this process by
which the Russian emigration is afflicted, except Bolshevization?

—Fedotov, *Nash Pozor* (Our shame)[8]

The Bolsheviks had expected the October Revolution to be the spark
that would ignite a revolution in Europe and then the world. The party's leaders envisioned the eventual establishment of a world federation of socialist states. Like Marx, they believed that the proletariat had
no nation of its own, that class determined consciousness, and that
economics ruled the heart and soul of mankind. The revolution, they
thought, must be a worldwide one in order to succeed. It didn't happen. The revolution in Germany was aborted. Europe's proletariat did
not rise up to destroy the capitalist national order. The Bolshevik
leadership, dominated by a hodgepodge of non-Russians, the most
conspicuous among them being Jews and Latvians, led by a de-nation-
alized Russian, had expected the proletarian internationalist consciousness to spread like a virus among the workers of Europe—Russia serving the purposes of history as the carrier of the internationalist bug.
Soviet Russia stood alone, a Bolshevik island in the capitalist sea. Particularist imperatives soon began to assert themselves: Socialism would
stand or fall in Russia. Radical economic measures in the form of War
Communism had been made during the Civil War period, but they
had proved disastrous. Production collapsed, the cities were starving,
the countryside ravaged by the war. In 1921 the New Economic Policy
(NEP) was proclaimed. Capitalist production measures were adopted,
small-scale private ownership tolerated, the Red Terror curtailed. Russian émigrés had reason to be hopeful. More than a million people had
left Russia after the October Revolution. In 1926, the League of Nations
estimated that 1.16 million had emigrated after the revolution, though
Lenin thought there had been as many as 2 million.[9] All classes and
professions were represented in the emigration, though former White
officers and the intelligentsia were the most prominent among them.
In 1920, Soviet Russia was invaded by Poland and old national animos-
ities were stirred up. E. A. Efimovskiy, editor of an émigré newspaper
based in Prague, called for the Russian emigration to rally to the "Russian" cause. Efimovskiy asserted that the Bolsheviks, by resisting the
Polish incursion, were de facto defending the national interests of Russia. Efimovskiy saw the Polish action as the first move by Europe
against Russia, the West's hostility for Russia being a given among
many nationalists. "In this conflict," Efimovskiy opined, "we will be
on the side of Soviet Russia. Not because it is Soviet but because it is
Russian."[10]

The trend was nothing new in itself: Many former czarist officers, disenchanted with the corruption and incompetence of the old regime, had served with the Reds during the Civil War, sensing that the imperatives of the state would eventually consume Bolshevism. Indeed, the Bolshevik forces would soon invade breakaway national republics, confirming the predictions of the *gosudarstvenniki* who had foreseen the rebirth of a great and indivisible Russia in a new, dynamic Soviet guise. British scholar Stephen Carter has noted that signs of a "gradual merger" of Bolshevism with "the more traditional Russian 'statism' " of the *gosudartsvenniki* had been evident for some time, with nationalists making distinctions between "Bolshevism" and "Communism." The writer Ivan Bunin reported overhearing a conversation among Red Army troops in 1919 that Carter summarized as follows: "Everything evil comes from the Jews, they are all Communists, but the Bolsheviks are all Russians."[11] The Bolshevik coup could not have succeeded without the cooperation of the common people, whether in the form of mass desertions, land seizures, or striking workers, but the Russian masses were keenly aware of the divide between them and the largely non-Russian leadership of the Bolshevik Party. They had their own agenda. In the Russian mind, the Jew Trotsky was identified with the leftist, internationalist, impulse they called "communism," whereas the Russian Lenin had brought down the old regime in the interests of a parochial "Bolshevik" social justice.[12]

Even before the NEP was announced, Lenin was veering away from Marxist orthodoxy. A full year before the introduction of the new policy, he wrote the pamphlet *Left Wing Communism: An Infantile Disorder*, "which urged upon Communists the necessity for intelligent compromise with their national political conditions." German leftists began to call this doctrine "National Bolshevism."[13] A man named Nikolay Ustrayalov had predicted that the Bolsheviks would pursue a national course, and he became the leading advocate of reconciliation with the Bolsheviks among Russian émigrés.[14] Professor Ustraylov was a former Kadet and one time supporter of Admiral Kolchak, leader of the anti-Bolshevik forces in Siberia during the Civil War. Stephen Carter maintains that Ustraylov was "strongly influenced by the ideas of Danilevsky, believing in the historic destiny of Russia and the incipient decay of the Western world" and that Russia "after an initial period of weakness and suffering" would "rise to the status of a great power in her new Soviet incarnation."[15]

In his book *The Struggle for Russia* (*V Borbe za Rossiu*, Harbin, 1920), Ustraylov argued for what later came to be called the single stream[16] version of Russian history, seeing the Bolshevik revolution as a "quintessentially Russian" phenomenon that had carried out its historic mission of sweeping away the moribund czarist order. The new regime

was destined to fulfill Russia's historic imperial mission in the form of
Bolshevik centralism. "Even if it were mathematically proven that 90%
of the Russian revolutionaries were foreigners, mainly Jews," he wrote,
"that would not dispute the essentially Russian character of the movement. Even if alien hands lent themselves to the cause, the soul of the
revolution, its inner nature . . . remains authentically Russian, proceeding from the ideas of the intelligentsia and refracted through the psyche of the people."[17] Ustraylov's ideology gave birth to a movement,
taking its name from an anthology published in Prague in 1921, *A
Change of Landmarks* [Smena Vek],[18] in which Ustraylov laid out the
essentials of the changing landmarks ideology, claiming that "it is not
the non-Russian revolutionaries who govern the Russian revolution,
but the Russian revolution which governs the non-Russian revolutionaries."[19] Other contributors criticized the Russian Right for its attachment to Orthodoxy, hoping instead for a "mystique of the Russian
state" to satisfy the religious impulse.[20] Writer Boris Pilnyak summarized the attitude of many *smenavekhovtsy:* "I am not a Communist and
therefore do not acknowledge that I ought to be a Communist or write
as a Communist. I acknowledge that the Communist power in Russia
is determined not by the will of the Communists, but by the historic
destinies of Russia; and insofar as I want to follow, according to my
ability and as my conscience and mind dictate, these Russian historical
destinies, I am with the Communists—that is, insofar as the Communists are with Russia, I am with them."[21]

The changing landmarks movement was to exert a great influence on
Soviet Russia in the 1920s. Its adherents eventually came to be called
"National Bolsheviks," though Ustraylov had not used the term in his
writings. Ustraylov proclaimed Soviet Russia a "radish," "Red on the
outside, White on the inside," and chastised the movement's critics for
confusing native Russian Bolshevism with internationalist, alien Communism.[22] The proclamation of the NEP in 1921 seemed to confirm the
predictions of the *smenavekhovtsy*. Between 1921 and 1931, over 180,000
émigrés returned to the Fatherland, with 121,000 returning in the first
year of the NEP alone. The returnees represented about 10 percent of
the émigré community, and they were welcomed by the Soviet authorities.[23] Who else would train the army, manage the factories, and coordinate the bureaucracy? Competent professionals had been in short
supply since the revolution, and the *smenavekhovtsy* made the trains
run on time, so to speak, in Soviet Russia. The changing landmarks
ideology also justified those professionals who, like the priests who
formed the government approved Living Church, remained and cooperated with the Soviet regime. The burgeoning bureaucracy needed
experienced hands. By 1925, the government apparatus alone num-

bered some 2.5 million (in 1917, there were fewer than one million), and the transportation system employed well over a million, compared to a prerevolution workforce a third smaller. The number of "civil servants" had more than doubled.[24] A 1922 *Pravda* survey hinted at the strength of the changing landmarks movement in Soviet Russia: of 230 professionals in state service surveyed, 110 claimed to be *smenavekhovtsy*.[25]

The Red Czar

> We think of terror as the reign of those who inspire terror; on the contrary it is the reign of people who are themselves terrified. Terror consists of useless cruelties perpetrated by frightened people in order to reassure themselves.
>
> —Marx to Engels during the Paris Commune[26]

Stalin had not been a supporter of the *smenavekhovtsy*. At the twelfth party congress in 1923 he had complained that the "great power ideas of the changing landmarks people are filtering all through the party" and that "Great Russian chauvinism" was threatening the internationalist traditions of the Communist movement.[27] Bukharin, a Russian, supported Stalin's criticisms.[28] Trotsky, however, supported the changing landmarks movement as a necessary prop for the regime, even going so far as to support continuing state subsidies for the National Bolshevik journal *Rossiya*, which Zinoviev had attempted to suppress. *Rossiya* had provided the writer I. Lezhnev (ironically, a Russified Jew) with a platform for his National Bolshevik ideas, which Lezhnev summarized as "Russian Imperialism (from ocean to ocean), Russian messianism . . . , and Russian Bolshevism (on the world scale)."[29] Lezhnev, who joined the party in the 1930s, may have been "typical of the kind of man who passionately sought a foothold in Russian identity, although he naturally excluded Russian Orthodoxy." A hardened Stalinist, he enjoyed a degree of prominence as a journalist until his death in 1955.[30]

The intricacies of the intraparty struggle of the 1920s need not concern us here. By 1924 Lenin was dead and the struggle for leadership of the party, which had been rumbling beneath the veneer of party unity since Lenin's poor health had taken day-to-day matters out of his hands a few years before, broke out in earnest. The various players— including Stalin, Trotsky, Zinoviev, Kamenev, and Bukharin—were engaged in a Byzantine political battle of shifting positions and alliances. One key element of Stalin's ultimate victory was the so-called Lenin enrollment of 1924. The party leadership, attempting to expand the support base for the regime, had brought in 200,000 new members, mostly industrial workers, increasing party membership to about 700,000.[31]

Stalin had never had the kind of appeal that Trotsky enjoyed within the party intelligentsia. "Koba," as he was known within the inner circle, was not considered much of a theorist or orator. He was thought rough, crude even, a worthy administrator but no real party leader. Stalin's earthiness and "common man" reputation may have helped him gain supporters among the inductees of the Lenin enrollment, but, as Adam Ulam relates, there was something else at work on his behalf as well—the notion of the Russianness of Bolshevism and the foreignness of communism: "All the rivals counted on this accession [the Lenin enrollment] to improve their political situation. The new members, Trotsky felt, would not be so critical of the idea that he had been a [party] member for only seven years; they would be respectful toward the *acknowledged* head of the Party, thought Zinoviev and Kamenev. But in fact the future was to show that the new members benefited Stalin more than anyone else. It would also become of some importance that the other three contenders were Jewish. The Lenin levy increased the proportion of Russians in the Party; new members were often politically ill educated and more prone to anti-Semitic bias than a Communist of long standing."[32]

The more Russified nature of the Bolshevik party came into play as Stalin, shifting positions as the power struggle required, became the chief proponent of a parochial policy of "socialism in one country," while Trotsky shifted to the classic internationalist position, "permanent revolution." One position put "Russia" first, the other emphasized the interests of the world revolution. Those enamored of Red patriotism tended to support Stalin against Trotsky, and Stalin used Jew-baiting techniques to neutralize his opponent. His hatchetmen (the Jew Kaganovich was one of them) undermined Trotsky with rumors of Jewish chicanery: Moscow party members claimed that "those Yids in the Politburo" were even paying Trotsky for his public speeches. Trotsky was furious and complained to Bukharin.[33] By the late 1920s, Bukharin could justly complain that National Bolshevism was gaining strength, perhaps even playing the leading role, within the party. "We tried to use them [the Red patriots and *smenavekhovtsy*], direct them, lead them. . . . However, it happens that according to Lenin's expression, the steering wheel is slipping from our hands. This is clearly manifested in our literature. A very considerable part of it is now howling in a genuine Russian fashion, though it is usually dressed in a Soviet cap for decency, decorated with Soviet trinkets and disguised as Communism."[34]

Scholars are divided over the sincerity of Stalin's brand of National Bolshevism. Mikhail Agursky thought Stalin a true convert to Russian chauvinism via National Bolshevism.[35] Most other scholars, including Carter, Dunlop, and Ulam, disagree. Simon-pure Stalinism would never go as far in the direction of the single stream as purist National Bolshevism would have liked. Stalin, for instance, approved of Mikhail Bulgakhov's play *The White Guard*, which depicted the travails of a White Russian family during the Civil War period. At the end of the play, the family accepts Bolshevik power as necessary for the preservation of order. "Stalin liked the play and saw it several times."[36]

Bulgakhov's next play (*Flight*, 1926), however, did not entirely meet with Stalin's approval. The play favorably portrayed the career of a former White general who chose to return to the Fatherland and serve the new regime. Stalin wanted Bulgakhov to make alterations in the play on ideological grounds.[37] Moreover, Stalinist ideology, although glorifying the revolutionary czars Ivan the Terrible and Peter the Great, and sanctioning Sergey Eisenstein's films on the two despots as well as on Aleksandr Nevskiy, continued to attack the legacy of the nineteenth century czars.[38] Stalinism barely tolerated the church (this only after the beginning of World War II), something that probably would not have disturbed the early *smenavekhovsty* and Red patriots, and was not as inclined, as many National Bolsheviks of more recent vintage appear to be, to embrace Orthodoxy as an essential element of the Russian experience. The Red czar never did appear to appreciate the importance of protecting national monuments, much less the environment in general, to the degree that latter-day Red patriots would.[39]

Stalin's embrace of "socialism in one country," although blunting the internationalist-radical element of the revolution, did not immediately begin a wholesale "national bolshevization" of the USSR. Attacks on the clergy and antireligious propaganda continued, for instance. The "Great Retreat"[40] from conventional Marxism-Leninism did not begin until 1934, when the older ideology was transformed into Marxism-Leninism-*Stalinism* by a rather far-reaching and unorthodox "change of landmarks." John Dunlop identifies two weighty considerations behind Stalin's decision to change course: "social catastrophe at home" and the "threat of impending war" in Europe.[41] At home, radical attacks on the "bourgeois family" through liberal divorce laws, abortion on demand, and de facto legalization of bigamy had led to plummeting birth rates and a general weakening of family ties that observers blamed for an explosion of juvenile delinquency. Traditional education had been shunted aside in favor of revolutionary indoctrination. Stalin was justly concerned that the USSR would lack the human material to carry out the rapid industrialization of the country. In order to become an industrial powerhouse, the USSR needed literate workers as well as competent specialists.[42] Divorce laws were tightened and a stiff law was passed against abortion on demand. Traditional teaching subjects and methods were reintroduced in the schools and, "in a throwback to czarist times," uniforms for the students were brought back.[43]

Stalin had apparently already concluded that Marxist-Leninist internationalism was ineffective in mobilizing the *narod*, the Russian masses who were the core of the Soviet population. His evil nature was once again complemented by his common sense, nonrational (rather than irrational) approach to fundamental questions of politics and human psychology. He had concluded that the Russian *narod* would be in no hurry to sacrifice themselves in a war to further the world revolution. Russian history and culture were rediscovered, as were the pre-Revolutionary terms (and all the powerful imagery associated with them) *Otechestvo* (Fatherland) and *Rodina* (Motherland or Homeland). Alex De Jonge has claimed that Stalin had other motives as well:

> In 1934 Stalin sought a new kind of popularity, as he began to encourage an upsurge in patriotism and Russian nationalism. . . . Hitherto it had been easy for foreign believers [in communism] to obtain Soviet citizenship. Now citizenship was hard to acquire, and foreign Communists were placed at a disadvantage, no longer being admitted to party meetings. This was put down partly to fear of spies and sabotage, partly to Stalin's understanding of the popularity of appeals to Great Russian Chauvinism. He wanted the support of the masses now because he was about to embark upon the next phase of his revolution, one to be directed at members of his own party. Over the next four years more than sixty percent of the delegates attending the Congress of Victors [the Seventeenth Party Congress in 1934] would be arrested and seventy percent of the Central Committee [of the Communist Party] would be shot.[44]

The extermination of much of the Bolshevik old guard not only ensured Stalin's supremacy but strengthened his claim to be *Vozhd* ("boss" or "leader"; the term, when applied to Stalin, at least, carried with it with some of the same mystique that *Duce* had in Italian or *Fuehrer* in German) of the Russian nation as National Bolsheviks saw it. Hadn't the *Vozhd*, by eliminating Zinoviev, Kamenev, and eventually Trotsky himself, declared war on the Jews? Trotskyism had become something of a codeword for many Russians for disloyalty, antipatriotism, and treachery, exactly the qualities Russian chauvinists attributed to the entire Jewish people, and Red patriots easily attributed all the negative aspects of the revolution and its aftermath to Jews like Kaganovich. Since Jews had served in high places in the secret police apparatus, it appeared plausible to blame them, not the leader, for the regime's excesses. It was even rumored that Beria, Stalin's most famous secret police chief, was a Georgian Jew![45] It became something of a truism that Jews were behind everything bad in Russia, Stalin behind the good, even long after the *Vozhd* had liquidated the old party hierarchy and Jews no longer played such a prominent role in party affairs. If it serves their purposes, human beings will believe in anything, even (maybe *especially*) in phantom enemies.

The popularity of the Stalin cult was assured by the Soviet victory in the second Great Patriotic War. The Wise Teacher, the Leader of the Peoples and Grand Strategist had not only led (Soviet) Russia to victory but had industrialized and modernized the country. The Fatherland was once more a feared and respected *derzhava*, a world power on a scale unimagined by Ivan or Peter. Stalin even singled out the Russian people during victory celebrations, praising them as the backbone of Soviet power. He commissioned a new anthem for Russia specifically, praising the "unbreakable union of free republics [that] was forged forever by Great Russia."[46] This was the period of high Stalinism, roughly from the end of the war until Stalin's death in 1953, when the aging tyrant's personality cult and the suspicion that he bred reached their bizarre height (or depth) and the leader himself, perhaps warped by the very terror he had unleashed, trusted no one. His health failing and the cold war developing, with Tito and his treachery preying on the evil genius's mind, Stalin hatched his final plot.

It is impossible to say what the source of Stalin's hatred of Jews was, exactly. He may have gradually converted, as Mikhail Agursky claimed, to a form of National Bolshevism, inheriting its suspicion of the Jews honestly, so to speak. Stalin's image had been one of a leader who identified himself with the common man, the rank and file, the workers, the rough-hewn Russians of the Lenin enrollment, and he may have shared their distaste for high-brow intellectual snobs like Zinoviev and Kamenev, so often men of Jewish origins. Stalin may have absorbed the lies and half truths of his own whisper campaign against his rival, Trotsky. Whatever the cause, by the period of high Stalinism the *Vozhd's* Jew hatred was evolving in a new direction. Trotsky had acquired the image of a devil, and Trotskyism the flavor of absolute evil. The move to "anticosmopolitanism," a term designating "rootless cosmopolitans" and "Zionists" as the main enemy, may have been a cover for a possible final purge of the Jews from Russian society. Stalin was plotting a new wave of terror, a purge of the party and state apparatus, and the climax of the campaign could well have been the deportation of the Jews to the nether regions of the Soviet Union, had not death spared the country by removing the tyrant from the scene.

The deportation would have meant death on the frozen steppes for many of them, as the Crimean Tartars and Chechens had discovered during the late war.

Stalin never became an anti-Semite in the full sense of the word.[47] The Jews did not stand at the center of his ideology as the focus and source of all evil in the world, and the purge he planned was not to be an exact replica of Hitler's Final Solution. The Jews appear to have been marked to share the fate of several other nations broken by the Man of Steel. It is fair to say, however, that the Jews occupied a central place in his *suspicions* during the period of high Stalinism. Adam Ulam speculated about Stalin's reasoning:

> And so now: a Jewish critic writes scathingly about a classic of Russian literature; his own daughter marries a Jew; Soviet Jews cry with joy at the appearance of the Israeli minister in Moscow; America, where Jews are so influential, adopts an increasingly anti-Soviet attitude. Were these separate phenomena which simply happened to coincide? Stalin had never believed that treason or dissent—and the two became identical in his mind—could be an isolated phenomenon springing from an individual's decision, and not also be a state of mind. Marxism-Leninism taught that whole classes are guilty. . . . Even the most altruistic and patriotic kulak was still an enemy. So, if classes, why not, at certain junctures in history, professions and nationalities?[48]

The final plot began with a newspaper campaign to unmask the Zionists and rootless cosmopolitans in the bosom of Mother Russia. The journal *Bolshevik* carried an article entitled "Hold Aloft the Banner of Russian Patriotism" that was typical for the time (1949): The machinations of the Capitalist-Zionist plot to undermine Russia were plain for all to see; the time for action had come.[49] The secret police were set to work unmasking and rounding up the plotters, mostly Jews. The Leningrad affair, ending with the execution of a number of high-ranking Soviet officials in 1950, signaled that something bigger might be afoot.[50] That something was the Doctors' Plot.[51]

The summer of 1952 marked the height of the anti-Zionist and anti-cosmopolitan campaign. A number of Jewish public figures who had been arrested in 1949 were tried and shot. "Anti-Zionist" propaganda was now standard fare in many of the Soviet satellites, particularly Czechoslovakia. In November 1952, fourteen high ranking party officials were arrested in Prague and were subsequently tried and convicted of being spies in the service of Zionism. Eleven were sentenced to death.[52] Eleven were Jews. It seemed apparent that Stalin was about to use the anti-Zionist campaign to simultaneously attack the Jews as a people and carry out another purge reminiscent of the Great Terror of the late 1930s. If he uncovered another conspiracy, he could unleash blood hounds of state security once again. On January 13, 1953, *Pravda* ominously noted that "some time ago agencies of state security discovered a terrorist group of doctors who had made it their aim to cut short the lives of active public figures of the Soviet Union through wrecking methods of medical treatment." The announcement went on to name V. N. Vinogradov, once Stalin's personal physician, as one of the plotters. The diabolical plot of the Kremlin doctors had been cooked up, so the story went, by international Jewry in league with British intelligence *and* "a Zionist-Titoist-American intelligence network of agents which penetrated the Communist movement and hence *had* to have people in the interstices of the Soviet system," people who were plotting against the Great Teacher himself.[53] The boss had covered all the bases, laying the groundwork for a purge of epic proportions, with the removal of the Jews thrown in for good measure. Being a history buff, he may have found inspiration for the phantasmagoria of the Doctors' Plot in the actions of fifteenth century czar Ivan III, who had Master Leon the Jew, his court physician, put to death for the alleged medical murder of his son and heir, supposedly on behalf of a cabal of wicked noblemen.[54]

The Doctors' Plot again demonstrated Stalin's ingenious capacity to plumb the depths of human psychology, the leader concocting a tale that was at once incredible and difficult to refute. Once the seeds of suspicion had been planted, who *didn't* wonder about the man in the white coat, the mysterious dispenser of tonics and elixirs who held the power of life and death in his hands? Miniature Doctors' Plots were duly uncovered across the Soviet Union, with anti-Semitism playing a supporting role in many of them. One doctor was dismissed on the strength of an allegation by a young woman that he had attempted to murder her baby during treatment. Since he was a Jew, the ritual murder element of the story apparently played well.[55] The Jews were poisoning the wells once again, and any unexplained illness or death could be laid at the doorstep of the grand conspiracy. Stalin had trumped the white czars by creating a serfdom, in the form of the collective farms, more suffocating, and much more deadly, than anything the peasants had previously known. Now he would outshine the most anti-Jewish czars by going a step further than the mere recreation of a pale of settlement. The potential deadliness of the deportation that was looming on the horizon was obvious: According to the plan, the Jews would never again play a role in Soviet-Russian public life, even if they survived as a people. Then on March 2, 1953, *Pravda* abruptly suspended the anti-Zionist campaign. "Something extraordinary must have taken place."[56]

The extraordinary event was a debilitating stroke that had incapacitated the Man of Steel. He had been ailing for some time in the first few weeks of 1953 but had refused the attention of his doctors. A tyrant can't be too careful. He lingered on for a few days and finally passed from this mortal coil on March 5, 1953. Some observers, De Jonge among them, have speculated that Stalin was given a bit of a push on his final descent over the abyss. Khrushchev and company surely had a motive: They were old Stalinist hands and could read the Doctors' Plot tea leaves well enough. The general reaction to the great man's death was a mixed one; some were joyous and others genuinely experienced a stunning combination of almost hysterical grief with a sense of emptiness and loss. Some cursed the dead man and others prayed to him like a god. The poet Joseph Brodsky, thirteen years old, was told of Stalin's demise at school. His hysterical teacher ordered the entire class to get down on their knees to receive the dreaded news.[57] Gulag prisoners danced and grieved as their ideologies or circumstances dictated. Ilya Ehrenburg "tried to think out what would happen to us all now but was quite unable to do so. Like so many of my compatriots at that moment I was in a state of shock."[58] A man who had surrounded himself with the trappings of a god-emperor, had cloaked himself in a veil of mystery, had formed an inner circle like a priesthood of initiates, and had used history and myth, symbol and word, so effectively had seemed immortal to many of his subjects. And now he had betrayed them by dying.[59] The one seemingly never changing element in their lives had passed away. The landmarks had surely changed this time.

On the morning of March 6, a crowd gathered on Red Square, probably the first spontaneous group action many of them had ever taken part in. Would Stalin's body come through the gates? The city itself had been sealed off, and MVD security forces were everywhere. Would there be an uprising, a spontaneous Russian riot, the wild and brutal *bunt* that Stalin's successors probably feared? March 6–9 had been declared a time of mourning. Thousands upon thousands paraded past the corpse of the Great Strategist. Some five hundred people were killed, trampled in the crush to see Stalin off.[60] "Human blood accompanied the Father of the Peoples to the grave."[61]

Stalin's Legacy

Stalin is very much inside of each one of us.

—Joseph Brodsky[62]

No matter how despotic the czar or how far reaching his thirst for power, the individual reach of the autocrat was limited by the regime's attachment to Orthodox Christianity. Even the bloodiest of czars was held in check by the lip service he was compelled to pay to his role as defender of the faith, as the paternalistic *batushkha* "little father" of his Christian realm and its inhabitants. It is not for nothing that Stalin, criticizing Ivan the Terrible's comparative restraint in dealing with opponents, real or potential, once commented that "God got in Ivan's way."[63] Nothing would get in Stalin's way. Modernity has seen both the weakening of religious faith and the strengthening of the integrated state in the developed world. Ideologies have seeped in to replace a belief in the transcendent, but the element of faith, as well as of self-subordination to an overriding imperative, has not in the least diminished. The modern era is in many respects the story of Man's attempt to immanentize objective reality, to fill it with purpose and meaning not otherwise evident. The era has witnessed the Christian view of purposeful history transformed into a quest for the temporal "end of history," an end point in Man's development that would signal the millennium.[64] Since the visible world is an end in itself and each individual is allowed by the laws of nature only a short time here, the desire of Utopians to remake reality has taken on a sense of urgency. Those who wish to satisfy ideology and personal amibition in a lifetime must not let anything get in the way.

It is not merely fortuitous that the simultaneous culmination of the development of the integrated state and secular faiths of the modern era should have been realized in the tyranny of Stalin, Hitler, and Mao. The time was right. Old beliefs swept aside, the twentieth century saw the further development of technologies that would enhance the power of the center and erode the ability of autonomous groups or associations to resist the encroachment of the integrated state on once privileged sanctuaries. If Stalin was Genghis Khan with a telegraph, one shudders to think of what a similar tyrant would do with computers. Moreover, modernization in the form of industrial development and state management of economies had created the sociopolitical conditions for the exploitation of such technologies by the agents of the integrated state. In that sense the competition of liberal democracy, communism, fascism, and Nazism has been over how to manage the awesome power of the modern state, not over fundamental assumptions. Stalin is the grand man of the era of the integrated state, a "great bad man" who recognized Leviathan's potential use as an agent for social transformation and acted accordingly.

Stalin's genius was his ability to manipulate the levers of power with a skill that was second to none, while realizing that the nonrational aspects of the human psychology, particularly Man's tribalist bent and penchant for self-justification, were the key to manipulating the

masses, for Stalin was certainly one of the most popular leaders of this
or any other century. The mythology of Stalinism was intoxicating, the
tangible rewards enticing. The case of opponents of the idea of total
depravity was not strengthened by the behavior of the Soviet masses
under Stalin. Stalin understood what Nietzsche called the will to
power—the urge to dominate others—that lurks in the darkest corners
of the human psyche. His system of power built millions of miniature
Stalins in every nook and cranny of his Gulag state, defending their
turf with ferocity, whether it be the factory party cell group boss, an
NKVD chief looking after the interests of the ministry, or the doorman
jealously guarding his tiny fiefdom. Nadezhda Mandelstam saw Stalin
in "anyone with a scrap of power, every investigator, every janitor. . . .
Petty dictatorships sprang up everywhere; our country swarmed with
them, and still does."[65]

Alex De Jonge maintained that Stalin "enjoyed nationwide support"
precisely because he and his style of governing were popular. Stalin
was truly a dictator of the people.[66] He was able to use nationalism's
populist element to great effect. Many Russians saw Stalin's dictatorship not as the destruction of the tradition of Moscow as the third
Rome, but as its fulfillment: "He converted this uniquely Russian feeling into Soviet man's acute sense that he is special."[67] The Soviet Union
that collapsed in 1991 was Stalin's Soviet Union, for if Lenin was the
father of Bolshevism, Stalin was the father of the USSR, the superpower that once was and could be again if Stalin's children have their
way. Stalinism was about power in the only manifestation that such
awesome centralism appeals to ordinary people. Stalin's USSR was
about national pride. The superpower days are lamented not even so
much because the former apparatchik or the janitor is nostalgic for his
own taste of power but because millions of Russians are nostalgic for
their collective sense of prestige. Stalin's creation defeated a Western
power, Germany (to which the leaders of a humiliated Russia had
looked for guidance and know-how in the past) in a deadly war. The
USSR launched the first man into orbit, demonstrating Russian prow-
ess in the sciences and technology and humiliating the West for a
change. The USSR was feared and respected, and the rejection of the
nomenklatura in August 1991 was not necessarily a rejection of the
Communist period or of the USSR as such. The events of the previous
fifty years, particularly the victory in the Great Patriotic War, had legit-
imized to a certain degree the Communists' rule and, for many Russians, that of the Wise Leader. It is not for nothing that the most popular portrait gracing the rallies of the patriots is Stalin's.

The Russian Communist Party and National Bolshevism

The National Bolshevik Revival

Khrushchev, a doctrinaire Marxist-Leninist, renewed the attacks on the church that Stalin had curtailed and generally blunted many of the manifestations of the cult of personality that had so defined Stalin's Soviet Union, as well as doing his level best to suppress any manifestations of bourgeois nationalism in Russia or elsewhere in the Soviet Union. Ironically, however, his efforts backfired. John Dunlop and Stephen Carter both have pointed to Khrushchev's neglect, even outright destruction, of Russian national monuments and churches—often one and the same—as perhaps the primary factor in the growth of nationalist oriented ecological, preservationist, and religious groups, official and otherwise, that sprang up under the Brezhnev regime.[68] The re-Stalinization of the Brezhnev period allowed elbow room for nationalist, preferably National Bolshevik, tendencies to openly display themselves within official institutions and publications; the activities of the "official" nationalists were matched by those of National Bolshevik-leaning dissidents writing in *samizdat*.

However sympathetic Brezhnev and company may have been to National Bolshevist ideas in principle, the regime was cautious in its approach to dealing with explicit manifestations of Russian nationalism. The *Molodaya Gvardiya* [Young Guard] affair is instructive on this score. Since the mid-1960s, Russian nationalist themes had begun to appear with increasing frequency in the arts. In 1964, for instance, director Andrey Tarkovskiy's celebrated film *Andrey Rublev* was released, whose namesake was an iconographer of the Middle Ages who had been canonized by the Orthodox Church.[69] The literary journal *Molodaya Gvardiya*, an official publication of the Komsomol, the Communist youth organization, provided a platform for nationalist oriented writers to push the limits of official tolerance. The writings of contributor Viktor Chalmaev, who argued openly for a single stream interpretation of Russian history, probably spurred the authorities to rein in *Molodaya Gvardiya*. "Young Guardism"[70] was going too far when its version of the single stream stressed the importance of the Slavophile current at the expense of the revolutionary one. In 1970, the journal's editor was removed, but the rest of the Young Guardist editorial board remained. A similar purge at the liberal oriented journal *Novy Mir* was far more thorough, and in 1972 Anatoliy Ivanov, who had been associated with *Molodaya Gvardiya* in the late 1960s, was named as editor of the nationalist journal. It became clear that Young Guardism had highly placed sympathizers.[71] By the early 1970s, the regime had established a sort of accord with neo-Stalinists and single stream nationalists, while continuing to persecute Christian nationalists such as Solzhenitsyn. Both Carter and Dunlop identify Mikhail Suslov, the party's chief ideologist during the Brezhnev period, as the probable promoter of the official nationalists. Moribund Marxism-Leninism needed nationalism, particularly in its Soviet patriotism mode, to prop up the regime. That and the regime's continuing emphasis on the party's role in the Great Patriotic War were to secure the Russian foundations of the Soviet regime.

Another inadvertent contribution that Khrushchev made to the nationalist cause in Russia was the creation of parallel party, professional, and publishing organizations in the Russian Federation. Heretofore, the Russian Federation had not enjoyed such particularist institutions, but in 1956 the Communist Party of the Soviet Union (CPSU) Central Committee created a Bureau for the Russian Federation. The Russian Council of Ministers soon began publication of a party newspaper for Russia, *Sovetskaya Rossiya* [Soviet Russia], as well as a publishing concern (also called *Sovetskaya Rossiya*) and a separate Russian Writers' Union. *Sovetskaya Rossiya* and the Russian Writers' Union would become hotbeds of nationalist (particularly official nationalist) sentiment by the 1970s.[72]

The Brezhnev regime even allowed exhibitions of paintings by the nationalist artist Ilya Glazunov in the late 1970s, which official nationalist journals praised to the skies. A sort of cease-fire in the war on the church was called as well, though the period did not see any significant official religious revival. Alain Besancon claimed that Brezhnev was "accomplishing the goals of National Bolshevism without admitting it."[73] Indeed, observers had adequate reason to draw such a conclusion:

1. The Russification program begun under Stalin continued apace in the non-Russian Soviet republics;
2. Stalin himself had been partially rehabilitated, a modest bust of the tyrant appearing by his grave in the Kremlin Wall, where the Great Strategist had been interred under the apostate Khrushchev;
3. In 1965, the Russian Federation Council of Ministers founded an official preservationist organization, the All-Russian Society for the Preservation of Historical and Cultural Monuments (VOO-PIK), and by 1972 the organization claimed seven million members;[74]
4. An All-Russian Society for the Protection of Nature claimed some 19 million members in 1971;[75]

5. Celebrations of Russian cultural achievements became regular fare for the Russian public;
6. Russians began organized pilgrimages to historical monuments and medieval monasteries.

Moreover, the Brezhnev regime, particularly following the Six Day War in the Middle East, renewed the attacks on Zionism and cosmopolitanism that Stalin had inaugurated. The campaign was probably connected to the regime's support of its Arab allies in their struggle with Israel, but hardened National Bolsheviks viewed it as a continuation of the struggle with the antipatriotic forces that were attempting to undermine the regime—particularly the dissidents. Thus the regime had recognized that "Russian nationalism could perhaps be 'harnessed' to official ideology," and that it remained a vital force in the Russified Soviet state.[76]

Dissident promoters of the single stream notion pushed the ideological envelope even further than Chalmaev, though few were persecuted by the authorities. Gennadiy Shimanov's *samizdat* writings one-upped Young Guardism, carrying National Bolshevism to new places by advocating a reconciliation of the party and Russian Orthodoxy. Shimanov also went beyond the preservationism of VOOPIK and the environmentalism of the official Soviet nature lovers, calling for a return to pastoralism as the basis of national life. Communism, in Shimanov's view, was the highest form of Orthodoxy. Like other nationalists, Shimanov was critical of Western materialism and capitalism but went so far as to hope for a future Orthodox-Communist Party state wherein all foreign influences would be purged. Shimanov repeated the familiar anti-Zionist and anti-cosmopolitan mantra of the official nationalists, and exulted in the power of the Soviet Russian *derzhava*. The Soviet Union, claimed Shimanov, was to be God's instrument for carrying out a great transformation of the world, and Russia would be the "spiritual trigger" for the "explosion" he predicted. He attacked all deviations from this path as the work of shadowy "kike-freemasonry" and maintained that Orthodoxy united with the Leninist Party was the only force capable of resisting the Satanic forces abroad in the world. The Civil War, collectivization, the Great Patriotic War, indeed, all of the trials of the Soviet period had been just that—trials sent by God to strengthen the Russian people. Moreover, they accomplished the historical task of building the Soviet system, Russia's surest defense against being infected by the Western materialist bug.[77]

The trend toward an assertion of Russian particularism gained strength during the Gorbachev period. The literary journals *Molodaya Gvardiya, Nash Sovremennik, Kuban,* and *Moskva* continued to promulgate Russian nationalist positions, often of the National Bolshevik or "single stream" variety. *Sovetskaya Rossiya* became a bastion of National Bolshevik ideology, and the Russian Writers' Union newspaper *Literaturnaya Rossiya* gave voice to the nationalism prevalent in the union's leadership. During the late Gorbachev period, Russian sovereignty was declared and the CPSU allowed the formation of a Russian Federation Party affiliate for the first time. This affiliate became the most numerous and well organized of the communist parties[78] and movements that came to life in the wake of the collapse of the Soviet Union and the fragmentation of the CPSU. The party's leader, Gennadiy Zyuganov, became the most prominent purveyor of National Bolshevism on the Russian political scene.

Zyuganov and the CPRF

Zyuganov, born in 1944 in the Orlov Oblast village of Mimrino, the son and grandson of teachers, joined the CPSU in 1966. He was trained at the Academy of Social Sciences and eventually taught there in the philosophy and mathematics departments, before beginning work as a CPSU Central Committee ideologist and eventually becoming a deputy to the chief of the ideology department concerning himself with "Russian [*Rossiyskie*] problems," that is, concerns of the party in the Russian Federation. He supported the creation of the Russian Communist Party in 1990, and he became a leading critic of the policies of Boris Yeltsin, chairman of the Russian Supreme Soviet.[79] The Russian Communists hated and attacked both Gorbachev and Yeltsin, seeing them as merely two sides of the same heretical coin. The CPRF at that early time had not fully shown its nationalist colors and tended to attack the apostates from a more or less conventional ideological position, rarely sharing the non-Communist nationalists' enthusiasm for Yeltsin and his works. Zyuganov and company were enthusiastic supporters of the State Emergency Committee, which attempted to overthrow Gorbachev and halt what they (correctly) saw as the slide toward the disintegration of the USSR. Zyuganov, in fact, had been one of the signatories of the notorious open letter "A Word to the People," widely viewed as a call to arms in the days before the coup attempt in August 1991.[80]

Zyuganov's words had graced the pages of *Sovetskaya Rossiya* earlier in the form of attacks on Yeltsin and the new Russian entrepreneurial class, which he derided as a "homegrown bourgeoisie,"[81] as well as on the reformist policies of Gorbachev. He had long warned that a "social explosion"[82] was just around the corner, and that perestroika's false prophets[83] were leading the USSR to national catastrophe.[84] After the collapse of the Soviet Union, Zyuganov assumed a leading role in the anti-Yeltsin opposition, attempting to forge alliances with patriots both White and Red in order to present a united "national-patriotic" front in opposition to the Westernizing reforms of the "Yeltsinoids." To that end, Zyuganov acted as cofounder of the Council of National Patriotic Forces (1992), a cochairman of the organizational committee of the National Salvation Front (from 1992 until the NSF was temporarily banned after the October 1993 violence at the Russian Supreme Soviet "White House"), and a cochairman of the Duma of the Russian National Assembly, a nationalist organization with Black Hundred leanings founded in 1992 by ex-KGB General Aleksandr Sterligov.

Zyuganov was elected chairman of the CPRF central executive committee by a party congress in February 1993. That same party congress adopted a "program statement" that included a section called "The Fatherland in Danger," which urged "the consolidation of all . . . patriotic forces, united by the idea of saving the Fatherland." Other sections of the document sidestepped long-held Marxist-Leninist dogmas by endorsing a mixed economy (although the state sector would still be the basis of the "multisector" economy) and calling for cooperation with all patriots, including active members of the Orthodox Church.[85] The nationalist weekly *Den* subsequently endorsed Zyuganov's election and characterized the "majority of the delegates" to the congress as "not just fans of the long dead writers Marx and Lenin" but as "ordinary citizens" who were concerned with the "fate of the Fatherland."[86] Zyuganov's single stream version of Russian history came more sharply into focus after he assumed the CPRF chairmanship. *Sovetskaya Rossiya* became the mouthpiece of the Zyuganov variant of the National Bolshevist line, serving as a platform for Zyuganov to elaborate his notion of the Russian Idea.

In an article entitled "The Russian Question," Zyuganov called on leaders of the "patriotic movement" to develop an "ideology of national rebirth" as part of a "national liberation" strategy for Russia. He called his opponents in the democratic camp "those who hate Russia" and saw the collapse of the USSR as just another chapter in the thousand-year history of efforts to destroy her.[87] He repeated his conviction that an ancient anti-Russian conspiracy was responsible for the woes of the Fatherland in a subsequent *Sovetskaya Rossiya* article that also argued for a single stream version of Russian history—the Soviet period was the culmination of the development of the Russian nation and empire.[88] *Sovetskaya Rossiya* cultivated ties with the church and frequently carried articles by Metropolitan Ioann of St. Petersburg, further illustrating the blood relation of Black Hundredism, Stalinism, and National Bolshevism, carried from generation to generation by an extreme mutation of the *gosudarstvennik* chromosome.

For the extreme *gosudarstvennik*, the powerful centralized state is not merely a necessary evil, something that Russia must endure in order to survive or even simply a manifestation of national pride, but something that has a value of its own, maybe the highest value of all, even if its consolidation comes at the expense of the *narod* whom the state ostensibly serves. The state *is* the nation, or the collective expression of the nation's will, a suprapersonal spirit that is embodied in the concrete realities of the land, the apparatus, the army, and national culture. This centralist expression of nationhood is what *gosudarstvenniki* like Zyuganov mean when they embrace Russian traditions like *sobornost*. *Sovetskaya Rossiya* in fact had attacked both Gorbachev and Yeltsin from a conspicuously *gosudarstvennik* stance, sharply differentiating itself from the more conventional Marxist-Leninist critique that *Pravda* offered. Following the failure of the August coup of 1991, *Sovetskaya Rossiya* lamented not so much the impending loss of the socialist system as the truly hateful prospect of losing the Soviet (read "Russian") superpower itself. The democrats were maligned as a foolish group of political adolescents, "mesmerized" by "pro-American, anti-Russian and anti-Soviet propaganda, camouflaged as anti-Communist." *Sovetskaya Rossiya* was certain that the democrats, if not witting agents of the conspiracy, were at least heavily infiltrated by agents of influence carrying out a plan that been worked out in Washington for the "destruction of the USSR, then Russia." Commentator Eduard Volodin called the aftermath of the August coup events as a loss of "national honor . . . and national dignity" rather than the liberation from "stagnation and dogmatism" that all patriots desired.[89] According to Volodin, the democrats were conscious agents of the "builders of the New World Order," who were seeking "the destruction of Russia's international authority" as well as the dismemberment of the Russian state.[90]

Zyuganov's Ideology: The Two Parties and the Grand Conspiracy

> It [the West] is afraid of our might as a world power. It has an interest in weakening, dismembering, and, if possible, enslaving Russia . . . [efforts to do so span] a period of more than a thousand years
>
> —Gennadiy Zyuganov.[91]

> In fact, there were two parties . . . [during] the Soviet period, and a fierce, but quiet, struggle between them took place. . . . The first was the party of "our country," the party to which . . . Zhukov and Gagarin belonged . . . the largest part of ordinary functionaries and administrators belonged to it . . . but there was a second party in the Soviet Union—the party of

"that country," . . . for whom "that country" and "those people" were merely the arena for the realization of their own . . . ambitions and . . . reckless social experiments. It was the party of Trotsky and Kaganovich, Beria, . . . Gorbachev and Yeltsin, Yakovlev and Shevardnaze. Its legal successor today is "Demrossiya."

—Gennadiy Zyuganov, *Derzhava*[92]

Derzhava, a collection of essays by Zyuganov published after the events of "Bloody October" in 1993, expounds on the CPRF leader's continuing efforts to unite the patriotic forces behind a single stream ideology that could work as the ideological foundation of a movement devoted to resurrecting the Russian great power in the guise of a renewed union. Only the resurrection of the union, Zyuganov claimed, which derives its strength from "people's power" in the form of renewed soviets, can make Russia a respected world power and foil the designs of ancient, implacable foes who are the agents of a thousand-year-old conspiracy to destroy Russia and establish a world dictatorship. In Zyuganov's convoluted conspiratology the Bolshevik coup is both disaster and blessing to the Russian nation, both part of the grand conspiracy and part of a great design, for the Soviet Union was the work of both criminals and heroes, meeting in the penultimate clash of opposites, the Soviet great power the synthesis of the clash that was made inevitable by the dialectics of history. The only way to fully explain the "patriotic" coalition in Russia is through Zyuganov's streamlined version of changing landmarks revisionism—the theory of the two parties.

Central to Zyuganov's single stream thesis is his dualistic view of the Soviet Communist Party. According to Zyuganov, the CPSU was divided internally between two philosophically antagonistic currents, the party of "our country" (*nasha strana*)—made up of populists and patriots—and the party of "that country" (*eta strana*) made up of internationalist, cosmopolitan, and mercenary elements, coming largely from national minorities, particularly Jews. According to Zyuganov, the party of "our country," the party of rank-and-file Communists and national heroes like Marshal Zhukov (hero of the Great Patriotic War) and cosmonaut Yuri Gagarin, was fundamentally patriotic and Russian. It never lost its affection for Russian tradition and its sympathy for the common man in whose name the Great October Revolution was made. The party of "our country" saw the particular talents and spiritual qualities of the Russian people rather than dogmatic adherence to Marxism as the essential element in the construction of the Soviet Russian *derzhava* and its socialist system, which for all its shortcomings achieved much that is worth preserving.

Zyuganov holds the party of "that country" responsible for all the bleak pages of Soviet history. The excesses of the Soviet regime were the work of the cosmopolitan non-Russians and their allies within the Bolshevik Party. These foreigners, according to Zyuganov, were simply incapable of drawing on traditions that were alien to them. Khrushchev and the Russophobes were able to "freeze the process of Russian national rebirth" that Stalin, who had rallied Russia to victory in the Great Patriotic War, had initiated.[93] The Russophobes' accomplices came from among the denationalized, mercenary, careerist elements within the party, elements exemplified in the late Soviet period by the likes of Mikhail Gorbachev and Boris Yeltsin.

Zyuganov identifies himself with the traditions of the party of "our country," a party that worked to "to modernize the economy, build new factories, and resurrect the armed forces." The party of "that country" persistently undermined the achievements of the patriots, and was responsible for organizing the Gulag system. The alien party of "that country" was entrusted by the world anti-Russian conspiracy with a great experiment, for Russia was to be the "proving ground for new world cataclysms . . . for inhuman experiments." If successful, the plotters would convert Russia into a "reserve of resources and 'human material' " for the new world order, the nascent global regime long anticipated by the conspirators.[94]

The United States is the locus of the conspiracy's seat in the modern world, but the cosmopolitan internationalist liberals running the West are but a facade for the ancient conspiracy. "In the final analysis," according to Zyuganov, "the Western states and the transnational banking and financial corporations are the obedient relayers of the aggressive anti-Russian policy" and no more. Russia, covering one-sixth of the earth's surface and heir to untapped natural resources, remains the final roadblock to the conspirators' plans to create a supranational world regime, a "maniacal idea" that "is closely linked to the development of secret political societies, religious sects, and mystical dogmas."[95] The conspirators, acting through their agents in Yeltsin's government and in the West, hope to first wreck Russia's economy by "reforming" it,[96] incidentally creating harsh living conditions that will decrease the population of the new colony. "It is easy to [reduce the Russian population] without need of concentration camps or gas chambers," according to Zyuganov, and in any event the population *has been dropping*, thus demonstrating "how economic 'reforms' can regulate demographic processes."[97] The world regime, long but a dream of the conspirators, has become possible through advances in technology in the post-World War II period, and Russia will be a desirable colony in the regime's world domain.

The environmentalism in post-Stalin Russian nationalism forms a part of Zyuganov's general thesis: The Western powers have raped the earth and are in need of the gas, oil, and minerals of Eurasia in order to sustain themselves.[98] This is the bait the world conspiracy waves on its internationalist hook, the mysterious "conductor" of the conspiracy remaining in the background orchestrating events, manipulating the "players" by organizing staged confrontations that heighten the social crisis and enable their players to liquidate the patriots. The confrontation between Yeltsin and Gorbachev was the first such staged event, the confrontation between Yeltsin and the Supreme Soviet the next act, a provocation designed to liquidate the system of soviets and pave the way for presidential rule.[99]

In Zyuganov's conspiratorial world both the Bolshevik Revolution and the disintegration of the Soviet Union are explicable as the fruits of the great plot. The party of "that country" perverted the struggle of honest Russians against the rapacious capitalist class and instituted a dictatorship designed to debilitate Russia and pave the way for the world rule of the conspirators. True, the *Zhidomasonstvo*, as well as the Zionists, have been replaced by a mysterious conductor, but the streamlined conspiracy theory propounded by Zyuganov is merely a slightly more sophisticated version of *The Protocols of the Elders of Zion*, one that has been modified by the experience of Bolshevik and Stalinist witch-hunts for the shadowy "wreckers" and "enemies of the people" that were supposedly behind every failure of the Soviet system. The Russians are still the chosen people, though chosen this time to provide a bulwark against the machinations of the conspirators, to ensure a balance among the great powers in an envisioned multipolar world,[100] and to build socialism as a beacon to the world. His opposition to presidential rule, as outlined in *Derzhava*, is not just a pragmatic position prompted by Yeltsin's position but a direct inheritance from *The Protocols*. The Elders of Zion plan to install a presidential system with one of their "players" as chief executive, acting on behalf of his unseen patrons.[101]

For Zyuganov, *derzhava* means the re-creation of the Soviet integrated state stretching from the Baltic to the Chinese border, a multinational unitary entity created and operated by Russians (and their Russified allies) in fulfillment of the nation's historical tasks. Russia will be a mighty garrison state again but will be free to operate pragmatically, exemplifying the socialist choice for the world but rejecting rigid Marxism.[102] The church will be revived—though, in view of many of the *gosudarstvenniki* interpreting *sobornost* as unanimity, probably as an arm of the state. Despite Zyuganov's assurances that the union will be reconstituted peacefully, as well as his public commitment to parlia-

mentarism and compromise with the authorities, one is justified in suspecting the intentions of a man who admires Joseph Stalin as the
builder of the Soviet Union. Division, disagreement, and dissent were
viewed as treason by the hard-line Soviet authorities, authorities Zyuganov supported until the bitter end. As a nationalist and *gosudarstvennik* in the tradition of the czarist official nationality policy, he defines
unity as strength and division as weakness. It is only logical for his
critics to conclude that he intends to return Russia to a state of mobilization, since her enemies, according to Zyuganov, are legion and will
settle for nothing less than her destruction. Zyuganov's actions have
not justified the worst fears of his critics, however, and it may be that
his brand of Red patriotism reflects the instrumental conservatism of
the Soviet apparatus that he served in.

Zyuganov and the Communist Movement

The CPRF is not the only successor to the CPSU. In Russia alone, there
are a host of communist parties and movements, ideologically ranging
from Viktor Anpilov's anarcho-communist Working Russia movement
to August 1991 putschist Oleg Shenin's orthodox Marxist Leninist
Union of Communist Parties (UCP) to Nina Andreeyva's Stalinist All-
Russian Communist Party of Bolsheviks. None of these parties enjoys
either the numbers or the prestige of the CPRF. Zyuganov has been
criticized by his fellow communists for "parliamentarism," that is, de-
ciding to participate in the parliamentary elections in December 1993
and December 1995 (largely restricting his activities to parliamentary
opposition to Yeltsin and the westernizers), "social democratism" in
the form of his willingness to tolerate an economic private sector and
to merely defend the interests of the proletariat legislatively, and
"bourgeois nationalism," the attacks coming from a purist Marxist-
Leninist position for the most part, of which Nina Andreeyva and company cannot be accused.

What the retro-Leninists cannot argue with is the CPRF's electoral
success to date, the CPRF becoming one of the more influential parliamentary parties after the December 1993 elections.[103] Zyuganov's campaigns have focused on everything but communist ideology. In 1993,
his TV campaign appearances stressed populist and nationalist
themes: Someone was attempting to remove a great power from the
world scene by destroying its economy through the destructive "reforms" of the Yeltsin government. Meanwhile, workers were laid off,
pensioners were humiliated by the miserly stipend allowed them,
overseas preachers threatened the hegemony of the Orthodox Church,
and "child pornography" proliferated. Crime was rampant. Civil war

was threatening the entire former Soviet Union, while Russians were being forced from their homes in the ex-Soviet republics. Russia must be reconstituted as an expansive state covering the former Soviet Union, her armed forces made second to none, her technologically advanced military-industrial complex revitalized. A music video accompanied the CPRF TV presentations, featuring a young man singing about the trials of his compatriots from the distant past to the present day. The singer himself was presented against a background of a church tower (he crossed himself before the song began), and images of Russian warriors from Aleksandr Nevskiy to Marshal Zhukov were contrasted with pictures of children begging in the streets and red banners waving at CPRF rallies. "God is with us, Rus!" he sang, implying that brighter days would follow the current struggle.[104]

Evaluating National Bolshevism

Recognizing the sense of common kinship that permeates the ethnonational bond clears a number of hurdles. First, it qualitatively distinguishes national consciousness from non-kinship identities (such as those based on religion or class) with which it has all too often been grouped. Secondly, an intuitive sense of kindredness or extended family would explain why nations are endowed with a very special psychological dimension—an emotional dimension—not enjoyed by essentially functional or juridical groupings, such as soci-economic classes or states.

—Walker Connor, *Ethnonationalism: the Quest for Understanding*[105]

Compatriots in the South and Southern part of Central Vietnam! The North, Center, and South are part and parcel of Vietnam! . . . We have the same ancestors, we are of the same family, we are all brothers and sisters. . . . No one can divide the children of the same family. Likewise, no one can divide Vietnam.

—Ho Chi Minh[106]

Mikhail Agursky defined National Bolshevism as

the Russian statist ideology that legitimizes the Soviet political system from the *etatiste* point of view, contrary to its exclusive Marxist legacy. . . . I would like to define *etatisme* as a powerful form of nationalism. . . . National Bolshevism does not reject Communist ideology though it strives to minimize its importance to the level necessary for legitimacy. Moreover, its objectives are different from those of Communist ideology. National Bolshevism in its original form strove for world domination conceived as the universal Russian Empire cemented by Communist ideology. It is not excluded that in some circumstances National Bolshevism might limit itself to the *etatiste* concept of a Russian superpower.[107]

John Dunlop has taken the definition a step further: National Bolshevism is essentially a fascist ideology.[108] Fascism was actually an extreme nationalist administrative variant of what political theorist James
Burnham called the "managerial state," the twentieth-century version
of the integrated state. Modern liberal democracies (that is, the capitalist welfare state), fascist states, communist states, and Germany's Nazi
order all have represented attempts at managing modernity. Their
structural attributes are economic and political centralism, industrialism, and urbanism, and their ideological variations are marked by secularism, statism, collectivism, and a faith in progress. Fascists glorified
the integrated state, as extreme Russian *gosudarstvenniki* do, as the embodiment of the national will; the nation was the fascist's deity, and
the grand projects of the state, from economic development and management to war, were glorified, as was the cult of brute force. The nation through the state simply takes what it wants under the rule of
might makes right—social Darwinism operating on the grand scale.
Fascism, like its Black Hundred ancestor, glorified the past as well—a
nation needs its mythology to cement the collective and mobilize the
population—but was not truly reactionary or conservative; in fact, it
was quite the opposite. Fascism harnessed the energy of the human
tribal impulse for building a new order that is led by a vanguard party
but is collectivist-populist at heart. Nostalgia for the distant past and
the values of the tribal warrior and village were inevitably subsumed
by the imperatives of the modern order. How could the nation be
strong if the antiliberal impulse in fascism turned into anti-urbanism
and anti-industrialism? Modern states need modern economies and
modern armies, and that means urban and industrial organization and
technological advancement. Democracy divided the nation into factions and weakened the collective, so the cult of the leader, who was
mystically tied to the people, was developed. The general will would
be transmitted through the leader from the bottom up, and his orders
were the will of the mystical body that is the nation. Naturally, alien
elements in the body politic could not be tolerated. Anticosmopolitanism wasn't invented by Stalin.

This should all sound familiar by now, for National Bolshevism in
its original form is fascism with a communist face. In fact *all* ostensibly
communist revolutions and "wars of national liberation" have either
turned to a form of National Bolshevism or have been essentially National Bolshevik from the start. "The people" are never very interested
in the fate of the world proletariat. Marxist-Leninist slogans were particularly attractive to third world revolutionaries who needed a convenient pile of rhetorical mud to sling at the Western capitalist powers
and "world imperialism." The Soviet model of modernization at one

time looked attractive to African, Latin American, and Asian revolutionaries cum nationalists who wanted to develop their countries and simultaneously throw off the onerous yoke of Western colonialism. Capitalist development for them (as it does for Zyuganov) meant domination by the transnational corporations and the Western bankers. A variation of socialism in one country satisfied their particularist impulses. The Ho Chi Minhs and Fidel Castros of the world were impatient for a "great leap forward" that only the organizational and mobilizational expertise of the communists could provide.

Zyuganov's brand of National Bolshevism appears to owe much to Shimanovism, especially his attempts to fuse Orthodoxy with communist ideology. To give him his due, his theory of the two parties is a cleverly streamlined version of an actual phenomenon and should be taken seriously by revisionist students of CPSU history. Furthermore, his theories concerning the nature of the new world order are only an exaggerated version of what is actually happening in the developed world—the move toward a transnational order that is encroaching on the interests of the nations is real enough and not the mere product of an overheated imagination. Zyuganovism isn't a pure form of communo-facism either but rather a variant of National Bolshevism that inclines toward Agursky's limited *"etatiste* concept of a Russian superpower"*: Zyuganov doesn't harp on the cult of the warrior as so many National Bolsheviks have and do, instead focusing his attention on the "heroic vitalism"[109] of the Soviet Russian project, which includes the martyrdom of the Communists during the Great Patriotic War as well as the epic tale of the country's forced industrialization, a tale taken by National Bolsheviks as the modern equivalent of the construction of the pyramids. The tale, the myth, and the ideology itself, like the state, is confused with the abstract "people," who themselves have turned out to be objectively expendable. How else can a man who idealizes the *narod* justify the butcher who slaughtered untold millions of them like so much livestock? The attachment to the National Bolshevik myth is strong, perhaps unbreakable, for people of Zyuganov's age and persuasion. If the myth is repudiated, then they cannot justify themselves or their parents. The glow of the victory in the Great Patriotic War would lose its luster, and the Great Teacher himself would be exposed as a pock-marked psychopath, an evil dwarf with a malignantly suspicious mind who bears no resemblance to the giant portrayed by the idealists.

Zyuganov, like so many of us, has never been able to love his people for what they *are*. Without the corrective of the doctrine of original sin, men have molded gods from the poor clay of the fallen earth. To give up their idols would be to commit suicide. National Bolsheviks delude themselves by imagining that the totalitarianism they are nostalgic for was merely the modernized variant of *sobornost*, the mass "collective" simply the Sovietized peasant commune, and Communist materialism the fulfillment of Christian theism. The Stalinist modernization they praise actually worked to undermine the very communitarian qualities they ascribe to Russians by destroying the village and what remained of the face-to-face aspect of Russian life. Self-delusion is self-preservation.

National Bolshevism as such is probably not long for this world. The electoral victories of Zyuganov's CPRF were built on a base of support made up disproportionately of old people. For them, the CPRF means the relative security of the Brezhnev stagnation period and the assurance that the banners they served under will not be desecrated.[110] This doesn't mean that some variation of the "single stream" version of history cannot prosper in the new Russia. Young people may not be particularly nostalgic for Brezhnev, but they are every bit as susceptible to the narcotic of *derzhava* as their parents and grandparents. Some may buy a version of Soviet-Russian history that recognizes the break that the October Revolution signified but still points to the victory in the Great Patriotic War as a victory of the Russian *narod*, and the achievements of the cosmonauts as a specifically *Russian* phenomenon. The Russian current simply overtook, and eventually obscured, the Soviet in this view. The difference is an important one, for this revisionist view does not stress the essential role of the party (as does National Bolshevism).[111] What National Bolshevism as popular ideology essentially does is legitimize nationalist revisionism. If young people aren't satisfied with the cult of the Great Patriotic War and Gagarin, or fascism with a communist face, the National Bolsheviks should at least get the credit for opening the door for the real thing, either aggressive populism in the guise of Zhirinovskiyism or what Russian radicals call the ideology of the "national revolution."

Notes

1. "Borba s tak nazyvaemym rusofilstvom, ili put gosudarstvennogo samoubiistva" (The struggle with the so-called 'Russophiles,' or the path to state suicide). Cited in John Dunlop, *The Faces of Contemporary Russian Nationalism* (Princeton: Princeton University Press, 1983), 232.

2. Cited in ibid., 3.

3. Aleksandr Solzhenitsyn, *The Oak and the Calf*, trans. Harry Willetts (New York: Harper & Row, 1979), 245.

4. The comments were made during the 1995 parliamentary election campaign.

5. *Washington Times*, 26 September 1995.
6. Stephen Carter, *Russian Nationalism: Yesterday, Today, Tomorrow* (New York: St. Martin's, 1990), 45.
7. Ibid.
8. Cited in Walter Laqueur, *Black Hundred: The Rise of the Extreme Right in Russia* (New York: HarperCollins, 1993), 76–77.
9. Cited in Mikhail Heller and Aleksandr M. Nekrich, *Utopia in Power: The History of the Soviet Union from 1917 to the Present*, trans. Phyllis B. Carlos (New York: Summit, 1986), 143.
10. Ibid., 144.
11. Carter, *Russian Nationalism*, 46.
12. Ibid.
13. Ibid.
14. For more on Ustraylov, see Carter, *Russian Nationalism*, 46–48, Heller and Nekrich, *Utopia in Power*, 145–151, and Dunlop, *Faces of Contemporary Russian Nationalism*, 255–258.
15. Carter, *Russian Nationalism*, 46.
16. Lenin had identified two streams of Russian thought in the pre-Revolutionary period, one left-leaning, progressive, and radical, that of the more radical westernizers, and the other, which he associated with the Slavophiles and Pan-Slavists, right wing and reactionary. Lenin thought it permissible to praise the progressive-radical current of Russia's particular history.
17. Cited in Heller and Nekrich, *Utopia in Power*, 146.
18. The title of the anthology was probably a conscious play on the title of the *Vekhi* ("Landmarks" or "Signposts") symposium.
19. Cited in Carter, *Russian Nationalism*, 47.
20. Ibid.
21. Ibid.
22. Heller and Nekrich, *Utopia in Power*, 148.
23. Ibid.
24. Ibid., 150.
25. Ibid.
26. Cited in Alex De Jonge, *Stalin and the Shaping of the Soviet Union* (New York: William Morrow, 1986), 485.
27. Heller and Nekrich, *Utopia in Power*, 150.
28. Carter, *Russian Nationalism*, 48. Carter asserts that Lenin, as well as Trotsky, was prepared to "exploit" the changing landmarks movement in the early 1920s. Lunacharsky, Commissar for Education, even coined a phrase, "Red patriotism," for the new National Bolshevism.
29. Ibid.
30. Ibid., 49.
31. Adam B. Ulam, *Stalin, The Man and His Era* (Boston: Beacon, 1973), 241.
32. Ibid.
33. Ibid., 266.
34. Cited in Carter, *Russian Nationalism*, 50.
35. Agursky examined National Bolshevism in *The Third Rome: National Bolshevism in the USSR* (Boulder, Colo.: Westview, 1987).

36. Carter, *Russian Nationalism*, 50.
37. Bulgakhov refused. Ibid.
38. But not their generals. See Laqueur, *Black Hundred*, 62.
39. Dunlop does note that Stalin did refurbish some monuments related to Russian military triumphs in the past, and that the Troitsa-Sergeyeva Lavra, Russia's oldest monastery, was restored as well. Dunlop, *Faces of Contemporary Russian Nationalism*, 12.
40. John Dunlop (p. 10) attributes this phrase to émigré sociologist Nicholas Timasheff.
41. Dunlop, *Faces of Contemporary Russian Nationalism*, 10.
42. Ibid.
43. Ibid.
44. De Jonge, *Stalin and the Shaping of the Soviet Union*, 305.
45. A false rumor, to be sure. Ulam, *Stalin*, 680.
46. Cited in ibid., 593.
47. Khrushchev gives a first hand view of Stalin's attitude toward Jews in his memoirs, *Khrushchev Remembers*, ed. and trans. Strobe Talbott (Boston: Little, Brown, 1970), 258–69.
48. Ulam, *Stalin*, 678. "Kulaks" were prosperous peasants who were the original targets of Soviet oppression in the countryside.
49. Ibid., 680.
50. See ibid., 706–7 for more on the origins of the Leningrad affair. Stalin's distaste for the Leningrad party organization furthered the image of the *Vozhd* as Russian nationalist. The Western-inspired architecture (not to mention the "progressive" atmosphere) of Saint Petersburg, later Leningrad, had been interpreted by many nationalists as insulting to Moscow, the very heart and soul of Russia, a rejection of all things Russian.
51. According to Heller and Nekrich, the plot would proceed like so: "Act One, sentencing [of the Kremlin doctors] after full confessions; Act Two, execution by hanging . . . ; Act Three, pogroms throughout the country; Act Four, Jewish personalities from the world of culture would turn to Stalin, asking that he protect the Jews from pogroms and give them permission to go back to the land; Act Five, mass deportation of Jews, 'at their own request,' to the countries' eastern territories. The philosopher D. Chesnokov, a member of the Presidium of the Central Committee, had written a book explaining the reasons for the deportation of the Jews. The book had been printed, and the original was being awaited for its distribution to the top party and government circles. As for the appeal by the country's leading Jews, not only had it been written: it had already been signed," *Utopia in Power*, 503–4.
52. Ibid., 727.
53. Ulam, *Stalin*, 736–737. Ulam, probably correctly, claims that this time Stalin, half-crazed by the suspicions that plagued him in his dotage, really believed this plot was at least half true—and Ulam believes he had good reason to be suspicious. The Soviet leadership had concluded, so the argument goes, that it was simply impossible to go on like this, each of them wondering if today might be his last. It is difficult to imagine what life under Stalin's thumb

must have been like. Why did it take so long for Stalin's henchmen to grow weary enough of the constant tension to imagine the boss's removal?

54. Ulam connects the two "Doctors' Plots" as well, *Stalin*, 736.

55. De Jonge, *Stalin and the Shaping of the Soviet Union*, 477.

56. Ibid., 478.

57. Ibid., 481.

58. Cited in Ibid., 481.

59. Heller and Nekrich note the following "titles" and honorifics, among others, attached to the name of Stalin: Leader and Teacher of the Workers of the World; Father of the Peoples; Wise and Intelligent Chief of the Soviet People; the Greatest Genius of All Times and Peoples; the Greatest Military Leader of All Times and Peoples; Corphaeus of the Sciences; Faithful Comrade-in-Arms of Lenin; Devoted Continuor of Lenin's Cause; the Lenin of Today; Mountain Eagle; and Best Friend of all Children. Not bad for a Georgian shoemaker's son. *Utopia in Power*, 507.

60. Ibid., 507–8.

61. Ibid., 508.

62. Cited in De Jonge, *Stalin and the Shaping of the Soviet Union*, 485.

63. Cited in Ulam, *Stalin*, 701.

64. For an elaboration of this view, see Robert Nisbet, *History of the Idea of Progress* (New York: Basic Books, 1980).

65. Cited in De Jonge, *Stalin and the Shaping of the Soviet Union*, 491.

66. Ibid.

67. Ibid.

68. For more on the Khrushchev period and its relation to the growth of Russian nationalism, see Dunlop, *Faces of Contemporary Russian Nationalism*, 29–37, and Carter, *Russian Nationalism*, 55–61.

69. The film is replete with religious and nationalist references and images. *Andrey Rublev* graphically depicts the rape of Holy Russia by foreigners—the Tartars in this case—and the long-suffering Russian people, some of whom have lost their faith, are redeemed by the saintly figure of the monk Andrey, himself a man who had been shaken by the savagery of the world around him. In a fascinating sequence, the neophyte bell maker Boriska, Andrey hovering in the background, successfully molds a bell for a church ravaged by the Tartars. The brutal grand prince decrees that if the bell doesn't ring properly, the boy will be beheaded, bringing a Slavophilish populist note to the film. In the end the bell rings, implying that the bells will once again ring in Holy Russia, and Andrey pledges to resume painting icons while Boriska molds bells for the church.

70. For more on Young Guardism, see Alexander Yanov, *The Russian Challenge and the Year 2000* (New York: Basil Blackwell, 1987), 105–127.

71. For more on the *Molodaya Gvardiya* episode, see Dunlop, *Faces of Contemporary Russian Nationalism*, 218–227. See also Carter, *Russian Nationalism*, 83–87.

72. Dunlop, *Faces of Contemporary Russian Nationalism*, 34–35.

73. Cited in ibid., 265.

74. Ibid., 38–39.

75. Carter, *Russian Nationalism*, 82.

76. Ibid., 83.

77. For more on Shimanov, see ibid., 71, 107–9. See also Ludmilla Alexeyeva, *Soviet Dissent: Contemporary Movements for National, Religious, and Human Rights* (Middletown, Conn.: Wesleyan University Press, 1985), 433–34; and Yanov, *Russian Challenge*, 231–48.

78. The CPRF claims between 500,000 and 600,000 members, making it the largest political party in Russia. Since the party still retains some property and has inherited what remains of the CPSU's Russian apparatus, as well as the Soviet Communist Party's organizational experience, it is fair to say that the CPRF enjoys a certain edge over parties that have more or less started from scratch in the last few years.

79. Biographical information is from Gennadiy Zyuganov, *Drama Vlasti* (The drama of power) (Moscow: Paleya, 1993), 3. *Drama Vlasti*, billed as a "political autobiography," is actually a collection of articles and interviews by and with Zyuganov, with commentary by the author. The articles chart Zyuganov's political evolution in the late *perestroika* period and the first two years of the Yeltsin regime in Russia.

80. The letter calls on Russians to defend the Homeland, the "united, indivisible" state, without which "we have no place under the sun." "A Word to the People" also set the example for the unsuccessful (so far) efforts of Zyuganov and others to unite "patriots" of all stripes against the Yeltsin regime, calling on workers, engineers, the army, the Orthodox Church, as well as liberals, monarchists, and communists to join together for the "salvation of the Fatherland." The Soviet Union was called "our home" and "stronghold" [oplot]." Three of the signatories of "A Word to the People" were imprisoned for their support of the coup. The letter was originally published in *Sovetskaya Rossiya*, 23 July 1991. The citations are from the version reproduced in *Drama Vlasti*, 40–44.

81. *Sovetskaya Rossiya*, 20 March 1991.

82. See especially *Sovetskaya Rossiya*, 7 May 1991.

83. *Sovetskaya Rossiya*, 6 June 1991.

84. *Sovetskaya Rossiya*, 25 June 1991.

85. *Pravda*, 26 February 1993.

86. *Den*, 21–27 February 1993.

87. *Sovetskaya Rossiya*, 3 July 1993.

88. *Sovetskaya Rossiya*, 28 August 1993.

89. The kind of reform the patriots had in mind was apparently something along the lines of Yuri Andropov's aborted program, one that allowed for deviations from Marxist-Leninist purism, but that would maintain discipline and order. Needless to say, the patriots of Volodin's stripe would also have allowed free reign for a single stream version of history, with modifications duly approved by the party, the vanguard of the nation, not the proletariat, especially, heaven forbid, the world proletariat.

90. *Sovetskaya Rossiya*, 20 August 1992.

91. Gennadiy Zyuganov, "The Russian Question," *Sovetskaya Rossiya*, 3 July 1993.

92. Gennadiy Zyuganov, *Derzhava* (Moscow: Informpechat, 1994), 66.

93. Ibid., 21.

94. Ibid., 19.

95. Zyuganov, "Russian Question."

96. Zyuganov, *Derzhava*, 23.

97. Ibid., 25.

98. See *Derzhava*, 8–9 for an example of the environmentalist current in Zyuganov's conspiratology.

99. Zyuganov supported the Supreme Soviet deputies during the crisis, but left the White House before the tanks blasted the deputies into submission, probably imagining that he must avoid direct confrontation with the Yeltsin regime for the time being in order to thwart the "conductor's" provocation. See *Derzhava*, 52–64, "Russia above the Abyss," for more on Zyuganov's view of the "conductor" and his provocational "planned explosions."

100. Zyuganov subscribes to Huntington's "clash of civilizations" thesis and hopes that Russia will provide a needed geopolitical counterweight to the West in the future. For more on this aspect of his ideology, see his book *Russia Is My Homeland* (Rossiya—rodina moya) (Moscow: Informpechat, 1996). Zyuganov explicitly connects himself with the ideas of Danilevskiy in this book, strengthening his claims of the single stream ideology's validity. Interestingly, Zyuganov also moves himself closer to the ideas of "sustainable development" championed by environmentalists (and Solzhenitsyn) in this book, a notion that contradicts his ideas about the necessity of industrialization and the militarization of the USSR, as well as his vision of the revival of the Russian superpower.

101. "From liberalism is born constitutional government . . . the President will be taken from among our creatures, our slaves." *The Protocols*, 149.

102. "From ancient times, Russia recognized itself as the successor and preserver of the imperial heritage. 'Moscow is the Third Rome.' . . . Russia is the continuation of the universal imperial tradition." Zyuganov, *Derzhava*, 15. Zyuganov goes on at some length about the need to reconcile the pre-Revolutionary and post-Revolutionary stages of Russian history: "Having united the 'red' ideal of social justice and the 'white' ideal of national . . . statehood [Russia will have] the might [necessary to reestablish] our Fatherland!" *Derzhava*, 33.

103. The CPRF carried the day in the December 1995 elections, winning nearly a quarter of the party list vote.

104. The particular references made in the text are to the November 22, 1993 CPRF presentation made on Ostankino state television.

105. Walker Connor, *Ethnonationalism: The Quest for Understanding* (Princeton: Princeton University Press, 1994), 74.

106. Cited in ibid., 199.

107. Cited in ibid., 48.

108. See Dunlop, *Faces of Contemporary Russian Nationalism*, 254–265.

109. Again I am indebted to John Dunlop for the phrase. See ibid., 263.

110. See, for instance, Jonathan Adler's "Pitching the President," *Newsweek*, 17 June 1996, on the aging communist electorate.

111. This is the middle-of-the-road gosudarstvennik line that is espoused by the current Russian regime. See chapter 9 for more on what I call "reform nationalism."

6

Zhirinovskiy and *The Last Drive to the South*

Russians are the most humiliated and insulted nation.

—Vladimir Zhirinovskiy[1]

What are Zhirinovskiy's positions and who are his followers? While campaigning for president in 1991, he promised that he would feed the country within 72 hours. How? "Very simply. I'll move the troops, about 1.5 million strong, into the former GDR; rattle my nuclear sabers; and they'll give me everything." By "them" he naturally means the West.

—Aleksandr Yanov[2]

The nationalist's claim of a people's uniqueness is the source of resistance to using foreign models of development and is based on an intuition that has some basis in reality. The real question for nationalists regarding the worth of any reform project is how it would channel the substance of national character into the framework of a given model. The Soviet model encouraged the worst features of the Russian national character, and Zhirinovskiy is the present-day politician who best manipulates the resentment and envy of Russians—both of them aggravated by seventy years of communist rule and by the competition with the West. His vision of tomorrow's Russia is modernist-statist and expansionist, traits that are inherited from past efforts to modernize Russia and from the imperatives of Russian history.

E xplaining the relative popularity of Vladimir Zhirinovskiy with Russian voters to Westerners unfamiliar with Russian and Soviet history can be a daunting task. Zhirinovksiy has (among other things) threatened Germany and Japan with nuclear annihilation, propositioned female reporters, and thrown flower pots at protesters

181

on a European trip. Many Westerners simply do not take him for a serious politician. Surely a vote for Zhirinovskiy is merely a protest against the increasing uncertainties of life in a reformist Russia, they reason. The Russian people must be humiliated by this grotesque figure. My answer to them is always the same: Guess again. To understand Zhirinovskiy's appeal for many Russians,[3] as well as his program of geopolitical expansionism and socioeconomic populism, one must bear in mind the cultural and historical peculiarities of the Russians, as well as a certain urge all people experience from time to time: the temptation to live at your neighbor's expense.

Russia and Zhirinovskiy

The Tenacity of Culture

Economist Thomas Sowell,[4] in attacking egalitarianism, has built his case for explaining socioeconomic statistical disparities among various national groups on the apparent tenacity of group cultural characteristics. "It is not a foregone conclusion," Sowell has written, "but an empirical question whether the Irish, the Chinese, the Germans, etc., in various lands are more like the other peoples of those lands or more like the people in their respective countries of origins and their kinsmen elsewhere around the globe."[5] Sowell notes that cultural characteristics appear to be extremely tenacious, various national groups retaining general group characteristics over periods of centuries in various environments. Ireland, for example, "spends a higher percentage of its income on alcohol than any other nation in Europe," and the Irish of Birmingham, England (7 percent of the city's population at the time) "constitute 60 percent of those arrested for drunkenness." More telling, perhaps, of the Irish taste for alcohol is Sowell's observation that "the rate of alcohol psychosis among Irish Americans" is five times that of Italian Americans and *fifty* times that of Jewish Americans.[6] Sowell explains the statistical disparity culturally: Italian and European Jewish cultures have historically made drunkenness a taboo: Italians and Jews are wine drinkers, consuming far less hard liquor.[7]

The Chinese have historically been disproportionately prevalent in the most "difficult and demanding" intellectual fields wherever they have been. "In Malaysia, where Malay college students outnumber the Chinese three-to-one in liberal arts, the Chinese outnumber the Malays eight-to-one in science and fifteen-to-one in engineering." Similar disparities are found in the United States.[8] The Chinese have justly earned a reputation as a hardworking and industrious people who have been willing to take on the most arduous physical labor under the most appalling of environmental conditions: In nineteenth century Siam, for instance, "the rickshaws were virtually all pulled by Chinese," and the Chinese performed some of the hardest physical labor in early twentieth-century South Africa as well. They were so diligent, in fact, that they "were later sent home" after other workers raised a fuss over their presence.[9]

The Germans too have demonstrated particular aptitudes in certain fields over time and space. Sowell observes that Germans have achieved notable successes as family farmers both at home and in Brazil, Australia, Ireland, and Mexico, as well as in fields involving technology and craftsmanship.[10] "Jewish peddlers followed in the wake of the Roman legions and sold goods in the conquered territories" and, Sowell notes, are found selling their wares "on the sidewalks of New York 2,000 years later."[11] Far from being mere stereotypes, group behavioral patterns transcend any given society. "[The tenacity of cultural peculiarities] does suggest that cultural patterns do not readily disappear, either with the passage of time or with social engineering. The very fact that there are still Jews in the world, after centuries of determined efforts to absorb them . . . implies that environmental influences extend well beyond immediate circumstances—and might be described as cultural inheritance."[12]

If Sowell is correct, and there is plenty of evidence suggesting he is, then nationalists, whose arguments for particularism often turn on the uniqueness of the nation, are justified in their wariness of foreign models of development. Russia, as the nationalists maintain, is a country of communalism, not individualism. The practices and habits of the community, and under the Soviet regime, its bastard cousin, the collective, are deeply ingrained in Russian culture. History, environment, geography, and national mythology have all played a role in perpetuating these habits, and these peculiarities have encouraged Russian expansionism and shaped Russia's image of itself and the West.

Geography, Environment, and Russian Culture

> In the case of Russia the geographic element is particularly important because . . . the country is so poor that it affords at best a precarious existence. This poverty gives the inhabitants little latitude for action; it compels them to operate within a very narrow band of options.
>
> —Richard Pipes[13]

> There are specific geopolitical factors that have played a part in the development of the Russian soul. Russia is situated in bad climate

zones, with bad neighbors. For 700 years there have always been
wars . . . The Tartar for 300 years . . . With Turkey alone, thirty
wars. With others, dozens, hundreds of wars. That is why there is
something animal-like about "Russianness." Our intention to
tame that instinct is the central point of our program. That's why
we need a strong army, so that no one should be in Russia's way.

—Vladimir Zhirinovskiy[14]

The Russian heartland around Moscow, the forest zone that is the central area where the modern-era Russian state had its beginnings, lies
just south of the Arctic tundra (which "cannot support organized
human life"[15]) and is part of a vast forest belt that stretches across
northern Eurasia. Until the middle of the sixteenth century, the Russians were largely confined to this area because the vast Eurasian
steppe to the south, with its coveted fertile black earth soil, was controlled by the Turkic conquers who had cut the trade route to Byzantium at the beginning of the thirteenth century, ending the salad days
of Kievan Rus.[16] The Russians would not become the lords of the steppe
to the south until the end of the eighteenth century. The vast Eurasian
expanse, north to south and east to west, is in fact a huge plain, a
relatively flat surface disturbed only by the "ancient and weather-
beaten" Urals, which "constitute no effective barrier between Europe
and Asia."[17] From north to south in European Russia flow the wide
rivers, the Dnieper, the Don, and the Volga, emptying into the Black
and Caspian Seas, providing Russia with ready made water arteries,
the hub of the Russian transportation system. The southward flowing
rivers had naturally turned Kievan Russian attention toward Byzantium, while the indefensible vastness of the steppe left the Russians
open to the depredations of the mounted hordes from the south and
east. Geographic and climatic conditions, along with poor soil, made
existence in the Moscovite heartland precarious: Crop yields in Moscovite Russia were low. If the weather held, the short growing season
yielded enough grain for subsistence but not enough to consistently
produce a significant surplus, making the peasants of old Russia poor
by comparison with those of Europe. A failed crop (and one in three
Russian crops have historically failed) might mean famine.[18] The harsh-
ness of the Russian winters is legendary; the Gulf Stream (which helps
warm western and northern Europe) barely reaches the northern coasts
of Russia.[19]

Richard Pipes has noted, however, that harsh climate and poor soil
cannot be entirely blamed for the low productivity of Russian agriculture: "Scandinavia, despite its northern location, attained already by
the eighteenth century yield ratios of 1:6, while the Baltic provinces of

the Russian Empire, where the land was in the hands of German barons, in the first half of the nineteenth century had yields from 1:4.3 to 1:5.1, that is, of a kind which made it possible to begin accumulating a surplus."[20] Another factor influencing low crop yields in Russia, according to Pipes, was the lack of markets for any surplus grain that might be produced. "Unfavorable natural conditions made for low yields; low yields resulted in poverty; poverty meant that there were no buyers for agricultural produce; the lack of buyers discouraged yield improvements. The net effect was the absence of incentives."[21] Incentives and technological innovation might have appeared had commercial contacts with outsiders been sustained, but time and again such contacts were cut off, first by the Central Asian nomads and later by the consolidation efforts of the expanding Muscovite state itself (it destroyed its rival Novgorod, which had become a member of the prosperous Hanseatic League of commercial city-states).[22] With lack of incentives added to harsh climatic conditions, poor soil, and the crudeness of Russian farming implements, it is small wonder that Russians failed to increase crop yields. The Russian peasant faced the additional burden (because of the long winters) of keeping his livestock indoors two months longer than his Western counterparts. "When finally set free in the meadow," Russian livestock was often "in a thoroughly emaciated condition," due to lost grazing time. Such difficulties discouraged livestock production and "caused perennial shortages of manure [for fertilization], especially in the north, where it is most needed."[23]

Of course, such environmental and economic conditions carried with them social consequences: "Everything indicates that fields lying in the north have been cultivated by people who conceive agricultural exploitation as collective labor, and those in the south by people determined to safeguard the independence and the freedom of initiative of each cultivator on his land."[24] The Russian peasants of the forest region had to complete their field work in four to six months, whereas European farmers had eight or nine months to do the same work. This situation led to the "pooling of resources, human as well as animal and material." Until the Bolshevik Revolution, most of the individual farms were found in the Ukraine and the Cossack regions.[25] The model that prevailed in the Russian heartland was that of the peasant commune, the *obshchina* or *mir*, where arable land and pasture was held in common. The commune "enjoyed peasant loyalty." It "provided a high degree of security without seriously inhibiting freedom of movement. It also allowed common access to meadow as well as co-ordination of field work which was highly desirable under the prevailing climatic conditions."[26]

The national character of a particular people is always manysided
and complex. Was Soviet collectivism, for example, merely the continuation of the *obshchina* tradition by other means? It is far too simplistic,
as Pipes has pointed out, to see the Soviet collective farm, the *kolkhoz*,
as merely the modern day equivalent of the peasant commune:

> The analogy has little to recommend it, except for a negative factor com-
> mon to both institutions, i.e. the absence of private ownership in land.
> The differences are quite basic. The mir was not a collective; farming on
> it was carried out privately, by households. Even more significantly, the
> peasant living in the mir owned the product of his labor, whereas in the
> *kolkhoz*, it belongs to the state which compensates the farmer for his
> work.[27]

Russian nationalists of the postcommunist era are given to describing the Russian national character as "collectivist," with all that word's
connotations of modern mass society, a society wherein the beehive
works on grand projects, the worker bees ready to sacrifice themselves
for the good of the hive as defined by the ultimate queen bee—the
Party, the state, or the *narod* as collective, transcendental spirit. Stalin
supposedly once observed that one man's death is a tragedy, a million
merely statistics; the Great Leader and Teacher seldom missed the essence of any particular political or social question: Collectivism is the
complete negation of individual personality and responsibility.

Soviet collectivism had a particular quality of its own, one that
tended to encourage the worst characteristics of the Russian past, for
the characteristics of a people will eventually be channeled into the
new forms, whatever they may be. Pipes has observed that climatic
conditions encouraged the Russian peasant to expend the least amount
of time, energy, and resources as possible in his field work.[28] He also
noted that, outside markets being practically absent for much of Russian history, whatever surplus grain remained would most likely be
distilled. Vodka is not the national drink of the Russians for nothing.[29]

Alex De Jonge went further than Pipes. Russia, according to De
Jonge, is a "grain belt country," one of those countries of northern latitudes where the drink of choice (and necessity) is hard liquor. The
harsh environment and living conditions of the northern latitudes may
well be what induces the drinker of grain spirits to "look for oblivion."
The grain-belt drinker "tries to get drunk as quickly as possible,
whereupon he tends to keel over." The grain-belt drinker is a man of
"extravagant excesses," who views beer as merely a chaser, a man attuned to bursts of energy and labor, followed by oblivion.[30] He is
uniquely unsuited to Soviet-style industrial labor discipline, the disci-

pline of the five-year plan, of exceeding production quotas and "voluntary" weekend work days. The grain belt is "the wrong place entirely to look for a willing and able industrial proletariat."[31] Soviet conditions apparently tended to push the Russian worker further in the direction of drunken oblivion and certainly encouraged irresponsibility.

It is probably more accurate to describe the traditional Russian social character as communal rather than collective. The old Russian commune was a cooperative, not a mass or collective endeavor. Thus Russian literature and folkways stressed the cooperative and the communal. The Slavophiles praised the commune as a bulwark against the selfish and materialistic brand of commercial individualism that was developing in the West, and Russia's agrarian economy, coupled with the traditionalism of the cooperative masses, encouraged a distrust of capitalism and profit seeking. Russian agro-economic social organization had accented community togetherness and the mutual responsibility of community members, one for the other. It was a more egalitarian way of life than that of the West: Communal division and periodic repartition was intended to "guarantee every peasant an equitable share of the land, and every household enough land to support itself and meet its responsibilities to the landlord and the state."[32]

What such social and economic arrangements did not serve to encourage, not so much by design as by practice, was initiative, innovation, entrepreneurship, and a sense of the individual's responsibility for his own fate. The image of the Russian masses held by some westernizers, past and present, as cowardly, indolent, besotted, barbaric, and envious children is, like all such simplistic images, insulting and wildly exaggerated. Still, stereotypes do contain a grain of truth, not the whole truth, but truth nevertheless. A frequently heard description of the Russian peasant mentality draws an unflattering picture of village life: Upon hearing that his neighbor has acquired a milk cow, the Russian peasant is more apt to pray for the cow's untimely death than for the will and good fortune to buy one of his own. True, old Russia had a merchant class, peasants frequently supplemented their incomes through cottage industries, medieval Novgorod was the Russian equivalent of a Italian merchant city-state, and the farmers and Cossacks of the black earth region and steppes were renowned for their independence and industry. But one of the overarching characteristics of Russian culture as it developed from the Muscovite period on was the stress on the group over the individual. Russian Orthodoxy, particularly after the Petrine period awakened conservative resistance to westernization, stressed almsgiving, aid to the poor, and the superiority of the spiritual over the temporal, further strengthening anti-individualist and anticapitalist tendencies among the Russians.

Suffering, purification, and redemption are recurrent themes in Russian literature, and in some Russian minds, at least, the sufferer gains a sort of moral superiority. Envy could not be far behind, since some Russians dismissed Western economic and political development as crass and demeaning, apparently as a means of reassuring themselves of suffering Russia's moral superiority. The mutiny of the peasant-soldiers during World War I, many of them abandoning the front and carrying out a spontaneous "land reform" through looting their more prosperous neighbors, aided the success of the Bolshevik coup. The mutiny was a traditional Russian *bunt*, a spontaneous and unorganized rebellion, destructive and uncontrolled. The long suffering Russian peasant felt he had suffered enough—the landlord and, in this case, the czar and the general staff, had gone too far for too long. That this was true enough did not necessarily justify pillage and robbery, but the logic of the notion of the moral superiority of the sufferer applied at home as well. For those who fell into this trap, it was quite natural to engage in the blame game: Since I (or we) am (or are) morally superior to him (or them), but he (or they) continues to live better than I (or we) do, then all of one's (or the Russian people's) ills were most probably the results of his (or their) plots and machinations. How else to explain his (or their) wealth and power? Thus the prospering neighbor (or country) must have come by his wealth illicitly. Because wealth is viewed as a finite pie (not something that can be created, perhaps a distorted reflection of the fact that the *obshchina* held a finite amount of land in common), it follows that he is wealthy at my expense—he has plotted to subjugate me.

Comparing Russia to the West on equal terms is akin to comparing apples and oranges, only worse: The psychological damage done to many Russian nationalists by such comparisons was and is dangerous to both Russia and the West. The need to imitate the West in order to "modernize" Russia socially, economically, diplomatically, and militarily stimulated a defensive reaction in Russian patriots to the criticism, even ridicule, of their homeland and people that one-to-one comparisons induced. In defending their people and homeland, some Russians resorted to outright lies that were told so often that the liar may have come to at least half-believe the untruth. Catherine the Great defended Russia in a letter to Voltaire by claiming that Russian peasants regularly had chicken for dinner, so often in fact, that they had turned to raising turkeys for variety.[33] The diplomat Antioch Katemir, in refuting the negative image of Russia offered in Locatelli's *Lettres moscovites*, claimed that Russian textiles matched those of Holland in quality and stressed the laudable qualities of patience and loyalty that typified the Russian peasant.[34]

Some Russian patriots were sensible enough to give the West its due but not anguish themselves with pointless inferiority-superiority questions: "I saw that in all countries there is more bad than good, that men are men everywhere; that intelligent people are everywhere rare, that there are everywhere plenty of fools, and, in a word, that our nation is no worse than any other," a Russian nobleman once observed.[35] For sensible people it was enough to claim that while their own people and country were no better than others, they were surely no worse. But for others, the lies weren't enough: "The problem with lies . . . is that the liar knows that they are untrue."[36] The result is what Liah Greenfeld identified as *ressentiment,* the resentment and hatred that come with feelings of inferiority, often accompanied by claims of superiority. It is an old feeling in Russia, that was if anything magnified under the Communists by cold war ideological competition. What student of Soviet affairs did not hear of claims that, among other superior qualities, the Soviet Union was crime-free, that top-flight free medical care was available to all, that Russians promoted the friendship of the peoples, or that Russians had invented everything from airplanes to telephones? If one accepts the view that wealth is a finite thing, then the Soviet image of a rapacious West tended to encourage a resentment of the comfortable circumstances of others: They had come by it illicitly, hadn't they? Still, no amount of empty boasting, half-baked theories, or half-believed lies could change the nature of the dilemma. The nationalist noble and playwright Denis Fonvisin put the Russian dilemma this way: "How can we remedy the two contradictory and most harmful prejudices: the first, that everything with us is awful, while in foreign lands everything is good; the second, that in foreign lands everything is awful, and with us everything is good?"[37]

The Economic and Historical Roots of Russian Expansion

Early Russian agricultural methods were not only comparatively unproductive but damaging to the soil as well. Until the nineteenth century, the Russian peasant used the three field method of cultivation (abandoned in Europe after the Middle Ages), which meant that one third of the arable land had to remain fallow in order to regain its fertility.[38] The history of Russian agriculture is thus "the tale of a land being mercilessly exploited without being given much if anything to nourish it and thus being driven to exhaustion."[39] Moreover, the amount of land available in the Russian heartland could not meet the needs of a population that was expanding already in the middle of the sixteenth century. By the middle of the eighteenth century, a population boom had begun. The population would quadruple in the next one hundred years (from about 17 million to about 68 million), partly as a result of the conquests made by the Russian state, conquests that were encouraged by the need for Russian peasants to colonize and cultivate virgin lands. The main thrust of Russian colonization and conquest has historically been to the south and east, to Siberia, the Central Asian steppe, and the southern black earth zone. The black earth region in particular offered better weather and richer soil for colonists.[40] Moreover, the southern steppe had

> served for centuries as the highway for Asiatic nomads to burst into Europe. The Mongol devastation was for the Russians only the most notable incident in a long series [of foreign intrusions], and it was followed by over two hundred years of Mongol rule. In effect, the steppe frontier, open for centuries, contributed hugely to the militarization of Russian society, a trend reinforced by the generally unprotected nature of the western border of the country.[41]

The Russian garrison state was born of a combination of Muscovite ambition and strategic and economic necessity: If Russia were to survive (much less prosper) and protect herself from invaders, she must become an invader herself. The Russian state in its original Kievan form in the tenth century was "under one three hundredth of its present extent. In 1462 it covered 15,000 square miles. By 1914 it occupied 8,660,000 square miles, the ethnic Russians establishing dominion over more than a hundred very different nationalities."[42] The Time of Troubles (1603–14) and the Bolshevik Revolution both ended in great losses of Russian territory and influence but were followed by periods of expansion as the state reconstituted itself and then some. Messianism abetted the expansionist efforts, and the very nature of Russian development cemented the tendency toward colonization, conquest, consolidation, and centralization. "Russian cities, few in number and, except for Moscow, small in population, came to serve primarily military and administrative purposes," fortresses and frontier outposts marked by their kremlins, the central citadel and administrative center of the city. Historian Nikolay Karamzin maintained that such circumstances encouraged autocracy: centralization of authority simplified administration and military preparedness. Russian expansion continued as the state gathered border areas, creating both opportunities for colonization and an ever widening protective buffer zone, which in the nineteenth century included Central Asia, Poland, and Alaska. Stalin extended the Russian buffer zone deep into Eastern Europe and the Balkans. The experience of the Civil War, allied intervention, the German invasion in 1941, and the terrible and heroic victory in the Great

Patriotic War have only served to harden two characteristics of the Russians and the Russian state already present before the Bolsheviks seized power: the suspicion of foreigners engendered by repeated invasions from the southeast (the Tartars in particular) and the west (Swedes, Poles, Frenchmen, Germans), and the glorification of the military and security services, whose regularization and modernization was begun under Peter the Great.

No politician in postcommunist Russia has more explicitly tied Russian survival and prosperity to territorial expansion than Vladimir Zhirinovskiy. No politician has exploited *ressentiment* regarding the West as effectively as Zhirinovskiy, and no other politician has managed to tap the Russian vice of neglecting personal responsibility and wallowing in envy of one's neighbor more skillfully than Zhirinovskiy. His weapons in the political battle are human frailty, chauvinism, envy, and self-pity, disguised as moral superiority and a seeking after justice and packaged as liberalism. What he is selling shares a number of characteristics with the selling points of other modern demagogues but is set off by his own personal style and policy prescriptions, which are uniquely Russian.

Who is Zhirinovskiy?[43]

> [After father's death] Mom was left without a livelihood. . . . She would grovelingly beg the cook [at the cafeteria where she worked] for some soup. . . . I never had enough to eat.[44]

> I myself am an ordinary citizen. . . . I am just like you, and I understand that these awful prices in the commercial and cooperative stores are beyond our pockets.[45]
>
> —Vladimir Zhirinovskiy

The facts of Zhirinovskiy's life and activities up until 1991 are fuzzy at best. What we know more or less certainly is that he was born in 1946 in the Kazakh city of Alma Alta, his father having died shortly before his birth. In 1964 he became a student at the Moscow Institute of Oriental Languages (later the name of the institute was changed to the Institute of Asian and African countries). Zhirinovskiy speaks four foreign languages—Turkish, English, French, and German. As a fifth year student he acted as an interpreter for a delegation of Soviet engineers sent to Turkey. He was expelled from Turkey for allegedly spreading Soviet propaganda, but Zhirinovskiy claims he was merely making gifts of Soviet lapel buttons to Turkish acquaintances. After graduating, Zhirinovskiy did his compulsory military service in the Caucasus (Georgia), serving in the staff headquarters and as a propagandist among the troops of the Caucasus Military District. In 1972 he moved to Moscow, where he worked with the Soviet Peace Committee, at the higher school of the trade unions, at the Foreign Law Collegium (he had taken a law degree from Moscow State University's night school program), and at the Mir publishing concern. He is married and has a son. Sometime in 1990 or 1991, he helped organize the Liberal Democratic Party (LDP).[46] In the 1991 presidential election, Zhirinovskiy made his first big political splash: virtually unknown a few short months before, he won about 6 million votes (roughly 7 percent of the total vote), placing him third behind Boris Yeltsin and former Soviet prime minister Nikolay Ryzhkov.

From the beginning, questions about Zhirinovskiy's background and personality have trailed him like an unwanted shadow. Is Zhirinovskiy Jewish? This is a question of no small importance to a man who purports to lead a "patriotic" organization, a man given to blaming Russia's ills on a "Zionist" plot as well as on the West. He has emphatically denied Jewish origins (his patronymic, Volfovich, is derived from a common Jewish name), claiming again and again that he is "Russian, Russian, Russian!"[47] Despite Zhirinovskiy's insistence that he is a "moderate in all things,"[48] Eduard Limonov, a former associate, has portrayed Zhirinovskiy as a cynical and unstable opportunist, a man given to some very immoderate sexual proclivities as well.[49] Zhirinovskiy's autobiography is in fact shot through with sexual references, including an account of his first attempted sexual encounter and references to politics in sexual terms.[50] Occasionally Zhirinovskiy throws fits of rage; among other incidents, he was involved in scuffles on the floor of the state Duma in 1995, struck Duma deputy Mark Goryachev in 1994 and attacked Duma candidate Telman Gdlyan in 1993.[51] If these incidents are considered along with his propensity for threatening other countries with nuclear annihilation, the question becomes, Is Zhirinovskiy crazy?

Zhirinovskiy claims that he is at once a political genius, a man of education and talent, a man of destiny and distinction, *and* a man of the people who can understand the plight of the ordinary citizen. He is a man envied by his doltish enemies ("An educated man with two university degrees who speaks European languages—where did he pop up from?"[52]) but is in touch with the concerns of ordinary Russians, a man who never was a member of the parasitical *nomenklatura* class:

> "They [the ruling class] are afraid of me," he once told Russian voters, "because I am the only one of all the republican presidential candidates who is not connected with the elite. I was never there at the top. I shall

represent you, millions of Russian citizens, those who receive, and still receive in these terrible years, only 200 rubles and live in two room apartments. There are the everlasting lines, from the maternity hospital to the grave. There is a total shortage of everything. You are made to do nothing but work—work so that those at the top get rich."[53]

The great man, however, cannot occupy himself with the mundane on a day-to-day basis, and he has attempted to explain what seems obvious (to him, anyway) to the Russian people: "Politics. You need a lot of free time for this. And a father with a lot of children will naturally be unable to go in for this because he has to devote all his emotional and physical efforts to his family. I have never been deeply in love with my wife. Our personal relationship has been OK, but we have not been head over heels in love. So I have been able to conserve my strength for politics."[54] Zhirinovskiy felt the call at a young age: "But even in early childhood something dawned on me," he claimed in his autobiography. "It was a kind of ultimate idea which was like the intellect governing the world . . . [even then] there was something . . . thoughts of something great were hovering over my head. . . . This was no accident."[55]

As an employee of the Soviet Peace Committee, Zhirinovskiy had not infrequently met with foreigners. He had specialized in "southern" affairs during his days at the university and in the army and had lived in Central Asia and the Caucasus. He learned Turkish and fancied himself an expert in geopolitics. Moreover, he had traveled more widely than the average Soviet citizen of the 1960s and 1970s. A man with a higher education, he had endured the deprivation that ordinary people experienced as the stuff of their daily lives. Surely his broad experience and education marked him for great things. Previous Russian bosses had, after all, been mediocre (at best) by comparison: "Gorbachev," Zhirinovskiy once wrote, "had an easy life. Why did he ruin the country? . . . He was the son of a kolkhoz chairman. . . . He lived like a little lord even then. Then he entered Moscow University and began to do Komsomol work. He got it all straightaway and enjoyed life. He did not have the potential to be a political leader. . . . [A]ll of Russia's rulers have lacked a classical education. Even Ulyanov [Lenin]. He was expelled from everywhere and eventually he passed his exams as an internal student. That is no education."[56]

The "ultimate idea" that came to occupy Zhirinovskiy's mind eventually took the form of his fundamental program: the drive to the south (*brosok na yug*). By the time he emerged on the political scene in the late Gorbachev period, the drive to the south was already formulated as the core of Zhirinovskiy's ideology. By 1991 he was certain that his time had come. During the presidential election campaign that year he told voters "If I do not win the election, I will not be the loser. You, the inhabitants of Russia, will be the losers."[57]

The Last Drive to the South

In his autobiography, *Posledniy Brosok Na Yug* [The last drive to the south], Zhirinovskiy lays out his vision of Russia as it is today—a humiliated country whose achievements have been denigrated and whose people are impoverished—and his strategy for restoring Russia to what he sees as her rightful place among the world's great powers. He sees Russia moving, under his leadership, from its current stage of humiliation through a stage of national, economic, and military regeneration, and ultimately to a stage he calls the end of Russian history, a millennium that marks the fulfillment of Russia's historic role. The millennium will be achieved when Russia consolidates control over its southern sphere of influence, stretching south to the Indian Ocean and thus ending military threats from the south, which have plagued Russia for much of her history, as well as ushering in a new era of peace and prosperity for the Russian people. In *The Last Drive to the South* Russia's regeneration, the prosperity of the Russian people, and the fulfillment of his own personal destiny are organically intertwined in this three-stage process. Humiliation, regeneration, and the promise of the millennium are the recurring themes, of the book as well as the outline of Zhirinovskiy's grand design.

The three stage historical process of regeneration that Zhirinovskiy describes in *The Last Drive to the South* is a comprehensive statement of a vision that he has been articulating since the 1991 presidential campaign.[58] His vision will be fulfilled, he believes, in distinct stages, a linear and progressive movement from humiliation through regeneration to consolidation and the Russian millennium. Zhirinovskiy does not regard politics, economics, or social issues as separate problems to be addressed through separate policies and sees himself a thinker on a grand scale rather than an ordinary politician who focuses on nuts and bolts sociopolitical prescriptions. He frequently makes contradictory statements on the specifics of his grand plan. As he sees it, the most important thing is to lead Russia to regeneration and the millennium; once that is done, the lesser problems will be solved. While inconsistent on matters of specific policy, Zhirinovskiy's vision is very consistent in the broad terms of his three-stage plan: Russia's present state of humiliation, Russia's regeneration in the near term, and the achievement of the millennium in the longer term.

Humiliation

> For decades you have been deceived, made fools of, and stuffed full of various dogmas![59]

> I will never allow anyone to humiliate Russians.[60]

> —Vladimir Zhirinovskiy

Zhirinovskiy's vision of Russia's humiliation is personal, national, and political-historical. The Russian people, a hardworking and noble nation as depicted by Zhirinovskiy, have been humiliated and impoverished at home, exploited and oppressed by corrupt rulers, and turned into second class citizens in the former Soviet republics. Zhirinovskiy often parallels his own personal humiliation and poverty with the daily struggles of the Russian people. Humiliation, he tells the Russians, has been the lot of the entire nation. His lot was that of the forgotten Russian, who, though a member of the Soviet *Staatvolk*, the backbone of both the Russian empire and its successor state, was reared in miserable conditions in a communal apartment.[61]

Moreover, Russians, who built the Soviet state, suffered at the hands of the minority nationalities, whom Zhirinovskiy depicts as favored by the Soviet bureaucracy.[62] It is true enough that the Soviet authorities practiced a sort of affirmative action in ensuring that local cadres were coopted by the system; it is equally true that Russians and other Eastern Slavs held the vast majority of top positions in the state and party apparatus. Jews in particular were blocked from most high state positions from the period of high Stalinism on. Russification continued under the Soviet regime. Though ordinary Russians had every right to wonder whether all the sacrifices of rapid industrialization, collectivization, and the war years were worth what they wound up with in the end, it is simply impossible for other nations formerly held by the Soviets to feel they have suffered any less than the Russians. In the eyes of Balts, Chechens, Crimean Tartars, and others, their own cultures were denigrated under Soviet rule even more than that of the Russians. In some cases, entire nations were deported to Siberia or the distant steppes of Central Asia, and the flower of the Baltic nations was eliminated in the Gulag by the Soviet (Balts read "Russian") "liberator." Russians resent the sacrifices their people had to make for the fulfillment of Soviet era projects in non-Russian areas, but the persistent view that Balts, Georgians, Jews, Volga Germans, and so on "live better" than Russians probably has its origins not only in resentment of Soviet projects designed to foster the "friendship of the peoples" but in the unrecognized (by many Russians) probability (as demonstrated by the work of Thomas Sowell) that many nations in the Soviet-Russian sphere of influence were *culturally* better able to improve themselves under *any socioeconomic* system. The Georgians, for example, were and are a conspicuous force in Russian open-air markets, earning a reputation as wily tradesmen. Some of the resentment is justified: The Georgians, like the Chechens, are renowned as racketeers. Much of the substance of Zhirinovskiy's attacks on "southerners" is based on the reality of one of the features of Caucasian life: clan based organized crime à la the Sicilian Mafia. On the other hand, the Baltic states were always more prosperous than Russia under both czars and commissars. Zhirinovskiy makes no such subtle distinctions, preferring to blend all together in a seething cauldron of Russian resentment. Be that as it may, Zhirinovskiy is no doubt invoking an image familiar to millions of Russians when he tells his readers that his mother "spent her whole life, all her seventy three years in torment." Shortly before her death she told him that she had "nothing to remember, not a single happy day." When she died in May 1985, Zhirinovskiy wrote that "I looked back over her life and I felt so bad that she had indeed experienced no joy. Nothing but humiliation and suffering all her life."[63]

Zhirinovskiy sees humiliation as pervasive and constantly reminds his audience of it. He also sees it as a stimulus to taking action to begin regeneration. *The Last Drive to the South* highlights Zhirinovskiy's personal struggle against hidebound bureaucracy, casting himself as the underappreciated and oppressed underdog. His path to the top is blocked by Jewish teachers, favored Kazakhs, and toadies who lie about him, jealous idiots bent on creating trouble for a bright boy who will not let his independent nature be squelched by a corrupt system. In his autobiography, the trials of Zhirinovskiy become a metaphor for the trials of the Russian nation, his rise to prominence a foreshadowing of future Russian regeneration and greatness.

Russia, like Zhirinovskiy himself, has been historically underappreciated. "Russia," he claims, "once saved the world from the Ottoman Empire by sending her troops to the south. . . . And seven centuries ago we stopped the Mongols. We could have let them pass and accepted their domination. And what would have been left of Europe then?" Indeed, Russia had saved the West not only from the Turks and Mongols but from Napoleon and Hitler, but the West is not grateful: "The Russians have carried freedom on their shoulders, whatever uniform they wear—that of the czarist army, the Soviet army, or the Russian army. . . . To this day we have not received adequate compensation from the Germans, from the French, from the Japanese, from the Swedes, from the Turks, from the Poles—from a single one of the aggressors who have trampled and destroyed our country and our people. . . . The world should be grateful to Russia for its role as savior."[64]

The West is attacked by Zhirinovskiy as an agent of Russia's continuing humiliation, a jealous body of ungrateful plotters who desire to turn Russia into an exploited colony, an appendage of the new world order designed by Russia's enemies to remove the only power capable of opposing the West's plan for global hegemony from the world stage forever.[65] The West, pretending to help Russia, sends "us the clothes you do not want to wear and the food you do not want to eat,"[66] while poisoning Russia culturally with "Pepsi-Cola and chewing gum."[67] The West, according to Zhirinovskiy, is weakening Russia spiritually, preparing the Russians for the hegemony of a new global regime.[68] Russia will have to make her own way in the world, and the path to regeneration and prosperity—as so often in the past—leads to the south.

Regeneration: The Drive to the South

> The Russian army will assemble for the last time for its southern campaign and will stop forever on the shores of the Indian Ocean. Beyond that there is nowhere to go, beyond that are the warm waters of the Indian Ocean which wash the shores of our eternal friend India, of Iraq, of our strategic allies. The warm Ocean breeze will soothe everyone living in this new geopolitical area, within these new borders of Russia. . . . The world gains the order it has long needed. . . . Guaranteed order [will come to pass] at long last. . . . We will be able to relax more, we will become calmer.[69]
>
> Why should we inflict suffering upon ourselves? Let's make others suffer.[70]
>
> —Vladimir Zhirinovskiy

Again tying Russia's fate to his own, Zhirinovskiy implies that Russia's restoration to her past glories and the revitalization of her military and economic strength will begin almost as soon as the voters bring the LDP—and Zhirinovskiy himself—to power. He will restore Russia to the borders of the former USSR (peacefully, he says),[71] while eliminating internal borders drawn on national lines. Russia will then turn her attention to the south—the region extending from Russia's present southern border to the shores of the Indian Ocean. Zhirinovskiy claims that the consolidation of Russian domination over this region will end the threat to her evident in the conflicts now taking place on Russia's southern borders in the Caucasus and Afghanistan, save Russia from the pan-Turkic designs of Central Asians and the Turkish state, and free the world from the "Islamic threat." "I dream of Russian soldiers washing their boots in the warm waters of the Indian Ocean and switching to summer uniforms forever," he wrote in his autobiography. Russian soldiers would keep the peace throughout the new Russia, stretching from the arctic to the Indian Ocean.[72] The drive to the south is "the normal movement of Russia," historically foreordained[73] by the geopolitical situation of the country and the dialectics of history. The drive to the south will free Russia, which has been pushed "into the tundra," where nothing "can breathe and develop," and will gain her a warm-water "platform" in the Indian Ocean and the Mediterranean Sea as well as access to the world's markets.[74]

The drive to the south will save the Russian nation, now confined to a truncated state enjoying only colonial status under the Western imperialists, from destruction, revitalize the Russian army—the guardian of the nation[75]—and stimulate the economy: Furthermore, the "southerners" will provide Russia with cheap labor.[76] In short, "Russia will grow rich," and the Russians will enjoy the benefits of the new territories' warmer climes while basking in the sun at seaside resorts and sanatoriums.[77] Of course, political elites in Turkey, Iran, Afghanistan, and Pakistan will resist. Zhirinovskiy appears not to envision a long campaign but rather a blitzkrieg to the south followed by the quick pacification of the new Russian territories.[78] Russia's allies India and Iraq will guard her flanks and Russia, now facing the Indian Ocean and the Mediterranean Sea in the south, will have secured what has been historically, in Zhirinovskiy's view, her most troublesome border region.[79]

Consolidation: Bringing the Millennium

In the longer term, Zhirinovskiy promises that LDP rule will bring Russia to the millennium, an era that he sees as the end point of Russian history, the resolution of a national task. Russia's last great historical mission having been fulfilled, a period of peace and stability will be ushered in. Russia and the other great powers—the United States, Germany, China, and Japan—will agree to divide the world into spheres of influence. This agreement will enable Russia to turn its attention from East-West relations to her true sphere of influence and concern—the region to the south. Zhirinovskiy sees the great powers' (all located in the Northern Hemisphere) turn to the North-South axis as the basis of a new period of peace in the world, since no clashes of interest in the East-West sphere will take place under Zhirinovskiy's version of the new world order.[80]

"How do I see Russia [in the future]?" he asks rhetorically in his autobiography. "I do not see Russia weeping. . . . I see a proud Russia, a Russia wherein the glorious traditions of her army will once again be realized, where talented Russian engineers and industrialists will create examples of the latest technology. . . . We have a huge number of inventors and rationalizers. . . . Russian mercantile traditions must be restored. . . . This is how I see Russia. It will have the world's strongest army, strategic forces, our missiles with multiple launchers. Our space combat platforms, our 'Buran' spaceship and 'Energiya' rockets. This is the country's rocket shield. . . . We will have no rival."

In fact, it is Russia's nuclear arsenal—and his threats to use it if necessary—that will persuade the other great powers, particularly the United States, to accept the new arrangements.[81] Indeed, he appears to be convinced that the West will not fight for Turkey, Iran, Afghanistan, or Pakistan.[82] The West, in Zhirinovskiy's stated view, is outwardly powerful but inwardly decadent and weak and will not put up a fight, thus justifying his bluster about playing the role of nuclear Robin Hood, robbing from the West to give to poor Russia.

Zhirinovskiy's Liberalism: Politics and Economics

> I will immediately declare a dictatorship [upon becoming president]—the country cannot afford democracy for now. I will stabilize the situation in just two months.[83]

> Without a party card and without joining the CPSU [Communist Party of the Soviet Union], my opportunities for promotion, for moving into other establishments, and for studies . . . were limited. All that was closed to me. You see the world as a world of apartheid when you are a nonparty person. From childhood I had experienced ethnic oppression since I had lived in non-Russian regions. Now I was living in Moscow. I seemed to be in Russia, in the capital, but here too there was oppression.[84]

> The important thing is pluralism in all things. . . . [A] multiplicity of views in everything. There cannot be a single line. . . . This totalitarian attitude is what I was sick of.[85]

> —Vladimir Zhirinovskiy

The drive to the south and the new millenarian world order would fulfill Zhirinovskiy's grand plan for Russia. But just what does he plan for Russia in the near term? Zhirinovskiy's plan for Russia economically appears to be paradoxical at first glance: He simultaneously supports the development of the Russian private economic sector *and* the maintenance of state control over long term planning, as well as the maintenance of a strong state economic sector, particularly in the military and space industries.[86] He also emphasizes his support for the welfare state, state support for both independent farmers and state farms (those that are productive), state support of science and culture, and protection of developing Russian industries and enterprises through both restrictions on imports and changes in the tax code.[87] This professed economic liberal goes so far as to guarantee free medical care and education, as well as "a guaranteed right to labor" (though he promises to break up illegal strikes)[88] and "adequate housing." He likes the instincts of the "new Russians," the new stratum of Russian entrepreneurs, and approves of their go-getter attitude. At the same time he embraces a Russian brand of state socialism, attuned, according to Zhirinovskiy, to Russian collectivist culture.[89] He promises to index savings accounts, adjusting the value of the accounts along with the rate of inflation, and to destroy the "bureaucratic mechanism of access to resources" in order to encourage the new Russians, though he promises that swindlers and speculators will be shot.[90] The Zhirinovskiy economic formula blends elements of populism, socialism, economic nationalism, and liberalism to produce a national socialist brew that is similar to that promised by the neocommunists but is more heavily reliant on entrepreneurship.

His sociopolitical prescriptions appear to be eclectic as well: He pledges that the LDP will come to power by legal means and promises "pluralism," equal protection of the laws for all, a multiparty system, freedom of expression and religion, and the abolition of national-territorial divisions in favor of provincial-administrative units. The new Russia will be united by the Russian language, by Russian law, and by civic citizenship for all, regardless of nationality.[91] However, a reasonable person (particularly a non-Russian) may question his veracity on the basis of his preoccupation with specifically Russian (*Russkiy*—"ethnic" Russian) questions, his glorification of the Russian nation, his promise that the Russian *Staatvolk* will no longer be humiliated under a national socialist LDP regime ("For Russia—For all Russians!" is an LDP slogan),[92] and his stated intention to rule the country by diktat (at least for a while), solving the crime and corruption problem by "shooting 100,000 people"[93] and shipping the reformist turncoats off in "the last [train] coach north."[94]

The key to understanding Zhirinovskiy's eclectic liberal-democratic/national socialist socioeconomic and political program may well be found in his interpretation of the career of former CPSU general secretary and KGB chief Yuriy Andropov. "Andropov," wrote Zhirinovskiy, "is connected to a most interesting political paradox." Both as KGB chief and as CPSU general secretary, Andropov brought to Moscow talented, mostly young operatives from around the Soviet Union, men who, after the beginning of *perestroika*, would face off in two opposing political camps—Gorbachev's cadre of westernizers and those who headed the anti*perestroika* forces. Both Gorbachev's *perestroika* ideologist, Aleksandr Yakovlev, and an up-and-coming KGB officer who would later play a prominent role in the anti-Yeltsin coalition, Aleksandr Sterligov, were groomed by Yuriy Andropov. The pro- and anti*perestroika* forces would eventually emerge as the core of the democrat-patriot dichotomy under Yeltsin.[95] Yet Zhirinovskiy claims that both camps still "respect the name of Yuriy Vladimirovich [Andropov]."[96]

On the one hand, Andropov supported market-driven economic experiments and patronized certain circles among the intelligentsia; on the other hand he cracked down on corruption and dissent. Andropov, in Zhirinovskiy's view the most gifted and shrewd of the Soviet leaders, balanced various forces, interests, and social strata, drawing the best ideas from each, bypassing the *nomenklatura* system to reward talented underlings, and innovating within the system, while slowly undermining the ossified party-state structures by tolerating a certain level of critical discussion of social issues.[97] Zhirinovskiy apparently views Andropov's methods as his model for administering the country by a carrot-and-stick approach. "For every weight there must be a counter weight. . . . [A]ny . . . political system needs elections and a free press," Zhirinovskiy once wrote, in order to prevent political, social, and economic stagnation.[98] The Communists failed to understand the importance of pluralism—the balancing of various social strata that Andropov was so successful at—and a multiparty system. "Under the one party system, anyone who did not join the CPSU experienced a sensation of political hunger."[99] Thus innovative ideas were stifled, and the urge of the educated and able to participate in the political life of the country was smothered. Under such a system, mediocre apparatchiks and untalented yes men flourished to the detriment of the nation and the state. Besides, the spectacle of elections, like sporting events, would channel social energy into more productive, or at least satisfying, channels.[100] "Totalitarianism—that's the rule of bureaucrats, democracy—the rule of politicians," chirps Zhirinovskiy.[101]

Judging from Zhirinovskiy's statements on carrot-and-stick rule, it appears that he plans—on assuming the presidency—to pursue a "balance of forces" administration, permitting other political parties to participate in and, perhaps, even to win Duma elections, tolerating a certain level of press freedom (as long as it does not interfere in state matters) and assuming emergency dictatorial powers when necessary. Such a scenario is not far-fetched. Yeltsin's own administration has from time to time operated in a similar manner, something it can do under the broad and vague powers of the constitution adopted in 1993. It is difficult to imagine Zhirinovskiy, a man of destiny in his own eyes,

voluntarily leaving the Kremlin, however, and his grandiose geopolitical plans would appear to require a centralization of power not seen in
Russia since Stalin. The question no one save Zhirinovskiy can answer
remains. Is he serious about his stated intentions?

His economic policies appear to combine a public-private partner-
ship more like Mussolini's Italy than Stalin's Russia together with welfare state measures—Russian national socialism. Acting in the best traditions of Russian anticapitalism, he cannot understand, much less
pursue, a full blown liberal economy. The goals of the nation, as defined by the state, come first. Full-blown capitalism is anathema to
Zhirinovskiy, as it is to most Russians.

Yeltsin and Zhirinovskiy

During the first session of the second postcommunist state Duma in
January 1996, some Western observers were startled to find Zhirinovskiy and the Yeltsin administration apparently working closely together to discredit the resurgent Zyuganovite Communists, who had
won the largest share of the party list vote in the parliamentary elections the previous December.[102] If Russia watchers were genuinely surprised, then they hadn't been paying attention to the evolving Yeltsin-
Zhirinovskiy symbiosis, something that had been going on for quite
some time. In fact, Zhirinovskiy's strong showing in the Duma elections two years earlier was partly due to the Yeltsin administration's
decision to treat the charismatic demagogue as an equal partner, even
an ally, in its efforts to secure acceptance of a "presidential" constitution, whose passage in a referendum held simultaneously with the parliamentary elections ensured the sitting president broad discretionary
powers—powers that enabled Yeltsin to intervene in Chechnya less
than a year later. Yeltsin and company may also have seen Zhirinovskiy
as a political prop, a useful idiot whom they could exploit either as
leverage in Russia's relations with the West[103] or as proof of their democratic tolerance of opposition. Zhirinovskiy shrewdly used the opportunity to further his own political aims, proving that he is a tough-
minded and calculating politician who saw his opportunity after the
demise of the Russian Supreme Soviet in October 1993 and took it.

The Yeltsin administration's change in attitude toward the bombastic
Zhirinovskiy began in summer 1993, after the LDP leader publicly supported Yeltsin's call for a referendum on a new constitution for the
Russian Federation. He had proclaimed that he was prepared to help
Yeltsin by supporting the presidential constitution and by backing him
against the recalcitrant Supreme Soviet.[104] When the constitutional conference, a body whose purpose was to present a draft constitution for

public discussion, met in summer 1993, Zhirinovskiy, sporting a new, sober-minded persona, dutifully took part.[105] It should not have been news to anyone that Zhirinovskiy had voiced support for the presidential constitution. He had never concealed either his thirst for power or his conviction that he would someday be elected president of Russia. He had seldom missed an opportunity to proclaim his preference for the presidential republic option for Russia, since such a system would suit his political designs. Zhirinovskiy had declared himself in favor of a presidential republic years earlier, in anticipation of the day when Russians would be "sick and tired" of the social and economic dislocations brought on by the reforms.[106]

Zhirinovskiy supported Yeltsin's decree of September 21, 1993, which dissolved the opposition-dominated Supreme Soviet and precipitated a crisis that culminated in the October 3 "Bloody Sunday" violence and the storming of the Russian White House. He did, however, prudently blame both sides for the violence. In any event, the road for an LDP victory in the December elections had been cleared by the administration's attempts at blocking other nationalist parties from participating in the elections. The Zyuganovite Communists, the only other nationalist opposition party allowed to participate, had not yet fully recovered from the shock of the crisis. Zhirinovskiy effectively filled the vacuum.

The democrats and the Yeltsin administration appeared not to have viewed Zhirinovskiy as a serious threat to their plans to dominate the new state Duma until less than two weeks prior to the elections. On December 1, then first deputy prime minister (and leader of the Russia's Choice Party), Yegor Gaydar, attacked Zhirinovskiy in the strongest possible terms. "Three years ago," Gaydar intoned, "Zhirinovskiy reminded me mostly of Hitler as depicted in Soviet films, but he now reminds me of the real-life, 1929 model Hitler."[107] State-run Ostankino television made a last-minute effort to discredit Zhirinovskiy with a similar (though implied) comparison in a documentary film entitled *Yastreb* [Hawk].[108] The efforts were to no avail. Still, as the revival of the Yeltsin-Zhirinovskiy axis during the early days of the Russian intervention in Chechnya, and their subsequent joint attacks on the Communists, revealed, both men continued to find the other useful.[109]

Zhirinovskiy's timely support of Yeltsin has sources other than mere political calculation. In Zhirinovskiy's view, Yeltsin is an objective ally in the historical dialectic. The course of recent Russian history has been set by a series of clashes, political struggles whose outcomes have determined the inevitable next stage of historical development.[110] Zhirinovskiy, tying these events to his grand theory, calls them "drives," each event and outcome a further "drive" toward history's goal. The starting point of the series of historical drives was the Brezhnev "stagnation" state, a state that could not hope to remain a world-class superpower. The foundation of that state had been created in the 1930s by Stalin. The "red monarch" recognized that under the then current historical circumstances, particularly the rise of Hitler in Germany, "Russia did not have the right to be weak." He had no choice but to forcibly modernize the country. It was a "terrible path" to follow to be sure, but the even worse alternative was the destruction of Russia by the Nazis.[111] Russia finds herself in a similar position today, weak and surrounded by enemies. There is one important difference, however. Today's Russia has a nuclear shield under which to safely carry out the process of reform. Moreover, the times call for a different type of change, one that does not require Stalinist methods. That historical process began with the undermining of CPSU power and the collapse of the Soviet Union (the first two drives), the destruction of the old system being a necessary prelude to the country's reconstruction. The last vestiges of Soviet power were removed from the historical stage when Yeltsin dissolved the system of soviets after his confrontation with the Supreme Soviet in fall 1993 (the third drive). The final three drives—the political and economic reorganization of the Russia Federation, the re-establishment of the union, and the drive to the south—will be accomplished after Zhirinovskiy is made president of Russia.

Evaluating Zhirinovskiy

Zhirinovskiy is no buffoon. He is a shrewd, calculating politician who is opportunistic but not an opportunist. He has a vision of a future Russia restored to greatness, and he has a plan for that restoration. Both strike a responsive chord among millions of Russians. Whether or not Zhirinovskiy is a fascist in the purest sense is immaterial. If he is serious about his stated aims, then the fact that his program is uniquely Russian and his own personal creation may merely represent a distinction without a difference between it and fascism in action: many of the results would be just the same. The plan itself is deeply rooted in Russia's historical experience and plays to weaknesses in human nature, one that is manifest in a particular way among the Russians. His initial appeal to Russians, however, is tied to something else—the distrust many of them feel toward the political class that ruled them as Communists during the Soviet era and continues to rule today in a different guise. His outrageous actions may well be appealing to those Russians who understandably identify with his hostility toward the powers that be. Every threat made and every punch thrown shakes the foundation of the power structure. If the "respectable" politicians and other elites hate him as much as they appear to, then he cannot be all bad.

Aleksandr Solzhenitsyn appeals to what is best in Russians and rejects expansionism and the cult of conquest. After a certain point, Russian expansion did nothing for the Russian people. They simply became a pawn in the great game played by ambitious men who, not unlike Zhirinovskiy, identified their own fortunes and the expansion of the state, as well as modernization via the creation of the integrated state, with the good of the nation. Solzhenitsyn and those like him know better. The grand themes of suffering, purification, and redemption are evident in the best of Solzhenitsyn's literature and hold out the promise of hope to Russia, a hope that is more spiritual than material. When Russians have united under such a banner, they have borne their suffering bravely and to great purpose, defeating Napoleon and Hitler and preserving the possibility of a better future for the nation. Russia will never match the West in wealth, but the Russian people are capable of building something that they can be proud of. Envy does not taint such a philosophy.

Zhirinovskiy transforms and secularizes the grand Russian themes into a personal saga of humiliation (suffering), regeneration (purification), and consolidation (redemption). Like Solzhenitsyn's literary themes, they are rooted in the Russian experience and Russian culture. It is perhaps expecting too much of men, particularly those living in the social wreckage that is postcommunist Russia, to buy a more noble version of the Russian Idea, one that is in the end much more difficult to fulfill in that it asks human beings to forget envy and revenge. Solzhenitsyn is a realist in that he recognizes that the rebuilding of Russia may take centuries and must be accomplished within the potentialities that Russian culture offers. Zhirinovskiy too is a realist. He recognizes that his nationalism is immediate and thus an easier sell in the short term. His message has broad appeal. Those who underestimate his abilities and the appeal of his message of *ressentiment* do so at their own risk. "I am one of you!" he proclaims. And so he is. That is not something that any of us can be proud of.

Notes

1. Vladimir Zhirinovskiy, Moscow radio broadcast, 11 June 1991.

2. Cited in Alexander Yanov, "The Zhirinovsky Phenomenon," *Chronicles*, August 1993, 28.

3. Zhirinovskiy's Liberal Democratic Party (LDP) carried some 11 percent of the party list vote in the December 1995 elections, after having been all but

written off by the pundits. He first defied predictions of his early political demise in December of 1993, when his party won about 23 percent of the party list vote. Despite the decrease of his proportion of the total vote, Zhirinovskiy still won 10 million votes in 1995, as compared to the 12 million he and his party garnered in 1993. His failure to make the second round of the 1996 presidential election has again led many analysts to believe that Zhirinovskiy is finished. For reasons that will become apparent, I am not so certain about such predictions.

4. Sowell, a Senior Fellow at the Hoover Institution, Stanford University, is the author of, among other works, *Civil Rights: Rhetoric or Reality*, *The Economics and Politics of Race*, *Ethnic America*, *Markets and Minorities*, and *Race and Economics*.

5. Thomas Sowell, *Civil Rights: Rhetoric or Reality* (New York: William Morrow, 1984), 26.

6. Ibid., 26–27.

7. Ibid., 27. Sowell does not attempt to explain the Irish propensity for alcoholism, though he does note that those "who see society as the cause of such phenomena would be hard pressed to find in the history of Irish Americans sufficient traumas not suffered by Jewish and Italian Americans as well to explain such differences" in the United States, at least. At any rate, the drinking patterns of the various groups "existed before American society existed."

8. Ibid., 28.

9. Ibid., 27.

10. Ibid., 28.

11. Ibid.

12. Ibid., 29.

13. Richard Pipes, *Russia Under the Old Regime* (New York: Scribner's, 1974), 3.

14. Vladimir Zhirinovskiy, cited in Graham Frazer and George Lancelle, *Absolute Zhirinovsky* (London: Penguin Books, 1994), 94.

15. Pipes, *Russia Under the Old Regime*, 3.

16. Ibid., 6–10. Kiev itself was overrun by the Mongols in 1240. See Nicholas Riasanovsky, *A History of Russia*, 5th ed. (Oxford: Oxford University Press, 1993), 80.

17. Riasanovsky, *History of Russia*, 4.

18. Pipes, *Russia Under the Old Regime*, 5.

19. Riasanovsky, *History of Russia*, 5.

20. Pipes, *Russia Under the Old Regime*, 9. The crop yield ratios indicate how many times the seed reproduces itself. When one grain sowed yields three at harvest, the ratio is 1:3, and so on.

21. Ibid., 9.

22. Ibid., 10.

23. Ibid., 7.

24. R. Dion, cited in ibid., 16.

25. Ibid.

26. Ibid., 19.
27. Ibid.
28. Ibid., 10.
29. "Where an urban market is absent, little can be done with the excess grain except distill it into spirits." Ibid., 9.
30. De Jonge was attempting to link the lack of grain belt industrial labor discipline to Stalinist forced labor—Stalin was attempting to force a grain belt culture to industrialize and overcome the West, which meant long hours of repetitive assembly line work. Terror was, in part, his answer to the problem of forcing the square Russian peg into the round industrial hole. See Alex De Jonge, *Stalin and the Shaping of the Soviet Union* (New York: William Morrow, 1986), 19.
31. Ibid.
32. Pipes, *Russia Under the Old Regime*, 19.
33. Liah Greenfeld, *Nationalism: Five Roads to Modernity* (Cambridge: Harvard University Press, 1992), 230.
34. Ibid., 231.
35. Denis Fonvisin, cited in ibid., 234.
36. Ibid., 232.
37. Cited in ibid., 223.
38. Pipes, *Russia Under the Old Regime*, 10.
39. Ibid., 12.
40. For more on the colonization process, see ibid., 13–16.
41. Riasanovsky, *History of Russia*, 9.
42. Frazer and Lancelle, *Absolute Zhirinovsky*, 1.
43. Zhirinovskiy's autobiography, *Posledniy Brosok Na Yug* (Moscow, 1993) is the single most useful source for information on his background, though the Russian (and foreign press) have published hundreds, if not thousands, of articles containing biographical material on our subject. See also Frazer and Lancelle, *Absolute Zhirinovsky*, James A. Morrison, *Vladimir Zhirinovsky: An Assessment of a Russian Ultra-Nationalist* (Washington, D.C.: National Defense University, 1994), and Sergey Plekhanov, *Zhirinovskiy: Khto On?* (Who is Zhirinovskiy?) (Moscow: Evrasiya Nord, 1994).
44. Vladimir Zhirinovskiy, *Posledniy Brosok Na Yug*, 9.
45. Cited in Frazer and Lancelle, *Absolute Zhirinovsky*, 133.
46. Morrison, *Vladimir Zhirinovsky*, 2–3. Morrison notes that "according to one report, an early Liberal Democratic Party was founded in March 1990 with Zhirinovsky as chairman, but he was expelled and in February 1991 he launched his own Liberal Democratic Party which in April 1991 was officially registered as the first party since 1917 to which the Communists granted official status." The LDP's early registration, along with Zhirinovskiy's foreign travel record (a rare thing for a young, unmarried man at the time), and uncertainties about the financing of his political campaigns have spurred allegations that Zhirinovskiy is a former KGB agent who has prospered from his contacts with the secret police. Indeed, some allege that the LDP was originally intended as a front "democratic" party that the KGB could control in the period

following the Communists' loss of an exclusive constitutional monopoly on power. Zhirinovskiy has denied the charges—and so did the KGB. See Morrison, 17–20; see also the *Washington Post*, 14 January 1994.

47. Zhirinovskiy is clearly uncomfortable with explaining his national origins: "I've had thousands of blood tests. If you have specialists who could find at least five percent Jewish blood in me, I would be proud. But there is none." (Cited in Frazer and Lancelle, *Absolute Zhirinovsky*, 133.) He rather lamely attempted to explain his patronymic (a middle name derived from the father's first name) in his autobiography: "I am Vladimir Zhirinovskiy. I have a Russian name—Vladimir—but my father's name was Volf; that is what his birth certificate and passport said. Mom used to call him simply Volodya, and it would have been simpler for me to have been called Vladimir Vladimirovich, but whether because of bureaucracy or red tape, I don't know, but one way or another I am Vladimir Volfovich. I'm proud of that name because it was my father's, although it sounds rather odd to Russian ears" (*Posledniy Brosok Na Yug*, 5). He has also attempted to explain his very un-Russian patronymic this way: "I am not a Jew. I am a Russian both on my mother's side and my father's. My father was born on the Russian-German border in western Ukraine in 1907. My grandfather loved German music. In this music one often encounters such names as Wolfgang, Wolf, and so forth" (*Svobodnaya Gruziya*, 3 June 1993).

When journalists claimed to have found evidence that Zhirinovskiy's real last name (until he had it changed in the 1960s) was Edelshtein, that he once applied to emigrate to Israel, and that he had done legal work for a late Soviet-era Jewish organization, he has usually claimed that these allegations are part of a smear campaign directed at him. Given the fact that documents were uncovered showing Zhirinovskiy had changed his name, that the Israeli government apparently confirmed an inquiry about a visa for Zhirinovskiy approved by the proper authorities, and that Zhirinovskiy has not denied performing some legal work for an organization that was called Shalom, we can reasonably assume that his father was Jewish. (For more on Zhirinovskiy's possible Jewish roots, as well as his connection with Shalom, see *Izvestiya*, 18 December 1993; see also *Novoye Russkoye Slovo*, 1 January 1994). Zhirinovskiy's unabashed Russian chauvinism is most likely an example of a man running headlong from the truth, a man who has identified himself with Russia and has to prove his patriotism. The rumors have not endeared Zhirinovskiy to the patriotic coalition: They continue to distrust him, and, in any event, Zhirinovskiy has run an independent one man show. He is not interested in coalitions.

48. Cited in Frazer and Lancelle, *Absolute Zhirinovsky*, 137.

49. Zhirinovskiy is purported to have a taste for peep shows, prostitutes, and pornography. Various press sources have seconded Limonov's charges; see, for example, *Qol Yisra'el*, 13 January 1994, and the German PRO Television report (on the program *Reporter*) of 18 January 1994. Limonov (a pseudonym, his actual family name is Saenko) once made a living for himself as a writer (he made a bit of a splash with the publication of a semi-autobiographical novel that explicitly highlighted the loose sexuality of young people) while residing as an expatriate in Paris. He became a member of Zhirinovskiy's

shadow cabinet, and later had a falling out with the LDP leader. Limonov now heads the National Bolshevik Party and edits a Moscow-based newspaper, *Limonka* (literally "lemon," Russian military slang for hand grenade). We will hear more from him in the next chapter. His charges against Zhirinovskiy are catalogued in a book, *Limonov Protiv Zhirinovskogo* (Limonov versus Zhirinovskiy) (Moscow: Konets Veka, 1994). See also the Limonov article in *Zavtra* 1 (January 1994).

50. In a TV speech directed at young people during the 1993 election campaign, Zhirinovskiy recounted a version of twentieth century Russian political history couched in sexual terms. The Bolshevik coup was thus an example of rape: The Bolsheviks "came into power during the night by using violence." "The next stage, the Stalin period, was a period when members of a party were being eliminated by that same party. . . . Compared with problems of sexual morality, this reminds one of the problems of homosexuality, where there are relationships between representatives of the same sex." The Khrushchev period was different: "He was always smiling, he was always happy and pleased. But, mostly, he was alone. . . . One can compare this with the problem of masturbation when a person satisfies himself alone." As for the time of Brezhnev, Chernenko, and Gorbachev, according to Zhirinovskiy, "it was a time of political impotence. They wanted to perform, but they could not. They proposed things but they could not achieve anything, just as in the case of physical impotence." Ostankino television, 26 November 1993. If that was not enough to raise questions about Zhirinovskiy's mental stability, his cavalier statements about wiping out the Baltic states, for example, only added fuel to the fire. In an interview with a Bulgarian reporter, Zhirinovskiy further claimed to have a secret weapon, code named "Ellipton," that could destroy the world: "[Q]: What is this 'Ellipton' weapon? [A]: It is my personal weapon. I can completely destroy buildings and people, not by fire, but with a laser beam that destroys all targets. [Q]: Can you destroy the world with this weapon? [A]: Of course I can, but I do not want to. It is important that we possess such a weapon. If any danger threatens us, in the case of extreme necessity there is nothing strange about us using it in certain regions—for defense." *Chasa*, 28 February 1994.

51. See, for example, the 14 January 1994 TASS report of a fight with Goryachev, as well as the AFP news service report of the same date.

52. Zhirinovskiy, *Posledniy Brosok*, 53.

53. Zhirinovskiy news conference, Russian television, 6 June 1991.

54. Zhirinovskiy, *Posledniy Brosok*, 60.

55. Ibid., 53.

56. Ibid., 49–50.

57. Interview with Zhirinovskiy, Russian television, 6 June 1991.

58. For earlier references to a "drive to the south," see Interfax news service report, 7 May 1992 and *Liberal* [LDP newspaper] 2 (1993) among many others.

59. Address by Zhirinovskiy, Russian television, 6 June 1991.

60. Headline in *Liberal* 1 (1993).

61. Zhirinovskiy, *Posledniy Brosok*, 19–20.

62. Ibid., 24.

63. Ibid., 19.

64. Ibid., 123–4.

65. See, for instance, the 18 December 1991 TASS report on a Zhirinovskiy press conference. See also Interfax news service reports of 7 May and 24 November 1992. In his autobiography, Zhirinovskiy implies that both the current regime and Gorbachev's reformers were (and are) agents of influence acting under orders from their Western masters: "Gorbachev and Yeltsin made all kinds of concessions to the West, the United States, the CIA, Israel. And what did they get for it? Nothing" (p. 140). Zhirinovskiy occasionally makes reference to Zionist machinations or Jewish plots (see *Posledniy Brosok*, 127, for instance). But such ideas, which have made Zhirinovskiy the target of accusations of anti-Semitism, appear not to play a central role in his ideology—he is not an anti-Semite as we have defined the term. The plotting of the "West," however, does play such an ideological role.

66. Cited in Frazer and Lancelle, *Absolute Zhirinovsky*, 71.

67. Ibid., 72.

68. For more on the threat to Russia of the West building a trans-state regime, see P. Valentinov's article in *LDPR* [the LDP Duma faction's newspaper], 9 (1995).

69. Zhirinovskiy, *Posledniy Brosok*, 124–125.

70. Cited in Frazer and Lancelle, *Absolute Zhirinovsky*, 9.

71. Zhirinovskiy, while making inflammatory stump speeches about laying waste to the Baltic states, for example, has maintained that the reunification of the former Soviet republics under a Russian flag will be achieved peacefully: "It will happen without force, through a voluntary unification of republics which want to return to Russia, first of all on economic grounds." (Patrick Bruno, *Besyedy Na Chistotu* [roughly, Speaking out] [Moscow: LDP, 1995], 54–55; the book is a transcript of numerous interviews with Zhirinovskiy. French journalist Patrick Bruno asks detailed and probing questions about Zhirinovskiy's intentions.) The gist of his argument, made frequently in response to accusations of militant expansionism directed at him by the press, is that Russia will tighten the economic screws, forcing the former USSR republics to pay world level-prices for oil and natural gas, for example, and the former republics, after suffering economic hardship and political instability, will beg Russia to return to the fold. See, for example, Frazer and Lancelle, *Absolute Zhirinovsky*, 8. He has, however, threatened to use force against Kazakhstan and Ukraine to bring them back into a new Russia: see Frazer and Lancelle, 11. In view of these threats, Zhirinovskiy's assertions (after the publication of his autobiography raised a firestorm of controversy over his warmongering) that the south, too, would join Russia voluntarily seem just as transparent as his stated hope for a peaceful reunification of the former Soviet republics.

72. Zhirinovskiy, *Posledniy Brosok*, 66.

73. Ibid., 103.

74. Ibid., 63–64.

75. "New armed forces can be reborn only as the result of a combat opera-

tion. The army cannot grow stronger in military commissariats and barracks. It needs a goal, a task." Ibid., 70.

76. Ibid. Zhirinovskiy acknowledges some rough spots on the way to the millennium—as southern laborers migrate north to man Russian factories, "part of the [southern] population will, unfortunately, die" due to an "absence of medicines" and a low "level of culture" among the southerners (71).

77. Ibid., 66, 70.

78. Zhirinovskiy calls the operation a form of military "shock therapy." Ibid., 64.

79. "All of Russia's problems are in the south. So until we resolve our southern problem we will never extricate ourselves from the protracted crisis, which will periodically worsen." Ibid., 45.

80. "For North America there will be Latin America, for Western Europe there will be Africa, for China, Japan, there will be Southeast Asia. . . . For Russia, only three states: Turkey, Iran, Afghanistan. It is a region of vitally important interests for Russia. . . . And further to the south, the warm Indian Ocean. . . . If we unite the Russian north (with its heavy industry) with the south, where there is basic food stuffs and raw materials for light industry, then yes, we will have a market economy." *Liberal* 2 (1993).

81. See Frazer and Lancelle, *Absolute Zhirinovsky*, 147.

82. See quotation on NATO and Turkey cited in Morrison, 104–105. Yanov, cited in Frazer and Lancelle (155), interprets Zhirinovskiy's intentions similarly: "What does Zhirinovsky think the rest of the world would do while his armies marched to the oil fields of the Middle East in order to monopolize this vital strategic resource? Zhirinovsky has quite an impressive answer to this. According to him, the rest of the world would do precisely what it did when Hitler marched around Europe—nothing. This is what Russia's 'nuclear shield' is all about: to ensure a new Munich on the part of the West. And, indeed, would any Western government risk annihilation for the sake of Turkey, let alone Iran?"

83. Vladimir Zhirinovskiy, cited in ibid., 102.

84. Zhirinovskiy, *Posledniy Brosok*, 48.

85. Ibid., 81.

86. Though he sometimes refers to privatizing the arms industry. See Vladimir Zhirinovskiy, *Posledniy Vagon Na Sevyer* (The last coach north) (Moscow: LDP, 1995), 26.

87. For an overview of Zhirinovkiy's economic plans, see *Rossiya I Reformiy* (Russia and reforms) (Moscow: LDP, 1995), a book he co-authored with A. G. Vinogradov. Judging by his pledges to jump-start the Russian economy by cranking up the now dormant Russian military-industrial complex through his "drive to the south," as well as his counting on Russian arms sales, the cutoff of aid to unworthy third world countries and former Soviet republics, as well as the collection of debts owed to Russia by other countries (since the December 1993 elections, and the charges of war-mongering leveled at him during the campaign, he rarely refers to nuclear "Robin Hood" operations), Zhirinovskiy appears to believe that creating prosperity for Russia is a relatively simple

matter. Many of his economic plans are frequently repeated in the pages of his party newspapers in a simple "Minimum Program" list of LDP promises. See, for example, _Pravda Zhirinovskogo_ [LDP party newspaper] 5 (1995). Since 1993, Zhirinovskiy appears to put less emphasis (in his stump speeches at any rate) on entrepreneurship and more on "social protection"—the maintenance of a cradle to grave welfare state.

88. See Morrison, _Vladimir Zhirinovsky_, 33. Morrison quotes a Russian newspaper article wherein Zhirinovskiy is characterized as willing to accept a certain minimum level of unemployment as "an incentive to ensure the maximum work capacity [of Russian industry]."

89. "Just what kind of society will we [the LDP] create? Will there be wealthy people? Of course. . . . We are not a proletarian party. Will we recognize private property? Yes, of course. Will we allow a pensioner or a child, abandoned and without parents, to die from hunger? Never. Subsidies, a roof over [one's] head, medical services, free bread and free milk must be found for the most unfortunate. This is socialism . . . our national [socialism] . . . built on the communal, corporate [national] psychology." _Posledniy Vagon_, 26.

90. _Posledniy Vagon_, 27–28.

91. See, for instance, _Posledniy Brosok_, 83–87, 94–98, 112–113, 118. These themes are repeated in most issues of the LDP's newspapers. Zhirinovskiy's attempt to graft Western civic measures onto the Russian state by promising a general citizenship without reference to nationality (something that was stamped on every Soviet citizen's internal passport) and abolishing national-territorial units (the Tartar republic, Chechnya, and Ukraine in the new state) appears to be a transparent attempt to establish Russian hegemony once and for all. Zhirinovskiy says the new state will be called simply "Russia." He appears to believe that the disappearance of the national-territorial units will dampen the territorial nationalist aspirations of the subject peoples. He is either naive or plans to use much more brute force to subjugate the republics—for that is how the titular peoples would undoubtedly view the effort—than he has heretofore let on.

92. See Morrison, _Vladimir Zhirinovsky_, 32.

93. He hastened to assure the public that the "other 300 million" would "live peacefully." Cited in Frazer and Lancelle, _Absolute Zhirinovsky_, 117.

94. He envisions reformers Gaydar, Chubays, Yakovlev, and Gorbachev, among others, taking their final train ride to exile in the Far North in his book _Posledniy Vagon Na Sevyer_, 7–9.

95. Ibid., 54.

96. Ibid.

97. Ibid., 55. Moreover, Andropov understood the historical necessity of the drive to the south—it was the KGB under his leadership, according to Zhirinovskiy, who initiated the "penultimate drive to the south," the invasion of Afghanistan.

98. Ibid., 87. As far as a free press goes, Zhirinovskiy sees no contradiction between his advocacy of such an idea while simultaneously threatening to close media that do not act in the interests of the state, 84–88.

99. Zhirinovskiy, *Posledniy Brosok*, 82.

100. Ibid., 85–86.

101. Ibid., 88.

102. See, for example, the *Washington Times*, 20 February 1996. Corespondent Martin Sieff ("Illness, Lack of Allies Cripple Yeltsin," p. A10) notes that Yeltsin has been accused of "abandoning the last vestiges of his democratic principles" by "forging an alliance" against the Communists with "ultranationalist Vladimir Zhirinovsky."

103. During the 1993 parliamentary election campaign, Nikolay Travkin, leader of the Democratic Party of Russia, charged that Zhirinovskiy was Yeltsin's creature, a scary figure wheeled out from time to time to frighten the West into unreservedly supporting the Yeltsin regime. Ostankino television, 23 November 1993.

104. "I told his advisers: 'Let him hold presidential elections, and he would help come to power a president [Zhirinovskiy] who would not put him against a wall.' And his name would last—as the first president of Russia." *Argumenty I Fakty*, 12 (March 1993); for Zhirinovskiy's declared support of a referendum on the presidential constitution, see *Nezavisimaya Gazeta*, 1 March 1994.

105. For more on Zhirinovskiy's participation in the constitutional conference see the RIA news service reports of 26 and 28 June 1993.

106. ITAR-TASS, 18 May 1993.

107. Moscow Ostankino Television, 1 December 1993.

108. Moscow Ostankino Television, 11 December 1993. The film was broadcast the day before the elections. "Hawk" included clips of Zhirinovskiy addressing crowds, including his usual outrageous rhetoric interspersed with footage of interviews of Zhirinovskiy and many of his followers. "Hitler's nationalities policy was a harsh one," one young man said, but the LDP, according to him at any rate, intended to "do the same for Russia." The film also raised the question of Zhirinovskiy's nationality, perhaps in an effort to discredit his Russian nationalist credentials.

109. Zhirinovskiy was an ardent supporter of the Chechen intervention. He sees the Caucasus war, no doubt, as but a preliminary "drive to the south." In any event, Russia must preserve her territorial integrity.

110. For more on Zhirinovskiy's historical theories, see *Posledniy Vagon*, 22–29.

111. Ibid., 23.

7

Neo-Nazism and the National Revolution

The National Revolution is a mature version of the Russian Idea that evolved from Black Hundredism and Stalinist National Bolshevism, a version of the idea that expresses itself in a new, racist mythomoteur and a myth-symbol complex that borrows heavily from fascism and German National Socialism. The alienation of modern technological-industrial society combined with the Soviet collapse set the stage for the appearance of the Russian national revolutionaries, young people whose quest for community has led them down a path that merges the new symbols with the old imperatives. The outrageous Zhirinovskiy paved the way for the national revolutionaries, but even his radical populism cannot satisfy the natural urge to action in a world where so many feel impotent and anonymous.

On May 8, 1995, President Boris Yeltsin addressed an auditorium filled with gray-haired war veterans, their chests bedecked with rows of ribbons and medals, and told them of the cost of victory in the Great Patriotic War. Citing new archival research, Yeltsin revealed the "terrifying figure" of 26,549,000 Soviet citizens lost in the war against "Hitlerite fascism." Yeltsin then closed his speech with remarks that may have seemed cryptic to some observers. "Many in Russia and beyond its borders are now wondering," he claimed, "why, half a century after the collapse of fascism, immunity to fascist and racist ideas in our society has weakened. . . . We must purge Russia of the fascist plague, completely and forever."[1]

Westerners may have believed that Yeltsin was referring to the bombastic Vladimir Zhirinovskiy or, perhaps, to the "red-brown" neocommunists who had done so well in the December 1993 elections and were already campaigning to expand their influence in the state Duma.

215

But the immediate cause of Yeltsin's concern was probably something else, a relatively new and far more radical force whose activities had prompted the president to issue a decree earlier that year on combating "fascism." This force, dubbed the "new opposition" by Russian journalists, is more willing to resort to violence than the old "patriotic" opposition. Like the Zhirinovskiyites, the new opposition boasts of having no ties to the discredited communist *nomenklatura* regime and has worked particularly hard to recruit young people. Unlike Zhirinovskiy, however, they are impatient and weary of talk. Russian greatness will be restored not by *boltuni* (windbags) in the state Duma but the implementation of what they call the "national revolution."

The September-October 1993 crisis, brought on by Boris Yeltsin's order to disband the recalcitrant Supreme Soviet, made the Russian White House—the seat of what the largely pro-Yeltsin media had dubbed the "irreconcilable opposition"—the locus of resistance to the president, the democrats, and all their works. The barricades surrounding the beleaguered and isolated deputies (Yeltsin cut off power and water to the White House) attracted what one could term the "usual suspects," the motley assortment of anti-Yeltsinites, pensioners, veterans, and imperialists of every shade and hue, from red to brown to white. Vladimir Zhirinovskiy, despite his subsequent support of the amnesty that would free all of the White House defenders, including former vice president Aleksandr Rutskoy and Supreme Soviet chairman Ruslan Khasbulatov, studiously avoided participation in what he apparently saw as a losing game being played by the Supreme Soviet supporters. But another band, far more radical than any other that had so far been accepted as legitimate by the nationalist opposition's leaders and promoters, made their very conspicuous debut as the most numerous and disciplined of the White House cohort. This particular band of irreconcilables was made all the more conspicuous by their unabashed display of their organization's symbol, an eight-pointed star embossed with a swastika, which they wore on the armbands of their paramilitary uniforms. The organization in question is Russian National Unity (RNU) and its leader, known within the movement as the chief "comrade in arms," is Aleksandr Barkashov.

Barkashov and his band of followers, who numbered somewhere between one hundred and three hundred RNU comrades-in-arms, provided what appeared to be the largest single contingent of White House defenders,[2] a contingent whose willingness to soldier on to the bitter end attests to their discipline and ideological commitment.[3] This steadfastness, as we shall see, won them a place in the heretofore hostile opposition forces, and Barkashov himself for a time was treated with respect by men who had once scorned his Nazi ideology as incompatible with the Russian Idea, however variously expressed, which is held as the ideal of the nationalist movement.

More importantly, Barkashov and the RNU may represent the first assault on the hoary Soviet-era based patriots of a new wave of oppositionists who are younger and more radical than the older opposition veterans, more willing to use force, and better able to connect with the alienated youth of postcommunist Russia.

The National Revolution

One cannot fail to see at the core of all . . . noble races the animal of prey, the splendid blond beast prowling about avidly in search of spoil and victory. . . . [This] herd of blond beasts of prey, a conqueror and a master race . . . is organized for war and . . . unhesitatingly lays its terrible claws upon a population . . . still formless and nomad.

—Nietzsche[4]

Barkashov's ideology is proto-Nazi and revolves around the notion of the "national revolution," which sets the nation (the Russian nation is seen as a distinct racial "genotype") and its aggrandizement as the highest value. Barkashov sees the racial purification of the national genotype as the logical first step toward the restoration of a powerful and feared Russian empire. The new Russia, cleansed of alien racial elements and transformed by the selection process of the national revolution, will then be able to fulfill what Barkashov has called Russia's national task: "The historical obligation of the Russian people is the creation of a powerful and just Russian state, through which the Russians are obligated to be the guarantor of justice (not to be confused with equality) in the world. When the Russian people becomes conscious of this chief obligation and strives to fulfill it, the Russian people will become the Russian nation. . . . [A] just order will be established in all the world."[5] RNU is to be the vanguard of this national revolution, a vanguard that stresses confrontation and violence as the means to achieve its aims. RNU, like other Nazi-like organizations in contemporary Russia, shares Nazism's ideological fusion of racialism-nationalism and socialism, which emphasizes the importance of the worker's movement in conjunction with youth groups and sympathetic elements in the military as the primary transmission belts of its populist *Volk* (*narod*)-based national revolution.[6]

The national revolution's primary enemies are Jews and other cosmopolitan and alien elements that the movement views as being bent on the dismemberment and exploitation of the Russian state and the eventual genocide of the Russian people, hence the emphasis of Russian national revolutionaries on immediate action, an emphasis coupled with a mystical faith in the deified *narod's* ability to save itself in a mobilized expression of will. In that regard, the national revolutionaries have much in common with the ideology of the more conventional radical populism of Vladimir Zhirinovskiy and the National Bolshevism of Russian Communist Party leader Gennadiy Zyuganov, both of whom also have made dark allusions to a planned genocide of Russians by sinister foreign forces and who espouse an ideology that likewise fuses nationalist and socialist elements. Nevertheless, Barkashov's ideology (and that of other national revolutionaries) is far more radical. Its racial element, which is the core of the national revolutionary ideology of all proto-Nazi organizations in Russia, transcends conventional nationalism in ways that cannot be other than chilling to the parochial Russian Right.

In her book *The Origins of Totalitarianism* Hannah Arendt cited Hitler's own reluctance to be confined by conventional nationalist ideology, an ideology that would be far too narrow to encompass his grandiose plans, which did not conform to conservative norms regarding what could be called particular "national" interests. Arendt noted a 1937 speech Hitler delivered before "future political leaders." According to Hitler, not "ridiculously small tribes, tiny countries, states or dynasties . . . but only races [can] function as world conquerors. A race, however—at least in a conscious sense—we have yet to become." In a 1941 decree, Hitler prohibited the further use of the term *German race,* fearing that such nomenclature would "sacrifice . . . the racial idea as such in favor of a mere nationality principle," which in turn would lead to the "destruction of important conceptual preconditions of our whole racial and folk policy." Arendt noted Hitler's real concern that such narrow nationalist concepts would "have constituted an impediment to the progressive 'selection' and extermination of undesirable parts among the German [ethnic] population which in those very years was being planned for the future."[7]

Indeed, Hitler's projected national health bill (never implemented) would have been the basis for the planned *creation* of the master race, which was still nascent, confined in the narrow national ghetto.[8] To be sure, the German nation, broadly defined, would be the genetic key to the creation of the Aryan racial hegemony Hitler foresaw, and for that reason otherwise more parochially minded fanatics like Ernst Rohm mistakenly identified Hitlerism with fascism or military dictatorship, a mistake that some, including Rohm, would pay for with their lives.[9]

The similar plans of the Russian national revolutionaries are made plain enough by programmatic discussions of the "national question" in their press organs, particularly newspapers like RNU's *Russkiy Pory-*

adok [Russian order], the National Social Movement's *Narodnoye Delo* [The national task], and *Russkoye Voskresyeniye* [Russian resurrection] whose front page banner depicts a drawing of Adolf Hitler, fist raised, screeching at an unseen crowd.

National revolutionaries envision the fulfillment of the revolution's primary national task (following the defeat of "anti-Russian" and "cosmopolitan" elements and the establishment of the national dictatorship) as contingent on the cleansing and strengthening of the Russian genotype's "genetic fund." The process would begin with the establishment of racial purity laws prohibiting the pollution of the Russian[10] genetic fund by intermarriage, proceeding through "national proportional" measures which would establish Russians in all leading positions in society, and concluding with the eradication of all unhealthy elements, which would begin with Jews and other despised groups and climax with a program of eugenics and the further elimination of mental defectives, alcoholics, drug addicts, and handicapped people of all genotypes.

Narodnoye Delo elaborated the benefits of such measures in an article entitled *Genetic Measures: The Norms of Life of a Healthy Society:*

> The democrats and communists always dismiss the biological factor in the development of the society, therefore their efforts to change society for the better are doomed to fail. In today's conditions, one may say with certainty that the genetic degradation of the population is the basic reason for all [of our] troubles. For seventy years of Soviet power and for the five years of *perestroika*, the genetic burden of society has grown so much that we observe it in everyday life. For example, while riding on public transportation, one may often observe [abnormal] . . . people: the debilitated, cretins, degenerates, the damaged children of alcoholics. . . . Their numbers grow with each passing year . . . our biological elite, people who could resist [such degradation] is becoming smaller each day. . . . It is necessary to liquidate in the shortest possible time this genetic baggage.[11]

Squaring Nazism and the Russian Idea

How do Russia's national revolutionaries square the swastika with their own Russian nationalist-racialist theories? After all, Hitler was responsible for the deaths of millions of Russians, and it has been the national revolutionaries' display of the swastika that has so alienated them from the more prominent oppositionists (who also view themselves as more respectable) of the now all but defunct National Salvation Front, the organization that was primarily responsible for the formation of the loose communist-nationalist alliance following the breakup of the Soviet Union. Indeed, the controversy over national identity with its various interpretations of history and views of Russian destiny has been a long one, spanning both the czarist and Soviet eras.

Since the Slavophile controversies of the nineteenth century, Russians have grappled with the question of national identity. Russia—a vast, multinational empire ruled by the autocrat who saw all the empire as dynastic patrimony—had survived well into the age of the "nation-state," our integrated state. The question for the nationalists, then as now, was one of the compatibility of modernization with the preservation of the traditional culture and identity of the Russians. For the first time in their history, the Russian question, or to be more precise, the Russian questions, became a primary concern of patriotic Russians who may never have had to contemplate the particulars of their loyalties and identity. Russian nationalists, infused with the romantic notions of the time, pondered the question What is Russia? Was she the huge, baggy expanse of the autocrat's holdings? If this was so, Who is a Russian? Were all the Russified inhabitants of the empire Russians? The nationalists who attempted to answer these questions groped for a unifying notion loosely termed the Russian Idea. What should Russia be? Her position as defender of the Orthodox states of the East raised the question of a national mission or destiny (as is often expressed in the notion of Russia as the third Rome, that is, the inheritor of a mission passed down from the Byzantine Empire). Still, however these questions were addressed by the thinkers of the day, Russian culture was intertwined with Orthodoxy and the monarchy.

Given the linkage of Russianness to Orthodoxy and the emotional attachment of Russian nationalists to the monarchy, the development of a fascist movement in Russia was problematic. Christianity stood in the way of fascism's celebration of violence and the will to power. The fascist's god was the nation, or rather their version of the ultimate idea immanent in the nation, whose collective will is expressed in the structures of the state and the personality of the leader. It goes without saying that the monarchy, bound to feudal social arrangements and traditionalist values, was a roadblock to fascism's relentless modernism or "futurism," which saw industrial advancement as the expression of the national Will to Power through technological and social progress. Class differentiation divided the nation and impeded the metaphysical unity of people, state, and leader as ordained by history. The national mission could not be fulfilled in the twentieth century by horse-drawn carts, localist hayseeds, and backward-looking priests. Fascism, then, was a form of right-wing modernism. Nineteenth-century romantic conservatives in Europe, Russia, and America posed a cultural question: Was modernization (the creation of the integrated state) compatible with traditional culture and the preservation of national identity? (They thought not.) In the eyes of fascist sympathizers, it was the wrong question. Nineteenth-century social Darwinism (not to mention Nietzsche's philosophy) had informed those nationalists, for whom the nation as a metaphysical constant was the highest value, that the story of history was the story of a struggle for dominance. The physical survival and advancement of the nation in the biological struggle for dominance was the real aim of patriots. The "national question" should read, How are we to win the struggle? What was needed was not reaction, not conservatism, and certainly not the emasculating strictures of Christianity, but a national revolution that saw the integrated state as the vehicle for the realization of national goals— thus Mussolini's "corporate state," an alliance of all social forces under the leadership of the Duce, and the eventual emergence of the ideology of national socialism in post-war Austria and Germany.[12]

Today's national revolutionaries can trace at least a part of their pedigree back to the Jew baiting of the Black Hundreds, particularly by spreading (along with other like-minded groups) the national revolutionary gospel in the guise of the ubiquitous *Protocols of the Elders of Zion*, now enjoying a revival in the land in which the lurid tale was first produced in that precise form. Still, the most direct antecedents of the doctrine of national revolution are to be found in the thinking of communist era National Bolsheviks, Russia's national communists, Russian chauvinists who see both the czarist and Soviet empires as part of an unbroken stream of Russian glory. National Bolshevism's development paralleled, and surely fed off, the evolution of fascism and national socialism.

The ideology of the National Bolsheviks is based on the theory of the two parties and is related to a proto-Russian fascism that dates back to the 1920s, when hopeful Russian nationalist exiles, living in the era of Mussolini, counted on a Russian Thermidor to implant a homegrown fascist regime in the land of the Bolshevik Revolution. The monarchy had proved itself outdated and incompetent, and Mussolini's fascist movement appeared to present a resolution of the modernist-nationalist dilemma by celebrating ancient symbols and virtues within the context of a dynamic and aggressive integrated state. Fascism was most attractive to the young, who had grown weary of hoary reactionary fantasies of a return to a past that had proved itself decrepit and impotent before the forces of history. The Young Russians movement (*Mladorossitsi*), organized in Paris and led by twenty-one year old Alexander Kazem Bek, was the first attempt at organizing a Russian fascist mass party. By the 1930s Russian Fascist and Nazi parties had been established in Manchuria, the United States, and Germany. Some forward-looking Russian émigrés saw Hitler as the possible liberator of

Russia from the Bolshevik Satan, while others suspected him of having expansionist designs toward the Russian homeland and thus preferred Mussolini.[13] In any event, by 1945 Konstantin Rodzayevskiy, who at age twenty-four had founded the Harbin-based Russian Fascist Party, admitted that he had misjudged Stalin and acknowledged the validity of the two parties theory. "Stalinism," he wrote, "is exactly what we mistakenly called 'Russian fascism.' It is our Russian fascism cleansed of extremes, illusions and errors." After being captured by the Soviets, he asked the Great Strategist to allow him to serve the Fatherland. Stalin was not the forgiving sort and he ignored the offer: Rodzayevskiy was executed in August 1946.[14] What had become apparent, however, was that nationalist forces were at work *within* the Soviet Communist Party as National Bolshevism consumed Marxism-Leninism via Stalinism.

National revolutionaries tend to go National Bolshevism (and its theory of the two parties) one step further, emphasizing the racial aspects of Russian identity and viewing both Hitler and Stalin as enemies of the cosmopolitan conspiracy against the Aryan peoples. Barkashov maintains that Russia "should become the center of consolidation of the healthy European nations," that is, the Aryans of Europe, particularly the Germans.[15] In the national revolutionaries' twisted version of history, only the machinations of the global conspiracy prevented the alliance of Nazi Germany and Stalin's Soviet Russia in an Aryan counterrevolution (how the national revolutionaries square this bit of revisionist history with either the domination of the Russian genotype in their projected New Order or Hitler's view of the Slavs as *untermenschen* remains a mystery) against the cosmopolitans. The Molotov-Ribbentrop pact is seen as evidence that the two dictators saw eye to eye on the subject of the world conspiracy.[16] World War II is explained as the fruit of the cosmopolitan infiltration of both regimes. One national revolutionary theorist singles out Admiral Wilhelm Canaris, chief of German military intelligence, and Stalin's secret police chief Lavrenti Beria as the conspiracy's agents of influence.[17] The war prevented the consolidation of the Aryan forces and averted the derailing of the global conspiracy. The collapse of the Soviet Union and the Yeltsin regime's efforts to westernize Russia manifest the continuance of the plotters' long-term plan to enslave, exploit, and eventually kill off the Russian nation.

Paganism and the National Revolution

> *For youthful, vigorous barbarians Christianity is poison.*
>
> —Nietzsche[18]

"The predisposition to religious belief," wrote sociobiologist Edward O. Wilson, "is the most complex and powerful force in the human mind and in all probability an ineradicable part of human nature."[19] Christians would agree with Mr. Wilson, but it is the neopagans, as well as his fellow atheists, who have dominated the religious (though not the truly spiritual) life of this unfortunate century. Like Emile Durkheim, modern barbarians see the religious ritual as a means of consecrating the group, the party, the class, or the race, the "core of society" as Wilson put it in *On Human Nature*,[20] and not as a liturgical mechanism for mediation with the Almighty. The intoxicating mix of myth, symbol, and ritual serves to subsume the individual in the collective, to bond him together with other adherents of the secular faith, the party hierarchy (Orwell's Inner Party) guarding and interpreting the sacred writings of the prophet (Lenin, Mao, Hitler), the leader (*Duce, Fuehrer,* or *Vozhd*) himself serving as the high priest, the remote keeper of the keys. Holy relics (Lenin's mummified corpse comes readily to mind) are put on display and serve as the focus of public rituals. The aura of the mystery of faith is retained.

The twentieth century, no less than the time of the Crusades or the turmoil of the Reformation, has been one of religious wars and revolutions. Ideologues of the revolutionary Left have harnessed humanity's hunger for transcendence to the yoke of a teleological Marxism, with History pinch-hitting for God and a communist future as the millennium. The revolutionary Right, without Marxism's convenient (and ready-made) pseudotranscendent underpinnings, has had to fall back on an older cache of symbolism and myth to mobilize the faithful. Thus paganism promotes progress as racism, the end of history being the perfection of the *Volk*, who will then inherit the earth. True, national churches can be useful for mobilization, but only the heroic mythology of paganism can free the race from the inhibiting fetters of Christianity. Fascism's and nazism's heroic vitalism, personified in warrior gods and Aryan heroes, was propagated through politicized revivals of paganism, the premodern mythology of the *Volk* or the race. Only the cult of the pagan warrior (as opposed to the Christian knight), so the avatars of neopaganism have reasoned, could prepare the people for the brutal actions necessary for the survival of the race in the merciless struggle for biological dominance.

The traumatic events of the last decade have left the Russian people shaken and adrift, and some ideologues of the revolutionary Right have sought to satiate the religious-ideological thirst of the people (particularly young people) with a heady political brew that disconnects the Russian nationalist impulse from traditional Christianity. The neopagan revival itself can be traced back to the 1960s, when a distinctly different breed of Russian nationalism reared its head, one that was an evolutionary step away from the Stalinist National Bolshevism that had satisfied the religious-tribal imperative within the Russified Soviet Union's elite and dominant nation up to that time.

Neopaganism's original prophet was Valeriy Skurlatov, who continues to play the role of philosopher-priest in Russian neopagan circles.[21] Skurlatov popularized the pagan mythology of *The Book of Vlas,* a forgery originally concocted by a Russian émigré in the Brezhnev-era Soviet press.[22] This chronicle cum folk epic depicted a Russian golden age in the pre-Christian era, complete with fabricated heroes Skoten and Igor the Elder. The Russians, according to the pagan priests who allegedly had authored *Vlas,* were the first Indo-Aryan people and had spread Aryan civilization to Europe. Their enemies the non-Aryans, especially the Jews, had contrived to subjugate the torchbearers of Aryanism, the Russians, since time immemorial. The subtext of Skurlatov's interpretation of ancient Slavdom's history was clear enough: Only a revival of the pagan culture of the golden age could harden the national fiber for the continuing struggle with the forces of darkness.

Skurlatov's ideas were picked up by other pagan ideologues and constituted a sort of semi-underground alternative to both conventional Russian nationalism and Soviet Marxism-Leninism. Valeriy Yemelyanov proved to be the most extraordinary of them. Later he would lead a pagan-oriented splinter Pamyat faction, foreshadowing, as we shall soon see, the birth of the national revolutionary movement.[23] Yemelyanov promoted an aggressively pagan doctrine that carried the rejection of the conventional nationalist worldview to bizarre extremes. He claimed, among other things, that Christianity was a Zionist sect and that Prince Vladimir was the grandson of a rabbi. In 1980 he was arrested for the murder of his wife (he dismembered the corpse for disposal, but the police found the remains) and was confined to a mental institution until 1987.

Little is actually known about pre-Christian paganism in Russia. The heathen Slavs deified the forces of nature (Perun, the god of thunder and lightening, headed up the pagan pantheon), and animism and ancestor worship appear to have played a part in their hodgepodge of ritual and myth. Russia's neopagans pay only cursory attention to the old gods, preferring to speculate about the mystical power of crystals, pyramids, eight-pointed stars and swastikas, the predictions of Nostradamus, or the energy fields that allegedly surround the Aryan Russians in the writings of the neopagans. There is little concerning the real mythology of the ancient Slavs. Russian paganism per se is not the point. Those Russians who dress up as ersatz Slavic warriors, sword in hand, and claim to re-create the ancient Slavic rituals are closer to the

Communists in spirit than they may realize: Russia's national revolutionaries' real aim in propagating their neopagan cultural system is much the same as the Bolsheviks' calculated antireligious propaganda coupled with their equally calculated cultivation of the pseudoreligious Lenin cult. Neopaganism, tailored to fit the political and social agenda of the national revolution, is aimed at eradicating real spiritual faith, particularly Christianity, as the first step toward the revolution they plan.

Thus Christianity in general and Orthodoxy as such, one of the pillars of conventional Russian nationalism, continues to be viewed with suspicion, if not outright hostility, by national revolutionaries. National revolutionary ideology, with its mystic faith in the triumph of the genotype, does, however, recognize the power of religious and quasi-religious symbolism as a part of the national-racial mythology, a manifestation of the unity and sanctity of the *narod*, chosen by history to dominate the world.[24] The swastika is frequently pointed to as an ancient national-racial symbol used in both Orthodox Russia and pagan times, and national revolutionary ideologists frequently mix aspects of both periods in their notions of the special spiritual qualities of the *narod*.

Barkashov himself professes what may be called Orthodox paganism.[25] The national revolution is antimaterialist and romantic (materialist philosophies cannot explain the powerful sense of will and belonging ingrained in the collective mind of the *narod*) and therefore rejects Marxist atheism. A higher will animates the universe, directs history, and finds its fullest expression in the collective, organic body of the Aryan race. Symbols both pagan and Orthodox Christian, the eight-pointed star and swastika in particular, radiate the life giving energy of this force, the Orthodox pagan god.[26] Thus Barkashov calls himself an Orthodox Christian, but Orthodoxy (for the Orthodox pagans) is merely one manifestation of Aryan Russia's special spirituality. The term Christian is virtually interchangeable with Aryan, a racial but not necessarily religious term in national revolutionary parlance. Orthodox paganism is idealism as racism.[27] Christ was an Aryan—a Galilean, not a Jew—and the Golden Rule need apply only to other Aryans.[28]

Since the Jews are portrayed as the most depraved and evil force on earth, the ideology of the national revolution suggests a certain dualism as well, with the Aryans being the bearers of the positive, creative and life-giving force of the universe and Jews being the physical realization of a negative, destructive force. In *Mein Kampf*, Hitler divided mankind into three categories—creators, bearers, and destroyers. The Aryans were the creators and the Jews the destroyers of culture and mankind's highest achievements. "The Aryan stock alone," he wrote, "can be considered as representing the first category."[29] Like the Nazis, Russian national revolutionaries identify capitalism with parasitism and the Jew. The finance capitalist doesn't make anything; he lives off the production of others by exerting the power of money over labor, of gold over blood, of mind over spirit, of artificial society over organic community, of individualism over collectivism. The Jew is death; the Aryan, life. We can thus extrapolate a national revolutionary line of the Russian Right's cultural system that looks like this:

Cultural System of the National Revolutionaries

God	Devil
Life Force	Death
Good	Evil
Creator race	Destroyer race
Russian nation	Isreal
"Christian" Aryan	Jew
Community	Society
Creation/production	Parasitism/destruction/finance[30]

For Barkashov and other national revolutionaries, the growth of the transnational regime is evidence of the Jews' age old plotting coming to fruition. "Up to 1914," Barkashov maintains, "Russia was the only state that was really independent of the trans-national financial oligarchy. . . . Russia potentially could have become the center of consolidation of all healthy European nations." The Bolshevik Revolution was designed to remove Russia as a roadblock to the foreseen dominance of the world "financial oligarchy," the controlling interest of which was (and is) in the hands of the Jews, the originators of the idea of world domination. The United States is today the primary platform for the realization of the Jews' plot, a tool in the hands of the "financial oligarchy."[31] The United States works in concert with the International Monetary Fund (IMF), the UN, NATO, and an internationalist-oriented elite in the mass media to undermine Russian sovereignty, military security, and cultural identity.[32]

Marxism professes materialism, while fascism and Nazism focus on a form of romantic pantheism. As we have seen, however, Marxism's materialism was "Hegelianized" and soon gained certain romantic qualities. It was "Hegelianized" Marxism that inspired the faithful, though the party's program was built on the foundation of "scientific materialism" and atheism.[33] The ideology of the national revolutionaries, like that of the Fascists and Nazis before them, partly derives its inspiration from pantheistic romanticism and thus declares itself to be antimaterialist. Even so, modernity again presents itself in one of its many Janus-like dualities: Nazism's pseudoscientific racism, the core of Nazi ideology, is nevertheless rooted in Enlightenment scientism. In Nazi ideology, race is not merely an objective category arrived at through human evolution but an "iron law" of history; the Nazis' racial classifications are as "structuralist" in their way as the materialist economic determinism of the Marxists. The Jew can no more overcome his blood than a given society can break the chains of its socioeconomic superstructure. Any sort of "conversion" is out of the question. The Jew, no matter what his personal opinions, is an "objective" enemy. It is as profound an error to identify Nazism with traditionalist conservatism or reaction as it is to deny that Marxism constitutes a secularized religious system.

In any event, national revolutionaries have made clear their intention to build a new Russia that in no way could be viewed as a revival of the Orthodox state that preceded the atheist Soviet regime. Thus one national revolutionary writer attacked Christianity as an anti-*narod* phenomenon: "The baton of proletarian internationalism," he wrote, "has been picked up by Christian internationalism. Total Christianization [is being carried out] through the mass media, [which] injures the health of society. The masses are inspired with the principles of a false humanism, love for the wretched and the deformed . . . the alcoholic and drug addict. . . . A society ruled by . . . such laws . . . will produce degenerates right up until the moment of its complete self destruction."[34]

Thus the ideology of the national revolution is the furthest extension of a line of ideological theorizing that spans the twentieth century, from the quasi-fascism of the Black Hundreds to Soviet National Bolshevism and German Nazism. The Stalin regime itself acted as the incubator in which quasi-fascism could gestate and mature to National Bolshevism before undergoing its final transformation to National Revolution. Today's national revolutionaries, despite their avowed anticommunism, are products, first and foremost, of the Soviet regime, though they first underwent an ideological trial period themselves in the ranks of the notorious nationalist organization Pamyat, an organization that acted as a halfway house for many conventional nationalists and National Bolsheviks on their ideological journey to the national revolution.

Common Roots of the National Revolutionaries

According to press accounts,[35] Aleksandr Petrovitch Barkashov was born in 1953 to a nurse and an engineer who worked in a thermal electric power center. Barkashov served in the Soviet Army and worked as an electrician afterward. A karate brown belt, he also taught martial arts classes. In 1987, Barkashov joined Pamyat, a nationalist organization of the Black Hundred persuasion, and quickly rose to a position of prominence, serving as a member of Pamyat's central council. In 1990, after a falling out with Pamyat leader Dmitriy Vasilyev, Barkashov left the organization and established Russian National Unity, having taken along with him one hundred Pamyat members, many of whom had been his karate students and had served with their former teacher in Pamyat's black-shirted "combat department."

Barkashov has never publicly described the nature of his falling out with Vasilyev, but a few clues about his past that dropped in a 1993 *Izvestiya* interview go a long way toward explaining his disgruntlement with Pamyat's outdated Black Hundred monarchism and its emphasis on conventional Russian Orthodoxy.[36] Barkashov told *Izvestiya* that he owed his worldview to his grandfather, who had served in the Stalin-era Communist Party Central Committee. According to Barkashov, his grandfather "was one of the organizers of the struggle with the cosmopolitan Yids in the late 40s," a struggle that took place in the twilight of the Stalin era, when the aging tyrant was hatching a plan to deport Soviet Jews to the nether regions. Having been immersed in Stalinist National Bolshevism at an early age, it is hardly surprising that RNU's founder would be dissatisfied with the narrow and parochial nationalism of Pamyat.

Barkashov was not alone in his dissatisfaction with the inadequacies of Pamyat. Two other men, younger still than Barkashov (who was 37 at the time of his break with Vasliyev), left Pamyat to form their own national revolutionary organizations at about the same time.[37] Nikolay Lysenko (born 1961) is a former biology teacher from the Irkutsk region who moved to Leningrad in 1986. In 1987, Lysenko joined Pamyat and became a member of the organization's central council. Lysenko, together with collaborator Viktor Antonov, left Pamyat after a conflict (again, of an unknown nature) with Vasiliyev and founded the People's Party of Russia. In January 1992, the party was reregistered as the National Republican Party of Russia, with its headquarters in the now renamed city of Saint Petersburg. The party claims 10,000 members, but the reasons for its notoriety lie elsewhere: The party has formed what the Russian press has described as "storm detachments," known collectively as the Russian National Legion, many of whom (like their counterparts in other national revolutionary organizations) have already been baptized by fire in the various hot spots of the former Soviet empire, particularly in the mini-civil war that has intermittently raged in the Dneister region of Moldova, pitting ethnic Eastern Slavs against the Romanian-Moldovans. In the December 1993 elections to the Russian National Assembly, Lysenko won a seat in that body's lower house, the state Duma.

The National Republicans' program stresses the importance of creating a "national regime" in Russia, one that would be "de-Zionized" and would wage a war on what the party terms the "Black Hydra," the most immediate threat being the "blacks," the Turkic and Caucasian hordes of the former Soviet empire's southern underbelly.[38] The party's members frequently dress in khaki uniforms with armbands bearing a lighting bolt symbol as their insignia.

Still, for all of this, Lysenko has cultivated a moderate image, maintaining cordial relations with Orthodox monarchists as well as with other national revolutionary groups. Like Zhirinovskiy, he kept his distance from the Russian White House during the September-October 1993 crisis, a decision that has not endeared him to other national revolutionaries, some of whom have outshone Barkashov in their commitment to violence and the national revolution.[39]

One of those groups, before its breakup by the Federal Counterintelligence Service in the summer of 1994, was known as the Legion of Werewolves. The Werewolves were quite ambitious in their plans and, having been blooded along with the RNU at the Russian White House, appear to have been eager to take the fight directly to the enemy, so to speak. Their aborted plans included a series of terrorist attacks directed at selected enemies of the race, including a Jews for Jesus rally, Moscow theaters showing Steven Spielberg's holocaust film *Schindler's List*, evangelical Christian communities, and leaders of various political parties, including those of the Russian Communist Workers' Party, the Russian Antifascist Center, and the Democratic Union. The Werewolves may also have seen Barkashov himself as a potential victim, presumably because even his radicalism was too squeamish from their point of view.[40]

The master of the Werewolf den was one Andrey Anokhin.[41] He was born in Estonia and, judging from press accounts, is probably in his early to mid thirties. Anokhin began his Nazi education in Estonia in 1982 by joining an underground proto-Nazi study group headed by an Estonian SS veteran. Sometime after that (the date is unclear), Anokhin left Estonia to study law at Moscow State University. In the late 1980s he too joined the ranks of Vasiliyev's Pamyat before leaving the group after an ideological clash with the Pamyat leader. Anokhin, like Barkashov and Lysenko, took along with him a cadre of fellow-travelers who would form the core of his Werewolf organization, Anokhin himself using the group to hatch his plans for his own version of the national revolution and to spread the national revolutionary gospel among the fringe underground in Russia, Ukraine, and Estonia.

Anokhin brought a group of Werewolves to the Russian White House during the September-October 1993 crisis, their avowed purpose being, according to Anokhin himself, to "shoot first the democrats and then the communists." The Werewolves, again like RNU and the Russian National Legion, had already seen action in the miniwars that have flared up in the collapsed Soviet empire, as well as in the Balkans, where Werewolf volunteers fought on the Croatian side of the Balkan War, probably judging the Croats, who lived under a Nazi puppet regime during World War II, the best upholders of the Aryan ideal.

The personal histories of Barkashov, Lysenko, and Anokhin show that since the late 1980s and early 1990s, when the disgruntled nascent national revolutionaries left Pamyat, postcommunist Russia has proved to be a fertile field for national revolutionary ideology. Alienation and atomization, so much a part of modernity's urbanized technological-industrial landscape, has been deepened by social and economic collapse. Workers, as well as military personnel and members of the police-security apparatus, have proved sympathetic to the national revolution. Among young people, who have no living memory of the World War II era, the message of national revolution and its violent promise of an assertion of national-racial (and personal) identity has proved to be most attractive.

Current Politics and the RNU

Barkashov claims thousands of RNU members across Russia and many more thousands of sympathizers, who carry out secondary functions such as distributing newspapers, leaflets, and other propaganda materials.[42] Most press accounts note the prominence of military, police, and security personnel among both RNU activists and sympathizers, including high ranking staff officers.[43] One press account claimed that RNU is not only "getting stronger and growing dynamically" but that it is the fourth largest political organization in Russia behind Zyuganov's CPRF, Zhirinovskiy's LDP, and former prime minister Yegor Gaydar's Russia's Choice party, claiming 70,000 members. Moreover, Barkashov at one time was judged the third most popular figure in the opposition, behind former vice-president Rutskoy and Vladimir Zhirinovskiy.[44]

In spring of 1994, Barkashov organized an alliance between the RNU and certain Russian labor unions and transformed the RNU movement into a political party. The Confederation of Russian Trade Unions, headed by Andrey Alekseyev, in March 1994 signed a declaration on "forming a National-Social movement aimed at introducing the Russian national idea into Russia's labor movement." The CRFTU claims 200,000 members.[45] By summer, RNU had registered itself as a political party and had held its founding conference as such in Novosibirsk with two hundred regional delegations in attendance.[46] In October 1994, RNU sponsored its first political candidate, party member Aleksandr Fedorov, in a six-way race for an empty State Duma (the Russian national legislature's lower house) seat in Moscow's Mytishchinskiy electoral district. Fedorov won 6 percent of the vote.[47] Barkashov has pledged to continue the struggle, and RNU has continued recruiting and training new members and propagandizing the national revolution since.

Barkashov's political ambitions may have been fueled by the respectability he apparently won in the eyes of some opposition figures, particularly Aleksandr Prokhanov, editor of *Zavtra*, perhaps Russia's most prominent nationalist newspaper, during the September–October 1993 crisis. Prokhanov, who has acted as a broker among various strains of patriotic oppositionists in hopes, apparently, of uniting the opposition forces, invited Barkashov to a May 12, 1994, meeting of opposition leaders and supporters sponsored by the *Zavtra* newspaper staff. It was the first such meeting Barkashov had attended. He was greeted warmly by participants, and Prokhanov subsequently praised his courage during the October 1993 shoot-out at the Russian White House.[48]

National revolutionary ideas have been particularly attractive to young people. Russian rock star Yegor Letov of the popular heavy metal band Civil Defense, along with other rockers of that ilk, has reportedly endorsed RNU's program of national revolution.[49] Other press accounts link Barkashov with ex-Zhirinovskiy[50] associate, writer, and denizen of the heavy metal rock scene, Eduard Limonov, former National Salvation Front luminary Ilya Konstantinov, supporters of anarcho-communist radical Viktor Anpilov, and nationalist-oriented businessmen.[51] Together they form what journalist Gleb Cherkasov dubbed the "new opposition."[52]

The Opposition's Third Wave

Russia's national revolutionaries constitute the third wave of opposition to the Yeltsin regime in the postcommunist era. They tend to be younger and far more radical than the more bureaucratic, staid opposition leaders of the first wave, many of whom held high positions under the old regime.[53] The opposition's most prominent first wave leaders, including the Russian Communist Party's Gennadiy Zyuganov, ex-factory director Petr Romanov, and *gosudarstvennik* former vice president Aleksandr Rutskoy, are all in some way attached to and perhaps nostalgic for the Soviet Union. In any event, they all advocate a reanimation of the union. Most were Soviet Communist Party members and, despite their fiery rhetoric, have at least attempted to distance themselves from more radical fringe elements.

Zhirinovskiy and his Liberal Democratic Party represent a second wave of opposition, an opposition proud of its outsider status, whose style is flamboyant and impetuous rather than conservative. In December 1993, Zhirinovskiy's LDP won nearly 23 percent of the vote in elections to state Duma seats allotted by a party list vote and he, at least for a time, eclipsed less provocative patriotic leaders in the public eye. Zhirinovskiy's rise to prominence came only in the Soviet Union's twilight era, shortly before its collapse. The LDP's leader himself constantly reminds the public that he was never a Communist Party member, that he never held any privileged position in the Soviet *nomenklatura*, and that he is one of them, a man born into deprivation and resentful of the arrogant fat cats who still rule the Russian people. Zhirinovskiy's outrageous and irreverent style has attracted some young people who are probably frustrated by the stodginess of conventional politics, but his core message is geared to people closer to middle age (Zhirinovskiy himself was born in 1946), people whose memories of the hardships of the past differ sharply from younger people—whose formative years were spent under Brezhnev and whose political views were shaped by Gorbachev's *perestroika* as well as by broadening contacts with the West, particularly through Western mass culture in the form of the culture of consumerism, films, television programs, and rock music.

The most important factor separating Zhirinovskiy from the national revolutionaries is the absence of overt racism from the LDP's program. Zhirinovskiy is a Russian chauvinist who demands a new Russian empire (rather than the reanimation of the Soviet Union), stability for its people, and a measure of economic freedom and prosperity to be achieved on the tried-and-true base of the military-industrial complex. He has never promulgated the ideology of "scientific" racism, though he, like many opposition figures, has made use of a variant of the Jewish-capitalist-Western plot theory when it suits him. Moreover, Zhirinovskiy has not participated in any of the violent clashes of the postcommunist period in Russia, something even the "respectable" first wavers cannot claim.

Historian Ian Kershaw has interpreted the Nazi movement as one of social protest whose appeal was strongest among young people.

Frustrated and alienated by the failure of the old semimodernized Germany and the tangle of social and economic problems which that failure spawned, they dreamed of a new order that would banish the "rigid immobility and sterility" of the old and offer increased social mobility and opportunity, prosperity and personal fulfillment, paradoxically, through a dynamic new collectivist movement whose "drive and elan" particularly appealed to them. Moreover, the Nazi movement provided a sense of entitlement—the new order's promise was their birthright as Germans.[54]

The violent, destructive impulse in Nazism proved to be a narcotic for those most alienated, for those who may have seen Germany's national revolution as an opportunity for self-assertion and affirmation through violence. For these people, violence was an assault on the hopelessness and despair of anonymous failure. They turned an old aphorism inside out, asserting, in effect, "I destroy, therefore I am." Thus war, both internal (racial cleansing) and external (conquest), was the irresistible essence of German Nazism and, indeed, is probably an important part of any movement that is truly revolutionary. Real revolutions, uprisings that intend the complete transformation of a society, have need of an irrational element that is both destructive and self-destructive, one that harnesses the impulse to destroy for destruction's sake.[55] A British student of Nazi ideology, Jeremy Noakes, has argued that "the Nazi revolution *was the war* [italics added] —not simply because the war accelerated political, economic, and social change . . . but more profoundly because in war Nazism was in its element. In this sense, Nazism was truly a 'revolution of destruction'—of itself and of others on a profound scale."[56]

It is no surprise then, that the national revolution has such appeal to young people, particularly those who identify with the nihilism of heavy metal rock music. Heavy metal rock is the music of destruction and self-destruction, the roar of despair, loneliness, and unrestrained, violent self-indulgence for young people throughout the developed world—orphans of rapid change who can find no place for themselves in societies where traditional roles and community stability have themselves been lost in the modern world's turbulent whirlwind. Social dislocations have spawned similar pathologies in Europe (skinheads and soccer thugs) and America (street gangs). Thus the impulses that produce violent miscreants organized as parties, movements, or gangs are not endemic to any particular culture, though their various manifestations and relative importance to their societies *are* particular. Seen this way, it may or may not be that Russia's national revolutionaries will eventually push Zhirinovskiy aside, as he did the opposition's first wave. But their chances will improve if instability persists and living conditions worsen. In such a scenario they too could capitalize on a political or economic crisis, as Zhirinovskiy, whose flamboyant radicalism helped to pave the way for them, did following the October 1993 violence in Moscow. Barring that, Russia's national revolutionaries, given their thirst for violence, will remain a dangerous and potentially destabilizing factor in Russian society. Even more disturbing is the possibility that even if the authorities moved to repress them, conditions are such that we would soon see their kind again.

Notes

1. Moscow, ORT, 8 May 1995.

2. For various claims of RNU participation in the White House defense, see *Izvestiya*, 14 October 1993; *Moscow News*, 21 April 1994; *Sovetskaya Rossiya*, 5 March 1994.

3. According to RNU leader Aleksandr Barkashov, two RNU members were killed and eleven were wounded in the fighting. Aleksandr Khinshteyn, "Humanist in a Black Shirt," *Moskovskiy Komsomolets*, 5 April 1994, 7.

4. *A Nietzsche Reader*, trans. R. J. Hollingdale (London: Penguin Books, 1977), 115–117.

5. Aleksandr Barkashov, *Azbuka Russkogo Natsionalista* [The ABCs of a Russian Nationalist] (Moscow: RNU, 1994), 27.

6. The phrase *national revolution* was used by the Nazis in the 1920s to describe their plans for Germany. F. L. Carsten, *The Rise of Fascism* (Berkeley: University of California Press, 1967), 138.

7. Hannah Arendt, *The Origins of Totalitarianism* (New York: Harcourt Brace & Company, 1979), 412.

8. Ibid., 416.

9. For a comment on the mistaken assumptions of Rohm and others, see Arendt, 317.

10. Eastern Slav may be a more accurate tag, since Ukrainians and Belorussians are viewed as Russians, broadly speaking, by all contemporary Russian nationalists, though national revolutionaries hint that other "Aryan" groups may be incorporated into the "genetic fund" of a broad Russian-Aryan hegemonic empire, hints that will be examined shortly.

11. *Narodnoye Delo*, 2 (1992), 1, 3.

12. For more on Mussolini, "futurism," modernization, and fascist aggression, see F. L. Carsten, *Rise of Fascism*, 9–81. See also Martin Blinkhorn, *Mussolini and Fascist Italy* (London: Routledge, 1984). Carsten outlines the rise of "national socialist" parties, 82–120.

13. For more on the émigré community and fascism, see Walter Laqueur, *Black Hundred* (New York: HarperCollins, 1993), 72–85 and John Dunlop, *The Faces of Contemporary Russian Nationalism* (Princeton: Princeton University Press, 1983), 5–6.

14. Laqueur, *Black Hundred*, 78–79.

15. Barkashov, *Azbuka Russkogo Natsionalista*, 7, 76–77.

16. In fact, the two dictators did share a mutual admiration and a certain ideological affinity, despite the political chasm that separated them. See Arendt, *Origins of Totalitarianism*, 309.

17. V. E. Kuzman, "Who Are the Judges?" *Narodnoye Delo*, 2 (1992): 4. Barkashov's personal view is a bit more complex. The unseen directors of the global conspiracy allowed the rise of a Russian oriented leadership cadre in Russia (while maintaining control of key posts in the Stalin regime) in order to rally the only force—the Russian *narod*—that could possibly defeat the Nazis. The world conspiracy's efforts to install a revolutionary regime in Germany had stalled after the failure of the post-World War I revolution. Hitler represented the insurgence of particularism and had to be destroyed. For the time being the conspirators had to forgo deepening the revolution in Russia, something that would resume after Stalin's death. Barkashov views Molotov and Zhadanov as the leaders of the pro-Russian faction in the Soviet regime under Stalin. See *Azbuka Russkogo Natsionalista*, 72–88.

18. *Nietzsche Reader*, 172.

19. Edward O. Wilson, *On Human Nature* (Cambridge: Harvard University Press, 1978), 169.

20. Wilson, *On Human Nature*, 169.

21. Skurlatov has had an interesting career. After serving in various Komsomol posts, he held a position at the Diplomatic Academy of the Soviet Foreign Ministry (Laqueur, 246–47, n. 6). A doctor of history, Skurlatov was expelled from the Communist Party as a result of his scandalous behavior but continued his activities nonetheless, perhaps indicating that he had found some supporters in Soviet officialdom. During the Gorbachev era he founded the Russian National Front. In a 1994 article published in the nationalist weekly *Zavtra* 32 (August 1994), Skurlatov praised both Stalin and Hitler, claimed that Russians were the "offshoot" of the Aryan race, and attacked conventional Russian nationalism for promoting racial inferiority.

22. Skurlatov's early antics are described in Laqueur, *Black Hundred*, 112–116. Laqueur notes that the Nazi SS set up a special department that collected (and sometimes fabricated) evidence of Germany's glory in the pagan past. Himmler was particularly enthusiastic about the promulgation of pagan mythology. He had been preceded in neopagan studies by none other than German World War I hero Erich Ludendorf, who celebrated the gods of Norse mythology, particularly the cult of Wotan (Odin), something that helped to frighten devout Christians away from the revolutionary Right in Germany. See Carsten, *Rise of Fascism*, 145.

23. Laqueur reviews Yemelyanov's career, *Black Hundred*, 210–212.

24. On the subject of religion, the RNU party program declares that "the freedom of activity of religious confessions [and] communities . . . will be provided for only to the degree that it strengthens the spiritual forces" of Russia. See *Azbuka Russkogo Natsionalista*, 104.

25. Barkashov's book, *Azbuka Russkogo Natsionalista*, is the best single source for an overview of Barkashov's "Orthodox paganism."

26. In fact, Barkashov claims to have had a vision of a gigantic swastika in the night sky during an RNU outing, obviously a sign of the energy produced when pure Aryans align themselves and their symbols properly. See *Azbuka Russkogo Natsionalista*, 96.

27. In the interest of maintaining terminological clarity, we will define racism as an ideology that reduces the complex story of human history to the category of race: Everything—politics, economics, art, and so on, is explicable via racial determinism alone. Race is not merely one factor among many in the shaping of human history, but the *single factor* by which all things are explicable, the key to history. Thus, racism is not mere race hatred, and is certainly not the view that race is an objective category. It is a full blown ideology. Racism is a phenomenon ideologically related to (since the object of veneration is the ancestrally related group) but distinct from nationalism. In that sense, the Nazis, as we have explained earlier, were racists, not nationalists.

28. See the article by Captain S. V. Rogozhin, "On the National Origins of Jesus Christ," *Azbuka Russkogo Natsionalista*, 68–71. Considering the eugenics and other racial measures envisioned by the national revolutionaries, one may question just how far the "Orthodox pagans" are prepared to go in observing the golden rule even for other "Aryans" in view of the need to purify the race. Nazi German propagandists attempted to establish Christ's alleged "Aryan" credentials as well.

29. Cited in Omar Dahbour and Micheline R. Ishay, *The Nationalism Reader* (Highlands: New Jersey, Humanities Press, 1995), 230.

30. I acknowledge my debt to Jeffery Herf and his interpretation of the "cultural system" of Nazism expressed in his important book *Reactionary Modernism: Technology, Culture, and Politics in Weimar and the Third Reich* (Cambridge: Cambridge University Press, 1984). I have followed his example in constructing a linear "cultural system" for the national revolutionaries. My linear system is based on the allusions to the vast differences between Aryans and Jews expressed in national revolutionary literature as a whole, not in any particular article, though a piece in *Azbuka Russkogo Natsionalista*, "Only a Young National Elite, Born of the Russian Nation, Can Save Russia from Enslavement" by Barkashov himself (89–92) is a good place to see the system at work in national revolutionary discourse.

31. *Azbuka Russkogo Natsionalista*, 7.

32. See *Russkiy Poryadok* [Russian Order], the RNU's press organ, 3–5 (1995), especially "The Chechen Crisis, Russia's Enemies and the Rebirth of the Russian People" (1) and "Empire of the Spirit" (4–5).

33. Bertrand Russell once offered this interpretation of Marxism: dialectical materialism is God; Marx the Messiah; Lenin and Stalin the apostles; the proletariat the elect; the Communist Party the church; Moscow the seat of the church; the revolution the second coming; the punishment of the capitalists hell; Trotsky the devil; and the communist commonwealth kingdom come. See Robert Nisbet, *The Quest for Community* (San Francisco: Institute for Contemporary Studies,1990), 33.

34. "Genetic Measures—The Norms of Life of a Healthy Society," *Narodnoye Delo* 2, (1992), 1, 3.

35. Biographical information on Barkashov is drawn from the following sources: Vladimir Ostrosvetov, "The Russian Order of Aleksandr Barkashov," *Moscow News*, 21 April 1994, 3; Sergey Tarchenko, "A Meeting with Aleksandr Barkashov," *Sovetskaya Rossiya*, 5 March 1994, 4; Aleksey Chelnokov, "A Man with a Swastika Two Paces from the Kremlin," *Izvestiya*, 30 July 1994, 5.

36. Aleksey Chelnokov, "A Man with a Swastika Two Paces from the Kremlin," *Izvestiya*, 30 July 1994, 5.

37. The description of the careers and ideologies of the following national revolutionary leaders is drawn from Vladimir Sirotin, "The National Republican Party," *Moscow News*, 3–9 June 1994, 6; Aleksey Chelnokov, "It's Not a Concentration Camp Yet," *Izvestiya*, 26 May 1994, 7; "Werewolves with Swastikas," *Trud*, 7 July 1994, 1; Aleksey Chelnokov and Arkadiy Zheludkov, "Where Werewolves Come From," *Izvestiya*, 9 July 1994, 1, 4.

38. The "Program Documents of the National-Republican Party" (Moscow 1994) are the most detailed of any of the national revolutionary parties. According to the party's program, the national socialist regime should simultaneously permit, even encourage, the growth of a private sector, while regulating the economy and maintaining a strong state economic sector that includes military industries (4). The state should guarantee "free housing, education, health care, [and] social insurance" for "all citizens of Russia" (4–5). The National Republican Party is also one of the more explicitly futurist national revolutionary parties, calling for the "unity of tradition and technological progress" (5). The new national ideology should not look to the past, but to a "new national future" (6). The National Republicans are committed to the struggle against the encroachment of the transnational oligarchy on Russian prerogatives and calls for Russia to regain superpower status in order to carry out the national mission of the Russians: first, to turn back the tide of "Turk-Islamic expansion" and second, to mount a world-wide resistance to "cosmopolitan 'American' expansion" (7). The National Republicans are among the least Nazi-like of the national revolutionaries (their program includes only a single provision for the improvement of the "genetic fund of the nation," 10) thus blurring the line between protofascist and proto-Nazi organizations in postcommunist Russia. Moreover, membership in the party is open to all Russians: In other words, there is no provision for a racial purity test for party cadres (23). The National Republicans, despite their more "futurist" orientation, are the also the most ecologically minded of the national revolutionaries, pledging among other things, to close "ecologically harmful" enterprises and to clean up the Volga and Don Rivers (18). Despite the activities of the party's "storm detachments," party documents declare the National Republicans to be committed to "constitutional means" of struggle (23).

39. Lysenko was formally ousted as the party leader at a party congress held in December 1994. His would-be replacement, Yuriy Belyayev, was wounded in an assassination attempt a few days later, probably as a result of the intraparty dispute. Lysenko kept his seat in the Duma and continued to be identified with the National Republican Party. He now heads a rival National Republican grouping opposed to the Belyayev faction. See *Izvestiya*, 9 December 1994 for more on the Lysenko-Belyayev squabble.

40. According to the news program *Vremya*, two Werewolves were sentenced to prison terms in March 1996 for their illegal activities. ORT television, 13 March 1996. Barkashov was shot in an assassination attempt on December 20, 1993. At the time he was still wanted in connection with the events at the Russian White House in September–October of that year (he, along with Khasbulatov and Rutskoy, was later amnestied by the state Duma). He spent some time in an MVD hospital before his recovery was complete. Barkashov later told *Zavtra* that a "special MVD unit" had arranged the attempted murder (*Zavtra* 12, March 1994). Others speculated that the attempt was the result of a dispute between Barkashov and his deputy, Viktor Krivov (*Izvestiya*, 6 January 1994). Some RNU members claimed that an Israeli "militarized unit" was behind the attempted murder (*Moskovskiy Komsomolets*, 30 March 1994). No connection between the Werewolves and the attempt on Barkashov has been made.

41. *Izvestiya* (9 July 1994) implied that "Andrey Anokhin" may be a *nom-de-guerre*, saying that this is the name "by which he is known in national patriotic circles in Russia, Ukraine, and Estonia."

42. Sergey Turchenko, "A Meeting with Aleksandr Barkashov," *Sovetskaya Rossiya*, 5 March 1994, 4.

43. Vladimir Ostrosvetov, "The Russian Order of Aleksandr Barkashov," *Moscow News*, 15–21 April 1994, 3; Aleksandr Khinshteyn, "Humanist in a Black Shirt," *Moskovskiy Komsomolets*, 5 April 1994, 7.

44. Andrey Zhukov, "The Nationalists' Fall Round Dance," *Rossiya*, 2 October 1994, 3.

45. For more on the transformation of RNU into a political party and its relations with the CRTU, see Olga Odintsova, "Trade Union Bosses Can Thwart the Signing of the General Agreement," *Nezavisimaya Gazeta*, 13 April 1994, 2, and Andrey Nikolayev, "Trade Unions and Fascists Are Forming a National Socialist Movement," *Segodnya*, 29 March 1994, 2.

46. "Provincial Chronicle," *Segodnya*, 5 May 1994, 2.

47. Andrey Semenov, "Revelation in Brown Tones," *Moskovskiye Novosti*, 30 October-6 November, 1994, 6.

48. Yegor Gaydar, "The Real Fascist Threat in Russia," *Liberation*, 20 June 1994, 6; "Aleksandr Barkashov: 'Heil Russia!'" *Zavtra* 12 (March 1994): 1, 2.

49. Andrey Zhukov, "The Nationalists' Fall Round Dance," 3.

50. Zhirinovskiy has long courted the youth vote, even going so far as to open a rock music emporium in Moscow. Limonov was his direct tie to Russia's (often) national revolutionary oriented heavy metal rock scene. The LDP has an affiliated youth organization known as the *Sokoli*, Zhirinovskiy's "Falcons" who sport black paramilitary uniforms. The Falcons, however, are not known to have engaged in any of the violent activities of the national revolutionary storm troopers.

51. Gleb Cherkasov, "Opposition Too Weak to Restore Lost Unity," *Segodnya*, 13 October 1994, 2; Aleksandr Burtin, "Fascists Speaking the Truth," *Novaya Yezhedenevnaya Gazeta*, 9 September 1994, 4; Aleksandr Barkashov, Aleksandr Dugin, Yegor Letov, Eduard Limonov, et al., "A Declaration of the Revolutionary Opposition," *Zavtra* 25 (June, 1994), 5.

52. Gleb Cherkasov, "Opposition Too Weak to Restore Lost Unity," 2.

53. Indeed, *Limonka*, the newspaper of Eduard Limonov's National Bolshevik Party and a mouthpiece of the "new opposition," carried a banner headline on the front page of issue 2 for 1995 that read "Long Live War!," a reference to Moscow's intervention in Chechnya. The "new opposition" supported the war, which is the only policy of the Yeltsin administration that has generated much enthusiasm among their ranks. Moreover, on 11 February 1996, Russian NTV reported that Limonov, apparently with the blessing of many national revolutionary comrades in arms, announced his support for Boris Yeltsin in the June 1996 presidential elections. RNU has been enthusiastic about the war as well. See *Russkiy Poryadok*, 3–5 (1995). The "old" opposition remains divided over the war, with the Zyuganovite communists (and Viktor Anpilov personally) denouncing the war as an attempt by the grand conspiracy to blacken the Russians in the eyes of the Muslim world and further the disintegration of Russia, and Zhirinovskiy and the national revolutionaries backing the war as necessary to *prevent* Russia's disintegration. The ins and outs of the various plot theories concerning the Chechen war are too convoluted to trace here, but the national revolutionaries judge Yeltsin's actions in this instance as objectively in the Russian national interest. Besides, what better way to harden the national fiber, promote solidarity, and hone the army's skills than war? War in fascist and Nazi ideology is the fullest expression of the national will to power and the most authentic experience of mankind, wherein man gives full reign to his will and emotions. Modern technology tied to war making helps to overcome the softness of bourgeois society and promotes "socialism of the trenches," the feeling of solidarity and belonging that the World War I generation experienced. Modern mass society offered only anonymity and atomization. See Jeffrey Herf, *Reactionary Modernism*, especially 70–108, for more on Nazism, the "trench generation," modern technology as expression of the nation's spirit, and the celebration of the "authenticity" of the war experience. See also Theodore Abel, *Why Hitler Came into Power* (Cambridge: Harvard University Press, 1986) for the importance of the war experience to the growth of Nazism in Germany, especially the sense of wartime national solidarity that the Nazi party attempted to recreate in the 1920s and 1930s. Originally published in 1938, Abel's book is an overlooked classic.

54. Ian Kershaw, *The Nazi Dictatorship: Problems and Perspectives of Interpretation* (London: Edward Arnold, 1985), 140–41.

55. Perhaps such behavior validates Konrad Lorenz's theories concerning man's particular penchant for unchecked aggression.

56. Cited in Kershaw, *Nazi Dictatorship*, 140.

8

The Nationalist Intelligentsia, Eurasia, and the Problem of Technology

Intellectuals, particularly writers, play the important role of codifying the nation's myth-symbol complex and mythomoteur once played by priests, scribes, and storytellers. In Russia, the intelligentsia associated with the communist-nationalist coalition is divided between collectivist Eurasianists— who occultize the geographical-cultural roots of the nation—and Russocentric elements, between modernizing "imperialists" and anti-modern, agrarian, communitarian neo-Luddites. The approach intellectuals take to the Russian question frames the nationalist debate and gives form to the unsystematized patriotic sentiments of ordinary people. Although the modern imperialists pay homage to Russian spirituality and traditional values, it is the neo-Luddites who best grasp the implications of the modern crisis of community and the dangers of globalization. Still, only Solzhenitsyn, who holds similar views, has offered a full-blown remedy for the modern disease.

I n the status-based world of the premodern era, priest, scribe, and storyteller formulated and promulgated the "high" (or dynastic) and "low" (or communal) traditions of a people, sometimes combining them to facilitate the cohesion of the clan and tribal-based groups that would form the organic body of the new nation. The nation's myth-symbol complex thus blends myths, memories, and symbols, the working material of scribe, priest, and storyteller, who codify the national mythomoteur that makes claims about the nation's origins and lines of descent. The mythomoteur thus provides "the focus of a community's identity" and "constitutive political myth."[1] Often the mythomoteur "centers around the image of a sacred people with a special relationship to the deity." "Typically, this *mythomoteur* posits

241

an ideal past in which that relationship was harmonious and natural, when the community of the faithful lived out God's dispensation in true faith and understanding." The people may have gone astray or may have fallen under the yoke of heathens, but it is their duty and destiny "to return to the ideal epoch of their history and become once again God's chosen emissaries on earth."[2]

The Russians are one such people, a people who inherited their sense of mission from the Byzantine Greeks. The Russian fusion of dynastic and communal elements to form the "Holy Russia" mythomoteur—the czar as defender of the faith and protector of the community of the faithful—originated in the Byzantine Greek restorative mythomoteur.[3] After Peter the Great's reforms, however, a deep tension in the national constitutive myth became evident, a tension that was made manifest in the Slavophile-Westernizer controversy.[4] The new post-Petrine mythomoteur of the westernizers competed with that of the Slavophiles and their epigones. To be sure, Russia still had a mission, but it was a secularized Hegelian mission, the sacral qualities of her purpose originating in History as the will of the Absolute. The controversy highlighted the rise of the new class, the intelligentsia, created by the Petrine reforms. In the quasi-modernized post-Petrine Russia of the nineteenth century, the intelligentsia assumed the role of arbiter of the national patrimony that the priest-scribe-storyteller triumvirate had fulfilled in an earlier period.

Prerevolutionary Russia never fully entered the modern world of the integrated state or settled the inevitable questions related to national identity in the face of a ubiquitous and often frightening modernity. Soviet repression subsequently subsumed the "Russian question(s)" within the communist mythomoteur, and the Russian question(s) went unresolved, only to resurface with a vengeance in the wake of the Soviet collapse. The intelligentsia, especially the writers (who have played the role of the nation's conscience and spiritual voice for two centuries in Russia), are destined to stand at the ideological eye of the storm in any modern-era nation's formative period. The communists' attempt at modernization failed and the nation, unsure of itself but fully self-aware, has once again been thrust into a new modernization effort, which has in turn opened the door for the intelligentsia to author a new constitutive myth, or resurrect an old one. The ideas of the politically active intelligentsia legitimize the various versions of the Russian Idea that are entertained in the popular imagination, and they inform the platforms of politicians of all stripes. Among the nationalists, the emotive, instinctual responses of ordinary people to the present day situation are given form, direction, and intellectual verification through the nationalist intellectuals' formulations. Arguments against westernization are made within the framework the nationalist-oriented intelligentsia has created, and that framework has guided the political content of the various nationalist programs.

The Russian intellectual of the Right is faced with a daunting task in the postcommunist period. Several competing mythomoteurs are available for inspiring a nationalist program—the National Bolshevik, the Holy Russia, and the National Revolutionary myths, as well as their numerous variations, complete with ready-made cultural systems, being examples of the diversity of Russian nationalisms. But each of the more popular variations of the Russian mythomoteur carries within itself elements that contradict some of the most important propositions of other variants of the Russian Idea. This competition on the Right has become particularly important among those whose overriding concern is antiwesternism and the restoration of empire and not so much the form that such a restoration may take. This is the attitude prevalent among a particular strain of the *gosudarstvenniki*. The "Russian" state (usually meaning the territory of the former Soviet Union) must be restored in order for Russia to fulfill her nature and regain her lost state of spiritual/political grace, and the various shades and hues evident in the nationalist coalition—red, brown, and white—must reconcile themselves to solidarity with other "patriots."[5] Such ideologues of the *gosudarstvo* have searched for a myth-symbol complex that would justify such a solidarity. They think that they have found it in a new version of Eurasianism, but the promotion of the Eurasian-Russian Idea has worked to divide the anti-Yeltsin coalition as much as unite it. Paradoxically, the language of the Eurasian cultural system has deeply penetrated the discourse of the Russian Right.

Eurasia, Prokhanov, Dugin, and Den

The Russian imperium once covered more than one-sixth of the earth's surface, preserving and spreading the pure Orthodox faith, protecting the Russian Orthodox people and their brethren in the Balkans. Holy Russia, so the myth asserts, was virtually unique among the world's empires: The Russian imperium was a tolerant place, allowing diverse peoples to fulfill themselves under the tutelage of the Russian *Staatvolk*. Holy Russia had united the vast landscape of Eurasia from Kamchatka to the Baltic, from China to the heart of Europe. She had evolved culturally as neither a fully Western state (the Great Schism had seen to that) nor an Eastern one, though Russia's deep religiosity brought her closer in many ways to the mystical East than to the materialistic West. Russia is in fact unique, between East and West, a state formed by a uniquely spiritual people whose long-term historical mission was to unite the Eurasian "world island" in a peaceful commonwealth—a mission that the geographic location of Russia, whose heartland lacked defensible borders in the form of natural barriers, made imperative, even to the Russophobic communists. Indeed, some of those inclined toward the original version of Eurasianism (developed in the 1920s and 1930s by Russian émigrés) were well disposed toward the *smenavekhovtsy* and Red patriotism.[6]

Within the parameters of a certain interpretation of the Eurasian principle, the *gosudartsvennik* could discern the makings of a new post-Soviet ideology, one that rehashed the single stream ideology of the National Bolsheviks in such a way as to avoid seeing communist rule per se as the Russian "end of history" but would appeal to the neo-communists just the same. What both White and Red (after the Stalinist "turn" at any rate) Russia had objectively accomplished, and a new Russia could continue, was a successful opposition to the nation destroying, homogenizing, uprooting tendencies inherent in materialistic Western capitalism, whose aim all along had been to establish a world government (mondialism[7]) via the destruction of Russia. Russian patriots must unite with all the antimondialist tendencies evident in the old empire's constituent peoples, especially the Muslim Turkic peoples (Islam is the deadly enemy of Western materialism), in order to revive the Russian state.

The foremost promoter of opposition unity, of reconciliation between Red and White (to say nothing of "brown"), and of the Eurasian/Russian Idea as the basis for such a reconciliation, has been the journalist and novelist Aleksandr Prokhanov.[8] Prokhanov, something of an avant-garde fictional stylist, was never a member of the Communist Party.[9] His devotion to ideological nonconformism has continued to this day, though his affinity for the Russian Right dates back to the mid-1960s.

Born in 1938 in Tbilisi, Georgia, to Russian parents, Prokhanov, like other leading figures of the anti-Yeltsin coalition, came naturally to his insistence that the non-Russian Soviet republics were inextricably tied to the larger Russian state and, he might say, spiritual body. Like other proponents of the neo-Eurasian synthesis (sometimes called the New Right), Prokhanov has alternately displayed a fascination with high technology (especially high-tech weaponry) and with the mystical qualities of ancient paganism and folklore. Trained at the Moscow Aeronautics Institute (graduating in 1960), he began his professional life working as a specialist in rocketry at a scientific institute but quit his position to work as a forester after he developed an interest in Russian folklore and the new environmentalism of the 1960s. During his two-year sojourn as a forester, Prokhanov observed the workings of nature at close quarters, recognizing in his observations "the natural pagan cycle [of life], the essence of which cannot be explained by words."[10] At that time Prokhanov claims to have had a "rather strong and intensive" spiritual experience, a "vision," perhaps even an "epiphany," and he considered retiring to a monastery.[11]

In the mid-1960s, Prokhanov decided to pursue a career as a writer. He initially followed the lead of the new school of Russian "village writers" such as Valentin Rasputin, Vladimir Soloukhin, and Vasily Shukshin, who celebrated the organic qualities of rural life and protested the despoliation of the natural world by Soviet development. His writings appeared under the rubric "folklore expeditions" in the journal *Krugozor*.[12] Prokhanov, however, did not remain on the trail blazed by the village writers. In 1980 he was sent to cover the war in Afghanistan (perhaps because of his past connections with the Soviet military-industrial complex) as a special correspondent of *Literaturnaya Gazeta*. In 1982, he published a novel, *A Tree in the Center of Kabul*, glorifying the exploits of the Soviet forces in Afghanistan. With the novel's publication, Prokhanov had found a special place for himself as the promoter of Soviet adventurism. John Dunlop elaborates: "With his dithyramb to the Soviet war effort, Prokhanov appeared to find his natural 'niche.' A latter day Rudyard Kipling, he seemed to sense that his role was to hymn the 'outer' Soviet empire in all its color and diversity, to show how intrepid Soviet representatives did battle with the nefarious West, and especially with the viperine United States, in a noble effort to expand the spheres of influence of a more just Soviet society."[13] Prokhanov was well thought of in the Soviet military and was called "the Nightingale of the general staff" in 1980s.[14] In 1985 he was made a secretary of the Russian Writers' Union.

Prokhanov's second career as political activist began in earnest after Mikhail Gorbachev launched his restructuring program in the mid-1980s, a program he and others saw as leading to the destruction of the Soviet empire and, therefore, to the demise of Russia/USSR as a great power, robbing the Russian people of their historic mission and destiny. As a writer and bearer of the historic Russian literary tradition, Prokhanov, among others, was particularly offended by the intrusion of Western pop culture that accompanied Gorbachev's policy of "openness." The Russian Fatherland was thus seen by nationalists of Prokhanov's persuasion as being under threat both strategically and culturally/spiritually: Western models did not apply to Russia; the degraded culture of fast food and rock music[15] was unwelcome in the land of the firebird. Western materialism would attack the very heart of Russia's strength—her unique spirituality, a special connectedness

with the extrasensoral realm that had manifested itself in forms both
pagan and Orthodox in Russian history. Prokhanov's interest in things
spiritual is heartfelt—he prides himself on his wide-ranging familiarity
with world religions and claims to have studied transcendental medi-
tation techniques.[16]

For all Prokhanov's superficially unmodern spiritual interests, however, he has not been willing to give in to the Luddite tendencies of a
certain strand of the Russian Right that emerged during the Gorbachev
years. According to Prokhanov, these people, whom he dubbed the
"preservers" (okhranitely), "repudiate civilization and organize the persecution of technocrats," a program that threatens to halt "technical
progress." This program would put not only future generations' living
standards at risk but, perhaps more importantly, would undermine the
Soviet military, the backbone of empire.[17] Early on, Prokhanov supported the National Bolshevik single stream ideology (particularly the
elements of a Zyuganovite two parties theory that identified the Communist Party as a Russian led "great power" movement after the Great
Patriotic War began)[18] as the best solution to the problem of reconciling
Russia's past with communism, though (in a foreshadowing of his embrace of Eurasianism) he worried that some versions of the Russian
Idea were too narrow, and perhaps would provoke a nationalist backlash among the small nations of the great Russian imperium. Moreover, Prokhanov (in the spirit of nonconformism) criticized the top-
heavy bureaucracy of the Brezhnevite-era nomenklatura and continued
to search for an acceptable post-Brezhnev-era ideology.[19]

In 1990 the nationalist journal Nash Sovremennik published Prokhanov's essay "The Ideology of Survival," in which the author appears
to have reached some preliminary conclusions in his ideological
quest.[20] Pre-Revolutionary Russia, according to Prokhanov, was "a
powerful, intensively developing state, with a full-blooded ethnos," a
mighty culture, and strong families. The pre-Soviet empire was destroyed by the machinations of plotters in the West, including Bolshevik radicals, New York bankers and German militarists. The Leninist
party fomented a revolution that was a catastrophe for Russia, but the
(more Russified) party of Stalin[21] followed the imperial imperative and
rebuilt Russian power. Prokhanov portrayed today's democrats as the
heirs of the Bolshevik radicals and as tainted by criminal associations.
Meanwhile, the West was encouraging the intrusion of Muslim fundamentalism into Soviet Central Asia in an effort to pit Slavic Russia
against the Islamic world in order to block Russia's traditional geopolitical route of expansion to the south, facilitate the dismemberment of
the Soviet Union, and distract anti-Western Islam.[22] In order to stave
off a disaster comparable to that of 1917, the Russian Communist Party

(and not the Soviet all-Union party, corrupted under the stagnation regime of Brezhnev) should jettison Marxism-Leninism in favor of "the ideology of national survival" and thereby achieve a "new, second fusion of the party and the people."

Prokhanov later identified three healthy political elements around which a Russian revivalist ideology could rally: The Russian Communist Party ("essentially a party of Russian people"), "national Orthodoxy," and the movement to revive the *zemstva* and the peasant commune. These three elements could assist the army in restoring order through a state of emergency. It is no surprise that Prokhanov signed the "word to the people" letter of July 1991,[23] supported the State Emergency Committee during the tense August 1991 coup attempt, and subsequently defended the coup organizers in his newspaper, *Den* [Day].[24]

Den (later appearing as *Zavtra* [Tomorrow] after the paper in its original incarnation, along with other anti-Yeltsin publications, was banned after the October 1993 confrontation between the president and the Supreme Soviet) began regular publication (a pilot issue had appeared earlier) in January 1991. *Den* was billed as "the newspaper of the USSR Writers' Union" (after the failed coup of 1991, *Den* dubbed itself "the newspaper of the spiritual opposition" and later began calling itself the "newspaper of the Russian state") and the first issue was devoted to attacking Gorbachev and his allies and warning of the international plot to dismember the USSR.[25] After the collapse of the Soviet Union, *Den*, which quickly became the leading organ of the communist-nationalist coalition, championed the rights of the new Russian Diaspora, particularly in the Baltic states, as well as the cause of empire.

From the beginning Prokhanov used the pages of *Den* to promote opposition unity and the Russian Communist Party—now led by Gennadiy Zyuganov—as the vehicle for securing the rebirth of the empire, a resurrection that could take place only *after* the Russian *Staatvolk* had reasserted itself by creating a "party of national interests" that would be animated by the "fire" of "national energy." All the same, he feared that the Red (those who stressed socialism above all as the element that would unite the people) and the White (those who relied on older national symbols and distrusted the red banner as a sign of neo-Bolshevik cosmopolitanism) elements of the coalition would "split the national energy" and hamstring the opposition. Zyuganov and Prokhanov agreed that only a movement that would unite the ideas of "social justice" and "national state development" could hope to integrate all patriots from monarchists to communists and reanimate the Russian consensus (*sobornost*), through which the empire would be re-integrated.[26] The two men have continued their cooperation, Zyuganov initially acting as the leading political figure in, and Prokhanov and *Den* as the cheerleader of, the National Salvation Front, which was, in its pre-October 1993 heyday, the most important vehicle of the patriotic coalition. *Zavtra* and Prokhanov subsequently vigorously campaigned for the Russian Communists during the electoral struggles of 1993, 1995, and 1996 and praised their victories.[27]

To be sure, *Den/Zavtra* has opened its pages to patriots of all conceivable stripes—including neo-Nazis such as Barkashov whom Prokhanov fulsomely praised for his violent opposition to Yeltsin's ultimately successful effort to suppress the Supreme Soviet.[28] It has entertained all sorts of takes on the grand anti-Russian conspiracy (under the rubric *Konspiritologiya*—"conspiritology"), and it courts the radical youth (via a regular column entitled "*Rok—Russkoye Soprotivleniye*"—[Rock [Music]—Russian Resistance]) whose support both the Zhirinovskiyites and the national revolutionaries coveted. Most importantly, *Den/Zavtra* has presented both sides of one of the most contentious debates within the anti-Yeltsin coalition, the question of Eurasianism as the guiding principle underlying the red-white synthesis, an ideology that Prokhanov himself has tirelessly promoted.

Dugin and Eurasianism

A race has roots. Race and landscape belong together. Where a plant takes root, there it dies also. . . . If in that home the race cannot be found, this means that the race has ceased to exist. A race does not migrate. Men migrate, and their successive generations are born in ever changing landscapes; but the landscape exercises a secret force upon the plant nature in them, and eventually the race-expression is completely transformed by the extinction of the old and the appearance of a new one.

World history is the history of the great Cultures, and people are but the symbolic forms and vessels in which the men of these cultures fulfill their Destinies. . . . [U]nderlying the nation there is an idea.

—Oswald Spengler[29]

In 1992, *Den* began touting the ideology of what Prokhanov and his supporters called the New Right, promoting a Red-White synthesis that was to be based on a revamped version of Eurasianism. The avatar of the New Right ideology was (and is) Aleksandr Dugin, a polemicist and theoretician formerly associated with Pamyat,[30] whose importance to the "patriotic" movement has not properly been acknowledged. In the pages of *Den* and his own journal, *Elementy*, Dugin elaborated a neo-Eurasianism that emphasized the importance of Russia's geographical location at the center of the Eurasian heartland in determining Russian culture and politics, and defended the urgency of Russia's imperial mission in the face of "mondialism."[31]

Dugin's claims about the culturally formative aspect of geography and climate are unremarkable (as shown in chapter 6). Dugin's geopolitics, however, are mystical and occult in nature, the shape of world civilizations and the clash of opposing vectors of historical development being portrayed as shaped by unseen spiritual forces beyond Man's comprehension. These forces exercise their influence through the land itself: "Geographic peculiarities of this or that region of the planet are in this way not mere 'dead,' 'material' phenomena, but a living reality, a natural expression of the 'supernatural.' "[32] The natural elements (*elementy*) determine the shape of a given civilization—its people, culture, worldview, and the form the state takes. The two most fundamental elements are earth (*zemlya*) and water (*voda*). Earth expresses stability and continuity, strength and solidity; earth is expanse, earth is space (*prostranstvo*). Water is movement, dynamics, pliable softness (*myagkost*); water is time.

The continental state or empire (*tellurokratiya*) and the seafaring state or empire (*talassokratiya*) are morphologically the two fundamental types of state that actively participate in history.[33] The great powers of the earth have all been seafaring or continental empires—*talassokratya* usually taking the form of the commercial, exploitive metropolitan with far flung colonies; *tellurokratiya* invariably acting as an integrative force, uniting adjacent territories and peoples in an imperial commonwealth, one that often is unprofitable (in material terms) to the formative people. The symbolic expressions of *talassokratiya* and *tellurokratiya* are island and continent. The island is expressed most vividly in the British empire and its successor sea power, the United States; Dugin calls the ideology of the island "Atlanticism." The most vital ideological expression of the continent in world history is Eurasianism. Atlanticism is Western and materialistic; Eurasianism is Eastern and spiritual.

Inevitably, the forces of island and continent have clashed as the two expansive forces met in world history. The prototype "Atlantic" power was Carthage, representing the forces of instability, rootlessness, commercialism, and chaos, whose religious-ideological essence expressed itself in the worship of the devil god Moloch. Rome was the prototype "Eurasian" empire, which reflected the primal forces of unity, rootedness, spirituality, and order, whose religious-ideological expression was most fully revealed in the cult of the parochial gods—the gods of hearth and home. One brought exploitation and degradation to the people within its imperium, the other harmony, fulfillment of national destiny, and autonomy.

For thousands of years, Dugin asserts, a special elite, spiritually attuned to the world historic nature of the clash of primal forces evident in the Atlanticist-Eurasian conflict, the conflict of chaos and order, rebellion against, and harmony with, the cosmic order, has acted out the great drama. The secret elite groupings, the "order of Atlanticists" and the "order of Eurasianists," have struggled for dominance since Man's first civilizations arose. The Germans and Russians have embodied the Indo-European ideal of rooted, spiritual, Aryan Eurasianism in more recent history; the Jews, British, and Americans, the rootless, materialistic, commercial Atlanticist idea.[34]

Both the Third Reich and Stalin's Soviet Union materialized to some degree the Eurasianist ideal of the unity of the world island in the face of the encroachments of the Atlanticist plot. Atlanticism works to subvert the traditional cultures of the Eurasian landmass through capitalism and the materialist ethic, which erodes the spiritual energy of the continental peoples. Unfortunately, the Atlanticists too were at work in both empires to head off the possible unification of the continental powers in a mighty second incarnation of the Holy Alliance[35] of the nineteenth century, an alliance that would have been built around a Germany-Russia-Japan triumvirate. In Germany, the Atlanticists diverted Hitler onto the path of a destructive biological racism that prevented the Fuehrer from following his natural inclinations, inclinations that had led to the Hitler-Stalin pact. In Russia, the agents of Atlanticism, after having been suppressed by Stalin in the great purges of the 1930s and the postwar campaign against cosmopolitanism, reasserted themselves following the *Vozhd's* death. Gorbachev and Yeltsin have been the contemporary agents of the Atlanticist plot to convert Eurasia into a colony, a raw materials source for the voracious and self destructive appetites of the consumerist new world order.

As Dugin sees it, Russia's long-term task is to unite the anti-Atlanticist, antimondialist forces of Eurasia in a new imperial alliance. Islam is a potential ally of Russia in this grand project, sharing with Russian Orthodoxy a deeply "Eastern," "continental" spirituality and rejection of materialism. A revived Europe, one cleansed of the poison of mondialist homogenization and consumerism, should unite with Russia and the Muslims in a titanic "Holy Alliance" against the Atlanticists. Only such an alliance, a uniting of the industrial power of Europe with the spiritual power (to say nothing of resources both human and material) of the East can save the distinct cultures of the continent from the demoralizing forces of the island in modern circumstances. Mobilization and organization, synchronization and coordination are vital in any struggle—economic, political, or military. None can survive alone. Dugin's envisioned continental imperial alliance will span the Eurasian landmass from Dublin to Vladivostok, with Moscow ("the third Rome") serving as the continental capital of the anti-Atlanticist alliance.[36]

In Dugin's ideology, history is destiny, which never stagnates but flows toward the fulfillment of itself. His spirituality is pantheistic, though respectful of Orthodoxy as the expression of the Russian people's peculiar spiritual qualities. Like Prokhanov, Dugin, despite his attraction to the primal call of the "elements," is not antimodernist or antitechnological. He is not a racist (as we defined the term), but is certain that the elements determine the consciousness and unique spirit of nations, that each, in its own way is an expression of an idea. "Scientific racism," with its dream of a biologically pure race created through eugenics, makes no sense to him. It is apparent that his New Right ideology is in part a streamlined package that combines elements of various Old Right systems cobbled together. Russia's historical mission, the uniqueness of Russia and the Russians, the theory of the two parties, the single stream, the grand conspiracy, Holy Russia, and the Third Rome are all evident in his Eurasianist idea. Dugin eschews the Old Right's conspiratology (the plot of the Jew-Masons, for example) as too crude and narrow, and he rejects Pan-Slavism for some of the same reasons that he rejects "scientific racism": Such ideologies are tools of the Atlanticists, designed to divide the antimondialist forces, as the secret "order of Atlanticists" was successful in doing in the case of Stalin and Hitler. Still, for the influences that have given Dugin's cultural system its terminology and framework, we have to look outside the Russian milieu to Europe.[37]

Dugin's Mentors: Russia and Germany

Dugin has appropriated (almost wholesale) the ideas of Belgian geopolitical theorist Jean Thiriart. Thiriart, pro-fascist in the 1940s, finally recognized the Russified Soviet Union as the final bastion of civilization in a Europe overrun by rootless Americanism and consumerism. He counseled the wisdom of a new Holy Alliance of the USSR and Europe—the "Euro-Soviet empire," one that would expand further to the south, since it required a port in the Indian Ocean—against the cosmopolitans.[38] Dugin has also borrowed ideas from the French "conspiratologist" Jean Parvulesco and the European geopolitical theorists of the first quarter of the twentieth century, especially Karl Haushofer.

Dugin and Prokhanov attempted to forge an alliance with the French-led European New Right (*Nouvelle Droite*) in 1992. The *Nouvelle*

Droite articulates a neopagan spirituality, an anticapitalist critique of
America and mass culture, and proposes a "third way" economic program for a united Europe without Euro-bureaucracy. New Right intellectuals, through their doctrine of "ethnopluralism," hope to preserve
the cultural autonomy of all nations in the new Europe. The *Nouvelle
Droite* movement amounts to an intellectual attempt to resurrect the
loose social relations of the premodern polity that most European conservatives identify with Christendom. Like others on the ideological
Right, the New Right is thereby intellectually struggling to stave off
the homogenizing, standardizing, and alienating effects of modernity.
At any rate, Prokahnov and Dugin (correctly, I think) in 1992 identified
the *Nouvelle Droite* as one of the many antimondialist forces arising in
the wake of the cold war, the particularist phoenix having arisen earlier
in Iran.[39] The attempted alliance appears to have fizzled out, but the
Nouvelle Droit and the Russian Eurasianists, particularly Dugin himself,
have both borrowed a great deal from the European, especially German, right-wing thinkers of the 1920s and 1930s, as well from Nietzsche. Dugin's pro-Germanism is really just one more instance of the
long standing ideological flirtation of Russia and Germany.[40]

Industrialization had come late to Germany, in the second half of the
nineteenth century, Britain and France having already "modernized"
themselves, and had been particularly disruptive by way of the accelerated pace that the great changes acquired, disturbing the peace of what
had been a more or less bucolic collection of pastoral German states
until Bismarck secured the reich. Germany, like Russia under Peter
(who imported German expertise and ideas to Russia—it is Peter who
is ultimately responsible for the influence of German Romanticism and
Hegelianism in his country), was dragged into the modern order
abruptly, and the resulting trauma raised the inevitable "German
questions" as the "Russian questions" had arisen in Peter's time.

For German nationalists of the period stretching from the mid-nine-
teenth century to Hitler's ascent to power, Germany was the land in
the middle—between the West corrupted by materialism and capitalism and a backward East. The avatars of German nationalism, however, were divided over the Russian question: Was Russia simply the
latest incarnation of the barbarian hordes who had threatened European civilization for centuries? Or were they, like the Germans, a spiritual people, a nation untainted by Western materialism and utilitarianism? Some Germans thought Russia a potential ally in the struggle
against capitalism and rootless cosmopolitanism.

The hard headed Bismarck, a geostrategist if there ever was one,
had originated the idea of a military-economic alliance with Russia. A
possible German-Russian alliance had been attractive to Kaiser Wil-

helm and Czar Nicholas II as well.[41] As anti-Semitism gained momentum in Germany prior to the Great War, many German nationalists saw Russia, with its Black Hundreds and pogroms, as the natural ally of a German *Volkstaat*, and the anti-Semitic Right in Germany was bolstered considerably by the European publication of *The Protocols of the Elders of Zion* during the interwar period.[42] Thus, "by a strange twist of history, German anti-Semitism, which had been exported to Russia in the early eighteen eighties, was re-imported into Germany from Russia after the First World War."[43]

For some time, German nationalist intellectuals had hoped to find a "third way" between capitalism, with its disruption of the traditional social order and tendency to replace aristocratic quality with the crass rule of money, and the proletarian internationalism of an equally materialist socialism. Some dreamed of a disciplined "Prussian socialism," a new order that would reconcile industrialism with the needs of the nation, while maintaining traditional Prussian order and discipline. The key to reconciling socialism with nationalism, so the Prussian socialists believed, was the notion of the "primacy of politics," the importance of the state (as the embodiment of the national spirit) directing and regulating the economy so as to develop society in accordance with its own vital interests and not those of comprador capital. Concrete "production" must therefore be disconnected from the abstract sphere of "circulation" and finance in order to accomplish the successful incorporation of modern technique with gemeinschaft. Thus Hitler did not originate the notion of national socialism in Germany. As the Prussian socialists saw it (and indeed, all thinkers on the Right before and since have shared this view) the purpose of the economic sphere is to support and nurture the community. Economic growth must not become a goal in itself, with the community treated as a mere unit in the production-consumption equation of capitalist rationalization.

Within Germany a new intellectual movement, "the conservative revolution," united more traditional-minded conservatives and reactionaries of *volkisch* agrarian persuasion with modernist right-wing thinkers in a romantic struggle against what they viewed as a corrupt Weimar state. The Weimar government, according to the conservative revolutionaries, had sold out German interests by accepting the Treaty of Versailles. Weimar's mass democracy was manipulating a disoriented people and promoting individualism. The new movement opposed both the capitalist-liberal revolution and the threat of a socialist one, which was constantly on the Right's collective mind after the aborted Red uprising of 1919.[44]

The conservative revolutionaries juxtaposed *Kultur* and *Zivilisation*, the one a reflection of organic gemeinschaft, the other that of an artificial gesellschaft, in their polemical tracts. The cultural system of the conservative revolution set the "symbolism and language of *Kultur*," community, blood, will, self, form, productivity, and, in some cases, race, against the symbolism and language of alien *Zivilisation*, reason, intellect, internationalism, materialism, and finance.[45]

The community of *Kultur* was form, which filled the community with direction and purpose. The mass of alienated, atomized individuals found in *Zivilisation*, by way of contrast, was thought to be formless, uprooted and directionless. Community offered a framework for proper ethics, the mass only individual satisfaction of base appetites. "Blood" (in many cases an expression of a people's spirit and not necessarily a racialist term) informed the member of the community a priori on matters of personal action, action that cold reason could deconstruct but not really explain or understand. The self was fully realized within the gemeinschaft, the organic community that provided the boundaries of the realizable world for mankind, fused with the community through a natural will. The community/*Volk*/nation was a specific morphological type, unrepeatable and unique, an organic outgrowth of its native soil. The *Kultur* self was alive and creative, expressing the essence of the particular *Volk* in the aesthetic forms of architecture, art, and handicrafts. The *Kultur* life was thus judged "authentic," an expression conveying the connectedness of the self through the community to the national spirit and thus to the life of the cosmos. Life was thus a spiritual and aesthetic experience, impossible to express authentically in the dead, life-negating embrace of cold reason, which could only justify empirically observable matter, individualism (and its ill-begotten twin, internationalism), and utilitarianism. Authentic production, in the sense of aesthetic creativity, was impossible under the sway of *Zivilisation*, where the efficient calculations of finance and profit outweighed the will to create.

The conservative revolution was itself divided over the question of the machine and technology: Did the machine cut off the self from nature and thus the wellsprings of *Kultur*? Or was it possible to find a means of producing authentically with industrial technology? Perhaps technics and the machines themselves were but expressions of the *Volk* spirit, the highest materialization yet seen of what Spengler called "Faustian Man's" impulse to control nature. Perhaps technics were organic in the sense that the machine was the will to power materialized in an instrumental sense, the drill press or turbine an extension of the *Volk* spirit and the machinist himself. If that was so, then under the right conditions the machine could produce authentically through an act of will—it could express the *Volk* spirit of *Kultur*—and could be put to the service of gemeinschaft. In this way, Jeffrey Herf's "reactionary modernists" embraced technology and diverted the German Right, as the fascists through "futurism" had done in Italy, away from the backward-looking longing of the agrarians and Christian moralists.[46]

The reactionary modernists tended to eschew Nazi scientific racism, preferring the Spengleresque morphological-idealistic explanation of the *Volk*. But some did embrace the cult of the will to power and exulted in war, the highest aesthetic achievement of modern man. Many of them had served in the World War and saw in the camaraderie and sense of community of the trenches the model for a new, specifically German socialism. Ernst Junger foresaw a coming worldwide mobilization of mankind by the forces of industry, technology, and the state as the culmination of the process of the regimentation and industrialization of human society—war itself had become industrialized. The symbolic figure of the new order in Junger's vision was the worker/ soldier. The eternal struggle for dominance would play itself out on gigantic scale—epic warfare, itself a natural event akin to hurricanes or earthquakes (one of Junger's books was entitled *Storm of Steel*), the machine merely the extension of the human will, embodied in the collective might of the national spirit. Junger's way to authenticity was the embrace of the new world, of the fusion of romanticism with technology, and of the ecstasy of the combat experience.[47]

Joseph Goebbels, after Junger, called for a new "steely romanticism" that would integrate the "reactionary modernist" synthesis with the ideology of race: Hitler's four year plan subsequently accelerated the industrialization and rearmament of Germany, and the autobahn and the great airships became the symbols of German technological superiority.[48] Technology and authentic production were uniquely German. Germans produced; Jews "financed" and swindled, thereby controlling capitalist society. Some of the reactionary modernists, particularly economist Werner Sombart, deduced that a German third way was possible if production were disconnected from finance and capitalism and reconnected with the spirit of the *Volk*. Sombart thus "reconciled 'German socialism' to technical advance by defending what he described as the realm of the concrete and productive against the tentacles of abstraction and unproductive circulation."[49]

Such ideas were manipulated by the Nazis to direct rage and resentment against modernity and the capitalist order into "rage at the Jews."[50] According to Nazi ideology, Jews were the true source of Germany's (and Europe's) troubles. In this way, German National Socialism was a "system of rule that used bureaucratic organization and modern propaganda to organize the 'revolt of nature' against abstraction."[51] The Nazis ironically used (and exalted) the integrated state system as a means of attacking capitalism and liberal or internationalist

modernity but not technological or political innovation, failing to see
that capitalism was but one face of modernity. The problems of social
dislocation, alienation, the disconnectedness from nature and authenticity that the reactionary modernists, and subsequently the Nazis,
railed against were not examined in sociological or structural terms.
The success of the "conservative" or "national" revolution depended
on will, mobilization, and identifying the enemy. It is not for nothing
that one so often hears the popular truism that states and nations have
need of enemies. It is, after all, much easier to lose oneself in the collective spirit of mobilization and war (and thereby briefly experience the
sense of lost community) than to effectively deal with complex and
difficult questions of social organization and spiritual rejuvenation.
The key to understanding early (and the style of later) Nazi mobilization was the psychology of the so-called front generation.

The phenomenon of the alienated veteran, the warrior who has experienced the heightened sensory awareness of the battlefield and is
faced with the prospect of aimless boredom in civilian life, is common
enough in the annals of warfare.[52] For many of the philosophically inclined members of the front generation, the war had been a welcome
relief from the inauthentic and life-negating boredom and disconnectedness of modern bourgeois existence. Following Nietzsche, they
thought of life as a fundamentally aesthetic experience; the war itself
had been a huge canvas on which the technology of modern warfare
had splashed the blazing colors of exploding artillery shells, the dark
hues of the clouds of gray and black pillars of smoke rising from the
ruins of smashed buildings and the craters of a transformed landscape,
one made strangely vital by the cacophony of the machinery of death.
The embrace of violence and death was the hallmark of Junger's philosophy, a philosophy that found expression outside Germany in Italian fascism and fascist-derived movements elsewhere. The longing of
those so inclined members of the front generation for the community
of the trenches, as well as for revenge against the Weimar government
that had betrayed the nation and the army, and the narcotic vitalism
of combat, found an outlet for expression in the street warfare of the
brownshirts against the reds, the sense of belonging generated by the
Nazi movement, and the promise of a new, heroic future under a man
who was one of them, Adolph Hitler.

Like all political movements, the Nazis were, especially early on, a
coalition of like-thinking national revolutionaries who represented
strands of German socialist ideology. Within the Nazi Party, "left" and
"right" wings developed, the Nazi "left" having been anticipated by
two members of the conservative revolution, Moeller van den Bruck
and Ernst Niekisch.[53] Van den Bruck asserted that the task of German

socialism was to fulfill the socialism of a misguided Marxism. He contrasted the "young peoples" of the East—Germany and Russia—with the decadent West. Niekisch and his followers called themselves National Bolsheviks, and advocated a German-Russian alliance against the West. In the Soviet Union, especially Stalin's Soviet Union, many German nationalists saw the logical fulfillment of the war against "Jewish capitalism" in the nationalization of the means of production and the central planning of social development. Goebbels and the Strasser brothers (Otto and Gregor) were associated with the Nazi "Left" for a time, Goebbels advocating cooperation with the anticapitalist Reds, who could eventually be fully converted into National Socialists, and voicing pro-Russian sentiments in his novel *Mikhail*.[54] Goering and Hitler tilted toward the Nazi "Right," which favored a system more akin to fascist corporatism.

Hitler, like Ernst Junger before him, saw the Bolshevik regime in Russia as being gradually appropriated by Russian nationalism. Indeed, the National Bolsheviks' desire for a Russian-German alliance was supported by the German geopoliticians and strategists who feared another two-front war (and another defeat) for the "nation between East and West." In any event, economic and military cooperation between Germany and the USSR had been going on for some time under the auspices of the secret clauses of the post-World War I Treaty of Rapallo. Geopolitical imperatives, not ideology, had secured the loose alliance of the Germans and Soviets. Following the signing of the Molotov-Ribbentrop pact and the subsequent division of Poland, Hitler himself once joked with party ideologist Alfred Rosenberg about the "Nazification" of Stalin's Russia. The coming convergence was "the sort of thing that a lot of people are thinking about nowadays," Rudolf Hess told the fuehrer. Hess thought that Stalin might follow the path of racial purity and that a "tremendous [anti-] Jewish pogrom" was a real possibility in the Soviet Union. Hitler found such a prospect singularly amusing. He told Rosenberg that if such a turn of events came about, then "Europe in its agony will ask me to take up the cause of humanity in Eastern Europe." Rosenberg himself "would have to write a report on the meeting I [Hitler] would chair on the humane treatment of the Jews."[55]

But convergence could not be a real prospect for Adolf Hitler. He had bought Rosenberg's characterization of Soviet communism as "Jewish Bolshevism." Communism in whatever form would always bear the burden of its Jewish origins, as would capitalism, liberalism, rationalism, and bourgeois softness and decadence. Besides that, the fuehrer had declared the Slavs *Untermenschen* and, perhaps influenced by the anti-Russian attitude of the Baltic German Rosenberg (transplanted Baltic Germans played an important role in the evolution of Nazism), had foreseen the expansion of the reich's lebensraum as the culmination of his plans for a *Drang nacht osten*. The East was judged to be Germany's natural directional path of expansion, an expansion that would be facilitated by the eventual destruction of the Soviet Union and the Slavs themselves.[56]

The influence of the German "conservative revolutionaries," especially the reactionary modernist wing of that movement, and other thinkers of the European Right of the 1920s and 1930s, particularly the profascist intellectual Julius Evola, is acknowledged by Dugin frequently in his writings. A revolution of the Right in Europe, especially in geopolitically strategic Germany, is a necessity in Dugin's ideology: How else can the new Holy Alliance and the third Rome stretching from Dublin to Vladivostok be fully secured? Dugin's mystical geopolitical speculations, tinged with gnostic overtones, his touting of a "third way" between cosmopolitan and materialistic capitalism and the equally cosmopolitan and materialistic ideology of communism, were common themes among the "conservative revolutionaries." The pro-Russian bias of the National Bolsheviks naturally has attracted an ideologist who is attempting to create a new synthesis, nonconformist in nature, that transcends the hoary and simplistic speculations of the Old Right, while preserving the special place of the Russians in the cosmic struggle.

The New Right embraces technology and geopolitics while celebrating romantic nationalism and spiritualism, expressing a Russian version of the "steely romanticism" the Nazis borrowed from the reactionary modernists of interwar Germany. Moreover, Prokhanov and Dugin glorify the warrior and the vitality of the struggle. Dugin, borrowing from Nietzsche and Junger, has even gone so far as to declare the eternal struggle between the Atlanticists and Eurasianists beyond good and evil. The approaching Armageddon-like battle for the world is expressed in eschatological but not moral terms in Dugin's discourse. The struggle is an end in itself, life an aesthetic experience, a cosmic drama in which individuals are merely players. Russia's role in history is a pivotal one, but one that may have no meaning beyond itself. Indeed, the only way to overcome the boredom of comfortable (a relative comfort in Russia, to be sure) modernity is to fully engage the struggle, to celebrate conflict and warfare, the dynamics of radicalism against the stunning complacency of "the system," the mondialist-bourgeois-liberal-materialist-internationalist prison that threatens to end history by homogenizing the key players—the nations of the island and the continent—thus making an "authentic" life impossible.[57]

The "Eurasian" Debate

The New Right, through its chief ideologist, Aleksandr Dugin, thus borrows heavily from the ideological arsenal of the European Right in an effort to renew the Russian Idea, but it has not repudiated those Russian thinkers of the past who are considered the precursors of the new synthesis. Dugin's ruminations on the nation forming aspects of geography may be Spengleresque, and he borrows heavily from the language of the conservative revolution's cultural system. But Danilev-skiy, Leontev, and especially Lev Gumilev[58] and the Eurasianists of the 1920s and 1930s are given their due.

The New Right's "patriotic" tone has not, however, prevented clashes within the communist-nationalist coalition over the nature of Eurasianism and its relationship to the Russian questions. To many on the Russian Right, it appears that the concrete interests of the Russian people themselves will once more be forgotten if Eurasianism is embraced as the coalition's new ideology. The *narod* would simply be one more ingredient in the Eurasian stew. The Russians would bear the burdens of empire but would be required to sublimate their Russian-ness, to defer to Muslims and Europeans in the interest of unity, in short, to repeat the Soviet experience. In Soviet Russia the explicit expression of Russian nationalism was virtually outlawed, watered down into the thin gruel of "Soviet patriotism" (this time as "Eurasian" patriotism?), which barely provided enough spiritual nourishment for the nation to survive, much less revitalize itself.[59] Others have attacked Eurasianism as merely another form of homogenizing mondialism—a mirror image of the Western mondialism of the new world order—in which all the peoples of the new imperial alliance will be subjected to a form of cultural standardization reminiscent of Sovietism, all in the name of tradition![60] Eurasianism is thus seen by some critics as incompatible with Russian nationalism, defined as the defense of one's own unique people and culture.

Dugin has defended the Eurasian variant of the Russian Idea by repeating Prokhanov's argument that the revitalization of the empire is impossible without the revitalization of Russian national consciousness and the strengthening of Russian statehood within the Russian Federation itself. For Dugin and Prokhanov, Russia can fulfill her historical mission only as empire. The empire, Red or White, *is* Russia. An empire is properly a nonexploitive, integrating polity, based on spiritual values and shaped by the geographic "space" (*prostranstvo*) that is the homeland. To deny the empire is to deny Russia and Russianness, to negate Russian identity. That identity by its very nature cannot focus on narrow, parochial interests but must be realized through taking up the burden of empire, whose task is the fulfillment of the promise of Holy Russia and the Third Rome, albeit in a somewhat secularized form. Dugin has maintained that "only those who share the basic tenets of [this] traditional Russian political self-consciousness can be Russian nationalists."[61] Putting Russia first means putting the historic imperial mission first—to be Russian is to be, in part, an imperialist as defined by Dugin and Prokhanov.

Since virtually all the members of the communist-nationalist patriotic coalition lament the collapse of the union and hope for a revival of Russian great power status, one may justly wonder what all the fuss is about. The answer lies in the question of the status of the non-Russian peoples and the related problem of determining a future Russia's borders. Will the ethnic republics be allowed to exist in a future empire—and possibly be a source of friction, as well as resuming the draining off of Russian blood and treasure, in the future as in the past? Or will Russia *be* Russia, meaning that the center will simply divide the territories of the revived union/empire into administrative provinces, ruling without shame?[62] More importantly, is the new Russia to include *all* of the territories of the former union? In order to better protect the Russian people from exploitation by the periphery and to avoid future nationality conflicts, it would perhaps be more productive to insist on the inclusion of only those territories that are predominately Russian (read *Slavic*) in population, leaving out troublesome hot spots in the Baltics, Central Asia, and the Caucasus.[63] Needless to say, such a program of political science nationalism, the creation of a more or less mononational Russian state, is anathema to Eurasianists, though a growing number of patriots (and, in view of the unpopularity and futility of the Chechen war, of ordinary Russians) seems prepared to accept the notion of a "Slavic union" or something similar. What remains is the notion of the "gathering of the lands" in some form, though imperialists remain convinced that a truncated Russia cannot be a great power, nor can Russia fulfill her nature without empire.

The priests, scribes, and storytellers of the past often described the history of their people as the gradual revelation of a special mission inspired by divine providence. Such stories not only helped to explain the historic turns of good fortune and misfortune (were the chosen ones following the path set for them?) but in some cases served to justify aggression and self-glorification. It was the misfortune of the Muscovite Russians to lack defensible borders in the form of natural barriers. That and the need for more arable land prompted Muscovite expansion; in the beginning such expansion was simply a matter of survival. The notion of Russia's mission as the carrier of the Orthodox tradition was appropriated to justify later expansion that somewhere along the historical road took on a life of its own. For many Russians, the imperial mission became an essential part of their sense of identity, to the great misfortune of their immediate neighbors. A sense of identity is inextricably bound up with any historic community's feeling of kinship and solidarity. Thus many ideas that appear esoteric and detached from the *Volk* themselves—Russia's historic mission, however defined—are ultimately a by-product of the national bond. It is true enough that such ideas can become so strong that the nation as idea can often outweigh the importance of the nation as concrete entity. Many instances of such a hypostatization have already been noted in this study. There is no reason to doubt either Prokhanov's or Dugin's Russian nationalism.

Dugin, Prokhanov, and Contemporary Russian Nationalisms

Neither Prokhanov nor Dugin has properly been recognized for the important role each has played in the molding of the communist-nationalist coalition that surfaced under Gorbachev and matured under Yeltsin. Prokhanov has engineered the various concrete forms the coalition has taken since the collapse of the Soviet Union (the National Salvation Front and the People's Patriotic Union that backed Zyuganov's 1996 presidential candidacy, for example). The founder of the most influential nationalist publication in Russia has worked diligently to promote opposition unity and is perhaps the only nationalist figure who has remained on good terms with his comrades across the political spectrum.

Prokhanov has also subtly spread the ideas of Aleksandr Dugin among his brethren via *Den/Zavtra*. Eurasianist or no, the term mondialism is heard from the lips of even the most vociferous critics of Dugin's ideology. It is Dugin, through Prokhanov, who broadened the horizons of the coalition: Mondialism, not simply the West or Yeltsin or Zionism, is the enemy. Gennadiy Zyuganov has wielded the language of Dugin's cultural system quite effectively, eschewing the classic Jewish-Masonic formula for a streamlined, modernized version of the grand conspiracy that transcends the conspiratology of the Old Right.[64] Zhirinovskiy's "drive to the South," as well as his notion of a possible strategic alliance with Germany, may have been inspired by Dugin's geopolitics, which are heavily influenced by the strategies of Thiriart and the German National Bolsheviks.[65]

Dugin was unsatisfied with Prokhanov's promotion of the Zyuganovite Communists and has joined forces with Eduard Limonov's neofascist National-Bolshevik Party, which has stressed the promotion of the warrior cult, violence as a means of experiencing authentic existence, and the ideology of a national revolution that draws heavily on the traditions of European fascism and the conservative revolution of the 1920s. Dugin probably judges Limonov's version of the national revolution as ideologically purer than Prokhanov's pragmatic flirtations with the mainstream Communists. In any event, Dugin and Limonov have promoted cooperation between radical Reds from Viktor Anpilov's "Working Russia" movement and the "browns" of Barkashov's neo-Nazi Russian National Unity organization.[66] Dugin apparently continues to hope for a truly radical fusion of "red" and "brown," one that the German National Bolsheviks were unable to secure, thus losing the day to the Atlanticists in the 1930s and 1940s.[67] For Dugin, such a fusion is the only means to secure the third way between the equally internationalist ideologies of liberal mondialism and communism that he has prescribed for Russia.

The fusion that both Prokhanov and Dugin hope for would go beyond Zyuganov's National Bolshevism but would not quite reach the neo-Nazi shoreline: How could it in view of the nature of their integrative imperialism? The important role played by Stalin's Communist Party in securing the empire is acknowledged by both men, but unlike Zyuganov, their version of the single stream take on Russian history denies the Communists themselves center stage. It simply isn't important whether the "party of national interests" is Red or not; it merely happens that Prokhanov (who, the reader will remember, was never a member of the party) sees Zyuganov's Communist Party as the best means of uniting the "patriots" at the present time. What is most important for Prokhanov is not the shade or hue of the Russian Idea's coloring, but its fulfillment in the form of "empire."

The Problem of Technology and the Nationalist Intelligentsia

Despite the reactionary modernist tack the chief ideologists of the patriotic coalition have taken, those Russophiles dubbed "the preservers" by Prokhanov continue to play a prominent public role in the opposition, for the most part taking the side of the Russocentrists in the debate over Eurasianism. The legacy of the village writers and their celebration of an organic, radiant past animates an important intellectual current in the nationalist movement, and a key element in the preservers' critique of the westernization of Russia is its neo-Luddism.

If technology is defined broadly as not merely applied science in the form of machinery but the automated and hypersystematized political economy that facilitates the dynamic of mechanization as well, then the passionate attacks of the preservers on both Soviet Communist and

Western capitalist prometheanism are readily explicable. The enemy of the Russian neo-Luddites is the technological society and progress itself, whose values are embodied in the machine and the destruction through development of the organic community and the natural world. The demise of the Soviet varieties of both, so the preservers reason, has merely exposed the Russian body politic to the possibility of infection by a different strain of the modernist disease in the form of the consumerist virus.

Russian neo-Luddism combines the celebration of traditional rural life with a heartfelt environmentalism and tends to promote the Russian peasant's ties to the soil of the *rodina,* animated by a deep religiosity, as the key to Russia's recovery. The radiant past will be restored when the Russian people once again revere the land of their forefathers as a gift from God and eschew the attacks that both communism and capitalism have and would make on the very soil of the Fatherland. Only faith in God can assure the rejection of technological man's machines, which despoil and exploit nature and uproot the people. The community will be revived only when these evils are rejected and the Russian people return to a life that is harmonious with the natural order.

Mathematician Igor Shafarevich and writer Valentin Rasputin are the two Russian neo-Luddites best known in the West. Both have participated in the activities of the patriotic coalition's public organizations, and Rasputin signed the now notorious "A Word to the People" open letter in 1991. Both have been critical of Eurasianism and have stressed the need for an assertion of the Russian nation's rights against a hostile world infected with "Russophobia."

Igor Shafarevich: The Modern Crisis and Russophobia

Igor Shafarevich has long been the odd man out in the patriotic coalition. Before the Eurasianist-Russocentrist debate flared within the coalition, Shafarevich told *Pravda* that "after the initial shock," thoughtful patriots could see an opportunity in the calamity of the union's collapse: "We [now] see that Russia can be a completely viable country within its new boundaries, can stand more firmly on its feet than did the previous USSR." The Communist Party had (temporarily) departed the scene; that was all to the good as far as Shafarevich was concerned. The party had "always played the role of the main destroyer, sacrificing Russian interests for the sake of igniting world revolution, building socialism, helping Communist China, or performing our international duty in Afghanistan." The new Russia now had the opportunity to freely develop in her own way, free of the burdens of empire.[68]

Shafarevich had earned his reputation as a dissident in the 1970s, when he joined Andrey Sakharov's Committee for the Defense of Human Rights and cooperated with Aleksandr Solzhenitsyn in the editing of the *From under the Rubble* symposium. Shafarevich himself contributed three articles to the collection, published in the West in 1975, and from early on shared many of the great writer's opinions on Russia, communism, and Russia's future. In his literary memoirs, *The Oak and the Calf*, Solzhenitsyn describes his friend as a man "[who] was from birth inseparably tied to Russia, the land and its history: they were one flesh, with a common bloodstream, a single heartbeat." Shafarevich's love for Russia is described by Solzhenitsyn as "a jealous love." He wonders whether his comrade's love was perhaps made so "to make up for the past carelessness of our generation?"[69]

A revealing anecdote about Shafarevich is related in *The Oak and the Calf*. On a walk with his friend "in the gently meandering valley between Ligachev and Serednikovo," the author tells Shafarevich, "How vividly we shall remember all this if . . . ever we are somewhere else, not in Russia. Shafarevich, who is always so restrained . . . answered as though his insides were being drawn out of him, as a fish's insides are drawn out by a hook. Life," answered the mathematician, "would be impossible anywhere but in Russia." Solzhenitsyn, who would himself be forced to leave his homeland, immediately grasped the anguish in his friend's voice—after all, "elsewhere there would be neither air nor water."[70] A Russian belongs in Russia, and Shafarevich is a man who would prefer "unhappiness here at home rather than happiness among strangers beyond the sea."[71]

This is a sentiment that may strike Westerners as bizarre, perhaps even xenophobic. After all, the weather is better in Crete, the food far superior in Paris, the strangers in Brussels or London far more interesting than the yokels of Peoria and Rapid City. But such a reaction would be understood by Shafarevich instantly—it merely confirms his opinion of what modernity has made of us. That opinion was outlined and developed in his major publicistic works, including his book-length *Socialism as a Phenomenon of World History* [Sotsializm kak yavlenie mirovoi istorii], a shorter version of this particular polemic appearing in *From under the Rubble*,[72] *Two Roads to One Precipice* [Dve dorogi k odnomy obrivu], *Russophobia*, and *Russia and the World Catastrophe* [Rossiya i Mirovaya Katastrofa].

Early on, while attacking socialism as an ideology that articulates the spirit of rebellion against God and the natural order—human hubris manifest in the desire to control nature and shape history—Shafarevich noticed similarities between capitalism and socialism, communism and Nazism. All, despite very different external attributes, are internally geared to converting human beings into components of the state, party, or production machinery; all tend to stress growth and expansion of the state, the controlling mechanisms of modern society, and the productive capacity of industry without regard to human nature or the environment. He noticed that the fulfillment of communism's fundamental aims, that is, the destruction of the family, religion, and tradition, were discernible in the *results* of Western imperialism in the case of primal peoples in the colonies. Modernization through contacts with the West had destroyed the natives' religious ideas and rituals, the very "way their life was arranged to give meaning to their existence." "Even when Europeans seemed to be helping by improving their living conditions, organizing medical aid, introducing new types of farm animals or obstructing tribal wars, the situation did not change. The natives became generally apathetic, they aged prematurely, lost their will to live. . . . The birth rate plummeted and the population dwindled." If communism "would amount to the destruction of Man," "*the withering away of mankind, and its death,*"[73] how did the evident *results* of other forms of modernization differ?[74]

By the 1990s, Shafarevich had concluded that the capitalist revolution in the offing was merely fulfilling the unfinished business of the earlier communist one. Technological civilization, in whatever form, is geared toward a dynamic of mechanization and conquest over nature that destroyed the natural world, eliminated Man's connections with the rhythms of life that animated his spiritual connectedness with God and nature, and uprooted face-to-face communities, replacing them with urban atomization. If Man lost these connections, the structural sinews of human existence themselves, life on earth would be threatened. We had been warned by Hiroshima and Chernobyl, by the social anomie evident in modern societies of every sort (had the empty—and endless—pursuit of material aggrandizement in both socialist and capitalist settings made human beings happier, more fulfilled, better able to experience life itself in all its richness and diversity?), of what was coming—a world catastrophe. Man is in danger of cutting himself off from reality, entangled in the suicidal embrace of technology. "The machine," wrote Shafarevich, "is merely the ideal that technics . . . is striving toward." Technological civilization destroyed "everything that is living and naturally growing," replacing it with the artificial and the unsustainable, the machinelike.[75] Thus both human beings and natural entities—lakes, rivers, forests, and animals—were transformed into raw materials fit only to be digested by the technological beast and regurgitated as goods and services in the endless cycle of production and consumption.[76]

The nature of technological civilization compels it to complete the rationalization of the world that began with the Enlightenment. To that end, all roadblocks on the path to the millennium must be shunted aside, and Russia, particularly spiritual and antimaterialist, is the single largest barrier blocking technological civilization's way. Russia, where Christianity had absorbed and, according to Shafarevich, magnified the pagan's sense of reverence and awe for nature, remained skeptical of progress. Unlike Protestantism, which had degenerated into individualism and materialism, Orthodoxy had retained its sense of community in *sobornost;* unlike Catholicism, Orthodoxy had not succumbed to the siren call of rationalism. The Russian, Shafarevich believes, still retains the seed of earlier peasant life within and is still capable of the spiritual renewal necessary to stave off the technological monoculture that is steadily absorbing Mankind.

Unlike traditional Russian culture, the technological monoculture would tolerate no difference, no expression of cultural individuality; the dynamic of modern technics saw to that. The West instinctively felt that Russia would not willingly be assimilated into the flesh and blood of the mechanized monoculture. Russophobia, a deep fear, suspicion, and hatred of all things Russian, was the natural spawn of this sense among Westerners and their allies, communist or democrat, both within and outside Russia herself.[77]

Valentin Rasputin: Living and Remembering

Igor Shafarevich's polemics point to the life of the peasant as the most authentic type of human existence; Valentin Rasputin has lived that life and given it vivid expression in his writing.[78] Rasputin is a native son of Siberia, born in 1937 in Ust-Uda on the Angara River. He was raised in nearby Atalanka. He left the village to attend secondary school and spent his university years in the Siberian city of Irkutsk. Kathleen Parthe, a scholar of Russian village prose, tells of the events of those years that inspired Rasputin's art: "During his years in college, the transformation of Siberia by the construction of the Angara hydroelectric system had begun. In order to provide energy for the projected growth of this region, the Angara River was to be dammed; the resulting inland seas would flood both the islands in the middle of the river and low lying villages along the shore, and Rasputin's own village of Atalanka was moved inland."[79]

Rasputin began a journalistic career in the 1960s and displayed an interest in the fate of Siberia's tribal peoples and their vanishing traditions in his early essays. Perhaps informed by his own sense of loss, his literature would take as its grand theme the contrast of the traditional village and the modern world, the disorientation and disruption of settled and time tested ways of living by progress, and the profound interconnectedness of human beings' lives with each other and the natural world. For Rasputin, each individual human being is an important thread in the tapestry of life. Being reveals itself within an interwoven pattern of such mutually dependent threads. The individual, the family, the village, the land, the sky, the animals, rivers and lakes, mountains and hills of each particular locality make up a natural, growing, living organic cell of life that is in turn woven into the larger pattern of kin and region, nation and country. Kinfolk and *Rodina*, one's native soil, is thus extended horizontally and vertically to nation and *Otechevstvo*, the Russian Fatherland. We can infer from Rasputin's art a heartfelt sentiment of organic patriotism: Love of the nation cannot be disconnected from the concrete realities of place. Particular places, as well as status and function within a particular community grounded in the seasonal rhythms of the natural world fill Man with the sense of reverence and attachment that is the essential foundation of a life that has meaning and direction. The artist's painful remembering was spurred by the sense that customs and traditions of the precollectivization village, which lingered on into the 1960s, were threatened with extinction by the hubris of technological Man.

Like all traditionalists, Rasputin compresses time into a relative phenomenon: past, present, and future are connected not only sequentially but in an eternal present. *Rod* (kin) are ever present in the lives of rooted people; the dead, the living, and the yet to be born are as real as the noonday sun. To live is to *remember*, even to *foresee*, for there can be no seeing without remembering. In his novel *Live and Remember*, a Soviet soldier, Andrey, foresees his own coming death at the front as the war nears its end. Since he has not fathered any children, he deserts to conceive a child with his wife, Nastyona. But his decision condemns both of them to death. Thus Rasputin, who does not overly idealize his peasant characters, captures in his art the clash of the procreative instinct with human intolerance and the barbarity of an unforgiving Soviet regime.[80]

Rasputin, who has been a leading spokesman for environmentalism in Russia (both communist and postcommunist) has passionately opposed the pollution of Siberia's lakes and rivers by indiscriminate development. His writing has connected the despoliation of the natural world with "the moral decline of a society"[81] and the deracinating influences of modernization. This theme is played out in what became a nonsequential trilogy of stories about the flooding of the Angara, the loss of the traditional village, and the uprooting of ancient communities.

In *Downstream* (1972), a writer named Viktor travels down the Angara by ship to visit his family, now living in a settlement made up of several villages that were forcibly moved by the flooding of the river's shoreline. But the new settlement is not home. Viktor and the villagers are displaced persons, refugees of modernity. In *Farewell to Matyora* (1976), Rasputin confronts the painful moment of loss itself as the inhabitants of Matyora, an island in the Angara, prepare for the moment of their own displacement. The three-hundred-year-old farming community, which had survived as a collective farm, is being broken up, the people themselves to be forced into urbanized, mechanized agricultural settlements, the Soviet versions of agribusiness and the company town. "Once more spring had come, one more in the never-ending cycle, but for Matyora this spring would be the last, the last for the island and the village that bore the same name."[82] The industrialization of agriculture is destroying an organic community, and the old ones especially grieve for Matyora as if for a living relative. In fact, the villagers react with horror at the prospect of abandoning the graves of their ancestors on the flooded island. For Darya, the story's chief protagonist, the desecration of the graves merely points to a deeper problem: the withering of the human conscience in the face of modern ideologies that stress utility over morality. "In the old days," muses Darya, "you could see it: whether a person had it [a conscience] or not. Those who had it were conscientious, those without it were conscienceless. And now only the devil can tell, everything is mixed up in one pile."[83]

In *The Fire* (1985), Rasputin follows displaced villagers into a new settlement, this time one that is centered on industrial logging rather than on agriculture, an enterprise that further distances the inhabitants from nature and from the harmony of organic life. Ivan Petrovich, the story's protagonist, conscientiously performs his work among people who are gradually losing contact with the sense of community that made the old villages viable for hundreds of years. In recent times the settlement has been overwhelmed by an influx of deracinated migrant workers. The migrants have few of the residual feelings of place that the old-timers have, and one night when the town's main warehouse catches fire, Ivan Petrovich catches a glimpse into modernity's heart of darkness as the migrants and finally some of the town's old-timers forgo attempts to put out the fire and indulge in an orgy of drunken looting. A brooding sense of disorientation and fatalism characterize the story's mood. Kathleen Parthe has observed that "the luminous ancestral memory of *Matyora* has given way in *The Fire* to a dark, angry pain."[84]

Russian neo-Luddism is not an isolated phenomenon, but a thread in a pattern of antimodern, antitechnological rejectionism that is evident all over the developed, and developing, world. In order to understand the shape of events unfolding in this last decade of the twentieth century, we must view Russian neo-Luddism from a proper perspective.

Shafarevich and Rasputin: Russian Neo-Luddism in Perspective

Britain is the home of the Industrial Revolution. Events there in the early nineteenth century foreshadowed a process that would repeat itself whenever and wherever the combination of Enlightenment ideologies, industrial technology, and bureaucratic social organization that is the essence of "modernization" has created the integrated state. As economic and political power in Britain became more centralized and systematized, the double blow of mechanization and enclosure,[85] followed by the repeal of British "corn laws" that had protected British agriculture, drove the English peasantry off the land and into the dreadful embrace of a brutally regimented factory system. Urban populations, and urban slums, swelled. The filth, disease, and overcrowding that accompanied the degradation of the English proletariat—the world's first modern underclass—would inspire the literature of Charles Dickens and the eventual efflorescence of Victorian reformism.

Britain was deforested, her rivers and streams, as well as the very air her people breathed, ravaged by the first Industrial Revolution. Dickens described industrial Manchester in *Hard Times* as "Coketown," a dreary place "shrouded in a haze of its own, which appeared impervious to the sun's rays. . . . [A] town of machinery and tall chimneys, out of which interminable serpents of smoke trailed themselves for ever and ever, and never got uncoiled." True, the worst would eventually pass away (though the threat of ecological catastrophe has been magnified by enhanced technology), but the settled and stable life of preindustrial Britain would be lost, perhaps forever, and the social pathologies that are endemic to modern societies would linger amid relative prosperity. Modernism had disrupted the community, and economic rationalism had transformed the self-sufficient villager into a dependent worker or consumer. Indeed, the very face-to-face quality that made community (and a measure of tranquillity) possible was swept away into the dustbin of history, replaced by the disorienting cacophony of mass society. Traditional notions of status and function, two of the keystones of individual fulfillment, were turned upside down by a society that determined the worth of humanity and all its works on the basis of economic utility. Indeed, "it is the task of industrial society to destroy all of that," to destroy "self-sufficiency, mutual aid, morality in the marketplace, stubborn tradition, regulation by custom, organic knowledge." The very notion of a household economy, wherein all the constituent members of the family realize their status and function in purposeful work, is the enemy of mechanized economic rationalization, whose ally is the bureaucratic state. All these *had to be destroyed* in order to convert society's "human resources" into "producers" and "consumers," and thereby grease the wheels of the gigantic automaton known as "the economy."[86]

The old Britain did not go gentle into that good night. From November 1811 to January 1813, a burst of violent opposition to modernization shone like a supernova in the English midlands, expending itself in a frenzy of passionate revolt in mere months, in what Kirkpatrick Sale has called the "Luddite triangle" from York in the northeast to Westhoughton in Lancashire in the west and extending south to Leicester, encompassing the heart of Derbyshire and Nottinghamshire, straddled by the Pennine Mountains. These "rebels against the future," known as "Luddites" in honor of their mythical captain, Ned Ludd, were, like Robin Hood and his merry men, whose legendary exploits were still part and parcel of Nottinghamshire life at the time, victims of what is generally called progress. Most of the Luddites were weavers, combers and dressers of wool, skilled artisans whose community life, dignity, and sense of groundedness in the world depended on the economic base provided by cottage industry supplemented by the meadows and woods of the commons. When the weavers became Luddites, attacking and burning the new factories that spread like a malignancy across the English heartland, breaking the hated machines that had helped reduce them to penury, they briefly imbibed the heady brew of Jacobin radicalism. In his sympathetic chronicle *Rebels Against the Future*, Kirkpatrick Sale rightly characterizes the Luddites' violent rejectionism as the passionate and primal reaction of a people who saw their world disintegrating before their very eyes. All the things that made the world make sense to these simple people, "their ordered society of craft and custom and community," was being eaten away by an outside force that was "beyond their ken and control."[87] Modernization for the Luddites was symbolized by the machine; thus machine breaking was the first manifestation of the Luddite impulse.

Nouvelle Droite publicist Alain de Benoist once called communism "a bad answer to a good question."[88] To his credit, Mr. Sale, a leftist and contributing editor to *The Nation*, does not make the same mistake of recommending different management for the integrated state as the

solution to modernity's particular pathologies. He recognizes that a
new decentralization is a key to reviving a society of human scale and
acknowledges that among the precursors of neo-Luddism were many
men of the Right, European romantic conservatives and American
southern agrarians among them, who shared his hatred of modern industrialism, urbanization and reverence for a life more attuned to the
rhythms of the natural world, if not his full-blown environmentalism.[89]
Furthermore, Sale discerns the scientific hubris (modern genetic research leading to the temptation to play God in the process of natural
development, nuclear power plants and waste that threaten to despoil
the earth, the atomizing potential of the computer) of modernity as
merely part of a larger pattern of rationalization that is reaching fruition in the transnational monoculture, as the "nation-state" itself has
now become a roadblock to globalization, the culmination of a second
industrial revolution, whose ancestor destroyed traditional society.
Global capitalism has won the war with fascism and communism over
management of the technological monoculture, whose expansion is fed
by ideologies that make the "end of history" a necessary fulfillment of
the dynamics of the new civilization.

What remains to be seen is if Luddite leftists like Kirkpatrick Sale
can follow the implications of their analysis to its logical conclusions.
If the Luddite revolt was an expression of revulsion at the destruction
of traditional society and if those societies were relatively homogeneous, held together in part by the social glue of the kinship bond
(many Luddites viewed the proliferation of factories as a sort of foreign
invasion), then that bond, in the form of nationalism, ethnocentrism,
tribalism, or what have you, must surely be an essential stabilizing
element of the communities (of indigenous peoples in South America,
for example) that Sale and other Luddite leftists celebrate. After all,
present-day disturbances in India, Mexico, Malaysia, and other third
world countries against Western intrusion in the form of GATT and
NAFTA interference in traditional agricultural practices are genetically
linked to some Europeans' resistance to the creation of a supranational
Europe in the form of the Maastricht Treaty, as well as to the populist/
nationalist/protectionist revolt of Ross Perot's and Pat Buchanan's followers in America, Muslim fundamentalists in Iran and the Arab
world, and the antiwesternism of Russian nationalists.[90]

Particularism in the form of nationalism, potentially the most effec-
tive force for backing a technology-skeptical environmentalism that
Luddite leftists link to resistance against global homogenization, is
making itself apparent around the world today. The late member of the
European parliament Sir James Goldsmith maintained (after George
Orwell) in his rumination on impending globalization, *The Trap*, that

272

Chapter 8

"it is characteristic of intellectuals to pass over in incomprehension the dominant political passion of the age. Today, that passion is the search for national identity. And this is the moment when European ruling elites are seeking to destroy the identity of every European nation."[91] Goldsmith was perceptive enough to link the vitality of a "Europe of nations" to a measured environmentalism. The ties between the two are evident in many locales. It is the Russian Right, for example, that first made protection of the environment a question of importance in the Soviet Union during the 1960s. What could patriotism be without respect for the soil of the *Rodina* (one's native land, the feminine Motherland)? How could a national consciousness exist without the preservation of the kremlins, forests, lakes, and steppes that are part of the symbolic vision of the larger Russian *Otechestvo*, the Russian Fatherland? It is on the Russian Right that skepticism of technological progress has flourished, finding artistic expression among the village writers and their heirs. If the Luddite Left could rid itself of its own antitribalist prejudices, then the prospect for a truly vital environmentalism, fueled by the fires of particularist passions and tied to the cultivation of economically viable communities, might not remain the dream of a few thoughtful intellectuals like Kirkpatrick Sale.

Martin Heidegger pondered the question of technology and modern industrialism as an essential element in his ontological quest for an authentic mode of living and producing. For Heidegger, production is an important means for Being to reveal itself, and the method and ideologies of producing determine to a large extent the degree to which Being is revealed and understood by Man. Heidegger, like Spengler, saw the West in decline. But unlike Spengler, Heidegger looked for the source of the West's decay in the stages of the history of Being, of the development from the Greeks to modern times of how Western Man understood what "to be" means. Man's primary occupation is work, and the way he works, the way he produces, is the key to understanding how Being is disclosed and understood in any particular period of Western history, which in large part determines the authenticity and vitality of Western civilization.

The Greeks invented "productionist metaphysics," the notion that "to be" means to be produced. That notion, flawed though it was, informed Greek culture's highest achievements. According to Heidegger, the flaw in Greek metaphysics—that same notion that for something "to be" means for it to be produced, and not *"brought forth," experienced, not disclosed or revealed*—devolved over the centuries into the technological-industrial view of Being. Man had developed a sense of domination over the universe—he was the producer, not a being "thrust" into the inexplicable "opening" or "clearing" that has made experience possible. That "productionist" metaphysic inevitably led to technological society, wherein "to be" means for an entity to be "enframed," reduced to the status of "raw material" or "standing reserve" for the subject, who is compelled by the ethos of the machine and modern productionist society to ceaselessly expand production for its own sake.

In his essay *The Question Concerning Technology*,[92] Heidegger contrasted the "productionist" view of the Rhine River, now dammed up as a "standing reserve" to drive the machinery of production through hydroelectric power, with the Rhine of poetry and historical memory, a natural work of art that reveals something of the majesty of improbable Being to the viewer not in the thrall of productionist metaphysics. Heidegger noted that some would object to his characterization of the Rhine as merely "standing reserve" for moderns: "But, it will be replied, the Rhine is still a river in the landscape, is it not? Perhaps. But how? In no other way than as an object on call for inspection by a tour group ordered there by the vacation industry."[93] Indeed, inauthentic producing spawned by the productionist metaphysic had warped Man's everyday existence, concealing Being as "standing reserve" or destroying the organic transmission belts of experience, nation, and community: "[For Heidegger] the homogenizing production processes of industrial technology and modernist political ideologies have destroyed the uniqueness of individual peoples and places."[94]

Heidegger's working life was the quest for the means to an authentic style of working and producing, and he eventually saw art, especially poetry, as the model for emulating the creative technique of the ancient Greeks while rejecting their metaphysic. The quest at one time led him to accept the premise of the "primacy of politics" and join the Nazi Party, which contained within its *volkisch* current a promise to defend traditional, preindustrial German folkways—essential to preservation of German identity and the possibility of evolving an authentic means of working and producing—from the onslaught of the modern industrial-technological society embodied in the twin evils of capitalism and communism, which threatened to crush "the nation in the middle" between them. Heidegger, wrote Michael Zimmerman,

did not regard himself as an "ordinary" Nazi, contending that such people were incapable of understanding the *metaphysical* issues involved in the question of modern technology. Rather, he believed that only a gifted and high-minded thinker could comprehend the metaphysical origins of the deadly "symptoms" afflicting Germany. . . . Heidegger became convinced that National Socialism represented a "third way" between the related evils of industrial capitalism and industrial communism. . . . He believed that his own philosophical version of National Socialism would make it possible for Germany to initiate a 'new beginning' comparable in scope to the beginning initiated by the ancient Greeks. This new beginning, so he hoped, would bring an end to the alienating and destructive modes of working and producing associated with industrial technology. It is no accident that he sought to become the spiritual Fuehrer of the National Socialist Democratic *Workers'* Party, for Heidegger longed for the emergence of a new social order in which work and workers would both regain their integrity and importance.[95]

Heidegger became disenchanted with the Nazi regime when the "reactionary modernist" current asserted itself and Hitler pursued a course of rapid industrialization and rearmament. He would be thereafter tainted by his association with an evil regime that had brought on the near destruction of Germany and the shame of the death camps. Heidegger, perhaps suffering from his own brand of hubris, had thought that he could direct the Nazis (who even in the early 1930s were a diverse lot) onto the correct path. He either failed to comprehend the depth and seriousness of the evil racism that was the core of Hitler's ideology or chose to ignore it.

The tragic example of Heidegger, one of the twentieth century's most important philosophers, might shed some light on the behavior of accomplished and humane intellectuals such as Shafarevich and Rasputin (and it would behoove men like these to be cognizant of that example) in the light of the ongoing crisis of modernization and identity, economic and spiritual exhaustion, and political collapse that is afflicting present-day Russia. These are desperate times, and many patriots have fallen into a state of shock and despair over the fate of their beloved country. Tens of millions of Russians have perished in this most bloody and disorienting period in the painful history of mankind, and Russia in the course of the last two hundred years has rarely experienced even a short period of respite from turmoil.

Today the West has the jitters about the revival of Russian chauvinism, but in the eyes of patriotic Russians like Shafarevich and Rasputin this reveals the West's Russophobia: The "civilized" countries say little or nothing about attacks on Russians in the Caucasus, anti-Russian discrimination in the Baltics and Central Asia, and the desire of Russians in the Crimea and the Dneister region to reunite with their countrymen, or at least, in the case of Ukraine, be allowed to hold dual citizenship.[96] Besides, the nationalists would argue, Western intellectuals showed a definite sympathy to communism. Many chose to ignore the Gulag and played down Soviet brutality, of which Russia was the first victim, while damning Hitler and the fascists. Is it any wonder that

Russians are fearful, anxious, even desperate when faced with the prospect of more of the same? Is it not amazing that even more Russians have not sought salvation in a Zhirinovskiy or a Barkashov? Many black Americans, and others besides, have been all too willing to overlook the racism of demagogues like Louis Farrakhan, preferring to emphasize the "healthy elements" in the black Muslim program (for example, the strengthening of family ties and self reliance) that might be cultivated at the expense of the more negative aspects of the movement. Men like Rasputin and Shafarevich undoubtedly see such healthy elements within the communist-nationalist coalition in Russia, and both have attacked the more extreme manifestations of anti-Westernism.[97] Shafarevich has even debunked one of the coalition's most widespread (and cherished) beliefs—that Russia has been the target of a gigantic conspiracy of one sort or another—while agreeing that the West and the Russian intelligentsia remain largely Russophobic.[98] Neither, however, offers any programmatic solutions to the modern crisis, as does Solzhenitsyn, who holds similar views, but has not engaged in partisan politics.

As of late, a number of Russian nationalists who have never displayed chauvinistic tendencies, including film director Stanislav Govorukhin and social-democratic politician Oleg Rumyantsev, have entered the ranks of the "irreconcilable opposition," joining in an all-out political war against the westernizing democrats and the Yeltsin regime. The nationalists call the ongoing capitalization of their country the "Snickersization" of Russia, a process whose symbols are the ubiquitous Snickers bar (seemingly available at every Moscow street vendor's kiosk), Russian knockoffs of *Penthouse* and *Playboy*, and McDonald's golden arches, which even now are looming over the statue of Russia's most revered poet on Moscow's Pushkin square.

I cannot and will not attempt to justify Rasputin, Shafarevich and company's association with the "patriotic" coalition that is led by the neocommunists. At least they can take comfort in the nationalist rhetoric that is now standard fare for the Reds. Still, when the crisis in today's Russia (as well as the "Snickersization" process they so strongly object to) is taken into account, one can grasp the fundamental motives of those Russians who now say "better the Communists than the democrats."[99]

Notes

1. Anthony D. Smith, *The Ethnic Origins of Nations* (Oxford: Basil Blackwell, 1986), 57–58.

2. Ibid., 63.

3. Ibid., 66.

4. We recall here that in classical Slavophile discourse, the "communal" element had overtaken the "dynastic" in importance since the monarchy in the person of Peter had disrupted the historical continuity of the traditional Russian "symphony" of czar, church, and people, each with its own autonomous sphere of activity but nevertheless united in an organic whole.

5. Indeed, the "patriots" have proved as inept as the "democrats" at forming lasting coalitions. Most national revolutionaries have remained outside the mainstream nationalist movement, denouncing the conventional patriots as has-beens and worse, while the patriots have shunned Zhirinovskiy as a loose cannon. The proliferation of political parties among both democrats and patriots is a manifestation of the infighting that plagues both camps.

6. For more on the Eurasianists of the 1920s and 1930s, see Nicholas Riasanovsky, "The Emergence of Eurasianism," *Collected Writings 1947–1994* (Los Angeles: Charles Schlacks, 1993), 126–151.

7. A term borrowed from the French speaking members of the European New Right, *monde* (world) being the root of a word meaning "globalism" or "one worldism," an idea that foresees the homogenization of the world's cultures and/or the creation of a world government.

8. Prokhanov's biography is drawn from John Dunlop, *The Rise of Russia and the Fall of the Soviet Union* (Princeton: Princeton University Press, 1993), 169–177, 186; *Elementy*, Prokhanov interview, 1 (1992): 9–11; Walter Laqueur, *Black Hundred* (New York: HarperCollins, 1993), 138–140, 248–249; and Vladimir Bondarenko, *Aleksandr Prokhanov* (Moscow, 1992).

9. In the *Elementy* interview, Prokhanov claims that he never enjoyed "the material privileges of the Writers' Union." Bondarenko (now the deputy editor of *Zavtra*, founded and edited by Prokhanov himself—see more about the importance of this weekly newspaper below) in his 1992 pamphlet on Prokhanov's life makes a similar claim. Judging from the fact that Prokhanov had (and has) public connections with the Russian Writers' Union, he must mean that he himself, a self-proclaimed nonconformist, never enjoyed the favor of the literary authorities.

10. *Elementy* Prokhanov interview.

11. Prokhanov interview.

12. Walter Laqueur asserts that Prokhanov began his literary activities as a protégé of the liberal Yuri Trifonov (*Black Hundred*, 139), and Bondarenko also makes allusions to a certain liberal phase in Prokhanov's career.

13. Dunlop, *Rise of Russia,* 170.

14. Prokhanov's fascination with war and the cult of the warrior has never abated. In spite of his initial alignment with Zyuganov in opposition to the Chechen war (a war between rival gangsters, perhaps designed by unseen anti-Russian forces to foment a Slavic-Islamic confrontation that would facilitate the further disintegration of the Russian Fatherland, or as a pretext for Yeltsin's introducing emergency rule and suppressing the opposition; see *Zavtra* 25 [1995] for Zyuganov's comments on the war), Prokhanov has visited the front

and praised the conduct of the Russian soldiers serving in Chechnya. In any event, the need to preserve Russian territorial integrity overcame any doubts the communist-nationalist opposition had about the war.

15. Paradoxically, Prokhanov has cultivated contacts with Russian rockers, apparently believing that "Russian rock" has subsumed Western influences within its (often nationalist) "nonconformist resistance" to the powers that be—perhaps as he too once expressed his dislike of the *nomenklatura* regime through his "avant-garde" literature. See below for more on *Den/Zavtra's* promotion of "Russian rock."

16. Prokhanov interview.

17. Dunlop, *Rise of Russia*, 171.

18. According to Prokhanov, "Stalin gathered together the remaining debris of Czarism . . . and created his own empire," an empire that reestablished Russian (rather than a cosmopolitan-revolutionary) hegemony "over the enormous territory of Europe and Asia." Cited in Dunlop, *Rise of Russia*, 173.

19. Ibid., 171–172.

20. All quotations are from ibid., 172–74.

21. Prokhanov once speculated that the Red czar Stalin may have contemplated marrying a Russian princess in order to fuse Red and White and underscore the historical continuity between the Russian empire and the USSR. Ibid., 176.

22. For more on Russian cooperation with the "Moslem world," especially the Turkic peoples of Central Asia, see, for example, *Den* (20), 1992, "Islam and the 'Right' '"; for a time, *Den* carried a page devoted to promoting cooperation between Islam and Russia under the rubric "Slav-Islamic Academy." *Den* contributor Geydar Jemal once claimed that Islam articulated a metaphysical anti-Americanism, which the New Right (the self styled "spiritual opposition") claims for itself. *Den* 38 (1992). *Den* 12 (1992) carried an article on Islamic revolution by Ayatolla Khomeini.

23. See chapter 5 for more on the letter. Dunlop believes that Prokhanov wrote "A Word to the People," whereas others have named Gennadiy Zyuganov as the primary author.

24. Prokhanov told *Elementy* that the State Emergency Committee members may well have been manipulated themselves so as to facilitate the subsequent collapse of the USSR. See Prokhanov interview cited earlier. Prokhanov's views sometimes appear to be contradictory, since he simultaneously attacked the Brezhnev "stagnation" regime and praised men who had been high-ranking apparatchiks. True, he tends to reserve his highest praise for military men, but no one could have possibly imagined that the graying dullards of the State Emergency Committee were anything but the rear echelon of Brezhnevism. As we have already noted, many Russian nationalists chose Yeltsin over the coup plotters when push came to shove, though some have lived to regret it. Prokhanov's focus on saving the "empire" proved to be prescient.

25. Laqueur asserts that *Den* was sponsored by "the chief political directorate of the armed forces," 139. The newspaper later became associated with the Russian Writers' Union. *Den's* first front page declared " 'No' to Civil War in the USSR!"

26. Prokhanov conversation with Zyuganov, *Den* 23 (1991).

27. See, for example, *Zavtra* 51 and 52 (1995).

28. Prokhanov, in his *Zavtra* interview with Barkashov (*Zavtra* 12 [March 1994]), gushed with admiration for the courage and fortitude of the RNU band during the October 1993 crisis. Prokhanov told Barkashov that the White House defenders "did not lose, but [had] won . . . spiritually and morally," and had "stood taller" after the smoke had cleared. For his part, Barkashov confirmed Prokhanov's intuition that the RNU *vozhd* was a deeply spiritual Russian leader—he had had a spiritual experience during his post-White House siege imprisonment.

29. Oswald Spengler, *The Decline of the West*, abridged ed. trans. Charles Francis Atkinson (Oxford: Oxford University Press, 1991), 254, 266.

30. Laqueur, *Black Hundred*, 139. Dugin was born in 1962 into a military family and he attended, as did his mentor, Prokhanov, the Moscow Aeronautics Institute (*Political Extremism in Russia* [Moscow: Panorama Analytical Group, 1996]).

31. *Elementy* 1 (January, 1992), the first issue, is something of a Eurasianist manifesto. *Den* serialized a Dugin book, *The Great War of the Continents* [Velikiya voina kontinentov] in issues 4–7, 9, 11, 13, and 15 in 1992. In 1997, Dugin published a book, *Osnovii Geopolitiki* (Fundamentals of geopolitics) (Moscow: Arktogeya, 1997) that gave a textbook description of Dugin's geopolitics. The fundamentals of Dugin's outlook are made clear in these writings.

32. Aleksandr Dugin, "From Sacred Geography to Geopolitics," *Elementy*, 1 (1992).

33. Switzerland, for one, is neither, but Switzerland is not an active participant in the unfolding of the cosmic drama and therefore remains outside "history."

34. Dugin opines on the alien qualities of the Jews at some length in "Understanding Means Victory," *Den* 18 (1992).

35. Originally formed in 1813 by the monarchs of Russia, Great Britain, Austria, and Prussia to defeat Napoleon, a mondialist of the first order, and preserve the old order against revolution. Dugin is apparently unperturbed by the compromised nature of the first alliance (he may think that Britain, as the quintessential "Atlanticist" power, subverted the alliance, which broke up in the 1820s). The new alliance will be truly "Holy," with Russia, as the "Third Rome," playing the leading role.

36. In fact, the cover of the first issue of *Elementy* carries a stylized map of the new empire, with Moscow conspicuously marked as the Third Rome.

37. A Duginesque cultural system might look like this:

Water	Earth
Island	Continent
Sea Power	Continental Empire
Atlanticism (Carthage, Britain, United States)	Eurasianism (Rome, Byzantium, Russia)
Materialism, mondialism	Spirituality, autonomy
Exploitation	Integration
Chaos	Order

38. Dugin frequently examines the ideas of Thiriart in his journalism. Articles by the self-styled geopolitician were carried in *Elementy* 1 (1992) and *Den* 34 (1992).

39. For a time, *Den* carried a regular column entitled *"Den"—Kontinent* on the activities of various antimondialist forces in Europe and Asia. The paper also carried interviews with the leading figures of the *Nouvelle Droit*, and an occasional reprint of one of Alain de Benoist's (the most prominent intellectual associated with the European New Right) articles. See, for example, *Den*, 22 (1992). The journals of the *Nouvelle Droit* include *Elements;* the Russians have not only appropriated the name of the movement but that of one of its leading journals as well! For more on the *Nouvelle Droit*, see *Chronicles*, April 1996, February 1995, and February 1993.

40. Walter Laqueur's book *Russia and Germany: A Century of Conflict* (Boston: Little, Brown, 1965), is the best single source on the German-Russian relationship. See also Ralph de Toledano's excellent article "The Russo-German Symbiosis in the First and Second World Wars," *Chronicles*, February 1995.

41. Ralph De Toledano speculates that "if the tinder that set off the Great War had not sparked in Serbia, a country with strong ties to Russia, Czar Nicholas—the record seems clear—might well have joined the Central Powers."

42. Laqueur examines the importance of *The Protocols* to Nazism in *Russia and Germany*, 79–104.

43. Ibid., 94. Laqueur also notes that "the existence of a Russian racialist group (Union of Christian Socialists) [inspired by similar groups in Germany] was mentioned by Gorky in *Novaya Zhizn*, May 20, 1918. It proclaimed the physical and moral superiority of the Aryan race; its slogan was: 'Anti-Semites of all peoples and countries, unite!' " (94).

44. The best single source on the conservative revolution and its relationship to reactionary modernism (which we will discuss shortly) is Jeffrey Herf's *Reactionary Modernism: Technology, Culture, and Politics in Weimar and the Third Reich* (Cambridge: Cambridge University Press, 1984). Dugin himself summarizes the basic tenets of the conservative revolution in an article in *Elementy* 1 (1992).

45. Herf, *Reactionary Modernism*,16.

46. I must here acknowledge a debt to Tulane University's Michael E. Zimmerman, who pursued Herf's lead regarding the reactionary modernists and technology in his examination of Martin Heidegger's philosophy of Being and its relation to the reactionary modernists and the philosopher's associations with the Nazis. See his excellent *Heidegger's Confrontation with Modernity: Technology, Politics, Art* (Indianapolis: Indiana University Press, 1990).

47. Junger's ideas are discussed in Herf, *Reactionary Modernism*, 70–108; see also Zimmerman, *Heidegger's Confrontation with Modernity*, for a discussion of Junger's influence on Heidegger's philosophy of Being.

48. The Nazis' program envisioned the technological progress of Germany as an act of will—basic science, especially "Jewish physics" was downplayed, to the detriment of the Nazi modernization program. The primacy of politics evident in Nazi antirationalism (but not anti-scientism) was paralleled in the

bizarre nature of Lysenkoism in Stalinist Russia. "Bourgeois" agro-biological science was attacked in favor of a new "socialist" variety that ultimately proved disastrous for Soviet agriculture. Totalitarian regimes' emphasis on ideology and politics over common sense was evident in both Brown and Red regimes. Herf discusses the effects of the Nazi ideology on the fate of the regime's weapons development program and the course of the war, 217–35.

49. Herf, *Reactionary Modernism*, 130.

50. Ibid., 131.

51. Ibid., 132.

52. Don Graham, in his biography of American World War II combat hero Audie Murphy, *No Name on the Bullet* (New York: Viking, 1989), describes the influence the addictive experience of combat had on Murphy's postwar life.

53. For more on van den Bruck and Niekisch, see Herf, *Reactionary Modernism*, 37; Zimmerman, *Heidegger's Confrontation With Modernity*, 9–10; and *Elementy* 1 (1992): 51–54.

54. Excerpts from *Mikhail* were published in *Limonka* 31 (1996) (as mentioned in chapter 7, this newspaper is associated with Eduard Limonov; Dugin's writings frequently appear in its pages). For more on the internal Nazi struggle between "left" and "right" factions and the conversion of Goebbels to Hitler's ideas on state and economy, see F. L. Carsten, *The Rise of Fascism* (Berkeley: University of California Press, 1967), 124–129. For more on the sometimes fluid lines between Red and Brown in pre-1933 Germany, see Theodore Abel's *Why Hitler Came into Power* (Cambridge: Harvard University Press, 1986).

55. Cited in George Watson, "Alfred Rosenberg: The Triumph of Tedium," *Chronicles*, February 1995. Judging by the unpreparedness of the Soviet Union when Hitler launched Operation Barbarossa, it appears Stalin may have been serious when he declared the pact "sealed in blood." Adolf Hitler was probably the only man the *Vozhd* had ever really trusted.

56. For more on the conflict between pro-Russian and anti-Russian factions in the Nazi movement, as well as Hitler's attitude toward Stalin, see Laqeur, *Russia and Germany*, 126–59.

57. See especially the final installment of Dugin's *The Great War of the Continents*, *Den* 15 (1992), for his opinions on eschatology and the notion of the "cosmic drama." Dugin's hatred of the "system" leads him to embrace radicals of all shades who are anti-"system," especially the French student radicals of the 1960s who mounted a violent assault on what radical ideologist Guy Debor called "the society of spectacle." For Dugin on the "society of spectacle" and his embrace of violent radicals from the 1960s, see *Limonka*, no. 14, 1995.

58. Gumilev was the son of the poet Anna Akhmatova. He spent time in the Stalinist Gulag, where he developed his theories of "ethnogenesis," which bear a striking resemblance to Spengler's and Danilevskiy's ideas on nations and cultures as unique types, as well as to Herder's celebration of the diversity of national cultures. Gumilev also agreed with the Eurasianists of the 1920s and 1930s on the closeness of Russia and the East. He even maintained that the Russian ethnos had experienced an infusion of "Eastern" blood during the

years of the "Tartar yoke," an idea that some Eurasianists shared but one that has been contested by certain quarters of the Russian Right. *Den/Zavtra* has published many articles by and about Gumilev. See, for example, *Den* 52 (1992). Gumilev died in June 1992.

59. See, for example, comments by Kseniya Myalo, Tatyana Glushkova, Valentin Rasputin, and Igor Shafarevich in their exchange with the Eurasianist Vadim Kozhinov, "What Condition Is the Russian Nation In?" *Nash Sovremennik* 3 (1993). Myalo ponders the absurdity of "Russia without Russians?" in *Moskva* 6 (1994).

60. See Geydar Jamal's article "Europe to Vladivostok, or Asia to Dublin?" *Den* 38 (1992).

61. Dugin's views on Eurasianism as a form of Russian nationalism were set out in "An Apology for Nationalism" ["Apology natsionalizma"], *Den* 38 (1993).

62. For more on the problem of the non-Russian republics, "Soviet patriotism," Eurasianism and Russian identity, see Kseniya Myalo and Nataliya Narochnitskaya, "The Re-establishment of Russia and the Eurasian Temptation," *Nash Sovremennik*, no. 11–12, 1994.

63. Nikolay Pavlov, formally associated with Sergey Baburin's Russian National Union, now an officer of Rutskoy's Derzhava movement and a member of the National Republican Party, made just such a proposal in *Zavtra* 24 (1995). Highlighting the confusion surrounding the fundamental question, What is Russia?, Tatyana Glushkova, herself a fierce critic of Eurasianism, subsequently attacked Pavlov's proposal for being *too exclusive* and anti-imperialist! See *Zavtra* (32) 1995. The debate over Russia's political future has been played out in *Zavtra* under the rubric "The 'Third Rome,' or the Republic 'Rus'?" Prokhanov, Dugin, and others of the Eurasian ideological persuasion are more likely to use the term *Rossiyskiy* in describing the nature of the Russian empire; their opponents are inclined to "call things by their right names" and use the word *Russkiy* to emphasize the "Russianness" of the state they wish to recreate.

64. For more on Zyuganov's rejection of the "Old Right" conspiratology, see "Russia at the Brink of the Abyss" in his book *Derzhava*. Zyuganov frequently uses the term mondialism and has described the anti-Russian conspiracy as an attempt to create an economically driven new world order. Like Prokhanov, he has viewed the Chechen war as an attempt to drive a wedge between Russian and anti-Western Islam. The Communist leader also has participated in many "roundtable discussions" in the nationalist press on Eurasianism as an ideological alternative for Russia. See *Den* 22 (1992), for example, a discussion in which Dugin, Prokhanov, and European New Rightists took part.

65. The link between Dugin and Zhirinovskiy is Eduard Limonov. Limonov once served as a member of Zhirinovskiy's shadow cabinet. See chapter 6. He has a long- standing friendship with Dugin. For a discussion of Zhirinovskiy's (sometime) desire for a German-Russian alliance, see Graham Frazer and George Lancelle, *Absolute Zhirinovsky*, (London: Penguin, 1994), 31–35. Thiriart

thought an Indian Ocean port to be a necessity for his "Euro-Soviet Empire." At any rate, Zhirinovskiy appears to have drawn heavily on the work of the geopoliticians in designing his grand strategy for Russia.

66. See chapter 7, note 58.

67. Dugin helped Limonov get *Limonka* off the ground in 1994, and the paper has been very critical of the parliamentarism and general pussyfooting of the Zyuganovite communists. Citing such criticism, Prokhanov announced in *Zavtra* 26 (1995) that Dugin's "leading role in the creation and functioning of the newspaper *Limonka*" had made his (Prokhanov's) continuing membership on the editorial board of *Elementy* "impossible." In doing so, however, Prokhanov acknowledged "the fruitful experience of our past cooperation." The announcement was signed "With respect, A. Prokhanov." Perusal of any issue of *Limonka* will confirm the paper's fascist nature, which is sometimes tinged with neo-Nazi overtones. One issue (28 [1995]) for example, contains an article on Stalin that asserts his Aryan ancestry, as well as an article on avant-garde art, eroticism, and "extremism," a label not disavowed by the paper's editors. In the spirit of avant-gardism, the paper's back page displays a photograph of a partially nude woman sporting a Swastika armband. The front page headline reads: "All Power to [a] Russian Caesar!" Rock music, revolution, fascist anthropology, and Dugin's philosophy, as well as sex and avant-garde art are frequent topics taken up by the "newspaper of direct action."

68. The *Pravda* interview is cited in Dunlop, *Rise of Russia*, 280–81.

69. Aleksandr Solzhenitsyn, *The Oak and the Calf*, trans. Harry Willets (New York: Harper & Row, 1975), 406.

70. Solzhenitsyn, *Oak and Calf*, 406–7.

71. Ibid., 406.

72. "Socialism in our Past and Future," trans. Max Hayward, in *From under the Rubble* (New York: Bantam, 1975), 24–65.

73. Ibid., 59.

74. C. S. Lewis called this phenomenon "the abolition of Man."

75. Igor Shafarevich, "Russia and the World Catastrophe," *Nash Sovremennik* 1 (1993): 101. Lewis Mumford, for one, would have agreed with Shafarevich. See, for example, his two volume *The Myth of the Machine* (New York: Harcourt, Brace, & World, 1964–70).

76. Following Konrad Lorenz, Shafarevich maintains that modern societies regard all living things as "dead" commodities to be exploited. They are therefore not subject to moral considerations. "Russia and the World Catastrophe," 102.

77. Ibid., 120–21.

78. Critical appraisals of Rasputin's work, as well as biographical sketches of the man himself, can be found in *Live and Remember*, trans. Antonina W. Bouis (Evanston, Ill.: Northwestern University Press, 1992), see the foreword by Kathleen Parthe; *Farewell to Matyora*, trans. Antonina W. Bouris (Evanston, Ill.: Northwestern University Press, 1991), foreword by Kathleen Parthe; and a collection of Rasputin's short stories, novellas, and essays, *Siberia on Fire*, trans. Gerald Mikkelson and Margaret Winchell (Dekalb, Ill.: Northern Illinois Uni-

versity Press, 1989), see the foreword by the translators. Other major works by Rasputin available in English include *Money for Maria and Borrowed Time*, trans. Kevin Windle and Margaret Wettlin (London: Quartet, 1981); "Downstream," trans. Valentina G. Brougher and Helen C. Poot, *Contemporary Russian Prose*, ed. Carl Proffer and Ellendea Proffer (Ann Arbor, Mich.: Ardis, 1982); and *You Live and Love and Other Stories*, trans. Alan Meyers (New York: Vanguard, 1986).

79. From the foreword to *Farewell to Matyora*.

80. The pregnant Nastyona, who has been hiding Andrey, commits suicide rather than betray him and expose their child to the hatred of both the villagers and the authorities. Rasputin's view of Man's nature, even that of his Siberian villagers, should give us pause when confronted with the charges of chauvinism leveled at him.

81. Kathleen Parthe, foreword to *Live and Remember*.

82. Rasputin, *Farewell to Matyora*, 1. This is the story's first line.

83. Ibid., 33.

84. Kathleen Parthe, foreword to *Farewell to Matyora*.

85. Britain's commons, meadows, fields, and forests that were open to common use, thereby providing supplemental fuel, pasture, and food sources that helped sustain the small freeholder, the tenant, and those engaged in cottage industry, were "enclosed," that is, closed to communal purposes and sold off to private, mostly industrial and commercial, interests.

86. Kirkpatrick Sale, *Rebels against the Future: The Luddites and Their War against the Industrial Revolution* (New York: Addison-Wesley, 1996), 38.

87. Sale, *Rebels against the Future*, 3.

88. *Den* 4 (1992).

89. Indeed, Harvard University's Barrington Moore once called the American Civil War "the last capitalist revolution" and has identified the fundamental conflict of the age as the clash between modernity in the form of the industrialized "nation-state" and the old agrarian order. His book on the subject, *Social Origins of Dictatorship and Democracy*, is subtitled *Lord and Peasant in the Making of the Modern World*. (Boston: Beacon, 1967).

90. Sale reviews these phenomena in *Rebels against the Future*, 241–248.

91. James Goldsmith, *The Trap* (New York: Carroll & Graf, 1993), 68.

92. The essay, translated by William Lovitt, is included in Martin Heidegger, *Basic Writings*, ed. David Farrell Krell (San Francisco: HarperCollins, 1993), 311–341.

93. Heidegger, *Basic Writings*, 321.

94. Zimmerman, *Heidegger's Confrontation with Modernity*, xvi.

95. Ibid., xvii.

96. See, for example, Igor Shafarevich, "Russian Resistance," *Den* 22 (1993) in which he lists the grievances of Russians and now seems less satisfied with the Russian Federation as the "real" Russia—repeating arguments similar to those made by others who assert that the federation is neither Russia nor a state for Russians. In his article "Separation or Reconciliation?: The Nationalities Question in the USSR," (included in *From Under the Rubble*), Shafarevich hoped for reconciliation among the nations of the union, implying that he had

hoped that the union would take on a new form after the collapse of communism. Rasputin too has wished the other nations well, but Russians' interest must come first—at least the Russian family, Russia, Ukraine, and Belorussia, should remain together in order to fulfill Russia's mission as spiritual exemplar—and he, like other nationalists, resents the concentration on Russian shortcomings when the rights of other nations are made the focus of Western concerns. See, for example, his article "What Next, Brother Slavs?" in *Den* 14, (1992). One can deduce that both men have become more attracted to the idea of a renewed union, or at least an expanded Russian state, as the only means to ensure peace among the nations and protect Russians outside the Russian Federation. At any rate, Shafarevich has endorsed the idea of a Russia somewhat larger than the present federation. See "What Is the Condition of the Russian Nation?" *Nash Sovremennik* 3 (1993), a roundtable discussion in which Rasputin also took part.

97. Shafarevich has asserted that nationalism—particularly Russian nationalism—must not be an "ideology of aggression" and that Russian nationalism should be interpreted as fundamentally "defensive" in character; he further asserts that Russian nationalism at the grassroots level is and always has been so. In any event, such a "defensive" attitude explains the ferocity of Russian resistance to Hitler and Napoleon, as well as Russian ineptness in Afghanistan. See the roundtable cited above. In the same discussion, Rasputin denounced Barkashov and Russian neo-Nazism.

98. Igor Shafarevich, "Was Perestroika a CIA Action?" *Nash Sovremennik* 7 (1995). The most controversial of Shafarevich's works is *Russophobia* (originally a *samizdat* piece, the long article was published in *Nash Sovremennik* in the June and November issues in 1989) in which the author names Jewish intellectuals as one of the most influential strata of the anti-Russian intelligentsia. Shafarevich claims that Jewish-Russian mutual hostility has a long and complicated history and that the Jewish radicals who were so disproportionately represented in the revolutionary parties acted out of sense of anti-Russian Jewish nationalism. That Russophobic tendency remains alive in the intelligentsia today, in which Jews are disproportionately represented. What is important here is what Shafarevich *does not* assert: "The Jews" are not collectively responsible for Russia's travails, there is no ancient "Jewish-Masonic" conspiracy, and Stalin's alleged Russian nationalism, as well as the "two parties thesis," are not part of Shafarevich's discourse. The historical fact of Jewish involvement in the revolutionary parties is indisputable and entirely understandable, given the history of Russian-Jewish relations. As far as mutual Jewish-Russian hostility and the role it played in the anti-Russian actions of the Bolshevik regime, Mikhail Agursky, a Jewish Zionist, acknowledged the same in an open letter published in the underground nationalist journal *Veche* in the 1970s. Agursky, who contributed to *From under the Rubble,* hoped that contacts with Russian nationalists would clear the air and open the door to a reconciliation between Jews and Russians, though he favored Jewish emigration to Israel. He died after himself emigrating to the Jewish state. John Dunlop analyzed the Agursky letter, its reception and the exchange that followed in his *The Faces of*

Contemporary Russian Nationalism (Princeton: Princeton University Press, 1983), 148–154. It is *Russophobia* that caused Shafarevich's ostracism by the Western scientific community (he had been a member of many international scientific organizations, including the American Academy of Arts and Sciences and the London Royal Society, and enjoyed an international reputation as an accomplished mathematician). Rasputin has made similar comments in the past. The evidence leads this analyst to ascribe such assertions to what in the West is now called "insensitivity," that is, the failure to observe the accepted norms of "political correctness" even when those norms stifle free discussion, rather than anti-Semitism. Both men's *actions,* their association with the communonationalists who are the heart and soul of the patriotic coalition, for instance, are what appear to me to be most questionable.

99. As Dunlop reports in *Rise of Russia and the Fall of the Soviet Empire,* 129.

9

———≡◦◦◦≡———

Reform Nationalism:
The Third Force

"I believe that Russia is not a choice, it is a fate."

—Vladimir Lukin[1]

Russia appears to be heading in a direction that so far has unevenly mixed elements of "westernizing" with nationalism. The reform nationalists take this trend to its logical conclusions, blending "westernizing" civic political elements with economic reform and a healthy, though not aggressive, Russian self-awareness. The success of a "third force" coalition of the future in part depends on the outside world's reactions to Russian attempts to both reform and assert a particular identity. Some of the reform nationalists appear to grasp the sources of modernity's social ailments and see current reforms as a halfway house to Russian revival.

T he "Russian question" that has perplexed Left and Right alike more than any other over the last two and a half centuries has been, What is to be done? The answer, as often as not, has been, Reform. The question of the content of reform—its rate, scope, and ultimate goal—has delineated the battle lines between reformers and radicals since the days of the Slavophile-Westernizer debate, resurfacing during the reform efforts of Count Witte and Stolypin. Under the Communists, the New Economic Policy, which countered the radicalism of War Communism, was undone by the Stalinist five-year plans. The de-Stalinizing reforms of Khrushchev and the economic reforms of Kosygin foreshadowed Gorbachev's *perestroika*. Indeed, it is common enough to hear from the mouths of Russian politicians that the *narod* are weary of reform, revolution, and the constant destabilization of society that has been the lot of Russia in grappling with the modernization demon. What the Russians want is stability, or so we hear. Thus only the most radical elements continue to (publicly, anyway) preach revolution over gradual reform, whatever its content may be.

Since the collapse of communism, a reform nationalism has taken shape. The nationalist reformers tend to be more secular than the Christian nationalists, more technocratic than the neo-Luddites, and anticommunist in political orientation. They tend to identify themselves as moderate and pragmatic *gosudarstvenniki*. Nationalist reformers distrust ideology and appeal to patriotism, convinced that Russia (or any country) must accept the cultural boundaries that history and fate has assigned her. Reforms must therefore be carried out within the parameters of Russia's own thousand-year-old culture for the good of Russians. Nationalist reformers are convinced that Russia must reform economically and politically in order to secure the country's future and catch up with the West. A liberal regime and democracy are not seen as ends in themselves but as the means to make Russia strong and prosperous in the future. Thus their westernizing is combined with a nationalist, Slavophile element.

Reform nationalism attacks instrumental idealism as utopian and destructive (No more revolutions!) and preaches realism as the only constructive alternative to messianic radicalism. Drawn from think tanks, the diplomatic corps, and the military for the most part, Russia's national interest, as defined previously, is the reform nationalist yardstick against which all proposed change must be measured. The Yeltsin regime has itself increasingly turned to its own brand of reform nationalism to justify its political, economic, and social programs. In postcommunist Russia no politician, and no party, has successfully propounded internationalism and an unequivocal pro-westernism in the electoral struggle. More importantly, the search for a "third way" that combines westernizing with a Slavophile element may eventually be the foundation of a political platform that could prove very attractive in postcommunist Russia. Those in search of a third way may see a reform nationalist coalition as a "third force" alternative to both the Yeltsin regime and the communist-nationalist "patriotic" coalition. So far, attempts to organize the network of such third way advocates into a "third force" have failed, but the overlap of views and associations of the nascent movement's leaders at least points out the possibility of a united third force alternative in the future.

Aksyuchits and Nemtsov

In spring 1997, Viktor Aksyuchits, Christian nationalist and follower of Solzhenitsyn and Erhard, joined the staff of the newly minted (he joined the government in March of that year) first vice premier of the Russian government, Boris Nemtsov. Nemtsov, who has a reputation as a strong westernizer, is a young (born in 1959) former governor of the showcase (for successful market-oriented economic reforms) Nizhegorod Oblast region. Beyond the shock and dismay displayed in some newspapers inclined toward the democrats, the most important aspect of Aksyuchits's appointment as a political adviser to Nemtsov is the possibility that their association may be a harbinger of the future coalescing of the third force. A third force capable of attracting anti-Yeltsin nationalists to the reform nationalist banner could well displace the rapidly diminishing ranks of the communist-led patriotic coalition as the democrats' opposition.[2]

Nemtsov himself is a fine example of the combination of westernism and nationalism that typifies reform nationalists. Before serving as a provincial governor, Nemtsov worked at a radiophysics institute in his native Nizhegorod Oblast and served in parliamentary posts. In 1988–90, Nemtsov took part in the activities of a local ecological movement that attempted to close down a nuclear power station. As a provincial governor, Nemtsov's reforms earned him the favor of Yeltsin. His westernizing, reformist reputation prompted some to see him as a "democratic" alternative to the ailing Yeltsin prior to the 1996 presidential elections, though Nemtsov remained loyal to his patron and refused to oppose him.[3]

What had largely gone unnoticed by Nemtsov's democratic admirers was his association with Viktor Aksyuchits and his nationalist tendencies. Nemtsov has maintained a personal relationship with Aksyuchits that has survived for seven years, despite a falling out over the former's steady (though not uncritical) support of Yeltsin.[4] Their friendship began in 1990, when Nemtsov was elected to the Russian Supreme Soviet and met Aksyuchits through their mutual association with the Democratic Russia movement. Nemtsov, whose father is Jewish, was baptized by his Orthodox grandmother as an infant, a fact unknown to him for many years. He joined Aksyuchits's Christian Democratic Movement (RCDM) in 1991.[5] Like many others of mixed heritage before him, Nemtsov affirmed the primacy of his Russian identity. Like other patriotic Orthodox Russians, he has commented on the "naturalness" of Orthodoxy for his people.[6] Nemtsov was highly critical of Gaydar's "shock therapy," claiming at that time that the democrats had made a "terrible mistake" by pinning Russia's hopes on foreign assistance, aid that Nemtsov feels "denigrates our entire people." If that were not enough to distance Nemtsov from the Gaydar democrats, he went on to attack the International Monetary Fund, whose aim at the time, as Nemtsov saw it, was to isolate Russia and prevent her from rising from her knees.[7]

Early on in his political career, Nemtsov also endorsed populist-sounding protection of Russian industry and slammed shock therapy's harsh treatment of ordinary Russians, emphasizing the Erhard-like social market aspects of his provincial economic reforms.[8] As a provincial governor, Nemtsov often sounded the populist-nationalist political note and carried out a Stolypin-like land reform that handed over rights to a parcel of land and a share of the collective farm's equipment to peasants willing to try individual or cooperative farming. "I respect the nation," Nemtsov said at the time, "and believe our people are capable of feeding themselves."[9] Nemtsov has also endorsed the revival of the *zemstvo* system of local self-rule backed by Solzhenitsyn and Aksyuchits.[10] He has praised the people's ties to their "little homeland," the province, town, or village, as the true backbone of a Russian polity. Like Solzhenitysn and Aksyuchits, Nemtsov as *gosudarstvennik* seems to have adopted the decentralized, premodernizing Russia as the ultimate historical-symbolic model for his version of reform, while disdaining the communist-nationalist coalition's view of the centralized state as the embodiment of the nation. Self-rule as endorsed by Nemtsov is about the unique identity and self-respect of the Russian people.[11] The popular provincial governor was made an honorary Cossack in 1995.[12]

The Radical Center: Yavlinskiy, "Yabloko," and Lukin[13]

As a provincial governor, Nemtsov developed another very important friendship, this time with Grigoriy Yavlinskiy, a westernizing economist who served in Gorbachev's last Soviet government. At the time, Yavlinskiy headed an economics think tank, the EPIcenter, which developed Nemtsov's overall plan for reforming the Nizhegorod Oblast economy.[14]

While hardly a Russian nationalist, Yavlinskiy, a secular Jew, shared many common views with Nemtsov and Aksyuchits. All three men had been disturbed by the breakup of the USSR and had attacked shock therapy. Like them, Yavlinskiy had been critical of both sides in the September-October 1993 standoff between Yeltsin and the recalcitrant Supreme Soviet.[15]

Following the 1993 shoot-out, Yavlinskiy, together with Yuriy Bolderyev and Vladimir Lukin, formed the "Yabloko" electoral block, winning a place in the state Duma that Yabloko has since maintained. Yabloko's reputation as a haven for democrats dissatisfied with Yegor Gaydar's Russia's Choice party has, however, obscured the nationalist, even Slavophile, element in the party's platform. Yabloko's founding statement, for instance, emphasized the party's intention to reform Russia while taking into account the social consequences of reform, as well as the "Russian mentality" and "Russian historical roots."

Yabloko cofounder and former ambassador to the United States, Vladimir Lukin, has postulated a third way which he calls "radical centrism," between "unbridled capitalism" and neocommunism, between East and West. His views—skeptical of Western models but not particularly hostile to the West—may have been influenced by a friendship with Solzhenitsyn struck up during Lukin's tenure as ambassador to the United States in the early 1990s.[16] Lukin's Eurasianism is not, to be sure, the Eurasianism of Dugin or the earlier Red patriots, but is, rather, representative of his view that Russia, as a Eurasian power, should develop ties with both East and West and should not depend on the West as the country's sole model for reform.[17] Like Aksyuchits, Nemtsov, and Yavlinskiy, Lukin has come to view the radical democrats as mutated Bolsheviks, ideologues whose search for the earthly heaven has led them back toward the postnational West.[18]

Lukin has been a strong proponent of an assertive Russian foreign policy line, defense of Russians in the "near abroad," and the traditionalist *zemstvo* movement.[19] He has warned the West that interference in Russian affairs, including Western insistence that Russia follow its model of reform, could result in a sharp nationalist backlash. For Russia, what is at stake are her national interests, her identity, and her "self-respect."[20] Russia will never allow herself to become a Western colony, though her interests are, according to Lukin, objectively in no way automatically are at odds with those of the West.[21]

Lukin asks for Westerners to attempt to see the world through Russian eyes: Russia saved the West from Napoleon and Hitler and blocked the path of the Mongols. Russia's attempts to show good will toward the West have gone unrewarded—Western aid has usually ended up in the pockets of the hordes of "advisers" sent to tell Russians how to reform a country they know nothing about. Westerners' condescending attitude toward Russia, a country with a thousand-year history and a people who have produced a unique culture that has spawned some of the world's greatest achievements, may yet bring on a wave of antiwesternism. Every great nation needs a national purpose, a national sense of identity that can be the foundation for the nation's life and development. Lukin maintains that the West should not view the Russian Idea as merely a mask for aggression, though it could well become that if the ideological aggression of the West itself is not curtailed.[22]

Lukin's views on the 1993 crisis, shock therapy, the cultural inva-

sion,[23] economic reforms (protectionism, land reform),[24] and decentralization[25] overlap to varying degrees with those of Aksyuchits, Nemtsov, and Yavlinskiy. But if each of these men brings something unique
to the nascent third force and though each in his own way could contribute to easing the country toward a decentralized, postmodern (à la
Solzhenitsyn), postimperial Russian order, one that does not view the
people as an abstraction, it has taken a man of action, a military man,
to successfully articulate the populist-nationalist line for the nationalist
reformers.

Lebed: A Man on a White Horse?

One of the most important nationalist reformers, Aleksandr Lebed, is
a former military officer. His emphasis on law and order as the only
real basis for proceeding with reforms has revived the specter of the
proverbial man on a white horse, the military savior whose iron-fisted
rule puts the national house in order. The image is not such an alien
one to post-Soviet Russians, many of whom remember well the charge
of Bonapartism made by Nikita Khrushchev against the popular Marshal Zhukov in the 1960s, despite the Russian and Soviet military's past
reluctance to involve itself in political matters. The war in Chechnya is
a case in point: Speculation concerning the ineffectiveness and the
snail's pace of the initial assault on Chechnya led many to believe that
the inauspicious beginning of the Russian action was partly due to the
reluctance of Russian officers to involve themselves in a matter properly assigned to the Ministry of Internal Affairs and the "Internal
troops."

Since the reins of state control over public expression were loosened
in the Gorbachev era, many Russian officers (both active and reserve)
have become involved in politics and have even run for office. By failing to support the coup attempt in August 1991, the Soviet military
effectively hastened the collapse of the Communist regime. Yeltsin's
use of regular army troops to suppress the Supreme Soviet in October
1993 highlighted the importance of military support for any prospective Russian leadership.

During the reformist era (beginning with Gorbachev and continuing
today) a number of issues involving military reform and the role of the
military in Russia have been raised in the public forum. Military officers, civilian experts, and politicians have debated the merits of an all-
volunteer military, the structure and mission of the Russian military in
the post-cold war period, the role of high technology in developing
weaponry, and military doctrine and strategy. The catalyst for much of
this debate was the Soviet defeat in Afghanistan, which exposed the

demoralized state of the army and the military's lack of preparedness for unconventional warfare. The army command system was judged too rigid; innovation and initiative had been stifled, and political ideology had often overridden common sense. The harsh and often brutal treatment of conscripts, the high peacetime casualty rates, the low pay and primitive housing conditions, and the corruption of the officer corps became common themes in Soviet and Russian public discourse. Russian officers began to organize to push for better pay, better living conditions, and much needed reforms. Committees of soldiers' mothers demanded that the state protect the enlisted men from the brutal (and often deadly) barracks hazing known as the *dedovshina*. The disillusioning loss in Afghanistan and the unfulfilled promises of the state to help returning veterans (and to find work and housing for officers mustered out as Russian military manpower was reduced) gave rise to politicized organizations of Afghan veterans and ex-officers. By the beginning of the postcommunist era, military participation in public life was a fact. Politicians now courted the votes of veterans' organizations and active military personnel.

Having had no experience of warfare on our native soil in more than a century, it is easy for Americans in particular to overlook or underestimate the symbolic importance of the military in Russian life. In the past, the army portrayed itself as an important social institution, the tie of military service was common to all Soviet era men, and army personnel were routinely used to help at harvest time in rural areas. The army of Holy Russia was tied inextricably to the church and the paternalistic czar, an army of the faithful that rose virtually spontaneously to defend the sacred soil of the homeland. Russia has a populist military tradition—irregulars had fought in the Great Patriotic Wars against the Napoleonic and Hitlerite invaders and the people had risen to defend the Russian Fatherland against the outlanders during the Time of Troubles. To this day the Russian military insists that it is the linear descendant of the armies of Aleksandr Nevskiy and Dimitriy Donskoy who repelled the Teutonic Knights and defeated the Tartars, respectively. The peasant was the backbone of the old Russian army, his endurance and stubborn ferocity the stuff of legend. It is small wonder that the peasant eyed the landlord's holdings with a covetous eye; if possession is nine tenths of the law, then sacrifice and suffering are surely nine-tenths of attachment. Since he had shed his blood for the soil of the Fatherland often enough by his own reckoning he had a right to think of the land as his own.

The special aura of the army and the mystical attachment between the Russian and his Fatherland was etched deeply in the popular imagination by the experience of the war against fascism. Millions died in the inferno of the Russian front; the legendary defense of Stalingrad and the march to Berlin strengthened the national bond as no other experience could. At home, every man, woman, and child was mobilized, their common cause welding tight the ties of blood and soil as only such a horrific crucible could. Whatever legitimacy the Communist regime would enjoy among the Russians thereafter was largely based on the sense of patriotism and nationalist fervor that the old ones, those surviving veterans who come out each year in May, weighted down by the rows of ribbons and medals that decorate their simple clothing, symbolized. They come to the parades to honor their fallen comrades and to be honored, but most of all to tell the tale, to remember, and by doing so pass on what had become a national epic. Their ranks are dwindling now, decimated by the one enemy that none will subdue, but the memory of mythic battles and heroes, of suffering and death, and of astonishing bravery remains. In postwar Russia, particularly from the 1960s to the late 1980s,[26] war memorials became as much a part of the tapestry of national life as the birch tree and the onion domed churches of the Fatherland.

Westerners may have been puzzled by Boris Yeltsin's decision to unfurl the red banners of the victorious Soviet army during the victory celebration in 1996—what of anti-Communism?—but, like his predecessors in the Kremlin, he recognized the importance of the banners so many had fought under, for there is no greater civic sacrament in Russia than the parade of the colors on Victory Day. As Yeltsin had told them before and would again that year, the victory was not so much the victory of communism, and surely not that of the *nomenklatura*, but of the *narod*. The army is mythologically the mobilized *narod*, its officers Slavic knights. Russia's army is a people's army. What institution could be more likely to raise up a man of the people?

Yeltsin, Russian Populism, and Rutskoy

The failed August 1991 coup made Boris Yeltsin the founder of Russian democracy and, for a time, left him with an enormous reservoir of goodwill among Russia's people. It was Yeltsin who had fought for Russian sovereignty, he who had repulsed the attack of the corrupt coup plotters, he who had made a specifically *Russian* policy possible. Boris Yeltsin was a most fortunate man. By being in the right place at the right time and by displaying courage and resolve during the coup attempt, he could quite rightly contend for the title of "father of his country." Yeltsin had placed himself above mere politics (though he plays this game with particular acumen) and had replaced the Democratic Russia movement as the symbolic fixture under which Russia's reformers of both Right and Left could take refuge.

His reputation as a man of the people, a Soviet-Russian populist of sorts, had been made during his days as a party boss in his native city of Sverdlovsk (now Yekaterinburg) and later in Moscow, where the swaggering Yeltsin, at once a rough-and-ready *muzhik* (peasant)[27] and a paternalistic father figure, rode the public transportation system while "taking the pulse of the city and its citizenry."[28] Yeltsin earned an exceptional degree of popularity among the people of both cities. A Sverdlovsk resident of the 1970s recalls that "no one had ever heard of *glasnost*, but he [Yeltsin] appeared on television to answer letters and take telephone calls. During these appearances, real questions about everyday life were discussed such as: Ought we to end rationing coupons for meat? Where ought we to build the new theater?"[29] What's more, Yeltsin followed through on his pledges to the people. In Sverdlovsk, for instance, he eliminated the special stores and rations reserved for the *nomenklatura* class as promised. Sverdlovsk rewarded her native son with a sweeping victory in the March 1990 elections to the Russian Congress of Peoples' Deputies (he won over 80 percent of the vote against twelve rivals),[30] a victory that helped to put Yeltsin in the driver's seat as Russian president in 1991.

Yeltsin's antiestablishment leanings and his battle with the Soviet center earned him the respect and support of the democrats and of a number of "enlightened patriots," reform nationalists of various stripes. Russian nationalists had good reason to see Yeltsin as an ally; after all, it was Yeltsin who had agitated for Russian sovereignty, and in 1991 he made a concerted effort to appeal to Orthodox believers and Russian traditionalists. On the day before the presidential election on June 12, 1991, Yeltsin promised that, if elected, he would return "churches, icons, crosses, and other objects of worship seized by the Bolsheviks" to the Orthodox Church.[31] In 1990, he told journalist Aleksandra Lugovskaya that he "felt pain and pity for Russia: for her history, her traditions, her culture." He did not mean to denigrate the non-Russian republics, but "if you look at history, you see that nonetheless the other republics joined her [Russia], they concluded a union with her." This was not necessarily a boon to Russia, since "under the new circumstances, she herself lost completely everything." Yeltsin, like other Russians, expressed dissatisfaction with "Russia's position."[32] The Sverdlovsk populist would come to be identified with the cosmopolitan democrats and westernization during the next two years, but many others, including the British journalist Barbara Amiel, thought him quintessentially Russian. "It may be," wrote Amiel, commenting on Yeltsin's ability to connect with the people, "that Yeltsin has this kind of oneness [with the Russian land and people] that Tolstoy ascribes to Kutuzov [the Russian victor in the war with Napoleon]."[33]

Two events tarnished Yeltsin's patriotic credentials in the eyes of the nationalists. First, Yeltsin and his young team of economic and political advisers, led by Yegor Gaydar and Gennadiy Burbulis, lobbied Russian deputies for approval of a Polish-style shock therapy program of rapid transition to market economic relations, a program that was overwhelmingly approved, much to the later regret of many deputies.[34] Second, and more importantly, in December 1991 the Soviet Union collapsed and the Commonwealth of Independent States, initially a loose confederation of Belarus, Ukraine, and Russia, was created. Thus the defense of the Russian Diaspora, some 25 million strong, became a cause common to all on the Russian Right.[35]

Yeltsin had not intended for the union to collapse but rather for the Russian Federation to gradually assume the powers that heretofore been reserved for the Soviet "center" and to play the leading role in a revamped union.[36] In September 1991, following the failure of the coup attempt, he gave notice to the non-Russian republics that the Russian Federation would ensure "strict guarantees of human rights on the whole territory" of a new entity to be called the Union of Sovereign States and that such a right would involve defending Russian citizens "beyond the borders of the republic."[37] The plans for a revised union were scuttled by the Ukrainian referendum of December 1, 1991. In part a reaction to reports of yet another revanchist coup attempt by unionist military officers and security personnel, more than 90 percent of the electorate chose to leave the Soviet Union and become an independent state. After that, Russia had no choice but to attempt to maintain what bonds between the republics as could be salvaged. On December 7–8, Russia, Ukraine, and Belarus signed an agreement to form the CIS and called for others to join. On January 1, 1992, the USSR was officially dissolved.[38]

It is true enough that the struggle between Russia and the Gorbachev-led "center" had played an important part in the collapse of the USSR, though it hardly seems fair that many Russian nationalists later blamed Yeltsin and Gorbachev for the dissolution of the union and all the bloody and painful confrontations that followed. The Soviet Union was not a viable state at any rate, and it had been the August coup that had set the wheels of collapse in motion, marginalizing Soviet president Gorbachev and increasing the authority of the republican presidents who filled the power vacuum. Gorbachev's subsequent frantic, and sincere, efforts to hold the union together had failed, and Yeltsin's plans for a revised Russian-led union were headed off by coup rumors and the Ukrainian referendum, among other factors.

Vice President Aleksandr Rutskoy's differences with the president on economic matters were only the first sign of a developing rift between Yeltsin and the reform nationalists. The enlightened patriots, among whom Rutskoy counted himself, criticized the shock therapy program pursued under Gaydar, fearing the possible breakup of the Russian Federation. Radical reforms, which in their minds had come too swiftly and without coordination from the center, had hastened the demise of the USSR. Rutskoy, like other reform nationalists, viewed the price reform program, which preceded demonopolization and privatization, as a step toward further anarchy and disorder. Pricing was largely left in the hands of bureaucrats, since no market mechanisms were in place. Production would not increase under such conditions; producers would simply raise prices to increase profits. Indeed, not only did production stagnate, it fell precipitously. In the meantime, the threat of "street dictatorship" and the possible unraveling of the Russian Federation increased as tensions rose.[39] Amid rumors that he was plotting an anti-Yeltsin coup (which he vehemently denied—there is no evidence that the former Soviet Air Force officer and Afghan veteran planned an overthrow of the Yeltsin regime) and attacked as a "fascist" in the pro-Yeltsin press, Rutskoy called on the president to restore order and fight the crime wave that threatened to further destabilize society.

Reform nationalists began warning of a coming "social explosion," and some joined others on the Right in wondering if the "pseudoreforms" under way were actually being done deliberately: Hadn't Yeltsin and company deferred to the West on every single important matter of policy? Perhaps the West gave such advice so as to ensure the collapse of the Russian Federation, prevent the reconstitution of the union, and permanently remove Russia as a potential international competitor.[40] Within a few years such views would be widespread. In fact, in one poll 60 percent of the respondents agreed that the West was attempting to "weaken" Russia through the economic reform that it was pushing.[41] Rutskoy himself sarcastically referred to Gaydar, Burbulis, and company as "young boys in pink shorts, red shirts, and yellow boots,"[42] inexperienced neophytes who were "completely removed from real life."[43]

Rutskoy later lamented the collapse of the union and the loss of Russian great power status, as well as the creeping influence of Western consumerist culture in his homeland. In a 1992 article entitled "Holy Communion at McDonald's,"[44] the Russian vice president expressed a sense of loss that was quite widespread at the time. Rutskoy wrote that he grew "more depressed" as he contemplated American dominance each time he saw the waiting lines—several blocks long—outside the McDonald's that faced Pushkin square in the heart of Moscow. Rutskoy wrote that the line "probably perplexes Aleksandr Sergeyevich [Pushkin], frozen on his pedestal" across the street. "There were times," after all, "when his [Pushkin's] compatriots formed similar massive crowds to catch a glimpse of the miraculous Iverskaya icon of the Holy Mother" or had waited outside the Pushkin Museum to see treasured works of art. The lines were a sign of Russia's spiritual decline under communism, and unchecked westernization might be just as bad. What "hurts me," intoned the Russian war hero, is the notion of Russians waiting hours outside McDonald's as if on a holy pilgrimage. This fascination with the trinkets of Western consumerism is "not like waiting for food," it is "like waiting for Holy Communion." Russia's spiritual decline is "more terrifying than the feebleness of our semi-ruined economy." He feared that the prophets of Russian revival, Solzhenitsyn among them, would "hardly be heard in today's babel of voices."

Rutskoy had not abandoned westernizing reforms entirely. In 1992, he founded the People's Party of Free Russia, whose platform included planks on parliamentary democracy, the (gradual) introduction of market relations, and a disavowal of attempts by unnamed parties to "reimpose the path of economic and cultural isolation on Russia." The party platform also stressed the need for cooperation with Europe, military reform, "Russia first" economics and foreign policy (former republics must pay market prices for oil and gas; Russia should protect the diaspora in the former Soviet republics; the navy should maintain Crimean bases; and the Russian Federation should actively take part in keeping the peace in Moldova's separatist Dneister region), and pledged to maintain the territorial integrity of the Russian Federation.[45] It was now obvious that Rutskoy had the presidency on his mind.

In February 1992, he attended the Congress of Civic and Patriotic Forces organized by Viktor Aksyuchits, Sergey Baburin, and other enlightened patriots. As rumored, the black-shirted storm troopers of Pamyat made an uninvited appearance. Rutskoy, speaking on the evolution of the nascent patriotic movement, directed pointed comments at Pamyat leader Dmitriy Vasilyev and his jackbooted followers. Eyeing the Pamyatniks, Rutskoy declared that the patriotic movement "should say 'no' to extremists in black colors."[46] The Pamyatniks subsequently drowned out the end of Rutskoy's speech with jeers and catcalls. Vasilyev later denounced the congress, calling its organizers "impostors."[47]

Rutskoy was no easier on the Gaydar government; employing standard Russian hyperbole, the vice president called shock therapy "a policy of economic genocide." The people, hardly living in the lap of luxury to begin with, were impoverished by shock therapy. What Russia needs is a strong patriotic sense, a sense of responsibility, and a love for the homeland in the implementation of reform. Rutskoy thought that a "great deal of what is being done today in politics and economics is being done without love, without love for one's people and one's Fatherland." Former professors of Marxism-Leninism, so the Afghan war hero claimed, now opportunistically experiment with shock therapy without any sense of "sinfulness and shame." He called for the revival of Russian tradition, the old Russian merchant class, and the village. Rutskoy wanted to restore the union as well, one freed from communism. He attacked the Gaydar privatization program that did not (in his eyes) give adequate opportunity for ordinary Russians to own what, after all, they had been told was theirs for more than seventy years.[48]

A "resurrected Russia" would "illuminate the world," he claimed, not through arrogant messianism, but by the path of "creative calm," itself brightened by a revived sense of spirituality among the people. He ended by referring to the East-West divide: "We are not the students nor the teachers of the West. We are the students of God and the teachers of ourselves. Our task is to create an original Russian spiritual culture, stemming from the Russian heart . . . leading to Russian freedom and revealing the substance of Russia. The word 'Russia' must be for us a word of unification. Such is the meaning of the Russian Idea. May God help us in our actions!"[49]

By summer 1993, Rutskoy had grown sharper in his attacks on the government and more explicit in his opposition to Yeltsin personally. Aligning himself with the Russian Supreme Soviet, increasingly dominated by anti-Yeltsin forces as pro-Yeltsin deputies abandoned their parliamentary duties to take posts in the government (now led by Viktor Chernomyrdin), Rutskoy joined in the critical chorus of "enlightened patriots" like Mikhail Astafyev and Viktor Aksyuchits who saw early elections, both parliamentary and presidential, as the only way out of the political dead end already evident. The president and deputies had frozen Russian politics in a fruitless gridlock. The standoff ended with Yeltsin's dissolution of the Supreme Soviet and the violence of "bloody October." Rutskoy, who had declared himself the rightful president of Russia, was led away from the ruins of the Russian White House a prisoner, only to be amnestied the following spring. In the aftermath of the debacle he founded the *Derzhava* movement, and drifted toward a Holy Russia ideological stance, perhaps influenced by his brief association with Viktor Aksyuchits. In any event, Rutskoy, who had once been a potential leader for a post-Yeltsin Russia, was now a marginal figure in electoral politics. Discredited by the October bloodshed, his movement failed to break the 5 percent barrier (necessary in order to gain seats in the state Duma) in December 1995. The following year, he found himself reluctantly joining the coalition of patriots backing Gennadiy Zyuganov's unsuccessful bid for the Russian presidency.[50] Whatever Rutskoy's political future, he did (inadvertently) accomplish one important task: pave the way for General Aleksandr Lebed.

Derzhavnost: Aleksandr Lebed and Yeltsin's "Turn"

Derzhavnost, "great powerness," is General Aleksandr Lebed's watchword, and in that word can be found all the ideology the general will ever need. "What is *derzhavnost?*" queried Aleksandr Prokhanov in a 1995 interview with Lebed.[51] "There is the citizen," opined the general, "a person, who has on the territory [of his] country a family, children, a home. . . . He has something to defend, something to fight for, and, if necessary, to die for. The vagrant is not given to understanding [the concept of] the homeland. . . . In wartime, . . . [the vagrant] disappears: 'I have nothing to defend,' [he says]. A man must stand on his own land; he must have something of his own." An army of such men, rooted and raised in the proper sense of patriotism, will defend their homeland and make her a great power. Self-respect in individuals breeds self-respect in a nation. The result is national greatness, *derzhavnost*.

Unfortunately, according to the general, in contemporary Russia imported goods, food, and pop culture from abroad are undermining the patriotic impulse, while foolish tax policies punish Russian producers. The privatization program, which is selling off state property in open auctions, merely enables the old *nomenklatura* to buy off the national patrimony. Such policies discourage *derzhavnost*. The military-industrial complex, once the pride of Russia, is being allowed to deteriorate. It may be true that Russia no longer needs "ten tank factories, but only three,"[52] but the state should regulate the transition of the seven to civilian production and take all necessary measures to ensure the viability of the three that Russia needs. Thus far the state has neglected vital Russian interests, and the average Russian may well wonder: Is this my state? If the citizen has nothing, if his state refuses to protect the nation's interests, he becomes a stranger in a strange land. The nation is an organism: the state is the natural growth of the developed nation. If the state deteriorates, so does the nation, and vice versa. Russians cannot look after themselves if the stability and security of the state is not looked after. Russians should not look to foreigners to save her but must use their own "technology, our brains, our hands" to revive the Russian nation and the Russian *derzhava*, but the state's minding its fundamental obligations is a prerequisite to Russian self-rule and self-regulation.[53]

While Lebed hopes that the creative ability of the "Russian scholar, the Russian entrepreneur, the Russian merchant, the worker, the soldier," once freed from the stranglehold of the *nomenklatura* bureaucracy, will revive Russia, he has acknowledged that the impulse to "look into your neighbor's pocket," to hate and envy the prosperous, is the bane of all Russian reforms. The Russian nation must "struggle," claims Lebed, not to ensure that "nobody will be rich" but to ensure that "nobody will be poor."[54]

Lebed sees *derzhavnost* as ensuring that the people will be "masters on their own land." "No foreign uncle" will save Russia. Only a self-reliant, self-respecting people on their own land, in their own shops, and in their own homes can be really be free and earn the respect of other nations.[55] This populist view informs the whole of Lebed's version of *derzhavnost*, from economics to politics to foreign policy. The state, says the general, has long used the people as the human material for economic and social experiments. Russia should forgo further revolutions, build *zemstvo*-like self-government, and institute Stolyipin-esque land reforms to revive the countryside, the repository of traditional values.[56] The crucial difference between Lebed's version of "great powerness" and others is his view of what makes a great power great. The state exists to serve the nation as the nation's vessel for self-development; for Lebed, the nation is not an abstraction embodied in the state.

Lebed has no love for the communists, though he is careful to distinguish between the rank and file and the hated *nomenklatura*. The general was once elected to the Central Committee of the Russian Communist Party but quickly swore off any active cooperation with the *nomenklatura*. Immediately, so the general claims, he saw that the party bigwigs seemed to be interested only in Byzantine political intrigues and feathering their own nests. "If these are Communists," thought Lebed, "then I am not a Communist."[57] During the 1996 presidential campaign, Lebed told reporters that "there will be no more Red commissars" in Russia.[58] It was communist incompetence and corruption that had destroyed the Soviet Union. Today the communist bosses had merely changed their stripes, fighting over a place at the trough of corruption marked "democracy" and "privatization." As a twelve-year-old boy in 1962, Lebed had witnessed the supression of popular protests in Novocherkassk, and his own father had spent two years in labor camps under the tutelage of the Great Teacher. The communists had never properly repented of their sins against the Russian nation.[59] More than once, the general has told reporters that he remains "allergic" to former communist bosses. Lebed himself is a tactical pragmatist and cares little for rigid ideologies, whether Red or White.[60] It is the nation, the people, that counts for him, not the fulfillment of abstract ideologies.

The Orthodox Russian nation had created the state, whose construction began, the general believes, with the army. "Russia existed as a military *derzhava*. She strengthened herself, prospered, and successfully defended herself through properly organized armed forces." Russia became a military power, and the Russian *narod* served in popularly raised units that repelled invaders from all points of the compass. The Russian military art was refined under Peter the Great, who professionalized military service, but the people rose up in support of the army at crucial times in Russian history. The Russian army is a people's army. The rituals, symbols, and organization (the regiment, for instance) of that army should be retained in order to maintain the sense of continuity between past, present, and future that is a necessary element of patriotism, of the sense that one owns a piece of the national patrimony.[61]

The Soviet army, says Lebed, was the carrier of the great Russian military tradition. The Great Patriotic War was won by the people's army fighting under the banners of the great Russian leaders of the past, such as Aleksandr Nevskiy, and not merely the red flag of communism.[62] It was the people's army that had made Russia (in the guise of the Soviet Union) a superpower. The democrats, as destructive in their ideological zeal as the communists had been (besides, many of them are former commissars), had kowtowed to the West. When the army had been strong, Russia had been a "strong and vital *derzhava*."[63] Now that Russia and her army are weak, NATO, with the blessings of the democrats, is planning to expand, despite the fact that Russia dissolved the Warsaw Pact. "Who is the enemy" that NATO expansion is directed against?[64] Russia.[65] Still, confrontation is not inevitable. Russia, says the general, can work with the West. Russia can deprive the West of its enemy by reforming and stabilizing herself.[66]

The general agrees that the Russian army, making use of its own rich heritage, needs reforming; but no real reform has taken place to date, merely destruction. Lebed himself has firsthand experience in reorganizing military units in action.[67] Army units should be mobile and flexible, smaller, but fully equipped and manned, according to the decorated veteran of the Afghan war. Quality is more important than quantity.

Military pay and living conditions should be a priority of state policy in Lebed's view. The Russian army is still one of the best at the level of the sergeant, but the officer corps has been abandoned by the state and is demoralized. *Derzhavnost* stresses the role of the military in Russian society, both as the defender and the inculcator of patriotic values. Military political instructors, formerly employed by the Communists to maintain ideological purity and consequently promote technical incompetence, should forgo political ideologies and teach *derzhavnost* to the troops. Indoctrination would be strengthened by the improvement of material conditions.

Russian vital interests, according to Lebed, should be clearly defined and military doctrine based on those interests. The regular army, the Internal troops, the border troops, and the regular police (presently engaged in a war with the criminal world), should be united in a single armed forces system under a reorganized general staff that works within the parameters of a national-interest-based doctrine.[68] At present, Russian policy is rudderless. Whatever form the new military doctrine takes, it must recognize that the only legitimate purpose of the armed forces is to defend the Homeland, not to further the aims of abstract ideologies or share in the costly glory of expansionism.[69] The Russian army will never again fire on its own people[70] nor ensure "constitutional order" with "fighter-bombers and howitzers" as in Chechnya.

It is self-evident, according to the general, that Russia should defend the diaspora in the ex-Soviet republics and that the Russian government should pursue the cause of peaceful reintegration of at least the Russian, Ukrainian, and Belorussian republics and Kazakhstan. It is the only realistic way to protect Russians and Russian national interests. In the meantime, any Russians wishing to return to their historic Fatherland should be aided in doing so by the state. Any republics remaining outside a future unionist or confederative structure should take note of Russia's determination to defend her sons and daughters abroad.[71]

Democracy, according to Lebed, will come to Russia, but it will be a distinctly *Russian* democracy, and it must evolve over time. Lebed once pronounced that presidential rule is appropriate to Russia under present-day conditions, but later shifted his position: too much power in the hands of one man could be dangerous. Democracy should be built from the ground up.[72] Democracy as a process is not an end in itself, but a means to strengthen the nation and Russian *derzhavnost*. The same can be said of market economics. All types of property—collective, state, individual, cooperative—will be protected by the new Russian democracy, but pragmatism, not revolutionary ideology, should guide Russian leaders.

Lebed's "formula" for economic revival is simple: "I will [as president] create conditions for honest work" for anyone willing to "work for the good and prosperity of Russia," but there can be no real reform without order.[73] For a time, Lebed appeared to endorse a period of Pinochet-like authoritarianism or a Gaullist type leadership as necessary to lay the foundations of the new Russia.[74] Later, however, he disavowed any such intentions, maintaining that a future Russia must be a law-based state and that the "era of czars and general secretaries" is over.[75]

Thus *derzhavnost* as explained by Lebed sums up the essence of his policy, his ideology, such as it is, and his most closely held beliefs about his country and his people. "I am," says the general, "a Russian (*Rossiysskiy*) general, but first of all I am a Russian (*Russkiy*) man. On Russian soil I was born, and to her I will return. . . . We cannot cancel out [*perecherkhnut*] our history. The past is with us, it is inside of us. Without the past, there is no future, but [we] cannot live with our heads turned," always looking back. "For the sake of [our] future," says Lebed, "we must become conscious of ourselves as a single people. The division [of the nation] into 'reds' and 'whites' led to no good earlier, and will not lead [us] anywhere" today.[76] The general's 1996 presidential campaign slogan was Truth and Order (*Pravda I Poryadok*).

"Russia . . . is returning to the search for self identification and confidence in her own special significance"
—from a 1995 campaign brochure from the Russia Is Our Home electoral bloc, led by then–Prime Minister Viktor Chernomyrdin.

Lebed's surprising third place showing in the first round of the 1996 presidential election won him a powerful position in the Yeltsin administration. Within a few days of the election, the now retired general officer was made secretary of the Russian Security Council and special adviser to the president on national security. Yeltsin granted Lebed wide powers to reform the state's security apparatus, including the army, and to deal with crime and corruption. Purges in the Defense Ministry started almost immediately.[77] Two days before the first round of the presidential election, Yeltsin had told reporters that he already had his eye on a possible successor, and that that man could be one of those taking part in the presidential campaign. Analysts had speculated that Yeltsin had Lebed in mind. Now it seemed obvious to all that he had.[78]

Lebed had been very critical of the decision to invade Chechnya. The war, according to Lebed, was started by the Moscow gangsters to punish the Chechen gangsters for taking more than their fair share of the corruption pie. Come what may, the war would drag on and engender hatred of the Moscow regime among Russia's Muslims. True, he had singled out then minister of defense Grachev as the chief culprit but had been none too kind to Yeltsin, either.[79] Yeltsin's apparent (brief) cultivation of the general as his successor is puzzling[80]—even in consideration of the fact that the president needed Lebed's 15 percent to ensure a victory in the runoff with Zyuganov—given the Russian leader's alleged affinity for the democrats. But Yeltsin's actions are only puzzling if the administration's turn to the right is not taken into account.

Yeltsin had won his political spurs in the Gorbachev era as a populist and a defender of particular Russian interests. Like so many other born-again democrats, he had used democracy as a political tool, a political bludgeon to pummel the hated *nomenklatura* regime into submission. He had been careful to distinguish between rank-and-file party members and the political "mafia" that controlled the Soviet Union. Although he attacked the oppressive nature of the Soviet *nomenklatura* regime, he never denigrated or intended to denigrate the entire legacy of the period, which, after all, included the people's victory in the Great Patriotic War and the achievements of *Russian* science, arts, and letters. It had paid in the beginning to cultivate the West as a partner in the struggle with the Soviet "center," and as an aid donor in the days after the collapse of the old union. In any event, Russia had been too distracted with internal matters to engage in active give and take with the West.

The democratic honeymoon was soon over. Western aid had not been as forthcoming as many Russians expected, and the disruptions and potential conflicts apparent in the shock therapy reform program made a slowing down of the liberal/democratic/capitalist revolution expedient. Moreover, as criticism of the administration's pro-Western foreign policy mounted, and the dividends of such a policy began to seem scant, the Russian leadership, probably smarting from what was widely perceived as Western arrogance and condescension, began to assert itself. Russia is a thousand-year-old civilization with her own traditions, and geography and history underscored the obvious divergence of Russia's interests from those of the West. What's more, the Western cultural invasion became disturbing to proud Russians, not all of them "patriots," who were encountering the Western Other at every turn.

The gleeful triumphalism of the West was too much to bear. The opening of McDonald's in Moscow and the appearance of sordid Western soap operas and tacky Western-style game shows on Russian television screens were events widely seen by Westerners as a sign of Russia's "progress." Many Western analysts and commentators seemed a bit *too* cheery about the collapse of the old union, which many, if not most, Russians *did not* identify with communist totalitarianism. Russians could see for themselves the ostentatious consumerism of the many Westerners in Russia, not to mention that of the "new Russians," the new rich who followed Western trends and fashions like bloodhounds on a scent. It is small wonder that many ordinary people appear to have grown more skeptical of Western intentions.

The decision to defend the territorial integrity of the Russian Federation by force in Chechnya had won the administration the support of some elements of the heretofore irreconcilable opposition. What's more, Zhirinovskiy had always offered his support to the regime at critical times and stood by the Kremlin during the early days of the operation in Chechnya, when the administration was under fire both at home and abroad. By this time, the Russian presidency had amassed the power to more or less rule the country by decree, the December 1993 referendum having confirmed Russia as a "presidential" regime, the State Duma notwithstanding. It is President Yeltsin who has pushed for the further integration of the CIS states, and any integrated CIS would surely be dominated by Russia.

Russia analyst S. Neil MacFarlane has noted that "from late 1992 onward, there appeared to be a coalescence of elite and policymaking opinion around" a more "centrist" approach to Russia's relationship with the West. From now on, there would be no more "one-sided tilt to the West" but rather "a focus on real national interests."[81] The move toward the center in foreign affairs was accompanied by a steady move away from radical shock therapy approaches to economic reform. The eventual adoption of a presidential constitution and the administration's forcible dissolution of the Russian Supreme Soviet evidenced a turn to a more gradualist approach to political reform as well. In January 1993 Yeltsin himself noted that "we are moving away from the Western emphasis" in foreign policy. Simultaneously one administration spokesman pointedly put the Baltic states, hotly debating at the time the terms of citizenship for the nonindigenous (mostly Russian) inhabitants of the newly independent republics, on notice that Russia would "take all necessary steps" to defend the Russian diaspora. By 1994, the foreign minister himself, Andrey Kozyrev, one of those most identified with a pro-Western line in the Russian administration, began advocating a special role for Russia in the "near abroad," the ex-Soviet republics, and began to negotiate the maintenance of Russian military bases in Georgia and other CIS states.[82] Russia increasingly took to defending the Serbian point of view in the Balkans conflict and became

highly critical of NATO's possible eastward expansion, while attempting to maintain cordial relations with the West.[83]

Although there have been many policy shifts, the direction of Russian
politics is toward a more generically nationalist stance as evidenced by
the replacement of Gaydar by Chernomyrdin,[84] the ouster of Kozyrev
as foreign minister, administration promises to shore up Russian cultural institutions and the sciences, promises to protect Russian producers from foreign competitors, the administration's cultivation of good
relations with the Orthodox Church, and the attempted forcible reten-
tion of Chechnya. Russians are a proud nation with their own unique
history and way of doing things. But Russia is also typical in that the
nation appears to be reacting to the intrusion of the Other and the
perception of a threat to her culture and identity as many other peoples
across time and space have reacted.[85]

Reform Nationalism and Russia's Future

Yeltsin's attempts at combining westernism with nationalism have
been marked by their haphazard and disjointed nature. By the 1996
presidential elections, however, he, like most other Russian politicians,
could read the political tea leaves well enough. It is true that what
the regime appears to be doing—mixing westernizing or modernizing
efforts with nationalism—is already an old game in Russia. The czarist
regime tried it and failed. Even the forced industrialization of the communist regime was, after all, an attempt to reconcile westernization/
modernization with the very peculiar interests of the Soviet regime.
Within the regime itself is a tension between its westernizing elements
and its nationalist turn, as evidenced by the broad-based Russian opposition to NATO expansion or Yeltsin's endorsement of granting the
Orthodox Church special status, even as Russia sought inclusion in
transstate organizations like the World Trade Organization. In the parliament, Zyuganov and the patriotic Duma opposition took to cooperating with a Chernomyrdin-led government that pledged to both protect Russian interests *and* continue "reform," presumably in a new way
and toward different ends.[86]

So what is different about reform nationalism? First, the reform nationalists' "great powerness" is not Yeltsin's generic version of *derzhavnost*. Yeltsin has refrained from directly addressing any of the important Russian questions, pushing a foggy "great powerness" without
explaining its roots or purpose.[87] National statehood presupposes the
nation and any state that ignores its national roots risks losing its legitimacy. The Soviets were forced to blur Russian nationalism with a col-

orless Soviet patriotism, and it failed. Likewise, any attempts to reconstitute the multinational union are doomed to failure. Modernity has
made the stability of empire obtainable only by mass terror, and postcommunist Russia has no stomach for it, as demonstrated by the unpopularity of the war in Chechnya.[88] A Slavic union of Russia, Belarus,
and eastern Ukraine may be viable, but the inclusion of nationalist
western Ukraine or Kazakhstan as such would only entangle Russia in
a quagmire as the nations clashed over national badges of identity such
as language and religion. The reform nationalists appear to be cognizant of such threats and are prepared to reconstitute Russia as a *derzhava* without empire. This is their answer to the territorial Russian
question, What is Russia?

The reform nationalists likewise are approaching an answer to the
question, Who is Russian? in a way consistent with their views on the
territorial question. Lebed, by calling himself both a *Rossiyskiy* general
and a *Russkiy chelovek* (Russian man), points the way. By grafting civic
elements, such as the westernizing notion of citizenship, onto the polity's predominantly Russian corpus, the reform nationalists, who eschew chauvinism and racism, are promoting a formulation that could
be a workable means of incorporating those of non-Russian heritage
into the nation. Loyalty and consciousness would be the touchstones
of identity. The key for the success of such a formula would be turning
away from expansionism once and for all. The day of empire is over.
Russia, as either the Russian Federation or a Slavic union, will likely
be strained within by the inevitable friction with its own minorities,
the Chechens being an extreme example. If Russia moves away from
her Eastern Slav origins, Russification inevitably will become problematic at best. The Russian impulse to "gather the lands" may, in any
case, be sufficiently satisfied by attempts to come to an understanding
on a future association with Ukraine, Belarus, and Kazakhstan.

The reform nationalists answer the final Russian question, What is
to be done?, by pointing to the Bolshevik coup as a forced break in
Russia's evolution. A program of Stolyipinesque reforms designed to
foster Russian self-reliance, self-confidence, and self-rule, together
with a view of the outside world that asserts Russian uniqueness but
eschews expansionism, would put the country back on its historical
track and at least present the possibility of a future Russia that is stable
and moderate in its dealings with foreign states. More importantly,
at least some of those in the reform nationalist camp seem to have a
reasonable idea of how modernity has distorted developed societies,
all of which, to varying degrees, suffer from the same social disintegration that afflicts postcommunist Russia. It is manifest in high crime
rates, family disintegration, declining birth rates, and other social pa-

thologies. To speak of a stable future Russia without considering the modern dilemma is a sociopolitical chimera.

Prospects for the Third Force

Lebed had kind words for Nemtsov after the latter's government appointment[89] and has continued efforts begun during the 1996 presidential campaign to form a "third force" alliance.[90] In 1997, Lebed founded the Third Force Union around his Russian Peoples' Republican Party and was able to gain the support of Yavlinskiy and third way advocate Svyataslav Fedorov in Samara's local elections.[91] Lebed, Nemtsov, and Yavlinskiy have consistently been placed among the leaders by respondents to polls on possible Russian presidential candidates, and both Yabloko and Lebed's party appeared to be gaining ground against the communists in 1997 polling. In May 1998, Lebed was elected governor of the vast Krasnoyarsk region, giving him an opportunity to build his political organization from the ground up.[92] Moreover, research on the Russian Idea conducted by the Moscow Institute of Sociological Analysis suggests that a third way coalition would be attractive to voters in that respondents appear to favor blending westernizing and nationalist elements within a democratic system with a mixed economy,[93] something that was borne out by Yeltsin's successful 1996 campaign. Only the reform nationalists have presented a more or less coherent program along those lines, something that makes them potentially an alternative to both the patriotic opposition and the uncertainty of today's muddling.

If the trend toward mixing westernism and nationalism continues, it appears that future debate over Russia's development will center around arguments over the extent of the state's role in regulating reform (within a context in which most agree that the state's role should be less than under the old regime), further devolution of political and economic power versus maintaining present levels of centralization (with most agreeing on the desirability of a mixed economy and at least some devolution of power to the regions), and authoritarian methods versus more democratic ones (a presidential versus a parliamentary system). Prospective answers to these questions will be, in turn, part and parcel of answers to the Russian questions mentioned above. Bearing in mind these developments, as well as this study's arguments for particularism, a winning formula for a future third force coalition, whether constituted by today's advocates of the third way or others, would include the following elements:

1. *Narodnost* "national roots." The new Russia Idea would stress Russian uniqueness and populism (the people are not a mere

ideological abstraction) but might equally stress the view that
Russia is a constituent part of the West that could lead the way to
civilization's renewal by making a new socioeconomic synthesis
à la the classical Slavophiles. Civic membership would solve the
Who is Russian? question while keeping in mind the desirability
of maintaining a dominant Russian (*Russkiy*) ethos.

2. *Dukhovnost* "spirituality." The Russian Orthodox Church will undoubtedly remain an important social institution in a country that
has always seen itself as particularly spiritual, but the Church
would not become a mere arm of the state or propagandist for an
expansionist *derzhavnost*.

3. *Sobornost* "Russian communalism." This could take many forms,
including *zemstva*, the revival of the Russian countryside, and opportunities for cooperative as well as private property relations
within a federation that accounts for regional differences.

4. *Derzhavnost* "Great powerness." As envisioned by Lebed.

The success of any third force coalition or even of continuing the
present trend toward a more or less reform nationalist approach depends, of course, on Russia's internal condition. If some unforeseen
disaster occurs or if conditions worsen, all of the elements of a new
Russian Idea, as demonstrated earlier, are subject to interpretations
quite at odds with those of the reform nationalists. The outside world
should bear in mind as well that its reactions to Russian particularism
are not without effect on the possible answers to the Russian questions.
More importantly, the evolution of a nascent world regime helps explain the current Russian reluctance to discard hope for a third way.

Notes

1. *Literaturnaya Gazeta* 47 (November 1993).

2. *Moskovskiy Komsomolets* (27 May 1997), for instance, badly distorted Aksyuchits's views and past history, comparing him to the most odious elements
in the nationalist movement, including Zhirinovskiy and Barkashov, and insin-
uating that he had supported the radicals during the October 1993 standoff
of the Supreme Soviet with Yeltsin. Aleksandr Khinshteyn, "Nemtsov's Right
Hand."

3. Nemtsov's biography and political career is outlined in the Panorama
analytical group's *Rossiyskiye Politiki Ot A Do Ya* (Russian politicians from A to
Z) (Moscow: Panorama, 1996), 2: 275–77. See also *Obshchaya Gazeta* 11, 16–22
March 1995.

4. The falling out took place after Aksyuchits went over to the "irreconcilable" opposition in 1992, though the two men apparently did not sever their

personal ties entirely (*Russian Politicians from A to Z*, 2: 276). For more on Nemtsov's sometimes rocky but admiring personal relationship with Yeltsin, see his autobiography, *Provintsial* (Moscow, 1997), 81–88.

5. Though he suspended his formal membership after he was elected a provincial governor later that year. Nemtsov had planned to be baptized in 1991 by Aksyuchits's RCDM associate, Father Gleb Yakunin but was told by his grandmother of his infant baptism at that time. *Provintsial*, 17–18.

6. See Nemtsov's comments on Orthodoxy and his visits to European cathedrals, *Provintsial*, 18.

7. Nemtsov interview, *Pravda*, 12 November 1992.

8. Paris, AFP, 31 January 1994; *Pravda*, 12 November 1992.

9. ITAR-TASS, 28 October 1993. The reform restricted the trade or sale of land parcels outside the collective as a way to protect the peasants from land hungry, Mafia-connected "new Russians" who might pressure—or threaten—the new landholders to sell out. For more on the land reform, see *Rossiyskaya Gazeta*, 12 March 1994, and *Izvestiya*, 3 September 1994.

10. *Segodnya*, 13 January 1994.

11. *Obshchaya Gazeta*, 11 (March, 1995).

12. *Leninskaya Smena*, 14 February 1995.

13. Lukin himself has dubbed his approach "radical centrism." See *Segodnya*, 6 July 1995.

14. *Russian Politicians from A to Z*, 2: 276. For a brief overview of Yavlinskiy's career, see 2: 494–96.

15. Though Aksyuchits would surely put more of the blame on Yeltsin than on his fellow deputies, however misguided they may have been.

16. Lukin was among those who greeted Solzhenitsyn upon his arrival in Moscow in 1994. Moscow, NTV, *Itogi*, 29 May 1994.

17. The best single source for more on Lukin's version of the "third way" is a book he coauthored with the U.S.A. and Canada Institute's Anatoliy Utlin, *Rossiya I Zapad: Obshchnost ili Otchyzheniye?* (Russia and the West: Community or estrangement?), (Moscow, SAMPO, 1995). For his views on Eurasianism, see *Mezhdunarodnaya Zhizn*, "Preobrazhennaya Rossiya v Novom Mire" (A transformed Russia in a new world), March-April, 1992.

18. *Russia and the West*, 43, 97.

19. For his involvement in defending the Russian diaspora, see the Ria news service report, 27 July 1994. For his association with the *zemstvo* movement, see *Delovoy Mir*, 27 February 1995.

20. *Moskovskiye Novosti*, 24 October 1993. For more on Lukin's view of a possible Russian backlash, see *Segodnya*, 3 September 1993. Lukin describes the essential elements of Russia's "Eastern European" identity in *Russia and the West*, 20.

21. *Russia and the West*, 104.

22. Ibid., 134–47.

23. Ibid., 14.

24. Ibid.

25. Though Lukin, like Aksyuchits, Nemtsov, Yavlinskiy, and Solzhenitsyn,

supports a strong presidency for the interim reform period. With the exception of Solzhenitsyn, all of these men have called themselves *gosudarstvenniki*. *Segodnya*, 6 July 1995.

26. Nina Tumarkin's *The Living and the Dead* is an excellent account of (as the book is subtitled) *The Rise and Fall of the Cult of World War II in Russia* (New York: Basic Books, 1994).

27. Yeltsin comes from peasant stock himself.

28. John Dunlop, *The Rise of Russia and the Fall of the Soviet Empire* (Princeton: Princeton University Press, 1993), 38. Dunlop's book is study of the Yeltsin-Gorbachev power struggle, the emergence of the Russian Federation as a Yeltsin power base, the events surrounding the August 1991 coup attempt, the collapse of the Soviet Union, and the creation of the Commonwealth of Independent States. Yeltsin's appeal in 1990–91 was very broad, encompassing both the Sakharov Left and a considerable number of nationalists. The description of Yeltsin's early period as leader of the Russian resistance to Soviet rule herein is drawn largely from Dunlop's excellent piece of scholarship.

29. Dunlop, *The Rise of Russia*, 38.

30. Ibid., 39.

31. Ibid., 54.

32. Ibid., 55.

33. Ibid., 38.

34. The vote in the Russian Congress of Peoples' Deputies was 876–16. Ibid., 265.

35. An August 1997 Russian poll showed that 71 percent of respondents "regretted" the collapse of the USSR. *Argumenty I Fakty* 34 (August 1997). This, of course, does not necessarily mean that those same respondents would support reviving the union as such.

36. Dunlop characterized Yeltsin's plan as "velvet imperialism," *Rise of Russia*, 265.

37. Ibid., 266.

38. The frenzy of political jockeying for position that accompanied the final days of the USSR is documented in ibid., 266–73.

39. *The Rutskoy Challenge*, 6.

40. When asked what he would say to Bill Clinton if they ever met, Rutskoy replied that "the current relations between our two countries are neither sincere nor honest. People think that the United States set out to weaken the USSR and Russia so that we would collapse. . . . The United States made a mistake in its dealings with us. . . . Every chemical reaction has its effects. The United States lays claim to a hegemonic role in the world, but the effects of this claim will have effects on Europe, too." *La Stampa*, 22 May 1994.

41. The poll was cited in Jerry Hough, "Why Ivan Mistrusts Us," *Washington Post*, 11 February 1996.

42. Cited in Dunlop, *Rise of Russia*, 263.

43. Cited in *The Rutskoy Challenge*, 8.

44. *Izvestiya*, 1 February 1992.

45. *The Rutskoy Challenge*, 5. The Dneister region of Moldova, mostly Slavic

in population, declared its independence from Moldova following the collapse of the USSR. Residents feared the possible union of Moldova with Romania, and they called for Russian protection. Fighting soon broke out, with the Russian 14th Army caught in the middle. Rutskoy visited the Crimea and the Dneister region in early 1992 and became an outspoken defender of Russian influence in both places.

46. *The Rutskoy Challenge,* 7.

47. Ibid.

48. Text of Rutskoy "Congress" speech, reprinted in *Obozvrevatel,* 2 (February 1992).

49. "Congress" speech.

50. Rutskoy found partial rehabilitation in his election as the Kursk Oblast governor in 1996.

51. *Zavtra,* 34 (August 1995).

52. *Zavtra* interview.

53. *Zavtra* interview.

54. *Za Derzhavu Obidno . . . (It's a pity for a great power . . .)* (Moscow: Komsomolskaya Pravda, 1995), 447. This is Lebed's engaging autobiography. For a more in-depth analysis of Lebed's views, see the author's "*Derzhavnost*: Aleksandr Lebed's Vision for Russia," *Problems of Post Communism,* March-April 1998.

55. *Za Derzhavu Obidno,* 447.

56. *Argumenty I Fakty* 22 (May 1996); *Pravda-Pyat,* 29 September–6 October 1995; *Trud-7,* 14–20 June 1996.

57. *Zavtra* interview.

58. *Washington Times,* 20 June 1996.

59. ORT news broadcast, *Vremya,* June 18, 1996. The arrest of Lebed's father is related in the *Washington Times,* 20 June 1996.

60. *Washington Times,* 20 June 1996. Lebed repeated his claim of an allergic reaction to communists, current and former, even after Boris Yeltsin appointed him secretary of the Russian Security Council a scant three days after the June 16, 1996, presidential election. Lebed won 15 percent of the vote, placing him third behind Yeltsin and Zyuganov in the first round. Interested in Lebed's endorsement, Yeltsin acted accordingly, but the general at first shrank from publicly backing the President. After all, Mr. Yeltsin had been a member of the CPSU Politburo. Lebed at first endorsed the idea of a coalition government, something that would seem to fit with his assertion made during the campaign that Russians should unite and seek a consensus on the important issues facing them. For more on the campaign, see the *Washington Post,* 18 June 1996.

61. From a Lebed speech made at the organizing conference (October 1995) of the reformist military organization *Chest i Rodina* (Honor and homeland). All further references to the speech will be identified as *Homeland.* A brochure with a reprint of the speech was published in Moscow in 1995. The speech roughly outlines Lebed's views, particularly on military reform.

62. Lebed has opined on military reform in most, if not all, of the press interviews he has granted in recent years. See, for instance, *Golos Regionov* 8–9

(November 1995); See also the *Zavtra* interview mentioned earlier, and the *Washington Times,* 2 June 1996. The *Homeland* speech covers most of the points Lebed usually makes in his references to military reform and the military's role in Russian society.

63. *Zavtra* interview.

64. *Zavtra* interview.

65. See, for instance, *Homeland.*

66. *Nezavismaya Gazeta,* 16 May 1996.

67. Lebed was made commander of the 14th Russian Army in the Dneister region of Moldova in 1992. He organized the defense of the Dneister republic against the Moldovans and then made peace, a peace that stuck. Lebed later refused to withdraw the 14th Army from the Dneister region, claiming that Russia had a special responsibility to defend the Slavs there. He was forced into retirement (1995), and into politics, following this episode. Along the way, the general made quite a reputation for himself for honesty and integrity. He quarreled with what he viewed as the corrupt Dneister leaders, and he publicly denounced corruption in the armed forces. Western analysts began referring to him as "Mr. Clean." He is certainly one of the most popular officers in the Russian army. See, for instance, the *Washington Times,* 2 June 1996; *Washington Times,* 6 October 1995 (a poll reported on at the time found Lebed to be the most popular political figure in Russia); and the *Washington Post,* 17 June 1996 (for a report on the election results).

68. Lebed favors an all-volunteer army but thinks it will take time to convert from the draft to an all volunteer force. *Washington Times,* 2 June 1996.

69. *Golos Regionov* 9 (1995).

70. *Za Derzhavu Obidno,* 414.

71. For more on Lebed's views on the diaspora and the former Soviet republics, see *Golos Regionov* 8 (November 1995).

72. *Russkiy Vostok,* 24 (December, 1995). Lebed later claimed that the presidency under Yeltsin had grown too strong. This is consistent with the general's disavowing of authoritarian methods (see below), *Segodnya,* 28 December 1996. It also reflects his growing commitment to political devolution and local self-rule.

73. The remarks were made during the 1996 presidential campaign. *Washington Times,* June 2, 1996.

74. See Martin Seiff's article "General's Support, Ideas Will Keep Him Powerful after Vote" for comments on Pinochet and "brick-by-brick" evolutionism. He also mentioned (in an interview that precedes Seiff's article) that he intends to come to power through elections and that he fears the "Latin-Americanization" of Russia's army, that is, the primary political role armies in "banana republics" have played. He is confident that this will not happen in Russia. He frequently mentions De Gaulle as a role model; see, for instance, *Russkiy Vostok* 24 (December 1995).

75. *Nezavisimya Gazeta,* 7 June 1996.

76. *Russkiy Vostok* 24 (December 1995).

77. ORT news program *Vremya,* 18 June and 26 June 1996.

78. ORT *Vremya*, 14 June 1996.

79. See, for instance, the *Zavtra* interview and *Homeland*. Lebed was very critical of the way the Russian mass media, which was perceived by him as being more anti-army than antiwar, covered the army's operations there. He told a foreign reporter that "the politicians have thrown the Russian army into Chechnya without necessary training, without a unified command structure. The army learned how to fight [there] in battle by having paid an unreasonably high price for this military experience. The politicians have taken victory from the army three times, and the Russian mass media have covered it [the army] with dirt." *Washington Times*, 2 June 1996.

80. Lebed was dismissed in fall 1996.

81. S. Neil MacFarlane, "Russian Conceptions of Europe," *Post Soviet Affairs*, July-September 1994, 250.

82. Ibid., 253.

83. Ibid., 250–258.

84. A 1995 campaign brochure for the Chernomyrdin-led "Russia Is Our Home" (*Nash Dom Rossiya*) parliamentary electoral bloc lists thirteen "priorities" of the bloc's policy line. Number one on the list is "spiritual rebirth of Russia." The list includes measures to ensure the "physical health of the nation," the "unity of the country," the "combat readiness and professionalism" of the army, the "integration" of the CIS states, the "defense of the rights and freedoms of our countrymen in the near abroad," and "conduct of an effective foreign policy." Moreover, the *domshiki* promise to conduct a "struggle" against crime and corruption and to combat "poverty and social inequality." Indeed, there are few points here that a nationalist of any stripe could disagree with. In an open letter to Russian voters included in the brochure, Viktor Chernomyrdin proclaims that *Nash Dom's* goals are "a great Russia, strong, stable, and confident." Russia will one day no longer be thought of as a "third world" country, and her citizens will no longer "envy Western Europeans, Americans, and Japanese." An especially important task of the movement is to "decrease the mortality rate and increase the birth rate." Russians are no longer attracted to "alien ways" and are "returning to the search for self-identification and confidence in their special significance," according to the brochure.

85. Addressing the Congress of Patriotic Forces on 27 June 1996, Aleksandr Lebed claimed that the invasion of foreign influences, including mass entertainment and the proselytizing of Western evangelists, represented a threat to Russian national security. ORT news program *Vremya*, 27 June 1996.

86. Zyuganov himself claimed that two "clans" are represented within the Russian leadership. One is cognizant of Russian interests, the other representative of "comprador" interests tied to the West. See, for instance, Ivan Rodin, "Zyuganov Berates Yeltsin Over Lenin and Clinton," *Nezavisimaya Gazeta*, 22 March 1997.

87. Though Yeltsin has not ignored the debate over the Russian Idea. In summer 1996, *Rossiyskaya Gazeta* (30 July 1996), a state-sponsored newspaper, announced a competition for formulating a "unifying national idea."

88. Polling indicates that Russians are prepared—indeed, would be

glad—to see Chechnya go. For attitudes on Chechnya and the Chechens, see The Russian Center for Public Opinion and Market Research's "Express Release" 6 June 1997, and 17 October 1997. See also the *Russkiy Telegraf*, 2 October 1997, report by Vladimir Todres.

89. Interfax, 18 April 1997.

90. Lebed had first approached Yavlinskiy about a possible coalition in spring 1996 (*Komsomolskaya Pravda*, 21 March 1996).

91. The "third force" alliance won a stunning upset victory over the "party of power." Moscow, NTV, 15 March 1997; *Izvestiya*, 1 July 1997. Fedorov, a prominent eye surgeon, has advocated a distributionist approach to economic reform. He was a presidential candidate in 1996 (*Komsomolskaya Pravda*, 21 March 1996).

92. See, for instance, the Interfax polling data published in *Argumenty I Fakty*, 12–22 June 1997. See also the Interfax report (30 August 1997) on the parties' relative popularity.

93. "Russkiye Idei: Bazovyye Tsennosti," *Ekspert*, 19 May 1997.

10

The Global Regime and the
Nationalist Reaction

The conclusive stage of the economic, political, and social rationalization that began in early modern Europe is its globalization. The fear that all nationalists express of the developing hegemonic global monoculture is inextricably tied to their intuitive grasp of the fundamental meaning of modernism's final drive toward dominance: The real question facing both the Russians and other nations is the question of survival.

It is easy enough for Westerners to dismiss Russian fears of cultural annihilation as the rantings of xenophobes. Who could be opposed to progress? That Russian fears are often expressed within cultural systems few Westerners understand or are formulated as crackpot conspiracy theories only allows the rational-minded (and self-satisfied) Westerner to ignore the inevitability of the clash of a native culture with the alien Other.

The fear of a hegemonic global monoculture swallowing Russia whole runs like a red thread through contemporary nationalist discourse. Nationalist nomenclature may designate the hegemon the "new world order," "mondialism," or simply the "West," but flippantly dismissing such fears as merely the latest incarnation of Russian xenophobia ignores the objective historic processes that have shaped the conspiratology and honest emotional reactions of Russian nationalists of whatever persuasion. Modernity has increased the likelihood of clashes between alien cultures, and the processes of economic, political, and social rationalization that began some hundreds of years ago in the West have now reached a new stage—globalization—that has brought Russia, and much of the under-(or un-) "developed" world face to face with a ubiquitous monoculture that appears to be a genetic trait of what may be called "westernization," "Americanization," "development," or "modernization," a process that is traumatic enough in itself. Just what is it that the nationalists fear?

A More "Modern" Modernity

In 1950, the Santa Clara valley of California, a showcase of commercial agriculture, was filled with orchards and dotted with towns bearing names like San Jose, Campbell, and the particularly Californiaesque Sunnyvale. By the 1980s the region had been transformed beyond recognition by the forces of what has come to be called "economic development." The Santa Clara valley became "Silicon" Valley, a hub of the world economy and leading symbol of postindustrial America. The social and economic revolution that the Santa Clara valley experienced in shifting from the production of fruit to the production of microchips was every bit as disorienting as the metamorphosis fostered by the enclosure of the commons during England's industrialization. The disruption of the economic base of the valley, euphemistically called "restructuring," had not merely restructured the Santa Clara valley, but virtually destroyed it.[1]

In thirty years, the population of the valley had exploded from some 290,000 to well over a million. What's more, "the nature of work, employment . . . , ethnic composition, and social structure underwent a stunning metamorphosis." At least a quarter of Silicon Valley's workers are illegal aliens, producing a demographic complexity that is indeed bewildering.[2] Bewilderment must by now be a familiar sensation to inhabitants of the Golden State. California has long been a testing ground for the various transformations that futurist gurus have hailed as a new beginning. Moreover, the confusing "restructuring" that had made its debut in California had left many an observer with the impression that the towns and cities of postindustrial America were less communities than scattered populations. The sense of particularity and place of the old towns had been lost amid the rush toward architectural and commercial homogenization that modern development brought with it. In his novel *The Crying of Lot 49*, novelist Thomas Pynchon described the fictional California city of San Narciso, a model of "postindustrial" development, as "less an identifiable city than a grouping of concepts—census tracts, special purpose bond issue districts, shopping nuclei all overlaid with access roads," less a real place than "a vast sprawl of houses which had grown all together."[3]

The creation of Silicon Valley was not without social costs. Human beings appear to thrive within a limited context, one that provides direction, purpose, status, and ultimate meaning for individuals who find their personalities fulfilled within a larger community, the family being the normal vehicle for the socialization of successive generations. Stability and continuity provide the social basis for a degree of certainty in the minds of the individuals who make up a given community, an unexamined feeling that the world makes sense and that the boundaries of right behavior are more or less clear. Internal and external badges of identity help demarcate the boundaries of the community, and a sense of commonality helps ease the frictions of social intercourse. Without such a context, we are left to our own devices, and chaos results. Sociologists have noted the "family turbulence" that accompanied the transformation of the Santa Clara valley. The degree of family disruption apparent in the transition from Santa Clara Valley to Silicon Valley was exaggerated even by California standards. While national divorce rates doubled between 1977 and 1985, sociologists Allan Pred and Michael Watts have observed that Silicon Valley divorce rates tripled; the number of "nonfamily households," especially households headed by single mothers, grew exponentially, and "abortion levels exceeded by one and a half times the U.S. figure."[4] Judith Stacey, dissecting the family crisis in Silicon Valley, asserted that the crisis has "a material basis in the new production system and in the highly segmented labor markets," labor markets that depend on the employment of women.[5]

Stacey's observations are nothing new. Allan Carlson's important work on family life, *From Cottage to Work Station,* paints a gloomy picture of modernism's effects on the family and thus on social stability in the developed world.[6] According to Carlson, "the introduction of machine technology and the factory system of production forced the reordering of Western social life beginning during the nineteenth century." For well over a millennium prior to the Industrial Revolution, home and workplace were most often one and the same: "Household production, ranging from tool making and weaving to the keeping of livestock and the garden patch, bound each family together as a basic economic unit, a 'community of work.'" Production and consumption, not being separated by the cash nexus, complemented one another, each family forming a more or less self-sufficient unit. "Wives and children stood beside husbands and fathers as coworkers in the family enterprise, with no debate over issues of work and dependency." Family life[7] was central to the stability of the clan, tribe, and nation; indeed, it was the nucleus of the broader communities that were each based on the kinship bond.[8] Religion, tradition, and custom reinforced both the socioeconomic and kinship bonds of the family unit and made explicit the understood function, status, obligations, and value of each family

member in an internal division of labor that made the family an important "cell of society."[9]

The Industrial Revolution undermined the economic viability of the
family. The head of household, who had shared child rearing functions
with his spouse, was removed from the home to the environs of the
factory, and the gradual transformation of self-sufficient households
into units of consumption began. As subsistence agriculture was displaced by commercial and industrial agribusiness, and as cottage industry was replaced by mass production, both women, as wives and
mothers, and children lost their essential economic functions. The
status of women was severely undermined, and children were no
longer important to the functioning of the family: The swift transition
of children from blessing to burden had begun. As the ideologies of
economic growth and individualism combined with the erosion of religion, tradition, and custom, a final assault on the home as the fortress
of the family was begun. In the United States, women poured into the
workforce, especially during and after World War II, either out of economic necessity as wages failed to keep pace with inflation and heavier
tax burdens or as a consequence of their declining status at home. Children, long wards of the state via "public schools," were targeted by
advertisers who promoted a new youth culture as the birthright of the
budding consumer. In the new America of the post-war era, the home
would be a bunking place for smaller and smaller families who saw
less and less of one another, the chief shared activity being the consumption of processed foods and other goods and services.[10]

No social transformations go unaccompanied (we will not attempt
to determine which came first) by ideologies that both promote and
justify the changes. Individualism, liberalism, democratism,[11] socialism,[12] fascism, Nazism, communism, and feminism are among those
ideologies that are surely modern, but evolved in different parts of the
modern world at different times. The formation of the integrated state,
the rise of industrialism, the dissolution of agrarian society, and the
growth of urban centers did not proceed in an orderly and uniform
pattern. Nevertheless, we have identified these phenomena as part and
parcel of what is usually called modernism, or development, in the
case of second and third world countries.[13] There has been some debate
over whether the first world is now "postmodern," about whether it
has entered a wholly new era as different from the modern as the modern was from the medieval, but it is probably more correct to say that
the process known as modernization is merely entering a new phase
in the first world, while it is completing the work of reformist autocrats
and communists in the second, and disrupting the third with a repeat
performance of the first Industrial Revolution. Writer Octavio Paz may

have had changes like those that took place in the Santa Clara valley of California in mind when he asked, "What is modernity?" He answered that it "is first of all, an ambiguous term; there are as many types of modernity as there are societies. Each has its own. . . . Since 1850 [modernity] has been our goddess and our demoness. In recent years there has been an attempt to exorcise her, and there has been much talk of 'postmodernism.' But what is postmodernism if not an even more modern modernity?"[14]

That "more modern modernity" that Paz noted is actually the continuation of a political-economic rationalization that began centuries ago in the West and is now proceeding to reorganize and rationalize the world in a new global division of labor that will further the logical ends of the process itself. Two theoretical models—the managerial revolution and the theory of the end of the nation state—will prove helpful in outlining the contours of the new order. The postmodern project of extending economic and political rationalization globally has certainly encouraged the explosion of nationalist phenomena that has erupted in the past several decades, particularly in the post-cold war era. It also helps explain the anti-Western course nationalist movements in Russia and elsewhere have taken.

The Managerial Revolution

In 1940, political theorist James Burnham wrote his most important book, *The Managerial Revolution*.[15] Burnham, after falling out with Trotsky, abandoned Marxism, thinking it inadequate to explain the new world that was coming into being in the two decades since the Great War. Burnham was impressed by broad similarities in social and political organization in fascist Italy (and Nazi Germany), Stalinist Russia, and New Deal America, and he discerned the outlines of a new type of society that was rising up to displace the capitalist world that had, in turn, displaced the feudal one.

Influenced by the work of Niccolo Macchiavelli, Max Weber, and Vilfredo Pareto, among others, Burnham retained a class-based analytical framework that focused on elites: The defining feature of any society is thus the elite class that dominates (through controlling the means of production) and sets the agenda for that society. The managers made up the dominant class of what Burnham called "managerial society." The fundamental sea change that was bringing the managers to the forefront of the new society was, in Burnham's view, the shift from "individually owned and controlled private property"[16] to corporate and state owned and controlled property. Technology had so increased the complexity of the productive process that the old capitalist class could not maintain proprietary control over the means of production. Moreover, improvements in communications and organizational techniques had made the possibility of an all-encompassing state bureaucracy a reality in the twentieth century.

In the United States, where Burnham judged that capitalism and the bourgeoisie were making a last stand against the new society, corporate property forms had yielded everyday control of production, finance, and even strategic planning to a class of engineers, executive officers, and financial managers who actually oversaw the productive process and even doled out dividends to the nominal owners. The advent of the New Deal broadened the base of the newly powerful managerial class to include government bureaucrats, technocrats, and central bankers, as well as certain members of the political class and labor union organizers, who were steadily joining in the management and control of the means of production. The New Deal's "alphabet soup" agencies told the tale of the gradual alignment and symbiotic relationship that was developing between the managers of the private sector and those of the public sector.

To be sure, Burnham did not assert that all mangers necessarily viewed the New Deal as a good thing; some, having absorbed the ideologies of classical liberalism and capitalism from the old elite, would resist the gradual reconciliation of the two supposedly antagonistic sectors. Nevertheless, Burnham even then detected a psychological merger in the works between the two wings of the managerial class. At first, the private sector elites would attempt to manipulate the public sector elites' programs for their own benefit (projects such as the Tennessee Valley Authority proved lucrative for private contractors, for instance) but would gradually come to see the public sector managers as their brethren. Often of similar educational background and status, the private sector managers operated in gigantic organizations not unlike the bureaucracies of the new Leviathan. Like their public sector counterparts, they believed that "they could run things, and they like[d] to run things."[17]

The New Deal, Burnham maintained, was slowly but surely turning the means of production over to the new class, who would regulate, manipulate, and coordinate the production process and formulate ideologies to justify the new order. Overall, Burnham thought the processes of the New Deal of the same nature as "corporate" managerial development in fascist Italy and Nazi Germany. Stalin's Russia was the managerial state perfected, with the entire socioeconomic structure rationalized via the nationalization of the means of production and the total bureaucratization of society. In Russia, the *nomenklatura* managerial class was in the driver's seat, pointing the way toward the brave new world for all. The various branches of managerial society would struggle for control of the world, for modern economies are expansive, and the natural inclination of the managers is to extend the rationalization process globally. But Burnham thought it unlikely that one of the managerial styles would dominate the entire world. The most probable scenario, so he thought, would be the gradual expansion of managerial domination over regions that could be physically, bureaucratically, and economically integrated, especially the Americas, Europe, and Asia, with the United States, Germany-Russia (the Hitler-Stalin pact was still operative at the time), and Japan acting as the nuclei of new managerial superstates. The struggles between the nascent managerial superstates, each with its own brand of managerial ideology, would not be unlike the clash of Christendom with Islam, or religious wars of the Reformation period, when the religions of the age, similar in origin, nevertheless clashed in a titanic struggle for dominance. The battle lines of the struggle would no doubt fluctuate, but no one managerial superstate and its justifying ideology would be able to establish a global regime.

In essence, Burnham thought of the embryonic managerial, liberal welfare state, Fascism-Nazism, and Stalinist communism as varying forms of the new society that was emerging in the wake of the Great War and the collapse of capitalism brought about by the Great Depression. Capitalism had been proprietary, truly "private," and centered on the dominance of the bourgeoisie, who justified their dominance via the ideology of classical liberalism, and the expansion of monopolies via the Enlightenment notion of rationalism.

In truth, the capitalists were "rationalizing" the economies of the developed world by expanding their domain through vertical and horizontal integration. Big business was the economic product of both the Industrial Revolution and the organizational revolution that had preceded it. Big business would, like big government, come to be organized along bureaucratic lines, the more so after the failure of proprietary capitalism in the 1920s. The most noticeable social hallmark of the emerging managerial order would be an expansive standardization and homogenization that destroyed nonstandard forms of social and economic life, the logical extension of processes that had begun in early modern Europe as the old feudal order was displaced by the emerging integrated state—so similar in reality to Burnham's description of the managerial state.

As insightful as it was, Burnham's analysis was nevertheless flawed. The new order that emerged triumphant after the Second World War (the cold war being here taken as the historical continuation of that struggle), which Burnham judged the first war of managerial society, would not be the one party monolith that he thought most likely. Rather, it was the New Dealist welfare state that promoted mass democracy, the maintenance of a broad private sector, modern liberalism, and consumerism as its defining features. The new system could well be called "managerial capitalism," or "managerial democracy," depending on which feature of the system the observer wished to highlight, the economic or the political. The public sector would be broader and more prevalent than ever, of course, managing and manipulating the means of production (as well as society itself) but not necessarily attempting to nationalize all the areas it influenced. Burnham also failed to include in his analysis the managerial strata that evolved in the public and semipublic educational institutions, especially the large universities, as well as the managers of big media and the semipublic foundations, themselves intermeshed with the public sector managers through state regulation and state funding. The large universities have tended to promote variations of the New Dealist ideology and have cranked out graduates who assumed posts in both public and private sectors. For their part, semipublic foundations and mass media have tended to promote the ideological aims of the managerial class.

The managerial class is not wholly monolithic. Struggles, sometimes quite bitter, are frequent among managerial elites of the "Right" and "Left," but the overall thrust of their ideologies is the same, stressing the importance of managerial control, rationalization, and consumerism, either in the form of the expansion of business (especially big business) activity or through the "empowerment" of the populace via economic redistribution and transfer payments. None question the fundamental assumptions of either modern liberalism (especially the egalitarianism of the ideology and its attachment to an expansive state apparatus) or the materialism that is called consumerism, which depends on market mechanisms to supply the bounty to be consumed. There is range for argument within such a framework, but it is an argument about how best to *manage* society, the development of a "global economy," and the expansion of "democracy." Both "Right" and "Left" embrace globalism and internationalism via the activity of transstate corporations and semigovernmental and supragovernmental bodies.

The ideological transformations that have occurred in the "West's" erstwhile internal opponents (Japan is often included in such speculations) raises a question: Does such a convergence of "Right" and "Left," the embrace by both of the global economy and internationalism, mean that the "nation-state" is doomed?[18]

The End of the Nation-State, the End of History, or the End of the Nation?[19]

Whether of the managerial "Right," which stresses the importance of the extension of the global economy as the agent of change, or of the managerial "Left," which stresses the importance of global democratization overseen by transstate quasigovernmental and supragovernmental bodies, observers who discern the outlines of a new order of global democratization and marketization are already writing off the "nation-state" as an obsolete barrier to the expansive rationalization ("democracy" and "the market," never adequately defined, are treated as the only rational alternatives to chaos and tyranny) that they foresee.[20]

Francis Fukuyama, the prophet of a universal "democratic capitalism" that embraces the economism of the "Right" and the democratism of the "Left," has written that the modernization of non-Western countries in the last few centuries has put the world on a path of global evolution that will make possible the writing of a universal history. As non-Western countries modernized themselves by employing Western techniques and technologies, writes Mr. Fukuyama, they bought into a mode of development whose logical end point is universalism and homogenization. "Technology," according to Fukuyama, "makes possible the limitless accumulation of wealth, and thus the satisfaction of an ever expanding set of human desires. This process guarantees an increasing homogenization of all human societies, *regardless of their historical origins or cultural inheritances* [emphasis added]."[21]

In Fukuyama's estimation, all countries that modernize pass through two developmental stages, first, a stage that roughly corresponds to the process developmental theorists have called nation building, and then, at a later time, a stage the first world may well be in now, a period of globalization as the "nation" unbuilds itself and becomes tied to the emerging global system. During the first stage of modernization, "all countries undergoing . . . modernization must increasingly resemble one another: they must unify nationally on the basis of a centralized state, urbanize, replace traditional forms of social organization as a tribe, sect, and family with economically rational ones based on function and efficiency, and provide for the universal education of their citizens." Eventually such societies will be ready to "become increasingly linked with one another through global markets and the spread of a universal consumer culture."[22] Indeed, "the logic of modern natural science would seem to dictate a universal evolution in the direction of capitalism," and the very act of development and modernization "seems to point in the direction of liberal democracy."

Citing the work of Seymour Martin Lipset, Fukuyama notes "an extremely high correlation between stable democracy and economic development."[23]

Fukuyama's observations more or less speak for the managerial consensus. Japanese "business guru"[24] Kenichi Ohmae, taking the globalization theory one step further, foresees a "borderless world" where transstate corporations can shift investment capital and factories wherever needed to enhance efficiency, finding cheaper labor sources, better access to natural resources, and more hospitable investment climates whenever necessary. New "information technology" has made the rapid shifts possible, and transstate corporations need no longer consider their country of origin more than a base for interaction with the "global economy." State borders, according to Ohmae, are mere "historical accident[s]" that are "irrelevant" in an age when the "nation-states" are no longer the "natural business units in a global economy."[25]

Distinctive national cultures figure in the arguments of proponents of the borderless world as a mere obstacle to a process of political and economic rationalization that presupposes social and cultural homogenization as part and parcel of the developing global system.[26] At any rate, culture, writes Ohmae, is a tool in the hands of "old-fashioned leaders" attempting to block the march of progress. "Enlightened" leaders of "nation states," and presumably of the transstate managerial class, can "make their people" set aside particularisms and begin "working together."[27] It is important to note at this juncture that it is not merely "nation-states" that are considered obsolete, but nations, tribes, clans, and families as well. According to Ohmae, the world is composed primarily of individual consumers who, when granted better access to global information networks, are much less likely to display signs of economic nationalism, preferring to make more rational choices based on individual taste, cost, and current fashions. Enlightened consumers would not buy "American or French or Japanese products merely because of their national associations."[28]

The "enlightened consumer" is an individual who has forsaken his nation's culture for that of the emerging global monoculture, one that is fundamentally consumerist. Ohmae notes that

> for more than a decade, some of us have been talking about the progressive globalization of markets for consumer goods like Levi's jeans, Nike athletic shoes, and Hermes scarves—a process driven by global exposure to the same information, the same cultural icons, and the same advertisements, that I have elsewhere referred to as the 'California-ization' of taste. Today, however, the process of convergence goes faster and deeper. It

reaches well beyond taste to much more fundamental dimensions of worldview, mind-set, and even thought process.

The globalization of "information technology" has made possible the culture revolution that is transforming the world:

> there are now . . . tens of millions of teenagers around the world who, having been raised in a multi-media-rich environment, have a lot more in common with each other than they do with members of older generations in their own cultures. For these budding consumers, technology-driven convergence does not take place at the sluggish rate dictated by yesterday's media. It is instantaneous—a nanosecond migration of ideas and innovations.[29]

In fact, the "well-informed citizen" and enlightened consumer of Ohmae's vision is driven entirely by his own material desires, concerned primarily with the ability of the global system to "deliver tangible improvements in lifestyle."[30] The atomization of global society is facilitated by the global social revolution, a revolution that has begun to eat away at "the essential continuity between generations, on which every society necessarily depends for its integrity and survival."[31]

Ohmae does not find such a trend alarming, nor does he ever pause to consider the effects of such social dissolution on the nations he thinks obsolete. How can any sort of social or political stability—as other "business gurus" have repeatedly pointed out is a necessity for the development of second and third world countries—be possible in a world where "creative destruction" disrupts the most fundamental unit of society, the family, day in and day out with ceaseless change that pits generation against generation and all against all in a fractured struggle for "tangible improvements in lifestyle"? Even Francis Fukuyama is troubled by the prospect of a world of Nietzschean "last men." Fukuyama calls the "last man" a "human being who is content with himself, and with a life of endless material accumulation, a being without striving, sacrifice, risk, or ideals." The problem of the "last man" is, according to Fukuyama, "the deepest problem of liberal democracy," which is in danger of leaving its citizens with "stunted souls."[32]

Fukuyama, perhaps the most thoughtful representative of the globalist school, has put his finger on the aspect of modernization that has done the most to spur the growth of anti-Western nationalism around the world in the post–cold war era. To modernize, in the sense that the term is now used, means to ultimately "Californiaize," to accept one's own national dissolution as the price of what may be a short term purchase of relative material prosperity, particularly as transstate corporations grow increasingly prone to shift plants and capital investment around the globe according to circumstance. Such modernization is naturally identified with its place of origin, and second and third world critics often call this process "westernization," or, more specifically, "Americanization," America being seen as the dynamic engine that drives the processes of the social-political-economic revolution.

In the third world, nations undergoing the process of development known erroneously as nation building (1) are forced by circumstance (and sometimes by governments) into associations with the national Other of sustained duration, associations that tend to exacerbate developmental friction as minority nations face the prospect of assimilation and cultural extinction (since few third world states are true nation states) and (2) experience severe social dislocation as a result of the abandonment of village-based agricultural for urbanized industrial society. Moreover, in both the second and third worlds, the "information technology" revolution has brought the populations of far-flung countries into constant contact with a global monoculture that propagates the ideology of consumerism and individualism, which has proved to be an attractive ideological narcotic for uprooted young people particularly, as the global economy makes at least some of the fruits of the system available, though often inaccessible, in their native countries. The Other is now an ever present Big Brother, and nationalist reactions to his omnipresent tutelage are predictable and inevitable.

What's more, the globalist Other, often identified with the West, is a difficult companion to shake off, as sociologist Leslie Sklair points out in her book *The Sociology of the Global System*. In fact, nationalist protests about cultural imperialism in the form of Western films, advertising, and TV programs assume something that is probably false, for such protests imply that "if American [or Western] influence could be excluded then cultural and media imperialism would end."[33] A more likely result of indigenizing mass media is merely the spawning of second and third world copies of the hated (by many) programming of the "cultural imperialists." Vacuous native-born soap operas, game shows, and advertising are as often as not the results of media indigenization efforts, as it appears that modern mass media are driven as much by their own limitations as by the desires of those who wish to turn the tools of cultural imperialism against themselves. The only model that second and third worlders have to follow is that of the West.[34]

Westerners might react to the hue and cry in the second and third worlds over the painful transformations of modernization and the "California-ization" of their cultures with a shrug: So what? The leaders of those "nations" are, in any case, merely giving the people what they themselves want, and the prospects for peace in a world where all of "us" are more alike, that is, homogenized, will improve, won't they?

The short answers to such reactions are that it is not at all clear what second and third world nations want (other than a higher standard of living, perhaps), and it is extremely unlikely that the utopia of the "end of history" will come to pass. It is a dreadful mistake to assume a universal desire for modernization on the part of non-Westerners as a given, for such an assumption ignores the conundrum of the "under-developed" world: To modernize will mean to disrupt, maybe destroy, societies that have preserved themselves for centuries. In order to modernize, people must be forced or persuaded to be less like themselves, to discard many, perhaps all, of the very things that had made the world make sense to them. To become "Western" for many a non-Westerner is to commit suicide. On the other hand, *not* to modernize may be just as deadly, for "backwardness" potentially leaves the nation's fate in the hands of the technologically superior Other. Thus the Slavophile-Westernizer controversy was indicative of the contradiction between modernization and what the Russians call *samobitnost*, originality, uniqueness, distinctiveness, or put differently, the specific ways that universal human nature has coped with a unique set of circumstances, the context of nationhood. The universal is thus found in the particular, which is ignored by the avatars of "end of history" utopianism. Even if the global monoculture appears to be claiming victory in many places, it is unlikely to last, for human nature will eventually intervene and the natural desire to communalize along lines marked "us" and "them" will reassert itself.[35] Particularism is a necessity for the flourishing of the community, for all real communities *are by nature particular and exclusive,* and the most potent and lasting particularism is one rooted in either the reality or myth of kinship. Even the communists, who, like the fascists and Nazis, attempted to recommunalize their modernizing societies along totalitarian lines, came to recognize this fact of life and accommodated themselves to it.

The proliferation of nationalist phenomena in the post–cold war era was brought on by the dissolution of the bipolar world of military-political blocs that tended to contain the nationalist imperative, but the anti-Westernism and anti-Americanism that is such a prominent part of Russian (and many other contemporary) nationalisms, that permeated "national liberation" movements in the postwar era and is an integral part of the ideologies of the Iranian revolution and Arab Islamic fundamentalism, has come to the fore in the last decade, showing itself for what it really is, with less need to cloak itself in the rhetorical dogmas of Marxism or liberation theology. Today, the *fact* of globalization is what stands behind the conspiratology of the ayatollahs and the

Black Hundreds, serving as an important catalyst to the various peoples' drive to self-recognition and self-definition. What historian Theodore H. Von Laue called "the world revolution of Westernization"[36]
did not begin after the fall of the Berlin Wall, of course, but the very
technological breakthroughs that facilitate globalization also appear to
be spurring on the inevitable conflicts between "us" and "them," as
avoiding the "Other" becomes virtually impossible. Matters are being
brought to a head.

The Russian question, like the nationalist question anywhere, is an
ontological one, a question of being. "To be" for the vast majority of
mankind means to be a member of a tribe, clan, or nation, to be a
Russian, Palestinian, Zulu, or Japanese. We Westerners could do worse
than to follow Heidegger's example and attempt to find a way to "let
things be," to let things be themselves. It is inevitable that the West
will continue to be, for a while at least, both a model to be copied and
an intruder to be feared and hated among the nations of the second
and third worlds. In any event, many a Westerner has come to appreciate the importance of the continuity, stability, and certainty of the community that we ourselves are losing, and that nationalists everywhere
fear losing. In that regard, we have as much to learn from them as they
from us.

Russian nationalists often describe the fate that awaits them with the
advent of globalism as "genocide." As the community dissolves, the
very bonds that ensured its survival unravel and the nation itself faces
extinction. The conspiratorialists again have a point, even if they miss
the mark in ascribing a purposefulness behind the declining birth rates
and rising death rates that have, after all, been evident in Russia since
at least the Brezhnev era. In the West, the same socioeconomic and
ideological forces are producing aging populations as birth rates decline below replacement levels and the family itself dissolves. As the
classical Slavophiles would have had it, Russia at the end of the second
millennium finds herself reunited with the West, a de facto part of the
developed world, facing the same, final question that that world must
face—and answer: To be or not to be?

Notes

1. The transformation of the Valley is described in Allan Pred and Michael
John Watts, *Reworking Modernity: Capitalisms and Symbolic Discontent* (New
Brunswick, N. J.: Rutgers University Press, 1992), 2–4.
2. Ibid., 3.
3. Cited in ibid.

4. Ibid., 4.

5. Ibid.

6. Allan C. Carlson, *From Cottage to Work Station: The Family's Search for Social Harmony in the Industrial Age* (San Francisco: Ignatius Press, 1993).

7. Here I am referring to what is commonly called the "nuclear" family and not the extended family of grandparents, aunts, uncles, and cousins that was probably more nearly the norm in preindustrial societies.

8. Carlson, *From Cottage to Work Station,* 1–4.

9. Carle Zimmerman, cited in ibid., 5.

10. Carlson, *From Cottage to Work Station,* 7–24.

11. It is worth mentioning here that democracy and liberalism are not the same thing. Democracy as it is understood today is a set of procedures and institutions (elections, universal suffrage, parliaments, courts), whereas liberalism is a philosophy about the ways things ought to be. Moreover, classical liberalism has evolved into modern liberalism. The latter tends to see state power as a positive force in promoting "individual rights," whereas the former disdained such actions, though not state actions in the interests of promoting trade and business interests. As noted in chapter 1, such a transformation is not necessarily inevitable, but the roots of the liberal metamorphosis were evident at the time of the French Revolution; indeed, classical liberalism has had a most difficult go at resisting the onslaught of the modern variety, since both forms share the same assumptions about progress and human nature. Such distinctions are rarely commented on and, especially in Russia, procedural democracy is viewed as an integral part of a liberal regime.

12. I use the term here to designate "leftist" socioeconomic agendas that fall short of the radicalism of Marxism-Leninism.

13. There is usually no debate in the literature on development about what the "first world" is, but it is often difficult to determine which states are in the "second world," states that are usually mostly industrialized but still are dependent on the agricultural sector to some degree (this term is used especially to identify former communist states and the People's Republic of China), and which are third world states, those that are sometimes called "lesser developed nations," or "developing countries." I admit to being stumped by this terminology myself and can only recommend the above stated guidelines to give the reader a rough idea of the subject of discussion.

14. From *In Search of the Present,* cited in Pred and Watts, *Reworking Modernity,* 1.

15. James Burnham, *The Managerial Revolution* (Bloomington: Ind.: Indiana University Press, 1966).

16. Ibid., viii.

17. Ibid., 255.

18. For an incisive review of the "Right"–"Left" convergence see Samuel Francis, "Left, Right, Up, Down," *Chronicles,* September 1989. The crusading Wilsonian element of Reagan-era anti-Communism, together with the Western triumphalism evident as the Soviet Union began to crumble, helped spur on an ideological flip-flop that made the terms right and left almost useless in

analyzing American (and, indeed, Western) politics in general. Mr. Francis
wrote that "what is called the 'right' in American politics today seems to in-
voke and take seriously all the slogans and clichés that derive from 'Liberty,
Equality, and Fraternity' and that would ordinarily locate their exponents on
the left. Its champions talk of the 'global democratic revolution,' universal
'human rights,' 'equality as a conservative principle,' and the final emancipation of mankind from war, racial and national prejudice, and poverty through
universal economic and technological progress." Francis notes that no leftist
of the past "would raise an eyebrow at the rhetoric and ideology of the contemporary American right." I am also indebted to Francis for his continuing
analysis of the American political scene in his syndicated newspaper column
and his monthly essay in *Chronicles;* both stress the rise of a managerial elite in
America. Francis sees both the Buchanan and Perot political insurgencies in
1992 and 1996 as evidence of a nationalist reaction to the rise of the new regime. His writings have contributed a great deal to my understanding of the
nature of contemporary nationalist movements. For more on the new American nationalism, see Samuel Francis, "From Household to Nation: The Middle
American Populism of Pat Buchanan," *Chronicles,* March 1996.

19. Two books bearing the same title in English translation, *The End of the
Nation State,* by Frenchman Jean-Marie Guehenno (Minneapolis: University of
Minnesota Press, 1995) and Kenichi Ohmae of Japan (New York: Free Press,
1995) respectively, offer the uninitiated an adequate primer on the doctrine of
the new global regime. Guehenno is not necessarily enthused at the thought
such a prospect, while Ohmae is a proponent of the global economic utopia,
whose main engine of development is the transstate corporation that objectively works to erode borders and cultural barriers through economic homogenization. Neither defines nation-state or nation and both are confused over just
what nationalism is, but that is to be expected. Of the two, Guehenno's is the
more thoughtful and penetrating.

20. The editors of a three-volume study called *Democracy in Developing Countries* claim that "democracy is the only model of government with any broad
legitimacy and appeal in the world today" and that "the role of the middle
class in fostering liberty and democracy" has been emphasized by both "the
laissez-faire disciples of Adam Smith and by the Marxists." The democracy
they speak of is the mass democracy of the Western liberal welfare state, which
makes their statement problematic in view of the way various countries have
employed the term. Larry Diamond, Juan J. Linz, and Seymour Martin Lipset,
eds., *Democracy in Developing Countries* (Boulder, Colo.: Lynne Rienner Publishers,1989), x–xi. Theoretician Giovanni Sartori has noted that "today Marxists
and non-Marxists alike speak of capitalist democracy as a matter of course."
The Theory of Democracy Revisited (Chatham, New Jersey: Chatham House Publishers, 1987), xi.

21. Francis Fukuyama, "On Writing a Universal History," in *History and the
Idea of Progress,* ed. Arthur Melzer, Jerry Weinberger, and M. Richard Zinman
(Ithaca, N. Y.: Cornell University Press,1995), 16.

22. Ibid., 16–17.

23. Ibid., 17.

24. This is how the dust jacket blurb on Ohmae's book *The End of the Nation State: The Rise of Regional Economies* describes the author. Ohmae is a former senior partner of a major transstate firm, McKinsey & Company, and "has counseled major corporations and governments on their international strategies and operations for twenty years."

25. Ohmae, *End of the Nation State*, 3–5.

26. The avatars of global homogenization do not necessarily see a centralized world regime as the outcome of the processes under way. Some, both Guehenno and Ohmae for instance, envision a looser set of regional associations cooperating within a global political-economic system. As anticipated by James Burnham, the globalist visionaries tend to see America, Europe (however defined), and Asia as the natural regional building blocks of the global system. Africa would presumably enter the picture after a period of "nation building." Australia is generally grouped with Asia in such schemes.

27. Ohmae, *End of the Nation State*, 11.

28. Ibid., 4.

29. Ibid., 15.

30. Ibid., 16.

31. Ibid., 30.

32. Fukuyama, "On Writing A Universal History," 28.

33. Leslie Sklair, *The Sociology of the Global Regime: Social Change in a Global Perspective* (Baltimore: Johns Hopkins University Press, 1991), 135.

34. Ibid., 134–36.

35. In *The Politics of Human Nature* (New Brunswick, N. J.: Transaction, 1988), 192, Thomas Fleming wrote that "if all forms of community association—including the family—were destroyed by the total state, they would be naturally reconstituted automatically, like origami flowers plunged into the water, as soon as the human survivors were revived in more natural circumstances."

36. Von Laue's study of the revolution and its effects is entitled *The World Revolution of Westernization: The Twentieth Century in Global Perspective* (Oxford: Oxford University Press, 1987).

References

Abel, Theodore. *Why Hitler Came into Power*. Cambridge: Harvard University Press, 1986.

Adler, Jonathan. "Pitching the President." *Newsweek*, 17 June 1996.

Agursky, Mikhail. *The Third Rome: National Bolshevism in the USSR*. Boulder, Colo.: Westview Press, 1987.

Aksyuchits, Viktor. *Ideokratiya V Rossii*, Moscow: Vybor, 1995.

——— *Miropraviteli Tmy Veka Sego*. Moscow: Vybor, 1994.

——— "Orden Russkoy Intelligentsii," *Moskva* no. 4, April 1994: 77–92.

Alexeyeva, Ludmilla. *Soviet Dissent: Contemporary Movements for National, Religious, and Human Rights*. Translated by Carol Pearce and John Glad. Middletown, Conn.: Wesleyan University Press, 1987.

Allensworth, Wayne. "Derzhavnost: Aleksandr Lebed's Vision for Russia," *Problems of Post–Communism*, March–April 1998.

Allensworth, Wayne. *The Rutskoy Challenge*. 1992 (unpublished).

Arendt, Hannah. *The Origins of Totalitarianism*. New York: Harcourt, Brace, 1975.

Arnold, John. "Patriarch Alexei: A Personal Impression." *Keston Journal*, 20 no. 2 (1992).

Barkashov, Aleksandr. *Azbuka Russkogo Natsionalista*. Moscow: RNU, 1994.

Berdyayev, Nicholay. *The Origin of Russian Communism*. Ann Arbor: University of Michigan Press, 1993.

Berdyayev, Nicholay, et al. *Vekhi*. Translated by Marshall Shatz and Judith Zimmerman. Armonk, N.Y.: M. E. Sharpe, 1994.

———. *Vekhi and Iz Glubiniy*. Moscow: Pravda, 1991.

Blinkhorn, Martin. *Mussolini and Fascist Italy*. London: Routledge, 1984.

Bondarenko, Vladimir. *Aleksandr Prokhanov*. Moscow, 1992.

Bruno, Patrick. *Besyedy Na Chistotu*. Moscow: LDP, 1995.

Burke, Edmund. *Reflections on the Revolution in France*. New York: Bobbs-Merrill, 1955.

Burnham, James. *The Managerial Revolution*. Bloomington: Indiana University Press, 1966.

Carlson, Allan C. *From Cottage to Work Station: The Family's Search for Social Harmony in the Industrial Age*. San Francisco: Ignatius, 1993.

Carston, F. L. *The Rise of Fascism.* Los Angeles: University of California Press, 1982.

Carter, Stephen. *Russian Nationalism: Yesterday, Today, Tomorrow.* New York: St. Martin's, 1990.

Connor, Walker. *Ethnonationalism: The Quest for Understanding.* Princeton: Princeton University Press, 1994.

Dahbour, Omar, and Micheline R. Ishay. *The Nationalism Reader.* Highlands, N.J.: Humanities, 1995.

Danilevskiy, Nicholay. *Russia and Europe.* St. Petersburg: St. Petersburg University Press, 1995.

De Jonge, Alex. *Stalin and the Shaping of the Soviet Union.* New York: William Morrow, 1986.

Diamond, Larry, Juan J. Linz, and Seymour Martin Lipset, eds. *Democracy in Developing Countries.* Boulder, Colo.: Lynne Rienner, 1989.

Dugin, Aleksandr. *Osnovii Geopolitiki.* Moscow: Arktogeya, 1997.

Dunlop, John. *The Faces of Contemporary Russian Nationalism.* Princeton: Princeton University Press, 1983.

———"The Growth of Fascist Tendencies in the Russian Orthodox Church." Paper delivered at an international forum on the Church in Russia, Moscow, 20–22 January 1995.

———*The New Russian Revolutionaries.* Belmont, Mass.: Norland, 1976.

———*The Rise of Russia and the Fall of the Soviet Empire.* Princeton: Princeton University Press, 1993.

Edwards, Roanne Thomas. "Russian Christian Democracy from a Regional Perspective: The Case of St. Petersburg." *Keston Journal: Religion, State, and Society* 20, no. 2, (1992): 201–11.

Ericson, Edward E. *Solzhenitsyn and the Modern World.* Washington, D.C.: Regnery Gateway, 1993.

Fleming, Thomas. *The Politics of Human Nature.* New Brunswick, N. J.: Transaction, 1988.

Francis, Samuel. "From Household to Nation: The Middle American Populism of Pat Buchanan." *Chronicles,* March 1996.

———"Left, Right, Up, Down." *Chronicles,* September 1989.

Frazer, Graham, and George Lancelle. *Absolute Zhirinovsky.* London: Penguin Books, 1994.

Fukuyama, Francis. "On Writing a Universal History." In *History and the Idea of Progress.* Edited by Arthur Melzer, Jerry Weinberger, and M. Richard Zinman. Ithaca, N.Y.: Cornell University Press, 1995.

"Fundamental Principles of the Political Program of the RCDM." *Keston Journal* 20, no. 2 (1992).

Gellner, Ernest. *Nations and Nationalism.* Ithaca, N.Y.: Cornell University Press, 1983.

Gilder, George. *Men and Marriage.* Gretna: Pelican, 1986.

Goldsmith, James. *The Trap.* New York: Carroll & Graf, 1993.

Graham, Don. *No Name on the Bullet.* New York: Viking, 1989.

Greenfeld, Liah. *Nationalism: Five Roads to Modernity.* Cambridge: Harvard University Press, 1992.

Guehenno, Jean-Marie. *The End of the Nation State.* Translated by Victoria Elliot. Minneapolis: University of Minnesota Press, 1995.

Heidegger, Martin. *Basic Writings.* Edited by David Ferrell Krell. Translated by William Lovitt. San Francisco: HarperCollins, 1993.

Heller, Mikhail, and Aleksandr M. Nekrich. *Utopia in Power: The History of the Soviet Union from 1917 to the Present.* Translated by Phyllis B. Carlos. New York: Summit Books, 1986.

Herf, Jeffrey. *Reactionary Moderism: Technology, Culture, and Politics in Weimar and the Third Reich.* Cambridge: Cambridge University Press, 1984.

Hilarion of Kiev. "Slovo o Zakonye I Blagodaty." In *Russkaya Idyeya.* Edited by Mikhail Maslin. Moscow: Respublika, 1992.

Ioann, Metropolitan of St. Petersburg and Logoda. "Rus Sobornaya." *Nash Sovremennik* 8–12, (1994).

Johnson, Paul. *A History of Christianity.* New York: Antheneum, 1976.

Kershaw, Ian. *The Nazi Dictatorship: Problems and Perspectives of Interpretation.* London: Edward Arnold, 1985.

Kirchner, Walter. *History of Russia.* New York: Barnes & Noble, 1976.

Kireevsky, Ivan. "V Otvet A. S. Khomyakovy." In *Russkaya Idyeya.* Edited by Mikhail Maslin. Moscow: Respublika, 1992.

Kirk, Russell. *The Conservative Mind: From Burke to Elliot.* 7th rev. ed., Washington, D.C.: Regnery Gateway, 1993.

Khrushchev, Nikita. *Khrushchev Remembers.* Edited and translated by Strobe Talbott. Boston: Little, Brown, 1970.

Laqueur, Walter. *Black Hundred: The Rise of the Extreme Right in Russia.* New York: HarperCollins, 1993.

———*Russia and Germany: A Century of Conflict.* Boston: Little, Brown, 1965.

Lebed, Aleksandr. *Chest i Rodina.* Moscow, 1995.

———. *Za Derzhavu Obidno.* Moscow: Komsomolskaya Pravda, 1995.

Lewis, C. S. *The Abolition of Man.* New York: Collier Books, 1955.

Lezov, Sergei. "The National Idea and Christianity." *Keston Journal,* 20, no. 1 (1992).

Limonov, Eduard. *Limonov Protiv Zhirinovskogo.* Moscow: Konets Veka, 1994.

Lorenz, Konrad. *On Aggression.* New York: Bantam Books, 1967.

Lukacs, John. "The Patriotic Impulse." *Chronicles,* July 1992: 19–21.

Lukin, Vladimir. "Preobrazhennaya Rossiya v Novom Mire." *Mezhdunarodnaya Zhizn,* March–April 1992.

Lukin, Vladimir, and Anatoliy Utlin. *Rossiya I Zapad: Obshchnost ili Otchyzheniye?* Moscow: SAMPO, 1995.

MacFarlane, S. Neil. "Russian Conceptions of Europe." *Post Soviet Affairs,* July–September 1994.

Massie, Robert K. *Nicholas and Alexandra.* New York: Antheneum, 1967.

———. *Peter the Great: His Life and World.* New York: Ballantine, 1980.

Moody, Christopher. *Solzhenitsyn.* New York: Harper & Row, 1975.

Moore, Barrington. *Social Origins of Dictatorship and Democracy: Lord and Peasant in the Making of the Modern World.* Boston: Beacon Press, 1967.

Morrison, James A. *Vladimir Zhirinovsky: An Assessment of a Russian Ultra-Nationalist.* Washington, D.C.: National Defense University, 1994.

Mumford, Lewis. *The Myth of the Machine.* Vols. 1–2. New York: Harcourt, Brace & World, 1964–70.

Myalo, Kseniya. "Rossiya Bez Russkikh." *Moskva* 6 (1994).

Myalo, Kseniya, and Nataliya Narochnitskaya. "The Re-establishment of Russia and the Eurasian Temptation." *Nash Sovremennik* 11–12 (1994).

Neitzsche, Friedrich. *A Nietzsche Reader.* Selected and translated by R. J. Hollingdale. London: Penguin, 1977.

Nemtsov, Boris. *Provintsial.* Moscow, 1997.

Nisbet, Robert. *History of the Idea of Progress.* New York: Basic Books, 1980.

———*The Quest for Community.* San Francisco: Institute for Contemporary Studies, 1990.

Ohmae, Kenichi. *The End of the Nation State: The Rise of Regional Economies.* New York: The Free Press, 1995.

Panorama Research Group. *Political Extremism in Russia.* Moscow: Panorama, 1996.

———. *Russian Politicians From A to Z* [Rossiyskiye Politiki Ot A Do Ya]. Vols. 1–2. Moscow: Panorama, 1996.

Paxton, John. *Companion to Russian History.* New York: Facts on File, 1983.

Pipes, Richard. *Russia Under the Old Regime.* New York: Charles Scribner's Sons, 1974.

Plekhanov, Sergey. *Zhirinovskiy: Khto On?* Moscow: Evrasiya Nord, 1994.

Pred, Allan, and Michael J. Watts. *Reworking Modernity: Capitalisms and Symbolic Discontent.* New Brunswick, N.J.: Rutgers University Press, 1992.

"Program Documents of the National-Republican Party." Moscow, 1994.

"Protocols of the Elders of Zion." *Molodaya Gvardiya* 10 (October 1993).

Rasputin, Valentin. "Downstream." In *Contemporary Russian Prose.* Translated by Valentina G. Brougher and Helen C. Poot. Edited by Carl and Ellendea Proffer. Ann Arbor, Mich: Ardis, 1982.

———*Farewell to Matyora.* Translated by Antonina W. Bouris. Evanston, Ill.: Northwestern University Press, 1991.

———*Live and Remember.* Translated by Antonina W. Bouis. Evanston, Ill.: Northwestern University Press, 1992.

———*Money for Maria and Borrowed Time.* Translated by Kevin Windle and Margaret Wettlin. London: Quartet Books, 1981.

———*Siberia on Fire.* Translated by Gerald Mikkelson and Margaret Winchell. Dekalb, Ill.: Northern Illinois University Press, 1989.

———*You Live and Love and Other Stories.* Translated by Alan Meyers. New York: Vanguard, 1986.

Riasanovsky, Nicholas. "The Emergence of Eurasianism." In *Collected Writings 1947–1994.* Los Angeles: Charles Schlacks, 1993.

———*The Emergence of Romanticism.* Oxford: Oxford University Press, 1992.

———*A History of Russia.* Fifth ed. Oxford: Oxford University Press, 1993.

Sakwa, Richard. "Christian Democracy in Russia." *Keston Journal: Religion, State and Society,* 20, no. 2 (1992): 135–200.

Sale, Kirkpatrick. *Rebels Against the Future: The Luddites and Their War Against the Industrial Revolution.* New York: Addison-Wesley, 1996.

Sartori, Giovanni. *The Theory of Democracy Revisited*. Chatham, N.J.: Chatham House Publishers, 1987.

Shafarevich, Igor. "Russia and the World Catastrophe." *Nash Sovremennik* 1 (1993).

———"Russophobia." *Nash Sovremennik* 6, 11 (1989).

———"Socialism in our Past and Future." Translated by Max Hayward. In *From under the Rubble*. New York: Bantam, 1975.

———"Was Perestroika a CIA Action?" *Nash Sovremennik* 7 (1995).

Sklair, Leslie. *The Sociology of the Global Regime: Social Change in a Global Perspective*. Baltimore: Johns Hopkins University Press, 1991.

Solzhenitsyn, Aleksandr. "As Breathing and Consciousness Return." Translated by Max Hayward. In *From under the Rubble*. New York: Bantam, 1975.

———*August 1914*. Translated by Michael Glenny. New York: Farrar, Straus & Giroux, 1972.

———*August 1914: The Red Wheel I*. Translated by H. T. Willets. London: Penguin Books, 1990.

———*The Gulag Archipelago I*. Translated by Thomas P. Whitney. New York: Harper & Row, 1973.

———*The Gulag Archipelago II*. Translated by Thomas P. Whitney. New York: Harper & Row, 1975.

———*The Oak and the Calf*. Translated by Harry Willetts. New York: Harper & Row, 1979.

———*One Day in the Life of Ivan Denisovich*. Translated by H.T. Willetts. New York: Alfred A. Knopf, 1991.

———*Rebuilding Russia*. New York: Farrar, Straus & Giroux, 1991.

———*The Russian Question at the End of the Twentieth Century*. Translated by Yermolai Solzhenitsyn. New York: Farrar, Straus & Giroux, 1995.

———"Russkiy Vopros v Kontse Dvadstatovo Veka." *Novy Mir* 7 (July 1994).

Sowell, Thomas. *Civil Rights: Rhetoric or Reality*. New York: William Morrow, 1984.

Spengler, Oswald. *The Decline of the West*. Abridged edition prepared by Helmut Werner and Arthur Helps. Translated by Charles Francis Atkinson. Oxford: Oxford University Press, 1991.

de Toledano, Ralph. "The Russo-German Symbiosis in the First and Second World Wars." *Chronicles*, February 1995.

Tumarkin, Nina. *The Living and the Dead: The Rise and Fall of the Cult of World War II in Russia*. New York: Basic Books, 1994.

Ulam, Adam B. *Stalin, The Man and His Era*. Boston: Beacon, 1973.

Vinogradov, A. G., and Vladimir Zhirinovskiy. *Rossiya I Reformiy*. Moscow: LDP, 1995.

Von Laue, Theodore H. *The World Revolution of Westernization: The Twentieth Century in Global Perspective*. Oxford: Oxford University Press, 1987.

Walicki, Andrezej. *A History of Russian Thought: From the Enlightenment to Marxism*. Stanford: Stanford University Press, 1979.

———*The Slavophile Controversy*. Notre Dame, Ind.: University of Notre Dame Press, 1989.

Watson, George. "Alfred Rosenberg: The Triumph of Tedium." *Chronicles*, February, 1995.
Weinberger, Jerry, and Arthur M. Melzer, eds. *History and the Idea of Progress.* Ithaca, N. Y.: Cornell University Press, 1995.
Wilson, Edward O. *On Human Nature.* Cambridge: Harvard University Press, 1978.
Yanov, Alexander. *The Russian Challenge and the Year 2000.* New York: Basil Blackwell, 1987.
———"The Zhirinovsky Phenomenon." *Chronicles*, August, 1993.
Zhirinovskiy, Vladimir. *Posledniy Brosok Na Yug.* Moscow, 1993.
———*Posledniy Vagon Na Sevyer.* Moscow: LDP, 1995.
Zyuganov, Gennadiy. *Derzhava.* Moscow: Informpechat, 1994.
———*Drama Vlasti.* Moscow: Paleya, 1993.
———*Rossiya—Rodina Moya.* Moscow: Informpechat, 1996.
Zimmerman, Michael E. *Heidegger's Confrontation with Modernity: Technology, Politics, Art.* Indianapolis, Ind.: Indiana University Press, 1990.

Periodicals Cited

Al-Ra'y, Amman, 29 March 1994.
Argumenty I Fakty 12 (March 1993).
Argumenty I Fakty 22 (May 1996).
Argumenty I Fakty 24 (June 1997).
Argumenty I Fakty 34 (August 1997).
Chernaya Sotnya 11 (1994).
Delovoy Mir, 27 February 1995.
Den, 23 (1991).
Den, 4 (1992).
Den, 5 (1992).
Den, 6 (1992).
Den, 7 (1992).
Den, 9 (1992).
Den, 11 (1992).
Den, 12 (1992).
Den, 13 (1992).
Den, 14 (1992).
Den, 15 (1992).
Den, 18 (1992).
Den, 20 (1992).
Den, 22 (1992).
Den, 38 (1992).
Den, 52 (1992).
Den, 21–27 February 1993.
Den, 22 (1993).
Den, 38 (1993).

Ekspert, 19 May 1997.
Elementy 1 (January 1992).
Golos Regionov 8 (November 1995).
Golos Regionov 9 (November 1995).
Izvestiya, 1 February 1992.
Izvestiya, 15 July 1993.
Izvestiya, 14 October 1993.
Izvestiya, 18 December 1993.
Izvestiya, 6 January 1994.
Izvestiya, 24 May 1994.
Izvestiya, 26 May 1994.
Izvestiya, 9 July 1994.
Izvestiya, 30 July 1994.
Izvestiya, 3 September 1994.
Izvestiya, 1 November 1994.
Izvestiya, 9 December 1994.
Izvestiya, 1 July 1997.
Kommersant, 29 October 1994.
Komsomolskaya Pravda, 20 September 1994.
Komsomolskaya Pravda, 21 March 1996.
La Stampa, 22 May 1994.
LDPR 9 (1995).
Leninskaya Smena, 14 February 1995.
Liberal 1 (1993).
Liberal 2 (1993).
Liberation, 20 June 1994.
Limonka 14 (1995).
Limonka 31 (1996).
Literaturnaya Gazeta 47 (1993).
Literaturnaya Rossiya, 21 February 1992.
Literaturnaya Rossiya, 6 December 1992.
Moskovskiy Komsomolets, 30 March 1994.
Moskovskiy Komsomolets, 5 April 1994.
Moskovskiy Komsomolets, 27 May 1997.
Moskovskiye Novosti, 33 (1992).
Moskovskiye Novosti, 43 (1993).
Moskovskiye Novosti, 52 (1994).
Moscow News, 15 (1994).
Moscow News, 22 (1994).
Narodnoye Delo 2 (1992).
Nezavisimaya Gazeta, 5 August 1992.
Nezavisimaya Gazeta, 23 October 1992.
Nezavisimaya Gazeta, 16 April 1993.
Nezavisimaya Gazeta, 1 March 1994.
Nezavisimaya Gazeta, 13 April 1994.
Nezavisimaya Gazeta, 27 April 1994.

Nezavisimaya Gazeta, 24 May 1994.
Nezavisimaya Gazeta, 28 May 1994.
Nezavisimaya Gazeta, 2 August 1994.
Nezavisimaya Gazeta, 1 November 1994.
Nezavismaya Gazeta, 16 May 1996.
Nezavisimaya Gazeta, 7 June 1996.
Nezavisimaya Gazeta, 22 March 1997.
Novaya Yezhedenevnaya Gazeta, 9 September 1994.
Novoye Russkoye Slovo, 1 January 1994.
Obozvrevatel 2 (February 1992).
Obshchaya Gazeta, 27 May 1994.
Obshchaya Gazeta, 11 March 1995.
Pamyat 1 (January 1995).
Pravda, 16 October 1992.
Pravda, 12 November 1992.
Pravda, 26 February 1993.
Pravda, 24 May 1994.
Pravda-Pyat, 29 September–6 October 1995.
Pravda Zhirinovskogo 5 (1995).
Put 1 (1991).
Qol Yisra'el, 13 January 1994.
Rossiya 37 (2 October 1994).
Rossiyskaya Gazeta, 12 March 1994.
Rossiyskaya Gazeta, 8 October 1994.
Rossiyskaya Gazeta, 11 March 1995.
Rossiyskaya Gazeta, 30 July 1996.
Rossiyskiye Vesti, 1 November 1994.
Russkiy Poryadok, 3–5 (1995).
Russkiy Telegraf, 2 October 1997.
Russkiy Vostok, 24 (December 1995).
Segodnya, 3 September 1993.
Segodnya, 13 January 1994.
Segodnya, 29 March 1994.
Segodnya, 5 May 1994.
Segodnya, 13 October 1994.
Segodnya, 6 July 1995.
Segodnya, 28 December 1996.
Segodnya, 16 May 1997.
Sovetskaya Rossiya, 20 March 1991.
Sovetskaya Rossiya, 7 May 1991.
Sovetskaya Rossiya, 6 June 1991.
Sovetskaya Rossiya, 25 June 1991.
Sovetskaya Rossiya, 23 July 1991.
Sovetskaya Rossiya, 3 July 1993.
Sovetskaya Rossiya, 28 August 1993.
Sovetskaya Rossiya, 20 August 1992.

Sovetskaya Rossiya, 5 March 1994.
Sovetskaya Rossiya, 9 April 1994.
Sovetskaya Rossiya, 2 June 1994.
Sovetskaya Rossiya, 9 June 1994.
Svobodnaya Gruziya, 3 June 1993.
Trud, 7 July 1994.
Trud, 14–20 June 1996.
Vecherniy Novosibirsk, 15 July 1994.
Washington Post, 14 January 1994.
Washington Post, 11 February 1996.
Washington Post, 17 June 1996.
Washington Post, 18 June 1996.
Washington Times, 26 September 1995.
Washington Times, 6 October 1995.
Washington Times, 20 February 1996.
Washington Times, 2 June 1996.
Washington Times, 20 June 1996.
Zavtra 1 (1994).
Zavtra 12 (1994).
Zavtra 21 (1994).
Zavtra 25 (1994).
Zavtra 30 (1994).
Zavtra 32 (1994).
Zavtra 24 (1995).
Zavtra 25 (1995).
Zavtra 26 (1995).
Zavtra 32 (1995).
Zavtra 34 (1995).
Zavtra 51 (1995).
Zavtra 52 (1995).

Other Sources (Radio, Television, News Services)

AFP, 14 January 1994.
AFP, 31 January 1994.
Aftenposten, 4 November 1991.
Chasa, 28 February 1994.
German PRO Television, *Reporter*, 18 January 1994.
Interfax, 7 May 1992.
Interfax, 24 November 1992.
Interfax, 20 July 1994.
Interfax, 18 April 1997.
Interfax, 30 August 1997.
ITAR-TASS, 18 May 1993.
ITAR-TASS, 28 October 1993.

Moscow NTV, *Itogi*, 29 May 1994.
Moscow NTV, *Itogi*, 24 July 1994.
Moscow NTV, 11 February 1996.
Moscow NTV, *Segodnya*, 15 March 1997.
Moscow ORT, 8 May 1995.
Moscow ORT, *Vremya*, 13 March 1996.
Moscow ORT, *Vremya*, 14 June 1996.
Moscow ORT, *Vremya*, 18 June 1996.
Moscow ORT, *Vremya*, 24 June 1996.
Moscow ORT, *Vremya*, 27 June 1996.
Moscow Ostankino Television, 23 November 1993.
Moscow Ostankino Television, 26 November 1993.
Moscow Ostankino Television, 1 December 1993.
Moscow Ostankino Television, 11 December 1993.
Moscow RTV, 6 June 1991.
Moscow RTV, *Vesti*, 15 June 1994.
Radio Moscow, 11 June 1991.
RIA, 26 June 1993.
RIA, 28 June 1993.
RIA, 27 July 1994.
RIA, 17 November 1994.
The Russian Center for Public Opinion and Market Research Express Release,
    6 June 1997 and 17 October 1997.
TASS, 18 December 1991.
TASS, 14 January 1994.

Index

About the Author

Wayne Allensworth is a Russia analyst at the Foreign Broadcast Information Service. His essays and articles have appeared in *Problems of Post Communism, Chronicles: A Magazine of American Culture,* and *The Family in America*. A native Texan, Mr. Allensworth currently lives in Purcellville, Virginia, with his wife, Stacy, and their three children.